The Pursuit of Harmony

The Pursuit of Harmony

Poetry and Power in Early Heian Japan

Gustav Heldt

East Asia Program
Cornell University
Ithaca, New York 14853

The Cornell East Asia Series is published by the Cornell University East Asia Program (distinct from Cornell University Press). We publish affordably priced books on a variety of scholarly topics relating to East Asia as a service to the academic community and the general public. Standing orders, which provide for automatic notification and invoicing of each title in the series upon publication, are accepted.

If after review by internal and external readers a manuscript is accepted for publication, it is published on the basis of camera-ready copy provided by the volume author. Each author is thus responsible for any necessary copy-editing and for manuscript formatting. Address submission inquiries to CEAS Editorial Board, East Asia Program, Cornell University, Ithaca, New York 14853-7601.

Number 139 in the Cornell East Asia Series

ISSN 1050-2955
ISBN: 978-1-933947-09-9 hc
ISBN: 978-1-933947-39-6 pb
Library of Congress Control Number: 2008929203

24 23 22 21 20 19 18 17 16 15 14 13 12 11 10 09 08 9 8 7 6 5 4 3 2 1

Cover illustration: *Hona'ami gire, from a portion of an eleventh-century manuscript of the Kokinshū*. Used with permission of the Kyoto National Museum.
Cover design by David Hopper, 2008.

To the memory of my sister,
Elizabeth Alma Heldt (1971–2005)

Contents

Abbreviations

DNK	*Dai nihon kokiroku*. Tokyo: Iwanami shoten, 1952–present. 93 volumes.
GR	*Gunsho ruijū*. Tokyo: Zoku gunsho ruijū kanseikai, 1959–1960. 25 volumes.
HJAS	*Harvard Journal of Asiatic Studies*.
IKKW	*Issatsu no kōza Kokin wakashū*. Tokyo: Yūseidō, 1987.
KST	*Shintei zōho kokushi taikei*. Tokyo: Yoshikawa kōbunkan, 1929–1967. 66 volumes.
KT	*Shinpen kokka taikan*. Tokyo: Kadokawa shoten, 1983–1992. 20 volumes.
MN	*Monumenta Nipponica*.
NKBT	*Nihon koten bungaku taikei*. Tokyo: Iwanami shoten, 1957–1968. 102 volumes.
NKT	*Nihon kagaku taikei*. Tokyo: Kazama shobō, 1956–1965. 10 volumes.
SKT	*Shinshaku kanbun taikei*. Tokyo: Meiji shoin, 1960–present. 114 volumes.
SNKBT	*Shin nihon koten bungaku taikei*. Tokyo: Iwanami shoten, 1989–2001. 100 volumes.
SNKBZ	*Shinpen nihon koten bungaku zenshū*. Tokyo: Shōgakkan, 1994–2002. 88 volumes.
ST	*Zōho shiryō taisei*. Kyoto: Rinsen shoten, 1965. 45 volumes.
TSZ	*Tsurayuki-shū zenshaku*. Eds. Tanaka Kimiharu and Tanaka Kyōko. Tokyo: Kazama shobō, 1998.

A Note to the Reader

Since Japanese poetry is the focus of this book, the conventions for representing it merit mention here. There has been some controversy over how to lineate *uta* poetry in English translation. Given the variety of calligraphic forms that any given poem could take when it was being written down, a standardized lineation representing contemporaneous conventions is impossible. Hiroaki Sato has noted that the concept of a metrical "line" as a spatially discrete written unit in pre-Meiji Japanese poetry is amorphous at best; consequently he has opted to translate poems in a single line.[1] While this point holds true in the most literal sense, as anyone who has looked at handwritten manuscripts can attest, the concept of discrete breaks within poems cannot be completely done away with. In fact, the notion that a 31-syllable Japanese poem is potentially divisible into separate "lines" (*ku*) of five and seven syllables was present from very early on.[2] In many cases, the 31-syllable *uta* poem was divided into two separate syntactic units called the "upper line" (*kami no ku* or *moto no ku*) of 17 syllables and the "lower line" (*shimo no ku* or *sue no ku*) of 14 syllables.[3] To emphasize this spatial sensibility in my own translations of poems, I have used five discrete lines to represent each metrical unit of five or seven syllables.

The semantic flow of *uta* perhaps presents a more serious challenge in translation. As Mark Morris has noted in a landmark essay on Japanese poetry, a large part of the beauty and complexity of these relatively brief poems lies in their ability to complicate the linear flow of standard Japanese sentence structures.[4] The poet and scholar Fujii Sadakazu sees these movements as, in their most extreme incarnations, a series of collisions and confrontations.[5] Such twists and turns in meaning as words (and lines) follow one another enable *uta* to construct multiple meanings in a dynamic manner both internally and through seriate arrangements or attachment to other objects. Although it is impossible to stay close to the word order of the original poem in all cases, I have attempted to do so when feasible out of a sense that this order was crucial to their intended effects.

A related challenge in translating Japanese poems is presented by the frequent ambiguity of their syntax. Verbs often simultaneously end one clause and form the heading for a new one, insofar as there was often no distinction between their sentence final forms (*shūshikei*) and their attributive forms (*rentaikei*). This allows the poem to create overlapping sets of phrases that both stand on their own and are simultaneously enclosed within a nested arrangement of ever more encompassing clauses, a characteristic that has also been identified by the noted linguist Tokieda Motoki as a signal feature of Japanese.[6] Although English requires distinctions between predicates that end a sentence and those that modify a nominal, the poems I have translated do not always observe such rules.

For the sake of making this book accessible to nonspecialists, I have provided modern romanized equivalents for most words rather than attempt to represent their original pronunciation or historical orthography. I have opted for the modern form of *kanji* with this same goal in mind. In particular cases where I have felt that orthography makes a significant difference in the way a poem can be read, I have drawn the reader's attention to it. Romanized transliterations are used when citing poems or brief passage of prose that were originally written in Japanese. Texts written exclusively in Chinese characters are cited in that same manner. Names and titles of works that originate in China are romanized according to the *pinyin* system. Chinese characters have been provided for proper nouns, titles of texts, and key words in the glossary. However, in those instances where there is no standard way of writing a particular word (such as *yomu*, for example) they have been omitted.

Accessibility has also informed my policy in selecting which version of a text to cite. Standard annotated editions in commonly available series have been chosen whenever possible, and among these, the most recent series featuring translations of the text in modern Japanese have been preferred. In the case of texts that were originally written in literary Chinese, Japanese editions that include either a translation into modern Japanese or a rendition in classical Japanese according to *yomikudashi* conventions have been selected for the same reason. Citations use one of the abbreviations for editions that are provided in the preceding section, including the volume and page number. For example, *SNKBZ*, 11: 105 would denote page 105 in volume 11 of the *Shin nihon koten bungaku zenshū* series. All translations, unless indicated otherwise, are my own. The one exception is the title of a work, where I have used standard renditions whenever possible. Quotation marks are used in the rare cases where I have provided my own versions.

To represent dates in the traditional calendrical system, the name of the regnal era is first mentioned, followed by numerals indicating the year of that era, the lunar month, and day; all are separated by slashes. Intercalary lunar months are further marked with an asterisk. Thus, Engi 6/3*/14 (906) would indicate the fourteenth day of the third intercalary lunar month of the sixth year of the Engi era. Dates in the Western calendar have been provided for people and texts in those cases where these are known.

Acknowledgments

Initial work on this book was made possible by a fellowship from the Fulbright Foundation for dissertation research in Japan in the years 1996–1998. I am greatly indebted to Fujii Sadakazu, who facilitated my affiliation with Tokyo University as a research student during that period. I also benefited from the support and example of Kawamoto Kōji, whose passion for poetry is truly one of a kind. A fellowship from the Whiting Foundation and a President's Fellowship from Columbia University allowed me to complete the dissertation in the subsequent two years. During that period, before, and since, my graduate adviser Haruo Shirane has been an unfailing source of counsel, encouragement, and patience. My debt of gratitude to him is, to echo an early lesson in reading Japanese, "higher than any mountain and deeper than the sea."

I have also been very fortunate to have been part of a truly extraordinary intellectual community of teachers and fellow graduate students at Columbia University, all of whom during and since that time have contributed in numbers and ways that far exceed what I can easily summarize here. In addition to this large group, other people who have helped me with words of encouragement and perceptive comments along the way include Monica Bethe, Robert Khan, Thomas LaMarre, Susan Matisoff, Joshua Mostow, Park Namgyu, Takahashi Tōru, Suzuki Yasue, and Tomiko Yoda.

The time needed to transform the dissertation into a book manuscript came in the form of a sabbatical from Bard College for the 2004–2005 academic year. I am grateful to the dean of the college for granting the leave, and to my colleague Michiko Baribeau for holding the fort while I was gone. I also thank the Japan Research Centre for providing me with an affiliation as a visiting researcher and access to the library at the School of Oriental and African Studies during this period. Stephen Dodd is owed a special word of thanks for making it possible for me to be in London in order to take advantage of this opportunity.

This book has benefited significantly from the close scrutiny and constructive suggestions of its anonymous readers. I am also grateful to G. S. Smith for his careful reading and inspired suggestion for its title. Anne Kinney and Paul Rouzer both took time out of their busy schedules to look over my translations to the prefaces of the first three imperial anthologies of *shi* poetry and provided numerous helpful suggestions. Joan Piggott offered crucial advice at a critical stage in preparing the manuscript. Jane Dieckmann worked diligently on both the manuscript proper and the index. Mai Shaikhanuar-Cota proved to be an ideal editor in her responsiveness to my suggestions and her help at every stage in the process.

Two grants from the University of Virginia have aided the publication of this book: a Research Support Grant from the dean of the College of Arts and Sciences gave financial help in the form of a subvention; a Faculty Summer Research Grant provided me with the time and resources to make final changes to the manuscript. The encouragement and support of my colleagues in the Department of East Asian Languages, Literatures and Cultures at the University of Virginia have been especially important, particularly that of Ellen Fuller, who was completing her own book at the time; Anne Kinney, who was always available to lend her expertise in classical Chinese poetry; and Michiko Wilson, who had faith in me from start to finish.

I am grateful to Stanford University Press for giving me permission to use the diagrams of the Heian palace provided in Helen Craig McCullough's translation of *Eiga monogatari*, and to the Kyoto National Museum for allowing me to use the cover image of this book, taken from the *Hon'ami gire* portion of an eleventh-century manuscript of the *Kokinshū*. David Hopper came up with the cover design, as well as numerous ways to make the whole process of completing this project more pleasurable than it might have been otherwise. The long journey entailed by this undertaking would not have begun without my mother, Barbara Heldt, who has always encouraged me to take the road less traveled by.

G.C.H.

Introduction

The Heian court of the late ninth and early tenth centuries represents one of the most innovative and influential periods in the history of Japanese poetry. It witnessed the creation of entirely new forms of verse in poetry matches, screen poems, and officially sponsored anthologies, none of which had a precedent in earlier times. At the apex of these phenomena lay the compilation of the *Kokin wakashū* (*Collection of Poems Ancient and Modern*), whose status as the first imperial anthology of native poetry would make it integral to Japanese court culture for centuries afterward.[1] Despite the enormous historical significance of these new forms of poetry and the marked interest displayed by powerful individuals in patronizing them, however, little sustained attention has been paid to the ties between the practices involved in producing and performing verse and processes of economic, ideological, political, and social change in this period. This book is intended to address such issues through an investigation of the ways in which different members of the Heian court community deployed poems in the pursuit of power.

One of the chief challenges in discussing the poetry of this period lies in determining how to approach texts from a time and place in which the modern category of "literature" possesses limited applicability. It has been argued that our current conception of literature has its origins in the latter half of the nineteenth century in Europe, and views it principally as a field of cultural activity that claims to be separate from the economics of bourgeois capitalism while observing many of its rules.[2] Literature, according to this theory, constructs writers as autonomous geniuses and readers who, during their nonproductive hours, enjoyed the fantasies sold to them. By contrast, the composition and reception of a significant portion of early Heian poetry was not intended for leisure or the consumption of fantasies, but rather as a ritualized expression of the court official's role in conveying royal words in writing.

The primary goal of this book is to broaden our understanding of poetic texts that have primarily been treated as part of an autonomous literary discourse, by highlighting their relations with other ostensibly nonliterary texts and practices. My focus on such elements stems from the belief that the social significance of early Heian court poetry can best be understood through attention to the ways in which it was produced, performed, and received in particular contexts. While such issues in many ways lie at the heart of understanding this cultural activity, only a few scholars have tackled them in depth, perhaps in part because the terms used to describe poetic activities are not always congruent with modern distinctions between orality and writing, or reception and production.[3] Such an approach is also difficult because it necessarily involves a degree of interpretation and inference, as the sources for reconstructing a detailed account are sparse, especially when compared with later periods. Nevertheless, there is a body of material from diaries, formularies of court ritual, and historical chronicles that can help flesh out our understanding of the social significances of the period's poetic practices. To date, the majority of these texts have not been discussed by Western scholars of Japanese literature and by only a few in Japan.

My chief focus will be on the connections between the poems produced in this period and the practice of "harmonization" (*wa*) with a superior's words through their citation and affirmation in banquets and other ritual observances at the early Heian court. Despite the importance of such events to poetic practices, most modern scholars have tended to neglect the ritual elements that informed the performative context in which poems were often produced.[4] This link between poems and banquets is perhaps most powerfully illustrated in the case of the *Kokinshū* anthology, discussion of which dominates literary historical accounts of the period and two chapters of this book. Due to its later history as the canonical model for court-commissioned poetry collections, the *Kokinshū* is often treated as a primarily aesthetic entity, with only an oblique relation to the expression of political and cultural authority.[5] My approach will focus on the anthology's relation to the royal banquets at which power and authority were enacted, in order to elucidate various formal features of the text identified by modern scholars, such as its nomenclature, topical categories, and sequencing of individual poems. The importance of poetic harmonization at banquet rituals to the anthology's self-definition can also help explain why it, unlike many earlier anthologies of *uta* such as the *Man'yōshū* (*Collection of Myriad Leaves*, ca. 759) and *Shinsen man'yōshū* (*Newly Selected Collection of Myriad Leaves*, 893), uses the word *waka* (harmonizing verse) in its title.

To say that the chief significance of early Heian court poetry lay in its affirmation of a cosmologically grounded view of the social order rather than the satisfaction of "nonproductive" pleasures is, however, not to say that aesthetic appreciation played no part in its reception at court. The challenge of harmonizing with another by echoing that person's words within the formal constraints engendered by poetic form entailed a degree of skill that must have been admired in its own right. In this sense, aesthetics and politics were closely implicated with one another. As a "courtly society" in which etiquette and rules of conduct provided the primary basis for evaluating one's peers, the ability to harmonize deftly, subtly, and quickly were often necessary to assuring one's place within such a social milieu. If this book tends to emphasize the political at the expense of the aesthetic, it is in part because it has been informed by the desire to redress an imbalance in the ways that early Heian poetry has been viewed in modern times.

Historicizing *Kokinshū* Period Poetry

Despite the enormous importance of early Heian poetry to Japanese cultural history, modern scholarly attempts to place it in its own historical context have been relatively limited and slow to develop. This is all the more remarkable given that one of the commonly acknowledged hallmarks of the period is its persistent claims to the "public" and "official" status of court poetry. To some degree, the slow pace of scholarship on this topic is a product of the more general neglect that has been suffered by the period's most representative work, the *Kokinshū* anthology. Although the *Kokinshū*—like other canonical Heian texts—has been studied and written about since medieval times, in the modern period it was deemed to be worthy of extended critical scrutiny in its own right only from the second half of the twentieth century. Ever since the Meiji-period critic Masaoka Shiki (1867–1902) famously dismissed the anthology as trite and hackneyed, readers have found it difficult to view the *Kokinshū* as an approachable work. The relative neglect it has suffered in modern times is particularly evident when compared with the level of interest that has been consistently lavished on literary texts of equal standing in Japanese history, such as the *Man'yōshū* or the *Genji monogatari* (*Tale of Genji*, ca. 1010). In contrast to the large number of monographs written about these two works, there are no more than a dozen or so book-length studies bearing the word *Kokinshū* in their titles, the majority of which date from the postwar period and most of which are collections of brief articles by individual scholars.

Scholarly neglect of the *Kokinshū* stems in part from the tendency among modern literary critics to emphasize the concern with artifice that Masaoka alleged to be the anthology's defining characteristic. Perhaps the most enduring and influential formulation of this critical stance was provided by Kubota Utsubo, one of a very few scholars from the 1930s who exerted significant influence on postwar studies. It was Kubota who first articulated the current critical commonplace that the *Kokinshū* exemplified a distanced, intellectualized stance toward the world of lived experience, one that stood in direct contrast to the supposedly more engaged approach of earlier *Man'yōshū* poets.[6] Unlike their predecessors, *Kokinshū* poets were seen as having laid primary emphasis on the selective appropriation of external phenomena and their reconfiguration into a self-contained interior world that was ruled by fictive rhetorical conceits rather than lived experience. Kubota attributed this gap between language and the external world to a Buddhist view of all phenomena as illusory and impermanent, and claimed this stance was embraced by poets who were often politically marginalized. In a similar vein, a later scholar characterized this poetics as an "aesthetics of despair" in which language's attempts at questioning the inexorable realities of the real world are doomed to failure in the same manner as the poets' efforts to control their social and political circumstances.[7]

This tendency to exile early Heian poetry from the realms of politics and power is perhaps most pronounced when it comes to the mid ninth century, an important moment in the development of court poetry.[8] Literary historians usually refer to this era as "the period of the six poetic immortals" (*rokkasen jidai*) after the famous six poets who are critiqued in the Kana Preface to the *Kokinshū*. Later works such as the *Ise monogatari* (*Tales of Ise*) portrayed its most famous representative Ariwara no Narihira (825–880) as a politically marginalized figure who turned to the pursuit of poetry as a way of expressing his discontent at being shut out of power.[9] Such a view, however, ignores the ways in which this period also saw a dramatic increase in the links between *uta* and court rituals designed to legitimate the authority of a newly established Fujiwara regency. In this book I will detail this and related historical phenomena in order to provide a much-needed corrective to a continuing perception of poetic composition during this period as an activity that was somehow divorced from the structures of power and authority. If anything, quite the opposite seems often to have been the case.

The introverted and subjective view of the world that Kubota Utsubo and later scholars have seen in *Kokinshū* poetry helps explain why it was not subject to the same sort of sociohistorical analyses that were enjoyed by other premodern literary works in the immediate postwar period. With its apparent lack of realism and seemingly trivial interest in wordplay, the *Kokinshū* made a far less appealing object of study for Marxist-influenced historians of this period than either the *Tale of Genji* or *Man'yōshū*, which could be more readily subsumed under the category of a realist form of literature that reflected to one degree or another the social circumstances of their times, the daily lived experiences of commoners, or resistance to the dominant ideology of the state.[10] One exception to this tendency in the late 1960s and early 1970s focused on "poetry circles" (*kadan*), emphasizing the role played by networks of patronage and political influence in the production of poetry. Even here, however, emphasis tended to be placed on mid-Heian and medieval poetry, perhaps in part because of the relatively larger amount of material available to reconstruct such networks in those instances.

In the case of the early Heian period, three book-length studies continue to provide the basis for the study of poetry circles: Murase

Toshio's *Kokinshū no kiban to sono shūhen*, Hashimoto Fumio's *Ōchō wakashi no kenkyū*, and Yamaguchi Hiroshi's monumental multivolume study *Ōchō kadan no kenkyū*. The wealth of detail provided by these scholars about the historical figures who were closely involved with court poetry at the time have been immensely valuable in reconstructing what was at stake and for whom in its composition. Due to their emphasis on the roles played by the individual tastes of particular patrons and informal "salons" of aesthetically like-minded people, however, these scholars have tended to neglect the ways in which the investment of institutions (such as the regency) in the political symbolism of ritual observances and a cosmologically oriented world view also helped constitute court poetry at the time.[11] Such poems were not produced or sponsored in a purely "literary" context, but rather were often intimately tied to a host of symbolic practices that helped project power and authority in communal settings.

Another influential approach to the history of *Kokinshū* during this period was provided by Ozawa Masao, whose work on the anthology has become authoritative on account of his wide-ranging and detailed approach. Ozawa's history is a classically literary one in the sense that it primarily focused on poetic rhetoric and drew heavily on the periodization provided in the *Kokinshū*'s own prefaces. It sketches out a three-stage development that begins with the poetry of high antiquity, proceeds to the late ninth century represented by the six poets critiqued in the anthology's prefaces, and ends with the anthologizers' own generation. The first of these stages bears a particularly close relationship to the anonymous songs found in the earlier *Man'yōshū* anthology.[12] Ozawa outlined these continuities by investigating the prefatory phrases (*jokotoba*) and place-names used to describe landscapes in verse. He demonstrated the ways in which anonymous *Kokinshū* poems drew on earlier traditions, followed by an interregnum during the *rokkasen* period in which these traditions were neglected, after which they were revived in the period during which the *Kokinshū*'s editors were active.[13] This scheme would prove immensely useful for other scholars reconstructing the history of early Heian poetry. The deliberately "neoclassical" stance of the *Kokinshū*'s editors in attempting to preserve earlier forms of poetic rhetoric, for example, has been viewed by the scholar Ueno Osamu as a signal feature of their role at court as "professional court poets" *(senmon kajin)* engaged in composing official court poetry.[14] Although later scholars have argued for modifications of this model, it remains a significant point of departure for analyzing the stylistic evolution of early Heian poetry.

Ozawa's approach anticipated a change in scholarly emphasis that began in the late 1970s, when Marxist historiography and its positivistic approach to texts receded and an emphasis on "style" (*buntai*) and "expression" (*hyōgen*) came to the foreground. The use of the latter term has been particularly widespread, covering a variety of topics that extend beyond a narrow definition of rhetorical technique to include such issues as the origins and modes of the intellectual and conceptual nature of early Heian poetry, the overall structure of the *Kokinshū*, and the arrangement of poems within it. Extensive work has been done on such topics as the changing nature of landscape depiction, the ways in which epithets and formulaic phrases were altered over time, and the evolution of particular connotations for particular items of poetic diction.[15]

Though detailed, informative, and rich in insights, the focus on language taken by these scholars has tended to separate early Heian poetry from the material and cultural practices that surrounded it. In this sense, one could argue, they have had the (perhaps unintended) effect of reinforcing Kubota's contention that the world of court poetry was largely self-contained. This is not to say that these scholars have not done valuable or useful work for my purposes, and I have drawn on many of them in this book. My chief concern in doing so, however, is to show how the changes that they identify often comment on the political and social forces at work in the historical moments in which they were produced.

As a result of the tendency for modern literary histories to focus on the continuities and breaks between the *Kokinshū* and *Man'yōshū*, innovative approaches to the former are often spurred on by developments in the study of the latter. Beginning in the 1980s, new connections between rhetoric and ritual in early Japanese poetry were identified by scholars engaged in innovative work on eighth-century texts. These scholars sought to illustrate ways in which the construction of a common language in early Japanese poetry and its use of incantatory rhetoric bound communities together as organic entities grounded in mythical origins.[16] While lavishing attention on the earliest Japanese texts, such accounts tend to be vague about how to position Heian poetry in relation to this prior period. Generally, literary historians view this supposed organic community (*kyōdōtai*) of the archaic past as steadily eroding over the course of the Heian period as the aristocracy's ties to clan and regional traditions were replaced by exclusively urban identities in the capital.[17]

This historical model, couched as it is in terms of loss and degeneration, runs the risk of downplaying the creative dimension to the development of court poetry in the Heian period. Furthermore, it could be argued that there were more continuities than discontinuities between Heian poetry and its precursors or, at least, that they coexisted synchronically rather than succeeding one another diachronically. We should remember in this regard that the texts through which a Japanese "antiquity" (*kodai*) has been posited—such as the mythohistorical *Nihon shoki* and the *Man'yōshū*—were themselves being recast during the first two centuries of the Heian period.

Poetry's performative power often lay in its ability to cite and legitimate new forms of older historical narratives in the interests of legitimating communal and individual claims to the state's wealth. This particular phenomenon, which has not been addressed by most modern scholars, reveals the need for us to revise our notion of the public purposes of court poetry by paying attention to the ways in which its ritual evocations of past precedent were often directly concerned with naturalizing and legitimating contemporaneous arrangements for organizing economic and political power. The means for producing these modes of authority—in the form of a communally recognized legitimization of the right to dispense resources—ultimately drew on a worldview that had its origins in continental culture rather than archaic native myths.

Heian Poetry and the Confucian World Order

Any reading of early Heian poetry that stresses its political and ideological effects entails discussion of the Confucian canon through which the Heian court's concept of ritual rulership was articulated. One aim of this book is to read this poetry through the lens of what I term a "continental" East Asian culture originating in China, but shared with a broad array of neighboring polities that included Yamato, Khitan, Koryo, Paekche, Parhae, and Silla. This view of a continental culture was sustained in part by the Heian cultural imagination, which used the term "Kara" (Tang) to refer to the mainland source of imported cultural forms, regardless of whether they originated with the Chinese dynasty that bore that name.[18] The literate members of this semi-global community shared concepts of self, society, and the universe that were articulated in a canon of historical narratives, philosophical discourses, cosmological treatises, and poetry written in a common language. Throughout this book, I refer to this common language as "literary Chinese" to emphasize its textual nature, which allowed it to cross boundaries of political geography, regional culture, and vernacular speech that otherwise separated people in East Asia.

Although it is universally acknowledged that continental culture played a profound role in shaping that of early Japan, those addressing its impact on native poetry have tended to limit their discussion of this influence to identifying allusions to particular words, tropes, or source texts. Such borrowings from continental poetry can be characterized as taking one of three forms of adoption: a line from a poem, a poetic technique, or the general meaning of a poem.[19] Most scholarship on the poetry of the early Heian period has focused on one of these three forms, documenting the similarities in rhetoric and wording between *shi* poems written in literary Chinese and *uta* written in *kana*.[20] At the same time, however, the similarities between the practices involved in producing both forms of poetry have received less attention. One result has been a general tendency to isolate the period's poetry from the broader array of cultural concepts and activities through which power and authority were produced and performed at the Heian court. A central argument of this book is that such elements suggest deeper ties between Heian poetry and continental culture than have been previously recognized.

At its most fundamental level, a shift in focus from text to practice entails a reconsideration of the terms employed by modern scholars to discuss Heian poetry. Today, the word *waka* is commonly used as a form of shorthand encompassing all 31-syllable poetry written in the native language, often in implicit or explicit contrast to poetry written in literary Chinese. One of the central arguments of this book is that *waka*'s prior history suggests that it was poetic praxis rather than ethno-linguistic status that often informed the definition of this word. Consequently, I shall refer to Japanese court poetry written in *kana* as *uta* rather than *waka* to highlight the fact that the latter term often referred to verse that "harmonized" (*wa*) hierarchical relations of social difference rather than to verse that was Japanese per se. This is, to the best of my knowledge, an understanding of the term which has not been pursued in modern scholarship.[21] It grows out of a reading of early Heian poetry that is informed by the ways in which *uta* are represented in contemporaneous court chronicles (a topic that has received little attention to date), and by a consideration of the similarities and distinctions between various forms of poetic practice, rather than rhetoric or diction, in determining the different ways in which different forms of verse were defined.

In the ninth century, harmonization in poetry was a practice most closely associated with the composition of *shi* poems on royal command. Like other forms of premodern poetry such as linked verse (*renga*), it was a practice that appears to have been taken up with greater alacrity in Japan than was the case in its original continental cultural context.[22] At the Heian court, poets would produce verses whose rhyme schemes and words echoed those of their sovereign, thereby signaling not only their accord with his will but also their fitness to transmit his words throughout the realm as officials representing his authority. These performances of poetic harmonization in *shi* poetry gained significance within the larger ritual contexts in which they were carried out. Chief among these settings were the annual banquets known as *sechien*, at which the sovereign dispensed the state's bounty to his officials in the form of food and stipends.

Such observances formed a core component of the Confucian concept of ritual rulership as the coordination of human activities with heavenly processes.[23] The importance of banquets to continental rites of kingship is attested to by the fact that the canonical Confucian ritual formulary, the *Record of Rites* (*Liji*), devotes an entire chapter to feasts presided over by the sovereign.[24] Because they were organized according to a precise calendrical schedule, they could claim to carry out the essential governmental function of harmonizing human actions with cosmological cycles. The bounty dispensed by the sovereign at these events was a paradigmatic ritual act that staged his "virtue" (*toku*), that is to say, his capacity to achieve this harmony. The resulting declarations of poetic accord by his subjects who echoed his words then testified to the social harmony that enabled material plenty and proper governance.

The performative significance of expressing harmony in verse drew on cosmological conceptions that were primarily intended to legitimate political authority.[25] In classical continental views of the universe, harmony produced phenomena through the varying relations it established between *yin* and *yang* forces. This emphasis on complementary opposites led to a correlation between the harmony governing relations between Heaven and Earth and that governing relations between sovereign and subject.

One of the earliest texts in Japan to articulate the ideal form of a centralized polity, the *Seventeen Article Constitution* (*Kenpō jūshichi jō*, 604), places the injunction to harmony at the very beginning of its governing principles. The import laid on this term can be traced back to a famous passage from the *Analects* in which a disciple of Confucius describes its intimate connection with ritual in the following manner: "Harmony is valued in using the rites. The beauty of the Way of former rulers lay in this. However, one cannot succeed in any matter, great or small, using only harmony. Attempting to harmonize affairs through a knowledge of harmony without also regulating them through the rites will not attain this goal."[26]

This emphasis on the role played by ritual in harmonizing human relationships takes on a discursive cast in the first article of the *Seventeen Article Constitution*, which is primarily concerned with the manner in which speech should be conducted between superiors and inferiors. The third article then proceeds to take this concern with proper speech and invest it with cosmological significance in the following terms:

> When the sovereign's command is given, obey it reverently. The sovereign is as Heaven and his subjects are as Earth. Heaven covers the world and Earth supports it, and so the four seasons proceed in order, thereby invigorating everything. If Earth were to seek to cover Heaven, this arrangement would be destroyed. Thus, the sovereign speaks and his ministers receive his words, while inferiors

> are swayed by the actions of their superiors. Therefore, you should respect any command from the sovereign that you receive. If you do not do so, ruin will result.[27]

Although the *Seventeen Article Constitution* predates the period I am discussing by two centuries, its pithy correlation of discursive, social, and cosmological harmony eloquently captures the connection among these three elements that informed the notion of statehood in the early Heian period as well. In the context of court banquets, the enactment of harmony between sovereign and a subject was intended to produce a shared sense of community among the court's multiple members, just as its cosmological corollary of a superior Heaven and inferior Earth were seen to sustain the physical world in its manifold variety. The court continually drew on such complementary opposites to generate and represent a political community whose multiplicity was ultimately organized around a single royal figure of authority, just as the cosmos's multiplicity originated in a singular ineffable source.

This play between multiplicity and unity in the harmonization of complementary opposites can be seen at work in many of the *uta* recorded in the court's official histories. In these texts, harmonization in *uta* usually takes the form of poetic dialogues, in which the responding party cited a word or phrase uttered by the initiator of the exchange within the first poem. Unity of wording between poems was balanced by the social differences between the actors involved in the context in which they were performed, leading to potentially different significances that various parties would attach to the same words. Like harmonization in *shi*, the effects of social harmony and accord that such dialogues sought to create did not depend solely on the parties involved in the exchange. In keeping with the cosmological concept of harmony as a process that generated multiple phenomena from the interplay of complementary forces, the harmonious exchanges of poems between two parties achieved closure only when multiple external witnesses to these speech-acts formally acknowledged their efficacy within particular ritual contexts.

The representation of *waka* as a form of "harmonizing" verse in historical texts can help us discern continuities among the diverse poetic forms of the period. Chief among these common elements is the practice of composing *uta* on "topics" (*dai*)—an activity that informs the majority of officially sponsored court poetry in the ninth and tenth centuries. Poems composed for royal processions, poetry matches, and screen paintings all incorporated words that were provided to the poet by a social superior in the form of lines from *shi* poems, individual words written in *kana*, or descriptions of landscape scenes.[28] These modes of topic-based composition in *uta* can be seen as a form of harmonization akin to that enacted in *shi* poems, insofar as both types of poetic composition involved the citation of words that were selected by a powerful figure and reproduced by the poet. As such, *waka*, or "harmonizing verse," were declarations of allegiance to and compliance with the will of figures of authority.

Another way in which this book attempts to situate early Heian *uta* within a larger East Asian context is by seeking to bring Western scholarship on *shi* poetry into productive dialogue with my topic. Broadly speaking, there are four means by which I have sought to do so. One is a consideration of the similar vision of language's relation to cosmology and society that was shared by both forms of poetry. Another is a consideration of similarities between the political context in Six Dynasties China (220–589) and that of early Heian Japan which informed the latter's selective borrowing of the former's poetic practices, such as anthologizing and group composition. I am also interested in the manner in which the *Kokinshū* made a claim to canonical status through various associations with the *Shijing* (*Classic of Poetry*) and its commentarial tradition of historically contextualizing individual verses. Finally, I consider the ways in which the formal parallelisms of *shi* poetics, which are usually contrasted with the metrical asymmetry of *uta*, also obtained within the latter group. Complementary binarisms in native poetry can be seen in both the rhetorical balancing of human and natural elements within individual poems and the ways in which individual poems often gained particular meanings when read in pairs with other poems.

Harmony and Its Discontents

My study of the historical forces at work in the production of early Heian court poetry will include attention to the ways in which the modes of expression (*hyōgen*) and networks of patronage (*kadan*) outlined by other scholars intersected with ritual and political elements of court culture. Another dimension to this sort of historicizing project is the need to emphasize the contested nature of claims to power and authority at any particular moment. My chief difference from scholars who have written about the incantatory aspects of early Japanese poetry, for example, lies in a desire to stress the ways in which tensions and divisions within groups can be as constitutive of community as claims to organic unity. Like the analyses of their seventh-century predecessors provided by Gary Ebersole, I view symbols of community and authority in Heian poetry as cultural resources that were exploited by different individuals and groups to different ends.[29]

The pursuit of harmony in Heian court poetry was itself often spurred on by the recognition of dissonance among its members. Poetic exchanges between high-ranking members of the court or poetry matches, for example, often sought to alleviate political tensions between different parties. In this sense, the practice of poetic harmony was inseparable from the political disruptions it sought to suppress. With this in mind, I have sought to foreground historical shifts in the political composition of the early Heian court that can more precisely delineate our understanding of what was at stake and for whom in the pursuit of harmony in poetry.

Tensions and divisions also inform the terms I use to describe the political topography of the court. In discussing this community, I frequently refer to the courts of individual rulers, regents, and retired sovereigns to denote loci of ritual and political authority around which larger groups of officials, kin, and followers clustered. Some of these courts succeeded one another in time. Over the course of the ninth century, however, they increasingly overlapped as political authority and economic power was shared between vying factions. Consequently, references to the "courts" of particular individuals are intended to emphasize their use of ritual to stage their authority as symbolic centers of community. They are not intended to suggest a monopoly on the forms of authority they projected.

Internal divisions within the court can help us understand one way in which the practice of harmonizing in *shi* differed from that of harmonizing in *uta*. Whereas the former was associated exclusively with rituals of royal governance, harmonization in *uta* through topic-based composition could assert the authority of various figures at court other than the sovereign, including consorts, retired sovereigns, and Fujiwara regents. This is partly due to the fact that the modes of poetic dialogue enacted through *uta* could take a variety of forms that were not always as strictly governed by hierarchy and decorum as their literary Chinese counterparts. Thus, the proliferation of poetic practices that sought to represent authority and power through *uta* in the period was due to the proliferation of parties claiming access to a shared body of resources and wealth, possession of which was legitimated and actualized through the administrative and legal structures of the state.

Although references to the Yamato court in this period were primarily cast in the singular as one sovereign, one calendar, one palace, one realm, and one law in the codes of the *ritsuryō* state, by the mid ninth century this same court came to accommodate multiple figures of authority who required a suppler means for representing community than those provided by a unitary Confucian model. Histories of the Heian period often describe this proliferation as a form of fragmentation or privatization in which different interest groups accumulated political and economic power outside the structures of the state. The period of the ninth and early tenth centuries on which I focus can be seen as occupying an ambiguous place within this narrative.[30] The authority of the primary actors at the early Heian court, such as the regent and retired sovereign, was contingent on their ability to mimic the prerogatives of the nominal ruler. As a result, these different figures of authority all drew on the structures of Confucian political and cosmological theory in order to legitimate their positions at court.

Written *uta* gave expression to these new positions by developing a new language for articulating models of time, space, humanity, and Heaven which echoed the singular forms of Confucian political cosmology while making them available to a plurality of social groups. One signal feature of this new poetic language was its articulation of a seasonal temporality. Although the seasons had been a longstanding feature of Japanese poetry, by the late ninth century they enjoyed unprecedented attention, as witnessed by their prominence as compositional topics in a variety of settings and texts. My approach to this phenomenon will emphasize its political implications, and the ways in which it created two cosmologies at the Heian court. Whereas the lunar calendar remained the prerogative of the reigning monarch and provided a paradigmatic instance of the Confucian ruler's role in harmonizing humanity with Heaven, the solar rhythms of seasonal time could be aligned with an alternative indigenous cosmology that was not regulated by the state.

Political symbolism informed this seasonal poetics in a variety of ways, for example, by associating the Fujiwara family with the royal family through the poetic motif of cherry blossoms. Attention to such symbolism can provide us with a more precise picture of the political interests at work in different poetic representations of power and authority. Because manuscripts of poetic texts were often produced as collaborative enterprises and exist in different recensions, there are limits to how precisely one can align political history with literary production. The *Kokinshū* is exemplary of this difficulty, insofar as it appears to have been a project involving more than one competing figure of authority. In such instances, I attempt to show how discrete features of the text intersect with particular historical moments and agents, rather than provide a comprehensive narrative of the stages in which the anthology evolved or an overly generalized attribution of its production to a single party.

Because the pursuit of harmony in early Heian poetry derived its political and symbolic effects from ritual structures, I have sought to emphasize the historically contingent and contested nature of these elements as well. Overall, my approach is informed by one influential theory of ritual that emphasizes its nature as a process (ritualization) that actively produces hierarchical relations of difference rather than simply reflecting them as a priori realities.[31] To naturalize these differences, however, rituals tend to represent themselves as atemporal and iterable rather than historically contingent and subject to change.[32] This contradiction informs my account of the way early Heian poetry often sought to assert harmony in the context of radical change. Established forms of ritual were constantly being adapted, and new ones created, to meet the changing political contours of the Heian court.[33]

Poetry often played a key role in legitimating these changes by asserting their links to the past through the citation of historical texts and "ancient words" (*furugoto*) that had their origins in mythic narratives.

This aspect of early Japanese poetry can be characterized as incantatory, but it also calls to mind the concept of "speech acts" outlined by John L. Austin to describe the performative social effects of language.[34] As some thinkers have noted, any form of speech-act—incantatory or otherwise—must present itself as the citation of words that already exist in order for it to claim authority. The importance of citation to the performative power of language has been most influentially asserted by the philosopher Jacques Derrida, who claims that it endows discourses with authority and efficacy by virtue of its claims to being iterable.[35] This facet of citation can be seen as informing much of court poetry, whether it took the form of the repetition of a final line in ritual songs or the repetition of a superior's words in the act of poetic harmonization. Just as the poetic act of citation could affirm the authority of particular individuals, it could also legitimate court rituals and the communities they created.

Poetry and Social Identity

Power in the cultural field can be seen as a productive force as well as one that constrains or limits action. With this axiom in mind, reading Heian verse in relation to the practice of harmonization also affords insights into the ways poetry produced social identities within the court community. The practices associated with the production, performance, and reception of court poetry constructed forms of social difference between figures of authority and the lower-ranking courtiers who wrote poems for their superiors. Of particular interest in this regard is the phenomenon of proxy composition, one of the distinctive features of early Heian poetry. Many poems produced for public gatherings by lower-ranking courtiers were used in turn by influential members of court society in their negotiations with one another. Because so much of court poetry was intended for different people in different settings, the relationship between language and the agents associated with it was neither static nor legible outside of the specific contexts in which it circulated.

Gender difference is one example of the limits imposed on discussing social identity in poetry when the analysis focuses solely on the text's language. As one Japanese scholar has recently noted, modern accounts of Heian court poetry have yet to analyze its historical and rhetorical production of gender in a sustained manner.[36] One difficulty involved in reading gender representations in *uta* lies in the radically open-ended nature of its language. Not only did most poetry not specify the modern categories of person, number, or gender through which subjects are typically specified, it also lacked the honorifics and humilifics through which social identities could be articulated in Heian prose. These ambiguities in any given poem permitted more than one person to speak through its language. Words expressing a lover's plaint in one instance, for example, could be used by a person of either gender to address his or her lord (or mistress) as a client to a patron in another situation.

The lack of social distinctions in the language of *uta* can be seen as the product of the same *yin-yang* metaphysics that correlated cosmological and human relations. In the case of gender, this metaphysics has been described as a system in which the categories of male and female were seen as analogical to other axes of social difference.[37] Moreover, this view of the world emphasized processes of transformation over static states of existence that are discrete and fixed. This ontological fluidity allowed correlative categories of being to shift into one another.[38] Appraising Heian poetry through this lens can help us understand that the goal of achieving harmony between subject and sovereign in poetry was often rhetorically indistinguishable from the goal of harmonizing the relations between men and women or between Heaven and Earth.

My approach to the social identities produced in the pursuit of harmony will take a cue from such correlations, and seek to emphasize the ways in which both class and gender were mutually implicated in one another, as well as in both the language and practices of Heian court poetry. The result is, I hope, a more nuanced picture of the period than totalizing concepts of public and private (or male and female) can provide. The ambiguous distinction between gender and social status in the language of *uta* was matched by the lack of clearly gendered distinctions in the settings associated with poetry matches and the composition of screen poetry in particular. Both genders composed verses and competed with one another for power, wealth, and prestige through these pursuits. Furthermore, both men and women could be the addressees to whom a poem's declarations of loyalty and longing were directed. The primary distinction in such cases was between poet and patron rather than between men and women, as suggested by the fact that the latter was often used to represent the former.

The primacy of the poet-patron relationship in the pursuit of harmony in court poetry also entails a need to reevaluate our modern notions of authorship vis-à-vis the Heian cultural and historical context. In the West, it has been noted by the historian Michel Foucault that the legal and textual status of the author is the product of a particular historical moment.[39] Foucault's account emphasizes the juridical notion of the text as a form of legal property, and is vague about its history prior to the Enlightenment. More recent historians have suggested that the concept of authorial identity as a normative category for texts can be traced back to the establishment of commercial presses.[40] As a way of classifying texts, however, the "author-function" that Foucault identifies stretches back to Socrates and Plato and thus cannot be entirely dispensed with in a premodern historical context.

Scholars have yet to detail the history of authorship in Japan prior to its own early-modern moment of print production. Manuscript cultures, where residual orality is a common characteristic and texts are often infinitely expandable, generally do not easily accommodate modern concepts of authorship as a normative feature of textuality. Even the classificatory function that Foucault claims as a minimal attribute of authorship is remarkably unstable within the Heian context, where a poem that is associated with one author in a particular text may appear as anonymous or the product of another author in alternate texts.[41] In Chapter 3 I shall propose one way of reading Heian poetry that addresses this question in its own historical moment through attention to one of the central practices that defined it as such. The verb *yomu* represented, among other things, the recitation of a text to a group of listeners. Unlike *miru* (silent reading) with its autoerotic and asocial connotations, *yomu* produced socially sanctioned communities of readers, listeners, and reciters. It did so, moreover, in a manner that did not distinguish between the original articulation of a poem by an individual and its rearticulation or verbatim citation by another. In these junctures between orality and textuality, author and reciter, and performers and audience, modern distinctions between a writer and a reader are less relevant than, for example, the degree of sociality implied by various discursive acts.

It could thus be argued that writers of Heian poetry were not authors, insofar as they were the product of neither a notion of the autonomous subject nor a modern capitalist system of print production. The case of poetry from the period is even more complex, because the same term that could identify one as the "composer of a poem" (*utayomi*) also frequently implied that the poem was claimed by someone else. The ubiquity of proxy compositions meant that poems were written in such a way as to address different subjects in different contexts. There might have been culpability, in the sense that a faulty or potentially insulting poem could have consequences for its author's career at court. There was no concept, however, of authorship as ownership. The *uta nushi* or "master of the verse" is the person who recites a poem, not the one who composes it.[42]

Distinctions between the acts of recitation and composition can be seen as also creating social distinctions between the agents engaged in these practices. This important development, which also will be taken up in Chapter 3, is closely tied to changes in the different performative modes associated with the word *yomu*. One result of these changes was that the pursuit of harmony in Heian poetry informed the creation of a new social identity: the poem composer who wrote *uta* for a social superior. Although both men and women engaged in this pursuit, texts such as the Kana Preface to the *Kokinshū* tend to create gendered distinctions between male writers of poetry and female performers of song. By paying attention to these slippages between text and practice, and the different ways that class and gender intersect in both arenas, we can gain some insight into what was at stake and for whom in the pursuit of harmony in Heian poetry.

Writing and Authority

Another area in which I will pursue the topic of harmony in Heian poetry is its relation to the phenomenon of writing. Although all extant early Japanese poetry is by definition written, the early Heian period is distinctive for its heightened interest in the material and visual properties of textuality. In fact, many of the new forms of poetry particular to the period, such as poetry matches and screen poems, depended on these properties for their ritual effects. The late ninth and early tenth centuries also mark a significant watershed in Japanese cultural history as a period in which the diffusion of the *kana* syllabary used to transcribe the Japanese language appears to have expanded exponentially. The history of this diffusion is complex and uneven. Up until the beginning of the tenth century, the modern script system in which one written sign represents one syllable was not universally observed in texts that used *kana* such as the *Shinsen man'yōshū*. At the same time, its growth in this period appears to have been explosive rather than gradual.[43]

Much innovative and important work on Heian *kana* writing has been done in recent years.[44] My own interest in the topic has to do with the particular ways in which the ideological, visual, and material aspects of writing identified by other scholars were manipulated to affirm a variety of political and ritual agendas in premodern Japanese history, as particular features of poetry's textuality were developed, suppressed, or ignored by different parties at different moments. The significance of the term *kana*, for example, is itself indicative of such political concerns. As many scholars have stressed, the concept of *kana* as a "provisional" form of script was implicitly articulated in relation to the more authoritative forms of literary Chinese that preceded it. It is no coincidence in this regard that the Fujiwara regents and retired sovereigns who first promulgated its use as a ritual medium were bent on establishing their equally "provisional" status as substitutes for the sovereign within the court's ceremonial regime.

Perhaps no form of poetic rhetoric is more characteristic of the period and its concerns with assigning human meanings to the natural world through written signs than the "pivot-word" (*kakekotoba*). Its prominent place in the poetry of the period has led to an engagement with this phenomenon at various points in this book. Pivot-words, it could be argued, enabled a peculiarly condensed form of poetic harmonization. In place of a single word or phrase that united two distinct texts (such as two poems, or a poem and a topic phrase), pivot-words merged two syntactically and semantically distinct phrases within a single poem by providing two meanings for a single set of letters. Pivot-words could simultaneously refer to human "aims" (*kokoro*) in the form of verbs and adjectives and landscape "objects" (*mono*) in the form of nouns, thereby linking mutually complementary cosmological phenomena in a manner that transcended normal grammatical rules. As one noted linguist has argued, the result in any given poem was to favor parallel contrastive relations over unity of syntax or meaning.[45] Another scholar describes the semantic enrichment provided by pivot-words, and the frequent attachment of the texts they appear in to other entities as a "rhetoric of supplementation" (*futaku no retorikku*) in which human intent is conveyed through its rhetorical and physical attachment to external objects representing the surrounding world.[46] These effects, as I argue at some length, were often achieved by manipulating the orthographic peculiarities of *kana* and by maximizing the potential for written texts to flatten out aural distinctions that normally obtained in the spoken language.

The harmonies between human activity and landscape scenes enabled through pivot-words in written poems were often deployed with political purposes in mind, reflecting the logic of a Confucian political economy in which the sovereign's harmonization of the human and heavenly spheres guaranteed his right to accumulate and distribute wealth. In many cases, pivot-words in poetry literally produced wealth, such as textiles, out of the places they named. Written *uta* were also manipulated to legitimate ownership by asserting the roles of various powerful figures at court in establishing harmony between Heaven and humanity. This phenomenon is especially evident in the case of poetry matches and screen poetry, where the written poem often interacted with other material objects to represent various figures of authority as the guarantors of harmony between Heaven and humanity. In poetry matches, the choreographed movement of poems as they were attached to different objects and people represented dynamic harmonies between the human and heavenly spheres. In the case of screen poetry, these harmonies took on a ritual cast through their literal placement onto landscape scenes, which in turn enveloped people who were the focus of attention in rituals such as birthday celebrations.

Just as poems often depended on *kana* to create their internal harmonies, the practice of producing harmony in verse was often carried out through a purely textual medium. Court poets typically wrote poems that harmonized with written words rather than spoken utterances or actual landscape scenes. In this sense, the phenomenon of writing poetry is deeply connected with the aforementioned issues of authorship and social identity. As mentioned earlier, one of the purposes behind some of the earliest forms of poetic harmonization at the Heian court was to affirm one's place as a court official, that is, as a writer whose texts represented the ruler's authority throughout the realm. At the same time, the practice of writing *uta* often entailed the alienation of the poet-composer from those public contexts in which membership in the court community was made visible. Compositional practices thus contained a double-edged nature, one that simultaneously provided a place for poets at court while rendering them invisible within its formal occasions. The tensions that such a situation could engender are particularly evident in the case of the period's most prominent court poet and critic Ki no Tsurayuki (ca. 868–945). Many of his writings suggest a lingering ambivalence toward his place at court, one that runs somewhat counter to later visions of this lower-ranking official as an authoritative figure. Such tensions will inform my discussion of his poetic theory and his poetry in Chapters 4 and 5.

One final aim of this book is to outline the broader historical contours of the relations between writing and court poetry, by comparing the significance attached to visual forms of rhetoric in Heian texts with their erasure from medieval recensions. Differences between the two comment on a general shift of emphasis away from vision and onto sound in the twelfth century. The forces driving this change can be seen as part of a broader attempt to create a pedagogical industry catering to a newly emerging political class at the end of the Heian period. This shift was also accompanied by changes in the significance of the word *waka*, as it evolved from a term that placed emphasis on achieving social or cosmological harmony into one that stressed the distinctive aural quality of Japanese words. In this manner, the pursuit of political and poetic harmony in Heian poetry was to metamorphose into a definition of Japanese verse that has continued to be operative up until the present day.

The Structure of This Book

Chapter 1 treats some of the ways in which *uta* represented the Heian court to itself in its first century of existence through a close reading of several instances in which that poetry is portrayed in the court's official historical chronicles, as well as through related materials pertaining to the practices associated with these instances. My aim is to shed light on both the forms that Heian poetic praxis took prior to the period in which the *Kokinshū* was compiled and the ways in which the history of this praxis was being constructed during that same period. I argue that texts from this time distinguish between *waka* as a practice of social harmonization and *yamato uta* as poems that cite Yamato history in written form. The distinct roles played by both forms of *uta* at the early Heian court, and their relation to other textual and ritual practices associated with them will provide a point of departure for further discussion in later chapters.

Chapter 2 focuses on the distinctive new forms of poetic praxis and community created in poetry matches at the court of Uda (867–931, r. 887–897). These contests are commonly viewed as setting the stage for the formal recognition of *uta* as a mode of public poetry in the tenth-century court. After an overview of scholarly conceptions of "formal court poetry" (*hare no uta*), I suggest the relation of this term to the social topographies produced in court ritual in general and poetry matches in particular. I then outline the historical context in which Uda's matches took place through attention to developments in language, ritual, palace architecture, social identity, succession politics, and the place of women at court in this period of dramatic cultural change. It will be argued that these matches responded to such changes by creating new visions of authority and community through the development of love and the seasons as topical categories, the ritual use of written poems, and the creation of the "composer" (*utayomi*) as a distinct social identity.

Chapter 3 describes the construction of a competing vision of court community in the *Kokinshū*. I approach this difference through attention to how and why the first imperial anthology of Japanese verse borrowed the language and practices of royal banquets to represent a view of the world from the palace. I then analyze certain features of the *Kokinshū* that are often seen as ancillary to individual poems but nonetheless provide a frame for reading them—including the anthology's categories and the language of its prose prefaces—in terms of the cosmological, social and political viewpoints they encoded. For the remainder of the chapter, I focus on the four categories in the *Kokinshū* that are mentioned in its Kana Preface: Blessings, Travel, the Seasons, and Love, and show the varying ways their internal structures created a particular vision of the court's geography, temporality, and sociality that would define it for centuries afterward.

Chapter 4 is intended to provide a new reading of the anthology's renowned Kana Preface. I argue that its account of "Yamato verse" (*yamato uta*) is a polemic for the written poem and the male composer. After explaining how similar prefaces written for royal peregrinations can elucidate our understanding of its social, political, and authorial characteristics, I show how the Kana Preface differs in subtle but significant ways from its literary Chinese counterpart. Whereas the former treats *yamato uta* as a written form poetry, with distinctive stylistic traits that depend on silent reading, the latter places more emphasis on song and the practice of harmonization in its definition of what it calls *waka*. I then discuss the way the textual nature of *yamato uta* further informs distinctions between male and female poetry by alluding to practices associated with royal banquets at which male officials inscribed poems while female entertainers danced and sang for them. The chapter concludes by suggesting that, far from being authoritative, the Kana Preface's distinctive vision of *yamato uta* was ignored by the pedagogical industry that arose around the *Kokinshū* in the twelfth century.

Chapter 5 turns to the development of screen poetry in the years surrounding the *Kokinshū*'s compilation. I argue for the need to reconsider issues of gender, genre, and perspective that have dominated scholarly discussions about this prominent form of court poetry, and offer an alternate history that begins with the ritual display of authority in palace paintings. Screen poetry provided new stages on which various men and women could lay claim to wealth. Insofar as it was composed by command on particular topics, moreover, screen poetry can be considered a form of "harmonizing verse." I follow this overview with an appraisal of the social implications involved in the act of producing and inscribing these poems. From these broader issues, the chapter turns to a close reading of poems by Tsurayuki who, in addition to being the chief compiler of the *Kokinshū* and the author of its Kana Preface, was also a prolific and much sought-after composer of screen poetry. I focus on his trademark use of reflective surfaces to complicate the visual doubles favored in court poetry by introducing a third mediating term between them. In conclusion, I suggest that this distinctive tripartite structure comments in turn on the visual and spatial features of screen poetry, and more generally on the mediating role of the court poet who produces topic-based proxy compositions.

The epilogue considers the place of early Heian poetry within the broader narratives through which the Heian period has been represented. In particular, I focus on the valences of the word "Yamato" as it was developed then, and show how they shed light on our contemporary understanding of Japanese court poetry. At the same time, an awareness of historical shifts in the place of poetry at court can also contribute toward our understanding of "early Heian Japan" as a distinct moment within the *longue durée* of the Heian period (794–1185), as well as within the broader cultural and institutional developments described in contemporary histories of the Japanese court. In this regard, I am particularly interested in the ways that the poetry under discussion in this book comments on and can contribute to our understanding of such contemporary historical categories as gender, empire, and the medieval as they relate to Japanese court culture.

Appendixes providing English translations of several texts that are cited frequently follow the epilogue. One intention in doing so is to offer translations of important texts that are not readily accessible to English speakers—such as the prefaces to the first three imperial anthologies of *shi* poetry and a *chōka* from one of the official court chronicles that is often cited by scholars in histories of early Japanese poetry. Although many of these texts—the two prefaces to the *Kokinshū* in particular[47]—have already been translated into English, I have provided new versions in order to emphasize the social function of poetry, and to incorporate insights into these important texts that have been afforded by scholarship in the intervening decades. My hope in all of these cases is to make the texts I translate accessible to both scholars and students of Heian literature, in order to further our understanding of a pivotal moment in Japanese cultural history.

Chapter One

Heian Histories of Poetic Harmony

Uta in Early Heian History

Conventional histories of Japanese poetry tend to begin their accounts of the Heian period with the years surrounding the compilation of the *Kokinshū* at the start of the tenth century. As an imperially sponsored anthology, this poetry collection is seen as epitomizing a newfound interest in the native language and culture that allegedly distinguish the Heian period from its more sinophilic predecessor. If we look closely at the preceding century, however, we see a more complex picture, one in which distinctions between genres such as *shi* or *uta* were less germane than distinctions in the performative contexts in which poems operated. Most of these practices have not been investigated in detail, and some of them have been virtually ignored in modern scholarship. This chapter will consider how these performative contexts developed as responses to political tensions and changes within the court community and the ways in which they can help provide new understandings of what made the later *Kokinshū* an imperial project.

Although the Heian period has typically been portrayed as the first sustained development of a native culture in the form of vernacular writing, painting, and architecture, it can perhaps best be distinguished from its immediate predecessor for its pronounced turn toward continental forms of political and social community. The reigns of the first four sovereigns of the Heian period, Kammu (781–806, r. 781–806), Heizei (806–809, r. 806–809), Saga (786–842, r. 809–823), and Junna (786–840, r. 823–833), witnessed a pronounced infusion of continental culture into the court's elite, from official garb to palace architecture, court ritual, and education. With the establishment of an urban center at Heiankyō, continental forms of literacy were disseminated through the capital's university to create a broader community of "men of letters" (*monnin*) composed of its graduates, men whose identities were largely defined by their facility with the writing brush.

Kammu and his sons were aided in their attempts to introduce new forms of government and culture through the extensive marital alliances they cultivated with immigrant clans whose familiarity with continental culture made them invaluable resources.[1] Kammu's own mother came from a family of immigrants from the former peninsular ally of Paekche. The location of this clan in Yamashiro influenced the decision to move the capital to that province.[2] The turn toward the continent in early Heian court culture was also spurred on by a rapid growth in the number of male officials who were responsible for meeting the needs of an expanding imperium. Another impetus for the new interest in continental culture at Kammu's court was an awareness of the ways in which written poetry had been used in other court communities to negotiate internal tensions. Similar stresses were endemic to the early Heian court, and their traces can be found in the texts and practices through which its members sought to pursue harmony in verse.

The ways in which poetry was used to create a sense of community at the early Heian court can be seen as indicative of this general turn to continental forms of culture. During the Nara period (710–794), native song had frequently been pressed into service in this capacity. In 734, for example, men and women belonging to six clans of immigrants from Paekche held a "song fence" (*utagaki*) in the western part of the capital in which they faced each other and sang six Japanese songs. The "song fence," which had originally referred to seasonal gatherings of young men and women from local communities, was being used here to create a similar sense of community in a new urban setting. When the capital was moved to Heiankyō in 795, however, these songs were replaced with quatrains of verse in literary Chinese (*jueju* or *zekku* in Japanese) which followed the latest continental style of heptasyllabic lines with elaborate rhyme schemes.[3]

In keeping with the continental turn in court culture during the early ninth century, the written record of the early Heian period mentions *shi* poetry more often than *uta*. What we know about the place of *uta* during the early Heian period is derived primarily from court histories, and these references become increasingly rare over time.[4] This paucity of native verse in the official record has been seen by the leading authority on the literature of the period, Kojima Noriyuki, as indicative of a "dark age of national culture" (*kokufū ankoku jidai*). We should keep in mind, however, that these historical texts place emphasis on annual banquets and other forms of court ritual, and that the actual popularity of *uta* in other settings cannot be gauged from such sources.

The picture, in fact, is more complex than the example of Kammu's *utagaki* or the official historical record might suggest. Both *shi* and *uta* coexisted in both the Nara and early Heian periods in many settings. By the reign of Shōmu (701–756, r. 724–749), these forms of poetry were being composed at numerologically significant junctures in the calendrical year, such as the New Year's Day, the Double Third, and the Double Seventh, all of which were designed to dramatize the Confucian ruler's ability to synchronize human cycles with those of Heaven.[5] At the same time, however, a general distinction was maintained between these two forms of poetry on the basis of their place within such rites. Whereas the formal first half of the banquet was devoted to commissioning and writing *shi*, *uta* were performed only at the end of the rite as an occasional supplement. Some scholars believe that the latter's location at the informal end of the banquet explains in part why extant *uta* from the period are so rare, since they were likely to have been composed on the spot and forgotten soon afterward.[6]

Given the relative infrequency with which *uta* are mentioned in early Heian court histories, it is significant that these instances often involve the Fujiwara regency. In this chapter I will argue that a significant shift took place at the time of the latter institution's establishment in the mid ninth century, when *uta* began to occupy the same spaces in such rituals that *shi* had previously monopolized. The regency's initial status as a contingent and provisional institution whose legitimacy was derived from the continuing existence of a reigning sovereign was reflected in the development of new forms of poetic practice that were deliberately modeled after their continental predecessors. One product of this shift was the articulation of "Yamato verse" (*yamato uta*) as a distinct form of *uta* written in the *kana* syllabary. A chief area of investigation here will be the ways in which the terms *waka* and *yamato uta* referred to different forms of verse in this setting.

One other source of early Heian *uta* represents a very different agenda from that of the Fujiwara regents. The *Ruijū kokushi* (*The History of the Realm Topically Arranged*, 892) is a historical encyclopedia compiled by the scholar-official Sugawara no Michizane (845–903) during the reign of Uda. This digest of historical material provides a rich source of insights into the uses of poetry to assert monarchical power and negotiate tensions within the court during the ninth century. Both functions would have been particularly germane to Uda, who was striving to reestablish the sovereign's authority after a long period of Fujiwara domination. The extensive categorizing of poetry composed during banquets and royal processions found in the *Ruijū kokushi* offered precedents for Uda's own rituals involving the composition of *uta*. In this sense, the *Ruijū kokushi* provides not only insights into the history of early Heian poetry but also a counterpoint to the official historical narratives produced by the Fujiwara.

My approach to these texts will be twofold. On the one hand, they can be used to track points at which political contexts and poetic acts intersected in the century prior to the *Kokinshū*. On the other, they provided past precedents and contemporary understandings of court poetry for the men and women involved in the construction of a court poetics during the time that the *Kokinshū* was being compiled. Insofar as the sources for constructing a history of early Heian *uta* were official historical chronicles produced by the ruling figures of the court, they provided a variety of ways for defining *uta* as a public and official form of poetry.

Harmonizing the Court in Kammu's Banquets

One of the earliest datable verses from the Heian court provides unusually detailed insights into the ways in which poetic ritual was deployed to establish Kammu's new regime at Heiankyō. During this time, *uta* were used to knit the elite together in the face of immense strains on the economic, social, and political fabric of court society, as the Yamato realm engaged in the two expensive projects of constructing a new capital and militarily expanding the imperium's northeast borders. One of the means for responding to such strains was through a poetic practice known as "harmonization" (*wa*) in which the sovereign's words were echoed in poems by his followers. This practice, and the banquets in which it took place, were in turn memorialized in the *Ruijū kokushi* compiled at Uda's court.

Poetic harmonization at Kammu's court appears to have largely taken place at *kyokuen* (curving banquets). In the *Shiji* (*Records of the Grand Historian*, ca. 109–91 B.C.E.) and other Chinese texts, the word refers to gatherings where the seating is arranged in a winding shape to facilitate the exchange of wine cups among the participants, thereby fostering intimacy among them. Such arrangements would have helped Kammu mobilize the powerful clans of the court behind his expensive projects. The occasional nature of these banquets provided a flexible medium for responding to political tensions, one that was not dependent on the architecture of the palace to stage them, or the calendrical schedule to which more formal annual observances adhered. Kammu's first *kyokuen* banquet was held in 795, just before he was to initiate the construction of the new capital at Heiankyō. The one he held in the following year took place during his fifth campaign against the Emishi tribes living on the imperium's eastern borders.

The most detailed account of Kammu's *kyokuen* verse can be found under a heading bearing the same name in Scroll 75 of the *Ruijū kokushi.* The banquet in question was held a month before the palace enclosure at Heiankyō was officially completed. No doubt, this *kyokuen* was intended to thank Kammu's ministers for their efforts in establishing the new capital.[7] The relatively detailed account of this event, the politically charged nature of its immediate context, and the curious description of a compulsory poetic exchange all make this entry a productive point of departure for considering the ways *uta* were put to work in constructing a community at the Heian court.

> Enryaku 14/4/11. Kyokuen. His Majesty intoned the following ancient verse:

Since ancient times has been	*inishie no*
the old way through Nonaka's fields.	*Nonaka no furumichi*
If we are to reform it	*aratameba*
let us reform it now!	*aratamaramu ya*
The old way through Nonaka's fields.	*Nonaka no furumichi*

He commanded the Imperial Handmaid of Junior Third Rank, Kudara no Kokishi Myōshin, to respond in harmony with this verse, but she was unable to, and so His Majesty harmonized with his previous verse in her place:

It is you, my lord,	*kimi koso wa*
who seem to have forgotten.	*wasuretaru rame*
Softly compliant	*nikitama no*
and frail of limb is this woman,	*tawayame ware wa*
who remains a constant pearl.	*tsune no shiratama*[8]

The setting of this *kyokuen* banquet, in which men and women faced each other across a small space, drank, and chanted verse, resembles the grand performance of *utagaki* rituals before an urban populace. In this case, however, the performance is on a more intimate scale, with the audience limited to the court elite. Both rites staged the creation of a human community through choreographed exchanges between male and female performers. Here, however, the nature of the performance is not decided ahead of time, making it a potentially fraught negotiation between parties in establishing their political, ritual, and gendered roles vis-à-vis one another.

The old song with which Kammu begins is rife with ritualistic repetitions in its wording and structure. The opening phrase *inishie no* (ancient times) is amplified by *furu* (old) in the next line. Amplification becomes repetition when the subsequent noun phrase *Nonaka no furu michi* appears again at the end of the poem. The two intervening lines provide variations of a single verb *aratamu* (to reform). Early songs often contained an element of formal repetition designed to enable their incantatory effects, and judging from the *Ruijū kokushi's* account, Kammu's performance has a similar intent. The use of the character 誦 (intone) to describe his recitation here suggests a somewhat archaic style of chanting. Such elements make Kammu's old verse a ritual speech act which "reforms" (*aratamu*) the multiple meanings latent in the phrase *Nonaka no furu michi* that ends each half of the poem. The result is to reshape an earlier verse to address, and perhaps influence, its speaker's immediate performative context. The phrase could refer to the trails that once passed through the fields of Furu in Yamato province. In the current context, it also alludes to the physical contours of Kammu's new capital. In addition to facilitating the flow of goods, information, and people, roads defined the capital's urban space as a grid radiating out from the palace. Another meaning of *furumichi* as "the Ways of Antiquity" suggests Kammu's desire to assert continuity in observing the moral and ritual practices of Confucian kingship. His recitation of an old song in the months prior to the establishment of a new ritual center for his sacerdotal duties also observes the Confucian imperative to preserve old ways while reforming them to suit new circumstances.

In addition to these trappings of rulership, the phrase that Kammu intones twice introduces sexual politics as well, drawing as it does on the conventions of *utagaki* exchanges in which a masculine speaker initiates a plea for feminine interest. The Kana Preface to the *Kokinshū* associates the phrase "drawing the waters of Nonaka" with the revival of a defunct love affair.[9] In this reading, the "old path through the fields" becomes a trail that a male lover once took in his visits to a woman's home, and the desire to "reform" it could contain a request that the relationship be renewed. By commanding Kudara no Kokishi Myōshin (737–815) to respond to this verse with one that "harmonizes with it" (令和之), Kammu overtly eroticizes the content of the old poem he has recited. The *Nihon kōki* in fact suggests that she was a favorite of his before she married the influential nobleman Fujiwara no Tsugutada (727–796).

Given Myōshin's position at court and the public nature of the gathering, however, more than purely erotic desire is likely to have been involved in Kammu's entreaty for her favors. In invoking Myōshin's past relationship with him, Kammu might also implicitly be asking for her support as he sets about reestablishing the court in a new locale. As *naishi no kami* (head of the Imperial Handmaids Office), Myōshin was in charge of the office entrusted with the sacred mirror representing the Yamato dynasty's divine ancestor. In keeping with her ritual role as a medium between the Sun Goddess and the court, she also played a similar role vis-à-vis the divine monarch and his courtiers. It was through her that communications passed between the sovereign and his ministers. The central political and ritual role accorded such women made their allegiances crucial to establishing the ruler's authority at court.

Myōshin's failure to reply with a poem of her own can be read in as many ways as Kammu's initiating poem. Perhaps she wishes to create an impression of independence before the men who depend on her favors for access to their sovereign. Perhaps she wishes to avoid any public performance that might remind her Fujiwara husband of her former allegiances. Or perhaps she is unable to come up with something appropriate to the polysemantic complexity of Kammu's old verse. Regardless, the historical account appears to be more focused on the importance of an exchange taking place rather than on Myōshin's own place within it. Most commentators tend to read Kammu's initial song as an attempt to elicit the woman's romantic interest.[10] However, this interpretation seems hard to reconcile with the way in which the exchange develops. Because Kammu seems to feel obliged to supply his own female respondent, the ritual performance of proper gendered relations in verse appears to be more important in this instance than the ability or desire of particular agents to enact them.

Kammu's response to his earlier song is described as "a harmonizing verse" (*wa suru uta*). There appear to be several dimensions to his act, at least one of which is political. His second poem's declaration of compliant loyalty, makes manifest his desire for the same qualities in his female partner. Kammu's poem is also a "harmonizing verse" in the sense that it echoes the syllables of its predecessor in a clever and subtle adaptation of the earlier song. In mentioning the "gentle spirit" (*nikitama*) of the woman in his response, Kammu implicitly evokes its complementary gendered opposite of *aratama* (rough spirit), a word that can be found in the syllables of the verb *aratamaramu* (let us reform them) that appeared in the first verse. Kammu's novel effort to echo syllables rather than semantically discrete words can be seen as a variant on the continental practice of harmonizing with a poem by replicating its sounds and rhyme schemes.

The overriding need for this poetic harmonization to take place, regardless of the actual desires or abilities of the participants, suggests it held a vital ritual role within the event, perhaps even as an act with cosmological significance. In continental models of the universe, "harmony" referred to the balanced exchange of energies between *yin* and *yang* from which the myriad phenomena of the world are created. One of the most succinct descriptions of this form of cosmogenesis can be found in the Daoist classic *Laozi* (ca. late third century B.C.E.):

"The Way gives birth to One. One gives birth to Two. Two give birth to Three. Three give birth to the myriad phenomena of the world. The myriad things in the world bear both *yin* and *yang* within themselves in harmony."[11] According to this model, all phenomena in the world are conceived of as arising from the balanced interaction of mutually complementary opposites. Similarly, harmony in poetic form was a generative act that produced its social world rather than simply representing it.

The court's foundational myths provide one variant of this principle in poetic form when they stress the importance of gendered propriety in verbal exchanges between the progenitor deities Izanami and Izanagi as a prerequisite for the proper generation of the myriad deities who go on to populate the land. This notion of discursive harmony as a generative model is reenacted through the narrative structure of the *Ruijū kokushi*'s account. Kammu's recitation of a poem leads to the creation of a complementary poem, and the combination of these two generates a host of chants for "a myriad more years" (*banzai*) from the assembled nobility. Insofar as many nobles traced their descent back to Izanami and Izanagi's divine progeny, this sequence of roles can be seen as a ritual reproduction of the court's mythic origins. Such a ritual assertion of continuities between the present genesis of a community at Heiankyō and the past production of Yamato ancestral deities must have resonated in a time when that court was experiencing profound dislocation.

Poetic acts of harmony were never assured of proper execution or stable meanings in their performative contexts. As with any prescribed ritual action, the possibility that individual agents might disrupt the performance by failing to carry out their assigned roles presents a constant threat. Izanami's initial failure to observe her proper place as the respondent rather than initiator in her verbal exchange with Izanagi leads to malformed progeny. The potential for Myōshin's silence to create an equally unfortunate result is implied by Kammu's efforts to provide the proper words in her stead. This is perhaps one reason why such performances were often recreated in textual form, where writing could stabilize the relations between poems in a fixed context that was no longer open to the poets' agency.

Kammu and his successors appear to have attributed great importance to *uta*'s potential for harmonizing and codifying relations between genders and political actors in the court's community. Although the word *waka* eventually became a generic term for Japanese poetry, the court's official dynastic chronicles often use it to refer to the act of poetic "harmonization" at formal banquets, in which loyal subjects cited the words of their sovereign. Like cosmological modes of harmonization, its poetic form was profoundly productive. In its many incarnations it helped affirm continuities with the past and create new communities during a period when the Yamato court was involved in the material, political, and ideological construction of a new capital at the heart of a new empire.

The Poetry of Royal Progressions

Although the palace constituted the inner core of Kammu's new capital, its immediate periphery was equally important for defining the imperium's center. This region was the site of frequent hunting expeditions during which Kammu inspected his new realm. In the banquet following one such hunt that took place in Enryaku 17/8/13 (798), *uta* generate harmonies that bind together the sovereign, his retinue at court, and the surrounding lands:

> On the thirteenth His Majesty went hunting in the fields of Kitano. Afterward he visited Prince Iyo in his mountain villa. Wine flowed and spirits were high. At dusk, His Majesty sang this song:
>
> | | |
> |---|---|
> | At break of dawn | *kesa no asake* |
> | the deer is said to cry. | *naku chō shika no* |
> | I'll not leave without hearing | *kono koe o* |
> | it give voice, | *kikazu wa yukaji* |
> | though deepest night may fall. | *yo wa fuken tomo* |
>
> Just then, a deer cried out keenly. He commanded his assembled ministers to harmonize with his verse. After night fell they returned.[12]

Once again, Kammu's verse displays his monarchical power by generating harmonies that proceed from the singular to the binary and then plural multiplicity. The deer's vocal act of fealty in responding to his verse, like the feminine response to Kammu at the previous *kyokuen* banquet, establishes a matrix for multiple declarations of fealty as the sovereign proceeds to "command his assembled courtiers to harmonize with this [verse]" (令群臣和之). In this case, the deer's demonstration of fealty also suggests Kammu's sovereignty over the spirits of the mountainsides and uncultivated areas. Access to the bounty provided by these spirits was traditionally a prerogative of the Yamato rulers.[13] By echoing his verse in their own "harmonizations," the poems of Kammu's entourage thus acknowledge his divine sovereignty.

Kammu's poetic performance of harmony here caps a royal excursion whose ritual characteristics preserved some of the most archaic forms of monarchical ritual associated with the Yamato dynasty. The composition of *uta* on royal hunts can be seen from as early as the seventh century.[14] In the early Heian period, these hunts took the form of hawking expeditions requiring a retinue of specialist handlers, unlike the hunting of deer or boar by commoners. Hunts were typically held in the Tenth or Eleventh Month, after the harvest and before the full onset of winter. Hunting grounds were designated as sacred spaces by placing boundary markers known as *shimeno* around their perimeter. At the end of the hunt, the sovereign traveled to the fields in a palanquin and viewed the kill. The rite then concluded with an informal banquet, such as the one at which Kammu composed the poem above.[15]

Royal hunts staged the sovereign's sway over the nonagricultural land of not only the capital but also the realm at large through the enactment of a rite known as "realm-viewing" (*kunimi*). By the early Heian period, such hunts were one of the few instances in which this archaic ritual was enacted. On these occasions, the sovereign would ascend a hill and gaze out over the surrounding landscape in order to mark his ownership of it.[16] The progression of the hunting party from court to countryside suggests a careful choreographed movement of both monarchical visibility and monarchical vision expanding outward from the palace to mark distinct zones around its immediate perimeter. The rite would begin with the sovereign appearing before his entourage, which, as it journeyed from the palace into the wilds, would observe the populace of the capital region and be observed by them. In the mountains and fields he viewed the game caught by his hunters, finally gazing out over his realm from a hill.

Kammu's hawking expeditions also staged his spiritual authority over the deities of the new capital region. Places such as Ōharano, Kitano, and Katano, in which the first Heian sovereign held his hunting expeditions, were all sacred sites marked by shrines to local deities. By establishing his hunting fields and their boundary poles in these sites, Kammu replaced local sacred spaces with markers of a larger one organized around his divine person. His collection of the surrounding land's bounty signaled the sovereign's primacy over the capital's boundaries by asserting his entitlement to the products of the mountains, forests, and fields and the services of the local spirits who provided them. In this context, the deer of Kammu's poem quite likely represents a local *kami* spirit.

The use of a poem to assert Kammu's rights to the land in this entry from the *Ruijū kokushi* would have held particular significance for that compendium's royal sponsor. Whereas royal hunts and processions had been a hallmark of earlier Heian courts, they had languished under Uda's immediate predecessors, when the center of ritual activity had shifted to the Fujiwara regents in the mid ninth century. These regents had used Buddhist prohibitions against the taking of life to curtail such exercises in monarchical authority. Uda was noticeably interested in reviving royal outings as a way of asserting his visibility and ritual authority. One hallmark of his peregrinations, like those of Kammu, was the frequency with which he commanded his entourage to harmonize in verse with his words. Such practices would feature prominently in the construction of a concept of formal *uta* during the time that the *Kokinshū* anthology was produced.

Confucian Visions of Harmony in Heizei's Reign

Kammu's son and successor Heizei holds an important, if ambivalent place in the history of *uta*. Despite the brevity of his reign, his presence within the larger Heian historical and poetic imagination looms large. In later generations he was seen as a champion of native verse in contrast to his more insistently sinophilic brother Saga.[17] Within the *Kokinshū* anthology, he became the symbol of a divided court, one used to allude to the binary polity in which that anthology took shape. In fact, Heizei's use of *waka* at his court suggests a continuity with the practices of Kammu and the active presence of an ideology that can be seen, in at least some respects, as continental in origin.

Heizei's reign was largely defined by political crisis and instability, forces that cast a shadow over later attempts to assert continuity within the new court community at Heiankyō. Although Heiankyō would serve as the capital for over a millennium, its status, like that of Nara before it, was far from assured in the initial years of its existence. Tensions between Kammu's two sons Heizei and Saga frayed the fabric of court society to the breaking point in what became known as the Kusuko Incident. Heizei was never in the best of health, and after only three years of government, he ceded the throne to his younger brother. The older brother continued to ensure that his interests were represented at the new sovereign's court through his consort Fujiwara no Kusuko (d. 810), who occupied the crucial post of *naishi no kami*. In order to undercut his female rival, Saga established the exclusively male post of *kurōdo no tō* (head of the Secretariat) as the chief intermediary between the ruler and his government. Heizei responded by declaring that the capital was to be moved to his official residence at Nara. Within the span of six days, Saga executed Kusuko's brother and then captured Heizei and Kusuko as they fled east. Heizei was forced to take the tonsure, his consort, to take poison.

Even prior to the dramatic events surrounding the Kusuko Incident, tensions can be detected in an exchange of poems between the brothers during a banquet held in Daidō 2/9/21 (807). As with Kammu's attempted exchange with Myōshin, the practice of poetic harmony here suggests frictions that are lying just beneath the surface.

> His Majesty went in procession to the Shinsen-en Park. Zither songs were performed and those of Fourth Rank and above placed chrysanthemums in their hair. His Majesty's younger brother then sang a song of praise:

Folk of the court	*miyabito no*
smitten by the fragrance	*sono ka ni mezuru*
of wisteria trousers	*fujibakama*
belonging to my lord	*kimo no ōmono*
are breaking them off today!	*te oritaru kyō*

His Majesty harmonized with this, saying:

In following the desires	*oribito no*
of those who break them off	*kokoro no ma ni ma*
these wisteria trousers	*fujibakama*
indeed shine forth	*ube iro fukaku*
in shades of deepest hue!	*nioitarikeri*

The assembled ministers all intoned "banzai." Robes were conferred upon those of Fifth Rank and above.[18]

The arrangement of these poems presents a carefully choreographed performance of fraternal harmony between Heizei and Saga. The younger brother sings the elder's praises by declaring that the courtiers are drawn to his glory. The elder responds by suggesting that the scenery's splendor can be attributed to the desires of his court. Once again, poetic harmonization engenders cheers from the watching courtiers that serve to signal the court's political harmony. Fraternal relations, however, appear to have involved a more delicate negotiation of position than Kammu's assertion of masculine authority over a female counterpart. Despite his stature as ruler and elder brother, Heizei is the one who responds in harmony with his younger brother's words. This ambiguity in status is amplified by the younger brother's eager assertion of his role in speaking for the sentiments of all the court's members in his song of praise.

In keeping with the conventions for *uta* exchanges, phrases that are especially polysemantic become the currency exchanged between the two parties. In this case, the pivotal word is "wisteria trousers" (*fujibakama*), which refers to a pale purple flower and a particular shade of clothing that Heizei could have worn for the event. In claiming that the courtiers are stirred and moved by the fragrance of flowers and by the charisma of the sovereign, Saga's poem evokes the vision of an idealized Confucian ruler who harmonizes the realms of Heaven and humanity to ensure prosperity and well-being among his subjects. Heizei in turn implies that the glory and bounty represented by his virtue stems from the desires of his subjects. As we shall see, blossoms also figure prominently in the *Kokinshū*'s poetic of imperial virtue.

The political implications of this poetic union of royal splendor and natural glory gained meaning within a larger Confucian system that encompassed cosmological, ritual, political, and economic dimensions. The scholar Ōmuro Mikio has described this system as an "economy of virtue," with "virtue" (*toku*) being the ruler's power to accumulate, refine, and redirect the energies of his subjects through his performance of ritual actions in synchrony with the celestial and seasonal cycles of Heaven, thereby ensuring material bounty and social harmony.[19] Ritual action transformed the state's wealth into a form of virtue that propitiated Heaven, ensured future bounty, and encouraged the realm's subjects to cleave to the social order. Through such actions, the ruler would manage the forces of transformation that moved the natural world, thereby ensuring that his people would behave toward one another in accordance with hierarchies of age, gender, kinship, and social status.

Heavenly and royal virtue are inseparable in the poems exchanged between Saga and Heizei, insofar as the sovereign's charisma is displayed in both his resplendent person and Heaven's manifestation of autumnal splendor. The accumulated energies of royal virtue in the human and celestial realms subsequently take material form in the textile gifts bestowed upon the courtiers at the banquet and the flowers they pluck in order to ingest the season's energies. Through the dispensation of state bounty in a seasonal setting, banquets such as this one enacted the classical continental vision of the ruler as the source and distributor of virtue. As we shall see, the practice of composing poetry on royal command codified and formalized the balanced exchange of virtue as it flowed between sovereign and subject at Saga's court.

Another poem in the *Ruijū kokushi* reveals a different dimension to the Confucian vision of a realm, one in which the ruler's virtue pacifies his subjects in a direct and overt manner. In this case, a courtier named Heguri no Kazemaro declares his loyalty by composing a *waka* verse at his sovereign's command during a procession in 808. Both the poem and its performative context suggest the importance of verse in codifying and harmonizing the relations between the Heian empire and its periphery.

How strong must be the force	*ika ni fuku*
with which these winds blow,	*kaze ni areba ka*
for plumes of pampas	*ōshima no*
on our great isle	*obana ga sue o*
to bunch together so!	*fukimusubitaru*[20]

Kazemaro's astonishment at the wind's ability to tangle plumes of pampas grass into clumps is more than simple awe at the power of natural forces. The image of grasses bending before the wind evokes a well-known passage from the *Analects* in which it is used to describe the suasive influence of the superior man's virtue over that of his inferiors.[21] In this regard, it is also significant that this poetic declaration of submission is made by the "head of the Hayato Office" (*hayato-shi no kami*), named after a tribe from southern Kyūshū who had been conquered by the early Yamato kings. Along with the Kuzu of Yoshino, the Hayato at court were not an actual ethnic group, but rather specialized court performers who enacted the submission of these peoples to Heian sovereigns through offerings of regional songs and dances at official rites.[22] These musicians, singers and dancers were usually members of the Inner Palace Guards (Konoefu) recruited from nearby provinces where the Hayato and Kuzu peoples had been resettled after the ancient Yamato rulers had conquered them. As such, they were actors who represented the court's imaginary Others to itself in the performance of a continental-style imperial geography whose necessary complement was a "barbarian" periphery.

This declaration of fealty by the official court representative of an ethnic group domesticated by the early Yamato kings must have resonated at Heizei's court, which had shifted from a policy of expansion on the Heian imperium's borders to one of assimilation. To stabilize the frequently contested northeastern frontier, Heizei's court forcibly removed the native inhabitants of conquered regions to villages across the rest of the realm, where they could be more easily controlled and absorbed into the general populace.[23] In the poetic performance of Kazemaro, the bloody disruptions and cultural genocide entailed by such policies are recast in a ritual reenactment of an earlier peoples' submission to their Yamato conquerors. The coercive policies of Heizei's present moment are thus smoothed over and cast as one instance of an eternal imperial order whose origins stretch back into myth.

In this account of poetic submission, the ruler's moral virtue is manifest in a balanced exchange of emotional energies between sovereign and subject. A royal command generates Kazemaro's declaration of his ruler's suasive powers, and this in turn moves the ruler to tears, leading him to promote the poet one grade in rank. In this Confucian economy of virtue, the loyal (conquered) subject's love for his sovereign engenders material rewards in the form of wealth and rank. By analogy, the use of Confucian political allegory through an allusion to the *Analects* here might also suggest the benefits of continental culture to the empire's new subjects. In this context, the use of the word *waka* to describe Kazemaro's poem refers as much, if not more, to its function in harmonizing the relations between sovereign and subject as to its being a native form of verse. Such harmonies help define the relations between the center and its newly conquered ethnic borderlands as ones that were beneficial to both parties.

The preservation of this poem in the *Ruijū kokushi* points to the enduring importance of its political vision of empire in later times. Although subsequent Heian rulers did not engage in aggressive territorial expansion on the scale pursued by Kammu, ritual demonstrations of the submission of "barbarians" in song and dance formed an integral part of the court's annual rituals. Even during the reigns of Saga and Junna, a period in which *shi* poetry was the most conspicuous form of verse at court, "songs of the Eastlands" (*azuma kuni no uta*) occupied a significant portion of the ritual repertoire. The symbolic geography of empire represented by such rites would play an especially important part in structuring the *Kokinshū*. The first imperial anthology of *uta*—which opens with an evocation of New Year's Day rites involving the Yoshino no Kuzu performers and ends with a shrine performance of music from the Eastlands—is framed by a Confucian vision of barbarian submission to the center similar to that seen in this poem from Heizei's reign.

The setting for Heizei's poetic harmonizations formed an integral part of their Confucian symbolism, insofar as they often took place on a ritual stage that was designed as a physical manifestation of the sovereign's ability to harmonize humanity's relations with Heaven. Modeled after the royal parklands of continental capitals, the Shinsen-en (Divine Spring Park) was an eighty-square kilometer enclosure surrounding one of the city's chief water sources.[24] During the reigns of Kammu and his sons it was the favored site for processions and annual banquets using the latest Tang forms of court ritual.[25] There, these sovereigns feted scholar-officials and aristocratic ministers, distributed their stipends, and ordered them to write poetry on preselected topics in a ritualized enactment of their bureaucratic work producing documents that expressed the royal will.

Every element in the arrangement of the park held geomantic significance, creating a world in miniature. Carefully coordinated arrangements of water, stones, and buildings were designed to place the ruler at the center of a harmonious composition of Heaven, Earth, and humanity. The spring for which the Shinsen-en was named lay in the geomantically vulnerable northeast corner of the park, where it became a small waterfall before flowing into a pond with an island at its center. On the geomantically dominant northern shore of this pond stood a pavilion in the latest Tang style where the sovereign held banquets for his officials and staged entertainments for them before distributing stipends. During these banquets, the sovereign would be seated with princes and senior ministers in the pavilion, below which were steps leading down to a dancing stage on which entertainers danced and sang "women's music" (*jogaku*). Seated to either side of this stage were nonaristocratic male officials—described as "men of letters" (*monnin*) in the court's official histories—who strove to demonstrate their masculine worth with the brush as they watched this erotic spectacle.

With its combination of carefully sculpted natural features and continental architecture, the Shinsen-en embodied the twin poles of Heaven and humanity over which the ruler presided. As a vital source of water, the park constituted a tangible juncture at which the cycles of Heaven and the well-being of the capital's population intersected. On its stage, the act of inscribing royal words in poetry would come to the fore as a way of binding the realm together. These means for expressing political and cosmological harmony represented a distinct new relationship among verse, writing, and ritual that came to define formal court poetry at the Heian court well into the next century. It was Heizei's successor who would provide their initial articulation through the promulgation of a textual culture in which writing sought to both represent and create social stability.

Binding the Realm in Writing

The reigns of Saga and his successor Junna hold a particularly important place in later Japanese cultural history as a period in which the practice of composing *shi* poetry attained new levels of sophistication. From the mid-Heian period onward, histories of *shi* poetry at the Yamato court would represent the fourteen years of Saga's reign in the Kōnin era (810–824) as the apex of literary achievement. Even modern scholars such as Kojima Noriyuki, who have typified this period as a nadir for Japanese literature, acknowledge the influence Saga's poetry exerted on the court's later tradition of native verse. In summarizing scholarship on the poetry of Saga, Andrew Pekarik claims that it is chiefly admired for its stylistic quality and the individuality of its sentiments.[26]

The importance of Saga's reign to the history of later poetry can also be measured by the ways in which this ruler invested new political significance in the practices associated with writing verse. This new relationship between poetry and polity, expressed in the slogan "patterned writing binds the realm" (*monjō keikoku*), was in part an attempt to bind together a broken community. Through practices such as inscribing poetry on a calendrical basis at the sovereign's command, and reinscribing them in anthologies, Saga's regime sought to project a sense of stability by drawing on conceptions of literary Chinese as something iterable and atemporal. Insofar as this regime provided a template for the imperial anthology in later periods, an understanding of the political contours of Saga's court can help us understand the motives behind compiling later versions of such collections, chief among which was the desire to contain the threat of political rupture.

Several features that would come to characterize the Heian court first emerge in Saga's reign, including the compilation of imperial poetry anthologies, the codification of annual rituals, the construction of countryside villas, and the diffusion of court culture to these and other sites outside the confines of the palace.[27] It was only beginning in this period, according to medieval writers such as Kamo no Chōmei (1153–1216), that Heiankyō truly became a permanent capital.[28] It was also from this period that the Northern House of the Fujiwara clan, who came to play such a prominent role at the Heian court, began their rise to power under Fujiwara no Fuyutsugu (775–826). In reward for this household's support during the Kusuko Incident, Saga made the Fujiwara nobleman the head of his new male-dominated bureaucracy, as head of the Secretariat, and allowed Fuyutsugu's son and daughter to marry his own children. Henceforth, male members of the Northern House effectively replaced female officials as the sovereign's chief intermediaries with the court.

On the poetic front, Saga's reign epitomizes another key feature of Heian court culture—the importance it placed on writing poetry in literary Chinese. To some extent, this was a continuation of earlier policies. Despite the political differences between the two brothers, Heizei and Saga shared their father's commitment to fostering literacy in literary Chinese. Heizei made study of the Confucian canon at the Heian capital's university compulsory for the sons of courtiers of Fifth Rank and above in Daidō 1/6/10 (804). In Daidō 3/2/4 (806), he established the study of poetry and other styles of formal writing (*monjō*) as a separate academic field from that of history (*kiden*). *Shi* poetry's newfound status within the curriculum reflected the importance of composing metrically regular, parallel prose in prefaces, examination essays, imperial proclamations, and other forms of official writing circulated among the ruler, his aristocratic ministers, and officials educated at the university.

Although *shi* poetry was already an established part of the curriculum, however, it was Saga who most insistently declared its importance to the state. His first such statement appears two years after the Kusuko Incident, in a rescript issued in 812: "For binding the realm and managing the state, nothing is more excellent than letters. For establishing oneself in one's own life and raising one's name to posterity, nothing is more reputable than learning."[29] Saga's faith in the lasting power of writing would be vindicated by history. It is largely on account of his anthologizing activities that this sovereign's hallowed place in the history of court poetry would be assured for later generations. Chief among these works were the three imperially sponsored anthologies of writings in literary Chinese: the *Ryōunshū* (*Collection Soaring Above the Clouds*, 814), the *Bunka shūreishū* (*Collection of Masterpieces of Literary Flowers*, 818), and the *Keikokushū* (*Collection for Governing the Country*, 827).

These three anthologies represent an entirely new form of writing. Unlike the *Kaifūsō* (*Nostalgic Recollections of Literature*, 751), the only earlier extant anthology of *shi*, they were expressly compiled at royal command. The importance of these new anthology forms to the concept that "patterned writings govern the realm" is made clear by the fact that the phrase *monjō keikoku* appeared in the preface to the first of these texts and inspired the title of the last one. Its locus classicus is the *Lunwen* (*Discourse on Literature*) written by Cao Pi (187–226), which opens with the declaration that writing is a major undertaking in the governance of the realm, one whose glory never fades. Cao Pi's assertion that writing preserves past legacies prefaces an extended eulogy for a group of fellow poets who have preceded the prince in death. As we shall see, this contrast between mortal time and the atemporality of state writing was a recurring theme at Saga's court as well.[30]

Given our modern tendency to associate the individual with the private realm, the fusion of collective stability and individual immortality represented by this theory of literature appears to join two unrelated concepts. Perhaps as a result, most readings of this slogan have tended to downplay the former element. In modern Chinese literary history, Cao Pi's essay is often seen as inaugurating a literary critical discourse in which poetry becomes the vehicle for intensely personal lyricism rather than the didactic expression of communally sanctioned political and moral values.[31] Similarly, scholarly accounts of Saga's court tend to assume the phrase *monjō keikoku* had little or no political value. Kojima Noriyuki, for example, characterizes its usage as haphazard and devoid of any overtly ideological content.[32] Helen McCullough likewise asserts that Saga's interest in the writings of Cao Pi had more to do with aesthetic than political considerations.[33]

Saga's choice of Cao Pi's phrase, however, could also have signaled his belief that the political context of his own times was similar to that of his continental predecessor. The latter's lamentation for his deceased poetic peers is set against a backdrop of intense political and social turmoil in the aftermath of the Han empire's collapse. As one scholar has argued, the practices of group composition, occasional social verse, and anthologizing that characterized the ensuing Six Dynasties can be seen as attempts to assert solidarity among the literate elite in the face of pronounced geographical mobility and rapidly shifting political alliances.[34] A similar conjunction of poetic practices and political context characterized Saga's reign. It is easy to imagine that a Heian court whose geographical locus and attendant social fabric had recently been called into question would have found useful precedents in this period's poetic practices.

Lingering trauma over the Kusuko Incident and the threat to court society that it had represented might also explain why the poetry of Saga's anthologies repeatedly expresses a desire for a community devoid of factionalism. One scholar has noted that the *shi* of Saga's court frequently declares itself uninterested in official affairs and work.[35] Many of these poems are composed for processions in which Saga led his entourage to one of his villas on the outskirts of the capital. Both features were probably borrowed directly from the early Tang court, where *shi* poems on Daoist escapism were frequently a part of imperial excursions to estates.[36] At Saga's court, the recurrence of this motif suggests an attempt to claim that the court is a community of like-minded individuals whose bonds with one another are shaped by shared sentiments, rather than competition for ranks and posts.

Similar declarations of political disinterest inform the prefaces to the anthologies in which these poems appear. The practice of collecting poems and organizing them into larger units itself suggests a political culture shared by the courts of Six Dynasties China and Heian Japan. Like Saga, Cao Pi was an avid anthologizer. He is known to have collected the writings of the poets whose passing he laments in his *Discourse on Literature*. In Saga's case, the act of anthologizing sought to bring poets together into textual communities that transcended the historical vagaries and political tensions of individual circumstance. As one scholar has noted, the first of Saga's anthologies pursues this goal by reintroducing Heizei and his coterie into a new harmonious scheme centered on his successor.[37] The decision to group poems by the rank and title of their authors removed their composers from any association with political factionalism. In fact, the anthology's preface goes out of its way to declare that those in power have not been placed above, nor are those out of favor placed below.[38]

Four years after the *Ryōunshū* was completed, a new anthology foregrounded new ways to assert political harmony through poetic ritual. The *Bunka shūreishū* showcased the latest forms of Tang court banquet poetry, including the poetic practice of "harmonization" (*he*) in which courtiers wrote poems sharing the rhyme schemes or wording of a verse or poetic topic provided by the sovereign. In place of ranks, the new anthology organized poems according to genre or the social contexts in which they were produced, such as excursions, banquets, partings, exchanges, historical lectures, or *yuefu* ballads. Although many of these categories were borrowed from the canonical sixth-century anthology *Wenxuan* (*Selections of Refined Literature*, ca. 351), Saga's anthology tended to favor those involving group composition. Within the textual world of the anthology, the individual's glory is always contingent on his or her participation in a larger social setting. In a similar manner, the expression of sentiments in the *shi* of Saga's court frequently takes place in public spaces such as processions and banquets, where his assembled followers would write poems that harmonized with those of their sovereign.[39] As we shall see in Chapter 3, the *Kokinshū* adopted a similar strategy in granting the status of a named identity to its poets.

The final imperial anthology, *Keikokushū,* modeled itself even more closely after the *Wenxuan*, and presented future generations with a broader panoply of genres, including *fu* rhapsodies, poem prefaces, and examination essays. Both the content and preface of this anthology are exercises in citations of the classical canon. Nearly every line of the anthology's preface alludes to continental classics such as the *Wenxuan*, the *Analects*, the *Wenfu* (*The Poetic Exposition on Literature*, ca. 300), and the *Shipin* (*Gradings of Poets*, ca. 500). As the anthology's title suggests, governing the realm through writing was a matter of intertextual practice and performance. The ambitious scope of the *Keikokushū* is also reflected in its preface's attempt to relate a broad history of poetry, beginning with the establishment of the Bureau of Music (Yuefu) in the Han dynasty (206 B.C.E.–220 C.E.) and ending with the Sui (581–618). Saga's *shi* are implicitly represented as a continuation of this continental tradition. At the same time as they assert their continuity with the past, however, the editors are acutely aware of the historical moment in which they are writing when they eulogize Saga's deceased elder brother. This indirect allusion to conflict between courts and brothers is balanced by a neutral scheme of organization in which poems are organized according to genre.[40] In this sense, Saga's *shi* anthologies provided a model for the *Kokinshū* as well, insofar as the later anthology of *uta* sought to negotiate, acknowledge, and ameliorate the competing claims of different royal figures by privileging topics instead of personalities in arranging its poems.

Anthologizing was only one way in which writing bound Saga's state together. The intensive ritualization of writing practices that accompanied his reign provided another means for subsuming the individual poetic act within a larger communal scheme. This investment of composition with ritual significance was achieved in two ways: by setting group compositional activities to a calendrical rhythm, and by emphasizing the intertextual nature of the poetic act. Writing a poem in literary Chinese provided an opportunity for distinction by displaying the individual's ability to draw on a network of meanings and texts associated with earlier poets. The composition of verse in such a context was a matter of stitching together phrases from canonical works in new patterns.

Given our modern tendency to ascribe central significance to the author in describing the process of textual production, it is important to stress that the concept of "writing binding the realm" did not emphasize the individual as the primary rubric for organizing texts or even producing them. In both settings, the texts of individual poets survived only when they were anthologized in larger collections involving multiple authors. The practice of resituating earlier texts in new multi-textual assemblages resembled the act of poetic composition itself. In the former case, individual texts took on new meanings within the larger context of a collection. In the latter, the individual poet's composition gained significance through its relation to a collage of intertextual allusions that supplied the poem's meaning and asserted its writer's connection with a communal textual tradition. Both practices bound the realm together through the act of reproducing earlier written texts, rather than creating entirely new ones sui generis.

The intertextual nature of composition and compilation at Saga's court can perhaps best be understood as an expression of political and ritual concerns. The creation of a court community at Heiankyō through writing was effected in part through the affirmation of a shared language whose constant iteration created continuity between past and present. The word *kei*, usually taken to mean "governance" when it appears in the phrase *monjō keikoku,* possesses both textual and ritual connotations tied to the concept of citation. As a noun, it is often used to refer to the Confucian canon, familiarity with which was a prerequisite for being functional in literary Chinese.[41]

By continually citing and reciting classical texts, state officials produced a ritualized effect of timelessness and repetition. This relates to yet another meaning of *kei* as a "thread" or "path" linking past precedents with current actions. The act of composing texts through citations created a line of continuity connecting past and present. The work of producing this atemporality bound the realm together in an endless cycle of textual reproduction. In the case of poetry, this cyclical effect was reinforced by the specification of the days in the calendrical year during which composition took place. Dates such as the Double Third, Double Fifth, Double Seventh, and Double Ninth held both numerological and seasonal significance. The act of writing *shi* poetry to the rhythms of this calendrical cycle thus synchronized the human world with that of Heaven. The ritual and cosmological significance of such activities was also derived from a new conception of poetic harmonization involving mass reproduction of the sovereign's words. It is in this area, as much as anthologizing, that Saga's contributions to the history of court poetry are most significant.

The Lord Intones, His Ministers Harmonize

Insofar as it was a constitutive element of writing in literary Chinese, textual citation was not an innovation of Saga's court. The frequency of compositional activity, however, and the degree to which this activity became set to a cyclical rhythm, suggests a self-conscious attempt to regularize and ritualize the practice. Saga's court witnessed the production and codification of court observances involving *shi* composition on an unprecedented scale. During his reign the *naien* (Inner Palace Banquet) and *hana no en* (Blossom Banquet) were established, and the *chōyō* (Double Ninth) observances was revived.[42] Together with the *kyokusui no en* (Winding Water Banquet) held on the third day of the Third Month, the *Tanabata* (Weavermaid) observances held on the seventh day of the Seventh Month, and banquets held in the Rear Palace

(Kōkyū) at the end of the Eighth Month, Saga's court was subjected to a relentless roster of annual events at which *shi* were composed.

At the same time as the court sought to preserve this new calendrical regimen of poetic performances in anthology form, its accompanying rituals were also being codified. Although the first two Heian sovereigns actively emulated Tang court culture, it was in Saga's reign that they were written down in ritual formularies. Known as *shiki* (procedures), these texts specified the manner in which rites were conducted, including the sequence of such physical actions as hand clapping, raising the voice in felicitation, bowing twice, and foot stamping which the assembled courtiers performed at such ceremonies. This desire to record ritual represents another instance of the belief that writing's longevity ensured its usefulness to the realm. Codification of these practices in written formularies facilitated their diffusion and replication at a time when the number of literate officials being produced by the university was increasing significantly.[43]

In order to bind together this burgeoning bureaucratic community, Saga's ritual formularies elaborated and stipulated a new calendrical roster of formal banquets. Known as *sechien*, these banquets included the dispensation of stipends known as *sechiroku* to officials on the calendrical dates 1/1, 1/7, 1/16, 5/5, 7/7, and 9/9. In such settings, under the personal aegis of the ruler, ministers and officials affirmed their ties to their sovereign and to the legal-administrative system over which he presided through the act of inscribing poems. The ritual forms codified at Saga's court thus endowed the composition of poetry with social, economic, and cosmological meanings that provided a template for imperial poetic texts and practices at the Heian court in succeeding centuries. These forms of poetic composition at *sechien* banquets involved an elaborate ritual in which the act of composition was only one feature. Our knowledge of these banquets is largely derived from tenth-century sources such as the *Saikyūki* and *Hokuzanshō*. In their accounts of *sechien*, these texts suggest that the rites were chiefly designed to foreground the ruler's role in overseeing his officials' textual labor.[44]

The beginning of the *sechien* banquet involved its own careful choreography of court hierarchy, with the participants arriving in order of rank. The ritual began with the sovereign's appearance at the Shinsen-en pavilion or the palace. Princes and nobility in regular attendance on him were then summoned to sit with their ruler. These were followed by *monnin*, who chiefly consisted of low-ranking officials educated in the forms of literary Chinese essential to the production and management of documents at core institutions of the Heian state such as the university, the Office of the Inner Scribes (Naiki-dokoro), the Palace Library (Uchi no Gosho-dokoro), and the Secretariat (Kurōdo-dokoro). Upon the arrival of the nobility and men of letters, paper, ink, and brushes were placed before them. The sovereign would then command his ministers to present a list of topics on which poems were to be composed. The topics typically consisted of lines from well-known poems. The ministers would then have a lecturer from the university, or some other man distinguished for his erudition, write the topics out in list form. The paper was then submitted to the sovereign for his inspection and approval. On occasion, he would reject the first list, and the rite would be reenacted to create a new one. In other cases, topics were designated in advance, and the lecturer would produce a clean copy and recite it aloud during the official rite.

After the list had been finalized, two additional copies were made and sent to the seats of the crown prince and ministers. The original list would be sent back to the preface writer so that he could incorporate its wording in his composition. Individual topics were selected at random by the participants in a procedure known as "searching for the topic" (*tandai*), which was designed to enable an unscripted virtuoso display of the official's poetic literacy. Each participant would approach a desk in the courtyard below the sovereign and draw a slip of paper, on which the topic was written out, from a bamboo basket. This procedure also went by order of rank, with those of the lowest echelons selecting a topic last.

Poems were composed during the banquet that followed this official rite of selection. There was a standard form these were expected to take: initial listings of characteristics of the topic that would be taken up (*daimoku*), an explanation of the topic's significance (*hadai*), a metaphorical equivalent for the topic (*hiyu*), and a final line relating the poet's feelings (*jukkai*).[45] While the second and third rounds of wine were being formally accepted by the participants, these same officials were entertained by women from the Naikyōbō (Palace Office of Female Performers).[46] As the men drank and wrote, these women danced and sang before them. This pairing of women entertainers with male composers provided a new gloss on the choreographed arrangement of gendered pairs in earlier ritual performances such as *utagaki* and *tōka* (foot-stamping songs).[47] Whereas both men and women engaged in the same mode of performance in those earlier rites, *sechien* banquets clearly delineated gender roles, showcasing the official's brush as a male implement that was distinct from the women's songs and gestures. Such distinctions, as we shall see, were deemed integral to the definition of a public poetic sphere in such later texts as the Kana Preface to the *Kokinshū.*

Surrounded by the sounds of musicians and the sights of dancers, officials would write their compositions and place them in a bamboo basket on the desk. Writers had approximately three hours or so in which to complete their compositions. Those unable to come up with a poem would raise their hands in defeat. Writers with completed poems would advance and place them in the basket as they declared their office, clan, and personal name. When all of the poems had been assembled, a captain from the Inner Palace Guard would take the basket up to the sovereign and write out a clean copy for him. A more informal banquet would then follow at which stipends were handed out.[48] During this banquet, members of the sovereign's intimate circle played music and sang songs for him. In some cases, he would join in the concert in a musical enactment of harmony between ruler and minister. At other times he would recite an old *uta* and have his ministers echo its words in their own responses, as was done at Kammu's banquets.

The *shi* poems composed during the main event appear to have been read aloud only occasionally. No mention is made of recitation in early ritual formularies such the *Dairi shiki* ("Procedures of the Palace," 821) and *Jōgan shiki* (*Procedures of the Jōgan Era*, ca. 870). When there were readings, they typically took place during the informal banquet held at the end of the event. The preface would be recited first, followed by poems in descending order of their composers' rank. Only a portion of the poems composed and presented would be included, perhaps ten or so, and often fewer if the recitation took place late at night.

The chief significance of such *sechien* banquets lay in the imperial act of overseeing and selecting topics, and in the subsequent act of re-inscribing the ruler's words in poems. These events thus condensed the textual labor of officialdom into a single poetic event. The choreographed movement of the piece of paper listing poetic topics from scribes through ministerial channels, the royal inspection of this list, and the subsequent writing out of copies for the sovereign and his ministers followed the same processes by which state documents were created.[49]

The importance placed on royal scrutiny in such gatherings can also be seen in the prefaces to the imperial *shi* anthologies compiled during this time. All three anthologies are written in the form of a report on the policies of the editors to their ruler. This genre of writing, known as *shangbiaowen* (writing presented to His Highness), was reserved for documents intended for personal viewing by the ruler.[50] In keeping with this generic emphasis on the ruler's role in overseeing textual production, all three prefaces note that poems whose merits are debatable have been submitted to the sovereign for final judgment. Anthologizing thus replicated the reigning sovereign's role at banquet rituals in selecting and approving words for subsequent inscription. As we shall see in Chapter 3, this connection between the practices of banquet poetry and anthologizing was apparent also in the creation of the *Kokinshū* in the tenth century.

By writing out the ruler's words (or at least attempting to) in exchange for stipends, *sechien* banquets provided a microcosmic enactment of the work of court officialdom. The term "bureaucracy," used so often in accounts of the Heian state, however, can suggest an instrumentalist and functional view of writing, in which its chief concern is to ensure the accumulation and circulation of information among officials. While the Heian polity undoubtedly required writing to sustain its political and economic operations, it could also function as a symbolic enactment of power and authority in ritual contexts. At *sechien* banquets, the aesthetics of skillful poetic writing in parallel meter also-signaled literal obeisance to, and reproduction of, the ruler's words in discursive harmony with his will.

Poetic harmonization at *sechien* was represented as a means for naturalizing social hierarchies by grounding them in the universe's fundamental structures. In the *Bunka shūreishū,* an anthology that foregrounds different forms of poetic harmonization, textual production is described with the phrase "Heaven is exalted and Earth lowly, the lord intones and his ministers harmonize with him."[51] Through topic-based poetic composition, sovereign and minister created discursive harmonies that paralleled cosmological ones between Heaven and Earth, thereby guaranteeing both social stability and material bounty. The use of the term "harmony" to describe this arrangement is particularly applicable to *sechien* banquets, where officials echoed words selected by their sovereign in their poems.

By the tenth century, this poetic ideal of harmonization between lord and minister was seen as a defining feature of the textual culture Saga had created. When the court of Daigo (885–930, r. 897–930) produced the *Engi shiki* (*Procedures of the Engi Era*, 927) in emulation of similar legal codes from Saga's reign, its preface characterized the latter's reign as one in which writing manifested the ruler's potency: "In the reign of the Kōnin sovereign, his virtue illuminated the marks of tortoise shells and uplifted the birds tracks scrawled across the sky. The lord intoned and his ministers harmonized, thereby gaining the loyalty of the talented. All above were at peace and those below happy, making it possible for them to coexist as intimately as fish in water."[52] In this eulogy to Saga, the ruler's vitality is manifested in a form of writing with cosmological rather than human origins. Like his father Uda and grandfather Kōkō, Daigo actively supported the ritual regime of writing *shi* at *sechien* that had been codified by Saga.

The connections between poetry and cosmology made in texts from the early Heian period reflect the central importance of the concept of harmony to cosmogenesis and phenomenology in continental thought. Continental cosmology posited a harmonious arrangement of binary elements in resonance with one another as the essential conditions for producing worldly phenomena. Although it may have been most consistently articulated in literary Chinese, this concept of poetic harmonization as a generative practice can also be seen in the *uta* exchanges performed at the courts of Kammu and his sons. Under Saga, the hierarchical nature of harmonization in *shi* was stressed, not only through the topic-based form of composition sponsored at *sechien* banquets but also more directly through the composition of poems whose words harmonized with the first line in a poem by their sovereign.[53] This practice, known as *hōwa,* first appears in Saga's anthologies, where it eclipses the earlier courtly paradigm of composing *shi* on imperial command *(ōsei* or *ōshō).*[54]

Unlike *uta*, however, *shi* reflected these cosmological principles in their internal structures. Poetry written in literary Chinese sought to embody the universe's paired relations through the parallel structures of the couplet, which as Stephen Owen puts it, "mediates between reductive generalities and the most complex particulars of concealed relations."[55] François Cheng, another Western scholar of Chinese poetry, has argued that *shi* provided a means of positing a fundamental correspondence between the material universe and the universe of signs. According to his account, the syntax of parallelism that largely defined such poetry reflected the complementary cosmological structures of *yin-yang* dualisms.[56] Given these scholars' claims that it captured the immanence of the world's structure in poetic form, *shi* would have proved a powerful tool for representing and legitimating a social hierarchy grounded in a corresponding cosmological order. The semiglobal reach of literary Chinese must have also invested *shi* with universal claims to truth and efficacy in representing the world.

Saga's court appears to have viewed the composition of *shi* as an especially effective means for asserting correspondences between the social world and the larger cosmos. By comparison, native poetry seems to have played a subsidiary role. At Saga's *sechien* banquets the recitation of *uta* appears to have taken place only rarely. When it did, however, it also often sought to assert harmony between ruler and minister. One instance can be found in the *Ruijū kokushi,* which describes the banquet following a procession by Saga in 813:

> His Majesty went in procession to the Crown Prince's mansion at the Southern Pond. Men of letters were commanded to compose *shi* poems. Minister of the Right Junior Second Rank Fujiwara no Sonondo sang this song to His Majesty:

Under today's sun,	*kyō no hi no*
here by the pond,	*ike no hotori ni*
we must have heard	*hototogisu*

hototogisu birds
chirping "chiyo" in level tones

taira wa chiyo to
naku wa kikitsu ya

His Majesty harmonized with this, saying:

When *hototogisu* birds
chirp "chiyo," then I hear
"a thousand more years"
for the verse's master and me
sounding in my ears.

hototogisu
naku koe kikeba
uta nushi to
tomo ni chiyo to
ware mo kikitari[57]

In this exchange, Saga compliments his Fujiwara ally by echoing Sonondo's verse in his own. Sonondo declares that the chirping cries of *chiyo* made by birds on a bright summer day carry the chant of "a thousand more years" to the assembled ministers. Saga's response declares that the blessings of Heaven manifested in these sounds are shared between the two men, in keeping with the Confucian economy of virtue which benefits both ruler and ruled. As with the earlier exchanges between Saga and Heizei, this graceful exchange of compliments pivots around a polysemantic phrase that aligns the human world with that of Heaven. *Chiyo* here could refer to both the chirps of birds and the chanting of *shi* poems by an official after the formal rite of composition at the banquet has been concluded.[58]

The simultaneous presence of both forms of poetry in this banquet reflects the ritual order of Saga's *sechien*, in which the predominant distinction was not between *shi* and *uta*, but between the act of poetic inscription—which constituted the core of the rite—and the act of recitation on its periphery. Sonondo's exchange with Saga constitutes an earlier form of harmonization at banquets that foregrounded the relationships between two individuals, rather than the mass replication of predetermined topics by a group. It also reverses the protocols of such forms of poetic harmonization by representing the social superior as the respondent rather than the initiator of the exchange. Sonondo's choice of native verse to publicly mark his own intimate relationship with his lord would be a harbinger of things to come. With the establishment of the first Fujiwara regency in the mid ninth century, *uta* came to assume the same role as *shi*, as texts composed "in harmony" with topics provided by the regent as well as the ruler. In the process, the concept of "Yamato verse" (*yamato uta*) would also come to the fore as a distinct genre of written poetry defined by its citation of the Yamato historical canon, in the same manner as *shi* cited continental classics.

Binding Yamato in Word-Spirits

With the passing of Saga and Junna from power and the accession of Ninmyō (810–850, r. 833–850), the poetic culture of the court underwent significant changes. Although Ninmyō's court continued to sponsor *shi* composition by scholars at annual banquets, these gatherings decreased drastically in scale and number. The increasing invisibility of male officials at the banquets of Ninmyō's reign was paralleled by a tendency to privilege kinship over qualifications in appointments.[59] By 848, no one on the Council of State was a graduate of the university. Instead, men and women of the Tachibana clan prospered under the patronage of Ninmyō's mother Kachiko (786–850), a woman who played a key role in enabling the ambitious Fujiwara no Yoshifusa (804–872) to install his own nephew as crown prince after the Jōwa Disturbance of 842.

During this time, *uta* appear to have been frequently performed at court banquets. Historical accounts of his reign represent Ninmyō as a patron of the arts, bestowing his favors upon courtiers who excelled at dance, song, and music rather than *shi* poetry.[60] Some of the earliest prominent poets in the *Kokinshū*, such as Henjō (816–890), Ariwara no Narihira, and his older brother Ariwara no Yukihira (818–893), embarked on their court careers at this time. Their exposure to the pageantry of Ninmyō's court left its legacy in later poetic practice as well, particularly in the development of props in poetry matches. The earliest known match, held by Yukihira some time in the mid ninth century on the topic of the *hototogisu* bird, featured an elaborate model of a mountain house and a hut amid paddy fields to represent the range of landscapes through which the bird moved as summer progressed. Such displays are likely to have been inspired by similar uses of props and poetry at Ninmyō's birthday celebration described below.

Elaborate material display was a hallmark of this sovereign's reign, beginning with his official enthronement. In contrast to the evergreen *sakaki* branches and plain strips of cloth adorning the pavilions at Junna's coronation, those of his successor involved an array of props including painted screens and artificial flowers. The elaborate forms of ritual display that characterized Ninmyō's court are epitomized by his fortieth birthday celebration, held over eight days in 849. Like similar events held in the reigns of Shōmu and Saga, *sutras* were recited by the priests of various temples to ensure the ruler's longevity. In Ninmyō's case, however, this took a distinctive form. As part of the celebration, Buddhist priests from the temple of Kōfuku-ji presented a *chōka* (long verse) of more than two hundred lines, along with forty images alluding to various tales of mortals and immortals and forty scrolls of the *Kongō jumyō darani-kyō* ("Scripture of Incantations for Adamantine Longevity").

Yoshifusa appears to have sponsored the priests who presented this text, even lodging them at his own mansion while they were in the capital. As the Buddhist temple affiliated with the Fujiwara clan shrine at Kasuga, Kōfuku-ji received significant patronage from that clan's patriarch.[61] The presence of its priests at Ninmyō's birthday thus suggests that the Fujiwara aristocrat identified himself closely with their activities at the event. Yoshifusa would have had much to celebrate at the time, having achieved new status as uncle to the crown prince. The birthday of his royal brother-in-law provided an opportunity for him to showcase the union of the two clans.

The importance of this event to Yoshifusa is also suggested by its lengthy treatment in the *Shoku nihon kōki,* a court history whose compilation he oversaw. Significantly, the chronicle's account of this event departs from convention by neglecting to describe the ruler's response to the poem. There is no exchange of verses, nor is the term *waka* used. Instead, attention is paid to elaborating a concept of Yamato verse as a form of poetry that shares the potential ability of *shi* to bind the realm together through writing.[62] The verse offered up by these priests is preserved in the *senmyōgaki* style of script, which uses *kana* to mark only particles and inflecting suffixes rather than entire words. Given its length, it is reasonable to assume that priests recited the *chōka* from a written text in the same manner as a *sutra.*[63]

The poem is archaic in its language, which draws on the rhetoric of divine rule developed two centuries earlier by royal bards to praise their sovereigns. Yoshifusa's priests set the current sovereign's reign within a larger mythic span of time, encompassing the creation of the land and the establishment of the ruling Yamato lineage. Their verse then proceeds to praise the peace and prosperity enjoyed under Ninmyō's reign. His virtue is manifest in the beauty and vitality of his surrounding lands, and illustrated by references to warblers, pine trees, cranes, and blooming wisteria. These poetic representations of monarchical virtue manifesting itself in the cosmos were given material form at the rite where the *chōka* was recited. Legendary figures mentioned in the poem, such as Urashimako, were accompanied by sculptures depicting them. Many of the natural objects mentioned in the poem possibly also appeared as props (*tsukurimono*). The felicitous associations with long life and monarchical virtue represented by these images are spelled out by the *chōka* in such a way as to endow them and their recipient with magical power.

Yoshifusa's use of a traditional form of native verse in place of Buddhist scripture made his contribution to Ninmyō's birthday celebration unique. The unusual nature of this poetic performance is reflected in the poem's own self-conscious description of its choice of language:

We have not borrowed the words	*Kara no*
of the Tang,	*kotoba o karazu*
nor employed scholars	*kakishirusu*
to write them down.	*hakase yatowazu*
In this realm	*kono kuni no*
has it been said from of old:	*iitsutauraku*
that the realm of Yamato,	*hi no moto no*
source of the sun,	*Yamato no kuni wa*
is a realm where flourish	*kotodama no*
the spirits of words.	*sakiwau kuni to zo*[64]

These lines have frequently been cited, most famously by Konishi Jin'ichi, as evidence of a longstanding belief in the oral performative power of native verse.[65] While such beliefs clearly existed in early Japan, the fact that this is one of only a few places where the term *kotodama* is used should give us pause in overstating its heuristic value for describing linguistic praxis in the early Heian period. If anything, the form of *kotodama* performed at Ninmyō's birthday involved a novel adaptation of earlier forms of poetic and ritual language to Buddhist technologies of textual recitation, which utilized diacritic marks to enable precise enunciation. This in turn would explain the apparent contradiction of having Buddhist priests educated in literary Chinese extol the virtues of native verse.

The development of such textual technologies, especially a systematized phonetic script, appears to have been closely tied to the establishment of Esoteric Buddhism and the introduction of treatises on Sanskrit phonology to the Heian court in the early ninth century. As Ryūichi Abe has argued, the diffusion of *kana* writing in particular posed a radical threat to the ideology of "writing binding the realm."[66] Confucian theories of writing claimed it had its origins in the natural order and asserted that the power of its graphs lay in their ability to "rectify names" (*zhengming*) by producing a fundamental correspondence between written signs and the world. *Sechien* banquets provided one instance of the belief that harmony in words produced harmony in the social order. As regent of a regime that had no precedent and must have generated resentment among his peers, Yoshifusa would have found *kana* a fitting form in which to represent the ways that writing bound together the realm. Just as *kana* were "provisional" names whose script borrowed the forms of literary Chinese to create a kind of writing both similar to and distinct from it, the regency sought to claim a similarly contingent relationship to the ruler as his temporary substitute. Yoshifusa's personal interest in *kana* can be inferred from the sort of Buddhist institutions he patronized. During the reign of his infant grandson Seiwa, the Fujiwara regent sponsored several temples engaged in the study of the Sanskrit phonetics and grammar and in the development of relative pitch markings known as "voice markings" *(shōten).*

Although the *chōka* for Ninmyō's birthday predates both the widespread diffusion of *kana* script and the formal inauguration of Yoshifusa's regency, it does suggest a certain self-reflexive awareness of its status as a written text, by drawing on the language of "writing binding the realm" to elaborate *kotodama*'s effects:

In the words of antiquity	*furugoto ni*
they flow down to us.	*nagarekitareru*

In the words of the gods	*kamigoto ni*
they are conveyed to us.	*tsutaekitareru*
Under the sway of these words,	*tsutaekoshi*
conveyed thus to us,	*koto no mani mani*
we revisit the affairs	*moto tsu yo no*
of the world at its origins.	*koto tazunureba*
And so each word of song	*utagoto ni*
is chanted over and over again.	*utaikaeshite*
We have come to use them	*kamigoto ni*
in matters concerning the gods.	*mochiikitareri*
We have come to use them	*kimigoto ni*
in matters concerning our lord.	*mochiikitareri*[67]

Kotodama is described here as an act of citation in which events and phenomena of the Yamato court stretching back to the age of the gods are brought into the present through the reiteration of ancient words and phrases (*furugoto*) that have existed from time immemorial. The resemblance to the practice of citing the literary Chinese canon that was operative in "writing binding the realm" is striking. In this case, the eternal present is sustained through the act of reciting ancient words over and over again, rather than inscribing them. Nevertheless, textuality is the condition of possibility for this form of binding as well. The use of *kana* diacritics in particular would have helped to ensure the mechanical and accurate reproduction of ancient incantatory phrases.

The same self-conscious attempt to assert a distinctly Yamato mode of state literature can be found in the *Shoku nihon kōki*'s ensuing account of *yamato uta*:

> Now as for the form of Yamato verse, it puts implicit and explicit metaphor first, from which it then proceeds to move people's feelings. This is what it is most accomplished at. As the state of affairs in the world falls into decline, this Way has also fallen from usage, reaching a state where now it can be found only among a few priests who have some knowledge of the old words. One could say in this case that when rites are lost at court they should be sought out in rustic surroundings. Therefore this verse has been selected for inclusion in the historical record.[68]

With the discussion of the rhetoric of Yamato verse, its power to move people, and a subsequent history of its neglect, this passage from the *Shoku nihon kōki* prefigures the better-known formulation of such matters in the prefaces to the *Kokinshū* anthology. The *Shoku nihon kōki*'s account also suggests parallels between *furugoto* and "writing binding the realm" when it declares Yamato verse to be a form of state literature whose changing status at court is a barometer of the realm's well-being.

Another similarity with *shi* is apparent in the terms used by the editors of the *Shoku nihon kōki* to describe Yamato verse. The noun *bixing* (implicit and explicit metaphor) with which they characterize its rhetoric can be found in Six Dynasties poetics treatises that could have been in circulation at the Heian court. Typically, these treatises favorably contrasted the tropological qualities of *bixing* with the rhetorically unadorned ones of *fu* (plain description). The *bixing* style crafted correspondences between human affairs and the surrounding world through the use of parallelism, overt simile, and implicit juxtaposition. Such harmonious arrangements of natural and human elements allowed Yamato verse, like its continental counterpart, to aid the state in its attempts to synchronize Heaven with humanity.

The chronicle in which this *chōka* and account of *yamato uta* both appear was compiled at the height of Yoshifusa's political dominance of the court in the reigns of Montoku and Seiwa. Its portrayal of his role in reviving Yamato verse coincided with unprecedented attempts to legitimate the Fujiwara household as an alternate center of ritual authority at court. Through its articulation of *furugoto* as a native form of "writing binding the realm," Yamato verse provided this new regime with a new textual technology, one that was not monopolized by established state institutions such as the university. During the Fujiwara regency, this new form of written *uta* would help transform the temporal, spatial, and symbolic dimensions of the Heian court.

Springtime for the Fujiwara

Yoshifusa's sponsorship of a new textual concept of Yamato verse went hand in hand with radical reformations of politics, ritual, and power at court. The Fujiwara patriarch's regency is often seen as heralding the advent of Heian court politics in their archetypal form. Whereas early Heian sovereigns such as Kammu and Saga are often viewed as aberrations on account of the degree to which they actively asserted their roles as monarchs, their successors Montoku (827–858, r. 850–858), Seiwa (850–880, r. 858–876), and Yōzei (868–949, r. 876–884) are typically seen as being in the classic mold of the Heian sovereign who delegated administrative power to his maternal Fujiwara relatives.

This shift traditionally has been attributed to Yoshifusa's ambitions and machinations, characteristics of his historical persona which are first fleshed out in mid-Heian historical tales (*rekishi monogatari*). Less frequently noted is the manner in which the Fujiwara patriarch developed a set of symbolic associations through native poetry which legitimated his regime. Although Yoshifusa was not the only person at court to foster the composition of *uta*, he and his female relatives were unique in the public and ritual uses to which they put it. By making the inscription of *uta* part of court ritual, his regency helped establish native verse in its quintessentially Heian incarnation as a form of poetry tuned to a solar cycle rather than the lunar calendar. Seasonal temporality, and the associations among spring, the sun, and cherry blossoms in particular, were hallmarks of this new regime.

Officially, Yoshifusa's rule dates from his receipt of the title of *sesshō* (regent) in Jōgan 8/8/19 (866), a promotion that took place in the aftermath of a political crisis involving the burning down of the palace's southern gate of Ōtenmon. Although historians often point to the "Ōtenmon Incident" as the prelude to the establishment of the Fujiwara regency, Yoshifusa's grip over the government was already assured in the final years of Ninmyō's reign, when he headed the Council of State as the maternal uncle of the crown prince. During this period, Yoshifusa first began to use *uta* and cherry trees to mark the transition from one regime to another and to establish a connection between the two that has lasted through the subsequent history of Japanese culture.

The importance of cherry trees to Yoshifusa appears to have been recognized by the editors of the *Kokinshū* who, in a rare departure from their general policy of omitting poems by male aristocrats, include a single verse by the patriarch of the Northern House on cherry blossoms in the Spring section of their anthology. In this poem, Yoshifusa likens a sprig of blossoming cherry placed in an ornamental vase at the residence he shared with his daughter Fujiwara no Akirakeiko (829–900) to the flowering fortunes of his family now that she is the mother of a future sovereign:

With the passage of time	*toshi fureba*
I've grown old.	*yowai wa oinu*
But though this be so,	*shika wa aredo*
when I see these blossoms,	*hana o shi mireba*
brooding thoughts disappear.	*mono omoi mo nashi*[69]

Yoshifusa's likening of his daughter to blooming flowers draws on established conventions for representing women in poetry. The use of cherry blossoms to denote Fujiwara fertility and political glory, however, was a more recent innovation at the time. Yoshifusa's regency, in fact, is the period in which this "quintessentially Japanese" motif first gained poetic prominence. By choosing this one poem, the editors of the *Kokinshū* mark an important moment in the history of both the regency and Japanese culture. The cherry blossom would be deployed extensively in the *Kokinshū*, in the process establishing it as the preeminent flower in Japanese court poetry.[70]

One factor that might have contributed to the tree's new prominence was its inclusion in the symbolic architecture of the palace in Ninmyō's reign. During this time, the plum tree growing in the courtyard before the inner palace's most formal ritual hall at the Shishinden died and was replaced with a cherry tree.[71] The new tree was paired with an evergreen *tachibana* to symbolize the complementary relations between change and eternity. The symbolism of this arrangement provided a fitting means by which to represent the regent's place at court as a temporary and provisional complement to the eternal sovereign. But the replacement of plum with cherry signified much more. The latter's new place at the physical center of the court heralded a shift in the temporal rhythms of the ritual regime away from the lunar calendrical cycles, regulated and run by the palace, to solar seasonal ones that could be enacted at the mansions of important personages other than the sovereign.

Cherry blossoms also feature prominently in the one instance when *uta* are mentioned in the official account of Montoku's reign compiled under Yoshifusa's heir, Fujiwara no Mototsune (836–891). In an entry from 851, the *Montoku jitsuroku* recounts a memorial service for the recently deceased Ninmyō at which the assembled aristocrats use poetry to acknowledge Yoshifusa's replacement of the ruler as the center of the court.

> Minister of the Right Lord Fujiwara no Yoshifusa assembled priests renowned for their wisdom and powers at his mansion in the east of the capital and had them deliver a lecture on the *Lotus Sutra* in offering to the former sovereign. The previous year, His Majesty had heard that the cherry trees at the minister's house were extremely lovely and had planned to enjoy them the following spring. However, his sudden passing made this impossible. Now that spring had come, and the blossoms had burst forth, Yoshifusa grieved, saying, "On this very day our former sovereign would have greeted spring here. Spring's arrival brings hope, but His Majesty has passed on and will not return. The blossoms are here, but the person is not. How hard it is to bear this grief!" There was not a single person, either priest or layperson, who failed to shed a tear. Some of the nobility composed *shi* to express their heartfelt sentiments, while others harmonized with the minister in *uta* that grieved for His Majesty's passing.[72]

Here, Yoshifusa uses the occasion of a memorial service for his former sovereign to draw attention to the closeness of his relationship with him, and then has this relationship acknowledged by everyone present in the ensuing poetry. The cherry tree of his mansion serves as a locus of memory and loss at which past and present meet, and the desires of a former ruler to see the blossoms and his minister to see his sovereign coincide. The ensuing *shi* and *uta* from the court nobility in attendance no doubt took up Yoshifusa's words, echoing and harmonizing with them. It is easy to imagine that the contrast between seasonal cycles and human impermanence suggested by the powerful man's remarks would have inspired many of these poems.

The act of composing poems in sympathy with Yoshifusa's declaration of grief resembles that of officials harmonizing with the words of their ruler at banquets. In this case, however, the current sovereign Montoku is absent, allowing Yoshifusa to assume the role of the lord intoning to his ministers. Perhaps the political import of poetic harmonization at this event explains why the term *waka* is used here rather than *yamato uta*. The parallel constructions of the final passage (或賦詩述懐或和歌歓逝) could suggest that 和 is working as a verb (to harmonize) in tandem with the character 賦 (to compose) that is used for *shi*. The wording of this passage also suggests that both forms of poetry are fulfilling the same function, in a striking departure from the norms of *sechien* banquets where the recitation of *uta* followed the formal inscription of *shi*.

Yoshifusa's staging of himself as the center of the court at his Somedono mansion took place at a time when the new sovereign remained conspicuously absent from the palace. Montoku appears to have spent the first three years of his reign at the crown prince's residence, and it is doubtful that he ever occupied the inner palace compound during the remainder of his time as sovereign.[73] The same historical chronicle that gives such prominence to Yoshifusa in the passage cited above makes no mention of his royal nephew. The cherry tree's prominence in the historical record thus marks not only the physical absence of a deceased monarch but also that of the current sovereign as the ritual locus of the realm.

To later generations, the Fujiwara patriarch's influence over his nominal ruler was most paradigmatically expressed by his success in ensuring that Montoku's favorite son Koretaka (844–897) was passed over in favor of Yoshifusa's own grandson, a boy who went on to become Emperor Seiwa at the age of nine in 858. Like his father, the new sovereign did not occupy the palace immediately. Only two days after he was enthroned, Seiwa returned to the crown prince's residence in his mother's carriage. The two continued to live there even after Seiwa underwent the capping ceremony on New Year's Day in 864 that officially marked his coming of age.

During the time in which these sovereigns were absent from the palace, Yoshifusa shifted the locus of ritual authority at court to his Somedono residence. Located on the capital's First Avenue, just south of the palace, this mansion was suitably positioned to claim geomantic preeminence above all other aristocratic houses, which were located south of it. Here Yoshifusa presided over *sechien* such as the White Horse Banquet (*aouma no sechie*) at which court ranks and titles for the new calendrical year were officially distributed. By staging palace rituals in his own mansion, the Fujiwara patriarch assumed the ruler's role of dispensing Heaven's bounty to his human subjects and officials.[74] The Somedono also featured prominently in royal visits that served to formalize the union between the imperial and Fujiwara clans before the entire court. Montoku made one such visit in 853.[75] His son continued this tradition of paying his respects to the Fujiwara patriarch during the cherry blossom season. According to the *Sandai jitsuroku*, Seiwa visited his Fujiwara grandfather's mansion to attend banquets under its cherry trees in 864 and 866.[76]

Such processions evoked the established practice of visits in the new year by the reigning sovereign to the residences of his father and mother, known as *chōkin no miyuki.* But whereas that rite was calendrical, this one combined filiality with prayers for the realm's fruitfulness in a seasonal context rather than on a fixed calendrical date. At the same time, these rites were carried out on a scale that rivaled that of any official state observance. The grandiose nature of Seiwa's visits inspired lengthy descriptions in the *Sandai jitsuroku* chronicle compiled under Yoshifusa's successor Fujiwara no Tokihira (871–909). Within the grounds of his mansion Yoshifusa staged agricultural rites that had previously been reserved for the formidable Great Hall of State (Daigokuden) inside the palace compound. During the royal visit, farmers planted rice seedlings, while music was performed before the sovereign in acknowledgment of his ritual oversight of the realm's agricultural bounty. For Seiwa's first visit in 864, Yoshifusa had the governor of Yamashiro province provide the farmers for this planting ceremony. The succeeding visit of 866 included performances of popular music and dance known as *zōgaku* (miscellaneous music). The cherry tree under which both of these events took place thus became a symbol of Heaven's approving fruitfulness, kinship links to a maternal Fujiwara grandfather, and the presence of the sovereign in a place other than the palace.

Officials composed poems on topics as part of the banquet that accompanied these elaborately choreographed agricultural rites. The *Sandai jitsuroku* does not mention any individual *shi* from these banquets, nor the precise manner in which they were composed. It is possible that they followed the etiquette of continental banquet poetry, according to which the guest first praises his host by describing the magnificence of the surroundings, followed by the host's responding compliment echoing the words of his guest.[77] A similar etiquette was involved in the harmonizing exchange of *uta* that occurred in earlier banquets. Given the large-scale nature of the event, however, and its evocation of the realm's bounty, it is more likely that poetic composition followed the forms of a *sechien* banquet, perhaps one that included topics involving cherry blossoms. Like Yoshifusa's earlier memorial service for Ninmyō, it appears that *uta* were composed along with *shi* at the event. According to the prose preface to a poem on cherry blossoms by Minamoto no Tōru (822–895), it was composed during an archery contest that accompanied the blossom banquet of 864.[78]

One of the appealing features of blossom banquets for Yoshifusa might have been their prior association with palace rituals. In Saga's reign, banquets held under plum blossoms on the first day of the lunar Second Month were elevated to the status of a *sechien* known as the *hana no en no sechi*. The rite was based on a similar observance inaugurated by the Tang Emperor Dezong (742–805, r. 780–805), at whose court the most recent Heian embassy had been observers. Dezong was a particularly avid sponsor of harmonizing verse during his reign, and it is believed that his activities in this area inspired Saga's own efforts.[79] It was during the latter's reign that blossom banquets became a fixture of Heian court ritual as the spring counterpart to the autumnal observances of the Double Ninth.

Whereas the Double Ninth banquet was invariably held on the same day each year, however, blossom banquets had no fixed place in the lunar calendar. As seasonal events dependent on the brief period in which particular trees bore flowers, these rites lay outside the calendrical cycle that determined the state's annual observances. Perhaps for this reason, blossom banquets failed to become an established fixture in the court's roster of *sechien* banquets. As early as Junna's reign, they had ceased to be held annually in the Shinsen-en Park and had moved to the imperial consorts' quarters in the Rear Palace, where they were held only occasionally.

The prior history of blossom banquets provided Yoshifusa with an established practice that was sufficiently flexible in its spatial and temporal features to accommodate his new position within the court's ritual regime. Their prior association with the women's quarters in the palace would have made the staging of such banquets at Yoshifusa's residence appear to be a natural extension of past precedent, insofar as the Somedono mansion was also the home of the Fujiwara consort. By remaining an occasional event, these banquets would have avoided the appearance of a permanent, outright usurpation of the sovereign's prerogative to ritually harmonize Heaven and humanity. At the same time, the precedence given to the cherry over the plum distinguished these gatherings from earlier blossom banquets that had featured literati in the Nara period. This preference for a native blossom in particular reflected Yoshifusa's interest in articulating a distinctly Yamato form of verse for his regime.

Another way in which the regency mimicked the ritual procedures of the state was its use of *uta* poets to compose verse on assigned topics. This practice inaugurated a tradition of patronizing *uta* poets by both male and female members of the Northern House that continued in the tenth century. Yoshifusa's niece Fujiwara no Takaiko (842–910), who was chief consort to Seiwa and mother of his heir Yōzei, appears to have been particularly active in commissioning poems from lower-ranking male courtiers. Many of these poems elaborated the seasonal symbolism of the regency. One verse, occupying the prestigious position of the first spring poem in the *Gosen wakashū* anthology, was composed by Fujiwara no Toshiyuki (d. 907) after he received a gift of white cloth at Takaiko's residence on New Year's Day. Poem 445 from the *Kokinshū* by Yasuhide was written for Takaiko on the topic of artificial blossoms when she was still the wife of the crown prince. As a *mono no na* (names of things) in which words are concealed with the letters of a poem, it is also a distinctly written form of verse, suggesting that it was inscribed on a topic in a manner similar to that of *shi* at *sechien* banquets. This in turn suggests that Takaiko occupied a place within the Fujiwara regime that was analogous to that of a ruling sovereign.

Perhaps the poem most emblematic of the springtime symbolism produced by court poets under the regency is the eighth verse in the *Kokinshū*, which was composed by the scholar-official Yasuhide on the third day of the new year, for Takaiko at a time when her husband was still crown prince:

Though I am	*haru no hi no*
bathed in the soft light	*hikari ni ataru*
of spring's sun,	*ware naredo*
my head, to my woe,	*kashira no yuki to*
is crowned with snow!	*naru zo wabishiki*[80]

This poem's mellifluous opening line, with its mention of "spring's sun" (*haru no hi*), merges the imperial clan descended from the solar deity Amaterasu no Ōmikami with the Fujiwara family, whose clan shrine, Kasuga, was represented with the Chinese characters for "spring" 春 and "sun" 日. Springtime is also associated with the Fujiwara crown prince, whose title is written with the graphs for "east" 東 (a direction geomantically associated with spring) and "palace" 宮. The fact that this poem's association between springtime sun and the Fujiwara clan was enabled through the interplay between *kana* and *kanji* reminds us that the latter writing system, with its "provisional" relationship to Chinese characters, eminently suited the ostensibly provisional nature of the new regime this script was deployed to legitimate.

The nature of Yasuhide's relationship with his patron is as important to understanding the historical significance of this poetic moment as the symbolism deployed in his poem. After his praise of the Fujiwara family's springtime glory, the remainder of Yasuhide's verse encodes a request for future promotion within the standard poetic plaint of old age. Yasuhide was a courtier of the lowly Sixth Rank when he composed this *uta* for the Fujiwara consort. His assiduous courting of Takaiko appears to have paid off when her son became sovereign. In 879, Yasuhide was assured continued access to his mistress when he was promoted in rank to Junior Fifth Lower Grade and given the post of assistant in the Office of Embroideries (*nuidono no suke*), which included such duties as keeping the registers of the princesses and female officials in the Rear Palace.[81] Through such relationships, lower-ranking courtiers like Yasuhide came to serve as "men of letters" for the Fujiwara court, and more particularly for its empresses. In place of a male sovereign, they could address a female co-ruler, and in place of literary Chinese, they could compose poems in *kana*.

Springtime for the Fujiwara thus signified more than simply a season of renewal. Its association with the solar cycle, the feminine trope of blossoms, the office of crown prince, and the name of their clan shrine worked together to produce a complex network of symbols through which the family's relation to monarchical institutions could be naturalized. The links among these symbols appears to have been widely recognized already in Yoshifusa's time, as is suggested in a well-known poem by Narihira that occurs after Yasuhide's springtime encomium in the *Kokinshū*.

If in our world	*yo no naka ni*
there was not	*taete sakura no*
a single cherry tree,	*nakariseba*
springtime hearts	*haru no kokoro wa*
would be at ease.	*nodokekaramashi*[82]

This poem is usually read as a paradigmatic statement of the regret that is supposed to accompany the evanescence of cherry blossoms. When read in light of the symbolism presented above, however, it takes on a more politicized cast as expressing a desire for the Fujiwara-dominated royal lineage to scatter and fall away. Such a reading becomes even more overt in the poem's retelling as part of episode 82 in *Tales of Ise*. There, Narihira is seen addressing this poem to Prince Koretaka, the man who was famously removed as crown prince by Yoshifusa in favor of his own Fujiwara kin.[83] The poem's "springtime hearts" (*haru no kokoro*) is usually read as a universal response to seasonal phenomena. But when we remember that *yo no naka* often meant more specifically the social world, and keeping in mind the associations between spring and future sovereigns, they might also suggest the feelings of the former (and perhaps hoped-for future) crown prince. The dangers involved in any suggestion of treasonous plotting require that it be further masked as an outrageously fanciful hypothesis. After all, everyone *knows* that cherry trees cannot cease to exist. Perhaps, as is often seen to be the case with his poetry, Narihira is acknowledging here his own powerlessness in the face of the political realities that Yoshifusa succeeded in establishing.

Significantly, the *Kokinshū* editors removed any explicit connection with Koretaka from this poem, providing instead only a laconic prose preface noting that it was composed by Narihira when he saw cherry blossoms at the Nagisa villa. The strategic nature of this omission in itself can be seen as an indirect testament to the degree to which the set of symbols and poetic practices established under Yoshifusa's regency were to continue in the period during which the *Kokinshū* was compiled. Yoshifusa's descendant Tokihira would stage similar banquets involving *uta* and wisteria blossoms to mark his house's unique position within the palace. Seasonal symbolism, blossoms, and a class of poets who gained access to and patronage from the nobility on the basis of their poetic skills all feature prominently in that anthology and in the subsequent history of court poetry. In this sense, Yoshifusa's regency marks a significant turn in the cultural as well as political history of the Heian court.

Reciting Yamato History in Verse

Traditional histories of Japanese court poetry tend to stress the absence of *uta* from the institutions and practices of the state in the period prior to the compilation of the *Kokinshū*. Whatever the degree to which blossom banquets and Yamato verse might mimic state-sponsored forms of poetic practice, they and their Fujiwara patrons could claim only an occasional, contingent, and supplementary role vis-à-vis the rituals of Confucian rulership associated with *shi* poetry. The historical record, however, suggests that at times the category of Yamato verse (as opposed to *waka*) was used in precisely the same manner as *shi*. In one practice that has been virtually ignored by modern scholars, *uta* can be seen playing a central role in the rituals of inscription established by Saga and his successors.

In addition to continuing the tradition of blossom banquets introduced by Yoshifusa, his heirs Mototsune and Tokihira initiated an entirely new form of poetic practice in which *uta* were composed to bind the realm through writing. Known to modern scholars as *Nihongi kyōen waka* (*waka* composed at banquets that concluded a series of lectures on the *Nihon shoki*), these *uta* took up topics from the court's foundational history. In the process, they asserted the importance of a phonetic script, a distinct form of poetry supported by it, and a place for the Fujiwara family within the dynastic myths of the Yamato regime. Such rituals, in which the term *yamato uta* features prominently, can help us understand the specific significance of this word at the time when Tsurayuki was providing his own definition in the *Kokinshū*'s Kana Preface.

These new rites of inscription instituted by Yoshifusa's successors took place at a time when their family's relationship to the monarchy was being redefined. The political preeminence for his house that Yoshifusa established during his grandson Seiwa's reign was extended into that of Yōzei, whose actions were overseen by his maternal uncle Mototsune, Yoshifusa's nephew and successor to the Northern House. Unlike his uncle, however, Mototsune did not appear to view the regency as a necessary institution, preferring the role of minister to that of maternal relative. If anything, the Fujiwara patriarch appears to have viewed Yōzei as an embarrassment. Mototsune is believed to have pushed for his retirement after the latter had the son of his own wet-nurse beaten to death.[84] Another sign of his lack of interest in continuing the regency can be seen in his decision to have an adult prince succeed the immature sovereign. This choice would lead to the establishment of a new line of adult rulers who would negotiate a more complex relationship with their Fujiwara peers than had been the case in Yoshifusa's time.

In his preferred capacity as loyal minister, Mototsune sponsored the writing of a new court history, the *Montoku jitsuroku*, and the expansion of the state's economic base through policies designed to increase the number of public fields (*handen*) and fields set aside for officials' incomes (*kanden*). The appearance of a new historiographic project in tandem with these economic policies suggests that the latter was intended in part to legitimate the former by establishing Mototsune's place at the head of an expanding state. Another link between these policies and the manipulation of historical discourse can be seen in Mototsune's pronounced interest in the Yamato dynasty's founding history during this time. One month prior to the issuing of the first rescript ordering the establishment of new public lands in Gangyō 2/3/15 (878), he launched a series of lectures on the *Nihon shoki* which concluded four years later at a banquet held in 882.

Banquets commemorating lectures on the *Nihon shoki* had long been an established practice at the Yamato court. In 720 one was held marking the completion of the chronicle; and in 812 and 839 banquets were held to commemorate the end of a series of lectures on the text. The *Sandai jitsuroku*'s description of Mototsune's banquet, however, is the first to explicitly mention *uta* that were written for the event:

> A banquet commemorating the end of the lectures on the *Nihon shoki* was held under the auspices of the Minister of the Right [Mototsune]. Previously, on Gangyō 2/2/25, Assistant Professor Yoshibuchi no Aisei had been ordered to read the *Nihon shoki* aloud under the eastern eaves of the Giyōden Hall. Lectures were conducted by Grand Outer Scribe Shimada no Yoshiomi and involved various students of literature and the classics. The Chancellor, Minister of the Right, and other nobility listened. Afterward, a banquet of fine writing was declared. The lectures ended on Gangyō 5/6/29. When the princes and those of Fifth Rank and above had taken their places, virtuous rulers and famed ministers were selected as topics from the *Nihon shoki*. Then everyone who had attended the lectures crafted a Yamato verse, from the Chancellor down to officials of Sixth Rank. The poems were based on topics drawn by each person that same day. Many songs accompanied by zither music were then performed. The banquet ended with much drink and good cheer. Stipends were distributed to the professors and lecturers, each according to their rank. Bolts of cotton from the palace storehouses were paid out to those of Fifth Rank and higher. A record of the event was made for the Office of Outer Scribes.[85]

All the elements of this description of the event—the dispensation of topics, the formal act of inscription, and the conclusion of the event with musical performances and the disbursement of stipends—closely follow the conventions of formal state banquets at which *shi* were composed. In fact, similar banquets following lectures on the Confucian canon had been a staple of Saga's reign. The *Ryōunshū* anthology, for example, includes *shi* written at a banquet concluding lectures on the *Classic of Poetry*. Such exercises exemplified the ideology of "writing binding the realm" in which the textual reinscription of earlier canonical works in poetic form sought to bind together past and present.

The textual regime of Saga's court did not distinguish between itself and its continental peers, chiefly because they shared the same language and thus the same canons and histories in which that language was articulated. By contrast, the banquet that Mototsune sponsored is significant for claiming that new forms of phonetic writing could bind together the Yamato realm in similar ways. They did so, moreover, by asserting the particularity of language and history that distinguished the Yamato court from its continental counterparts. At Mototsune's banquet, the poetic reinscription of names and events from the court's canonical history asserted the state's unchanging ties to its mythic origins, as well as the shared history of its aristocratic clans, whose divine ancestors were each accorded a place in the *Nihon shoki*'s mythology.

In this regard, it is especially significant that the chief historical precedent from the *Nihon shoki* cited in the poetry composed at this banquet concerned Mototsune's position at court. The choice of loyal ministers as a topic for poetic composition was no doubt intended to affirm the legitimacy of Mototsune's position as the ruler's representative. Shōtoku Taishi (574–622), who appears to have been a favorite subject in poems composed at the banquet, would have been a particularly apt model in this regard. Like Mototsune, he sought actively to enlarge the state on behalf of a royal relative. By citing this famous figure, *uta* composed at the *Nihon shoki* banquet implicitly legitimated Mototsune's claims to power and prerogative within the state.

Another striking feature of the event is the way in which *yamato uta* are distinguished from other forms of native verse on account of their textuality. In its description of the banquet, the *Sandai jitsuroku* appears to make a clear distinction between "Yamato verses that are crafted" (作倭歌) in written form during the formal event, and "zither songs" (*kinka* 琴歌) that are sung to musical accompaniment at its more relaxed end. This distinction suggests that the very act of inscription, and its attendant goal of binding the realm to its written past, defined *yamato uta* verse as such. Within the space of a few decades during which the Fujiwara had come to dominate the imperial household, written *uta* had been transformed from a curiosity at Ninmyō's birthday to a distinct ritual technology with its own formal acts of inscription and canons for citation.

The citation and inscription of the court's oldest historical chronicle in poetic form at Mototsune's banquet might also have been intended in part to legitimate a new version of this text. One of the goals of the lectures that preceded it appears to have been the establishment of authoritative new *kana* glosses for the literary Chinese in which the *Nihon shoki* was written. According to the fragmentary "personal records" (*shiki*) of attendees that were compiled in the Kamakura period (1183–1333), Mototsune is said to have brought a *kana* version of the *Nihon shoki* to lectures on the text.[86] Although it is unclear whether the phonetic script in Mototsune's version of the *Nihon shoki* was reserved for its *uta*, or whether it was intended to provide a gloss to the entire text, the latter possibility is more likely. While modern versions of the *Nihon shoki* all record the texts of songs in *kana*, there is scattered evidence that they could be inscribed in a variety of formats. The record of one lecture from the Kōnin era, for example, represents a famous poem about the tragic prince Hayabusawake in three pentasyllabic lines of literary Chinese.

A hawk climbs toward Heaven, 隼鳥昇天兮

(ハヤフサハア メニノホリ)

beating wings above the zelkova tree, 飛翔衡槫兮

(トヒカケリイツキカウヘノ)

it grasps the sparrow. 鷦鷯所摯焉

(ササキトラセネ)[87]

Except for the odd number of three lines, the above poem appears to adhere to the grammatical, lexical, and metrical conventions of literary Chinese. Perhaps this asymmetry was the chief means for signaling the poem's Yamato qualities. Insofar as there could potentially be more than one *kana* version of this literary Chinese text, the attempt in *Nihon shoki* lectures to establish new textual versions of earlier poems resembles the act of composing new ones on topics at the final banquet.

Both practices took a text written in literary Chinese as their point of departure for a *kana* version, both drew on that earlier text's words and contexts in their poetic reworkings, and both claimed continuity with the past through this act.

Despite their fragmentary nature, accounts of *Nihon shoki* lectures can tell us much about both the fluid qualities of the historical narrative's textual form in the early Heian period, and the politics of its reformulations. The very fluidity of the historical text itself is a testament to the power of poetry, which, through the act of citing new versions of the past, recast them as an authoritative touchstone. At least one scholar has noted that the poems composed for this banquet work to subtly reorganize the chronicle's account.[88] Such revisions of the *Nihon shoki* reaffirmed its status as the founding narrative of the Yamato realm and helped define the role of male Fujiwara aristocrats within that enterprise by virtue of the prominent place it accorded their Nakatomi ancestors in its mytho-history. Far from being ancillary to public ritual, *yamato uta* in this instance are crucial to both its practices and purposes. Perhaps for this reason it was customary for the leading Fujiwara statesman at court to oversee the compilation of official chronicles. Ostensibly a practice designed to legitimate the Yamato dynasty, these activities also provided a means for the Fujiwara to represent themselves as loyal ministers integral to the state.

In keeping with this stratagem for controlling official historical discourse, Mototsune oversaw the compilation of the *Montoku jitsuroku*, and his own son Tokihira was given the task of compiling the next official history, the *Sandai jitsuroku*. Tokihira's assumption of editorship sealed his political triumph over Michizane, who had previously been designated as the court's official historiographer. In both cases, revisions of the *Nihon shoki* and inscriptions of *yamato uta* accompanied the writing of new court histories. Yamato verse provided an opportunity to legitimate revisions to the historical record by citing them in ritualized acts of inscription. The link between a distinctly Yamato form of poetry and "old words" (*furugoto*) preserved in written texts that was first developed under Yoshifusa, was thus expanded and strengthened by his successors. Just as *shi* poetry "bound the realm" together in a web of atemporal textual allusions, Yamato verse under the regency "returned the world to its origins" as it cited the canon of historical narrative and its verses. The use of *kana* to create this continuity would make it equivalent to literary Chinese as a ritually effective medium.

Although Yamato verse appears to have established itself in both the national histories and the ritual spaces of the court prior to the compilation of the *Kokinshū*, events such as the *Nihongi kyōen* banquets lie outside the mainstream of Japanese literary history.[89] None of the poets in the *Kokinshū* that are commonly associated with this period participated in them. Men such as Narihira and Yasuhide were not part of the community of scholars and officials who inscribe *uta* in the *Sandai jitsuroku*. This omission is especially noteworthy because similar rites were being held in the years surrounding the compilation of the *Kokinshū*. In 906 Daigo sponsored another *Nihon shoki* lecture banquet. All the men attending this event were graduates of the university, and all of them were of Fifth Rank and higher. Within this ritual hierarchy, men such as Tsurayuki were excluded from the court's most formal occasions for composing *yamato uta*. This gap between the fantasies of lower-ranking courtiers seeking to claim a place beside their ruler and the realities of a court in which they were placed on the ritual and political margins would come to inform the *Kokinshū*'s own distinctive vision of Yamato verse.

Chapter Two

Household Harmony in Uda's Poetry Matches

Placing Poetry Matches at the Heian Court

In most histories of Japanese literature, court poetry first comes into its own with the compilation of the *Kokinshū*. By virtue of its being an imperial anthology, this text is often said to have elevated *uta* to the status of a public form of poetry akin to *shi*. Both before and during the time in which the *Kokinshū* was creating a vision of the court community that drew on the practices associated with continental poetry and politics, however, gatherings known as "poetry matches" (*uta-awase*) were helping to define another form of court community in the shape of a household. Like its predecessors at court, this new social formation drew on Confucian models of political cosmology and ritual. Unlike them, however, it gave equal prominence to men and women, thereby influencing conceptions of communal identity at the Heian court for centuries afterward.

The poetry matches of the late ninth century are often seen as a bridge between the "dark age" of native verse and its "renaissance" in the tenth century. By the Kamakura period, the Kanpyō era (889–898) in which Uda reigned was being treated as a significant historical epoch for court poetry in treatises such as the *Kindai shūka* (*Superior Poems of Our Time*, 1209). Connections between the poetic activities of the Kanpyō era and the development of a new form of public court poetry are suggested by the characteristics the former share with the *Kokinshū*. Like the first imperial anthology of *uta*, Uda's poetry matches give prominent attention to the seasons and love, display an interest in forms of rhetoric associated with written verse, and rely on lower-ranking courtiers to supply their poems. All these features are often identified as hallmarks of "public" Heian court poetry.

Although it is frequently claimed that these matches played a crucial role in the development of Heian court poetry, the nature of that role has been left largely unexplored by modern scholars. One difficulty in assessing the import of early poetry matches is the paucity of detailed documentation. While over forty poetry matches are known to have taken place during the reigns of Uda and Daigo, extant manuscripts usually consist of nothing more than a short list of the poems presented by each team. Moreover, these manuscripts are more than a century older than the events they record.[1] In only a few cases are the circumstances surrounding the presentation of poems provided. In fact, it is during the period when the *Kokinshū* anthology was being shaped that extended records of such matches first appear. Despite this lack of information, however, enough features of Uda's earlier poetry matches exist to give a sense of the general significance of these events. The major part of this chapter will be devoted to an account of what we can glean from such information, especially when it is correlated with a variety of ritual and political features of Uda's court that have not been extensively discussed in literary-historical accounts of its poetic practices. Taken together, these features of poetry matches contributed to a new concept of political community centered in the household and mansion rather than officialdom and palace.

One important element of my approach is an emphasis on the connections between poetry matches and ritual, which can help illuminate the significance of not only this particular form of Heian verse but also the categories used to discuss the period's poetry in general. Modern scholarship often divides court *uta* into "formal poetry" (*hare no uta*), and "informal poetry" (*ke no uta*). One representative scholar defines formal poetry as the product of professional poets who worked on commission, like a painter or craftsman, to produce poems whose public nature was reflected in their emphasis on novel forms of expression. By contrast, informal poetry was produced by amateur poets for utilitarian communicative purposes, typically in epistolary correspondences, and relied on formulaic phrasing to make it intelligible to the recipient.[2]

Most scholars who write about the so-called *Kokinshū* period emphasize at least one of these elements to define the formality or informality of its poetry, a procedure that tends to privilege poetic style and authorial identity as a means for defining *hare* and *ke*. One result of this approach is to isolate the text from the varying contexts in which it was produced, circulated, and received. The same poem could appear in a personal collection or an imperial anthology with very different meanings. In addition to appearing in different texts, the same poem could appear in connection with different people, often being composed by one and performed by another. Within this fluid and context-based setting, neither authorship nor style is a reliable means in and of itself for ascertaining whether a given poem is formal or informal.

Another approach to distinguishing *hare* and *ke* has been proposed more recently by Thomas LaMarre, who associates them with distinctions in modes of appearance that in turn represent different political formations. Whereas *hare* modes were associated with the daytime rites of the court, *ke* forms of culture represented the nighttime alliances formed by aristocratic families which took place outside these visual, temporal, and architectural structures.[3] Part of the political import of Uda's poetry matches, I suggest, lay in the strategic ways in which they combined the symbols associated with these two modes of display. My approach, however, focuses on their connections not so much to diurnal forms of time as to seasonal ones.

Early poetry matches can be seen as an intrinsically formal mode of poetic display insofar as they participated in the larger ritual topographies through which the court constituted itself. The history of the terms *hare* and *ke* in itself suggests the importance of performative context in determining any given poem's status as formal or informal. The word *hare* first appears in ritual formularies and diaries as a way of denoting court observances that were fully carried out in clear weather (*seigi*) as opposed to ones abbreviated or otherwise altered due to rain (*ugi*). Both *hare* and *ke* were first used to describe poetry in the twelfth century, when the act of composing *uta* in competitive matches had become extensively codified. Such terms marked the locale at which a poetry match took place or the rank of its sponsor, with one held under the reigning sovereign in the palace as the most exemplary instance of *hare*.[4] A notable example of this usage occurs in an anecdote from the *Mumyōshō* (ca. 1211–1216), a compendium of poetic lore written by Kamo no Chōmei, where one poem elicits the remark that "it should have been recited for some terribly formal gathering or before the sovereign and his grand ministers. What a shame that it was composed in such informal circumstances!" (*kayō no koto wa imijikaran hare no awase, moshi wa kokuō daijin no onmae nado nite koso yomame. Kakaru kegoto ni yomitaru munen naru koto nari*).[5] Behind this lament lies the assumption that neither poets nor poems can be considered *hare* unless they appear before the sovereign.

Early Heian poetry matches primarily took place in settings where sovereigns and retired sovereigns presided. As with other forms of court ritual, status in such contexts was defined through proximity to the imperial person who, in accordance with Confucian conceptions of political cosmology, was seen as the organizing locus between homologous structures that extended from the macrocosmic level of cosmos and polity down to the microcosmic level of individual bodies.[6] Likewise, the physical geography of the palace and capital city were organized around the imperial body and treated as an extension of his person.[7] Complex networks of *qi* energy exchanged and circulated between these different registers of the world in a sympathetic resonance that was constantly modulated by the Confucian "Son of Heaven" through daily and annual ritual actions. Kingship involved harmonizing the movements and actions of humanity with the world surrounding them through rites whose performance was synchronized by a court-mandated calendar. Consequently, regulations concerning the dress, activities, food, government, and activities of the court and its sovereign were all set to a calendrical cycle designed to ensure harmony between society and the cosmos.

The outwardly expanding topography of this political cosmology linking the sovereign to his subjects and the realm was represented in court ritual through a spatial order in which those closest to him physically were also highest in status. In official observances, ministers of Third Rank and higher typically were seated in the hall with the sovereign, while those of Fourth and Fifth Rank were placed below this space in curtained partitions to the east and west.[8] What one saw was determined by one's position within a strictly defined seating arrangement at banquets and other formal gatherings attended by the sovereign. The significance placed on such positioning is indirectly attested to by diaries from the period, which record the position and point of view of participants with a frequency bordering on the obsessive.[9] Unlike the women and men who attended the sovereign in such settings, the majority of officials within the palace compound labored in anonymity and usually were not participants in court ritual. They are largely absent from descriptions of court observances found in the ritual codes, aristocrats' diaries, and historical chronicles of the Heian period.[10] By the time of Uda's reign, they were even excluded from the New Year's Day court blessing at which they had previously been visible. In its place, new rites enacted within his household would create a more intimate and circumscribed definition of status.

Scattered evidence suggests that early poetry matches often reflected the social topography of court rituals. A detailed account of one such gathering held in 977 at the mansion of Minister of the Left Fujiwara no Yoritada (924–989) gives an especially detailed account of the placement of its participants.

> The masters of the house, and the upper nobility were in the hall. Those of Fourth and Fifth Rank were seated on the verandah of the eastern wing, with those of Fifth Rank in the rear. Those of Sixth Rank were seated inside the Tang-style room. [. . .] Toward daybreak, lamps were refreshed and each composer presented a poem. A lamp was set up and a reciter summoned from each team. During these preparations, those of Fourth and Fifth Rank all drew closer to hear the recitation.[11]

According to this account, courtiers of the lowest ranks were placed at the periphery of the poetry match. They could neither see the event nor hear the recitations that followed. This marginalization was even more pronounced at Uda's earlier matches, where the lower-ranking male officials who produced poems did not participate at all.[12] In their stead, upper nobility and intimates of the retired sovereign would recite the poems that had been presented. This division between composer and reciter, as will be argued at the end of this chapter, was further reflected in changing definitions of the poetic act of *yomu* (composition/recitation) which were taking place during the same period.

While the social hierarchies encoded in poetry matches were no less formal than those of other court rituals, there were significant differences in the composition of the communities they created. Whereas the latter drew on a continental political cosmology that conceived of ruler and court as exclusively male, the former provided many opportunities for women to claim status through proximity to the sovereign's person. Poetry matches created a space in which both male and female attendants could gather around their ruler and vie with one another for his favors. By contrast, only high-ranking male courtiers represented the opposing teams in other formal arenas of social competition, such as archery meets, horse races, and wrestling matches.

The presence of both men and women at Uda's poetry matches reflects the emphasis these events laid on kinship filiations rather than court ranks in determining what was at stake. Unlike other ritual forms of competition, where membership in a team was determined by one's place within the state's official structures of post and rank, membership in the team of a poetry match was determined by one's relations. Many of the earliest poetry matches, for example, involve the sisters, daughters, and consorts of Uda at moments when the issue of succession to the throne was being negotiated at court. Such gatherings thus provided a means for formally acknowledging and managing the interests of different factions within the imperial family. In doing so, they also recognized the crucial role played by women in determining the outcome.

The unprecedented nature of these communities and forms of competition was reflected in the media they used. With their combination of written *uta*, landscape dioramas, and musical performances, poetry matches provided a truly novel form of theatrical display in a reign distinguished for its inventiveness. The active sponsorship of these new forms of display by Uda was in keeping with his pronounced interest in constructing new rituals both during and after his abdication in response to the increasing fragmentation of political and economic authority at court in the late ninth century. One outcome of this larger strategy, in which poetry matches played a part, was the development of the household as a site for displaying new forms of wealth and authority which did not depend on the placement of the ruler in his palace for their organizing locus.

Ritual, Language, and Politics in Uda's Reign

The political context informing Uda's reign and the important role played by ritual within it are essential to understanding the process by which poetry matches first took shape. Accounts of Heian *uta* tend to link its rise to prominence at court to a period of rule by a more assertive line of sovereigns which began in 884 with the ascendancy of Kōkō (830–887, r. 884–887) and continued in the reigns of Uda and Daigo. As we saw in the last chapter, however, Yoshifusa and Mototsune already had laid the groundwork for these later developments. The germinal role played by these Fujiwara men in developing *uta* as a new form of state literature complicates the distinctions typically made by modern scholars between their clan's dominance of the "private" realm of marriage and family and the ruler's prerogative to oversee the "public" realm of court ritual. Uda's poetry matches reflect the complexity of this state of affairs in their attempt to conflate the two spheres by making highly public claims for the retired sovereign's prerogative in overseeing his household's marital alliances and descent within the imperial family.

Uda's particular blending of public and private symbolism in the new modes of ritual that he established comment eloquently on the complexity of court politics during his reign. Although scholars often discuss the late ninth and early tenth centuries in terms of a restoration of monarchical influence, the political history of this period suggests a more ambivalent balance of power between the reigning sovereign and the Fujiwara Northern House, one that would characterize the intensely bifurcated nature of court culture throughout the Heian period. In such a situation, an ambitious monarch such as Uda could not simply return to a pre-Fujiwara past. Rather, his response to the political realities of a divided court was to revive continental ritual modes of sovereignty developed in Saga's reign while also adapting and appropriating the new Yamato modes established under the regency.

This process would begin with the enthronement of Uda's father Kōkō in 884. For the first time in recent memory, an adult sovereign with no maternal connections to Yoshifusa's family now headed the court. Although Mototsune continued to hold important posts at court, his influence over the Council of State became increasingly diluted as men from Kōkō's own Minamoto kin and other non-Fujiwara families replaced his supporters. In his study of the early Heian court, Robert Borgen characterizes this period as one in which minister and ruler shared power in an amicable manner.[13] While this was no doubt true in terms of their negotiations over court appointments and positions within the bureaucracy, in the realm of ritual Kōkō appears to have been more assertive of his royal prerogatives. The reappearance of an adult ruler at court saw a resurgence of interest in elaborating his role as the sacral intermediary between Heaven and humanity. One noteworthy characteristic of Kōkō's four-year reign was the importance given to *yin-yang* prognostication as a means for interpreting and responding to celestial phenomena. The number of such portents reported during this time noticeably increased. According to the official chronicle covering the period, Kōkō was also committed to reviving annual observances associated with Saga's reign.[14] In acknowledgment of his sovereign's newly active role in this area, Mototsune wrote out the court's annual ritual regimen on a screen placed in his sovereign's personal residence.

Kōkō's assertion of the monarch's prerogatives had important consequences when he succeeded in having his favorite son, previously relegated to commoner status as a Minamoto, reaffiliated with the royal family and made crown prince. Uda's subsequent enthronement established a new line of rulers whose relations with the Northern House were called into question. Struggles over the definition of Mototsune's place at court burst into the open at the beginning of Uda's reign in the so-called Akō Debate. This incident involved a dispute between the Fujiwara minister and his sovereign over the meaning of Mototsune's newly conferred title of *akō* (*aheng* in Chinese), an ancient Chinese post that had never been used before at the Heian court. Disagreement over the precise duties that came with this title led Mototsune to stay away from Uda's court until its significance was defined to his advantage.

In addition to the immediate political repercussions described by historians, the Akō Debate can be seen as playing a part in shaping the court's linguistic culture, in particular its concern with the names of things. Uda's reign was characterized by a heightened awareness of language's role in establishing the political order. One overt example of his interest in this issue can be seen in his "Notes on the Classic of Changes" (*Shoekishō*, ca. 897), a compilation of passages from the Confucian classic of prognostication the *Yijing* and its commentaries that he personally completed just prior to his abdication.

> Words issue from one's self and spread to the people. Conduct rises near at hand and is seen far off. Words and conduct are the piv-

> ots that move a gentleman. The results of this pivot determine both glory and defamation. It is by means of his words and deeds that the gentleman moves Heaven and Earth. How can one not be cautious in this regard?[15]

Language here is described as having both political and cosmological consequences. Its effects spread outward from the royal person to influence both his subjects and the nonhuman world. In Confucian conceptions of governance, one of the ruler's duties was to ensure that written signs corresponded with the material universe.[16] Uda's marked interest in the manipulation of language both before and after his reign can be seen as an extension of such concerns. Within the poetry matches he held in both periods, *kana* writing would be used in novel ways to rectify names and redefine community.

Uda's interest in the connections between language and political authority can be seen in his active sponsorship of annual banquets at which officials echoed their ruler's words in *shi* poems. Although he is chiefly known for his patronage of *uta*, he was equally concerned with established continental rituals of poetic inscription. During his time on the throne, Uda expanded the yearly repertoire of such events from the four held in Kōkō's reign—the Inner Palace Banquet (*naien*), the Double Ninth (*chōyō*), and two lectures on the Confucian classics (*sekiten*)—to include a purification ritual held on the first Day of the Snake in the Third Month (*jōshi*), and the *Tanabata* observances of the Double Seventh. Moreover, he continued to host these annual observances at his Suzaku-in mansion after his abdication.[17] Through such rituals of writing, the retired sovereign asserted his continuing right to rule and to constitute a court around his person.

Another aspect of the Akō Debate that influenced Uda's strategies for asserting his power and authority at court can be inferred from the prominent role played by mansions in the struggle between him and his Fujiwara minister. Mototsune manifested his dissatisfaction with Uda not only by staying at home, but also by persuading a sizable number of the court's influential members to attend on him there. This demonstration of his personal residence's continuing role as an alternate locus of authority at court might have spurred on Uda's creation during this same period of his own household government at his living quarters within the palace. Like its Fujiwara counterpart in the Somedono mansion, Uda's new ritual locus in the palace was defined through appeals to a distinctly Yamato tradition and close connections to imperial consorts. It was in this new household space that a new poetics would first come to prominence.

Uda's Household Government

Uda's reign witnessed a radical reordering of the palace's ritual topography, one that would define court culture for centuries to come. Status at court and the rites encoding it both shifted to the ruler's living quarters in the Seiryōden. This new locale created a new community in which male and female members of the court strove to assert their status through intimate access to the sovereign's person within his domestic space. The radical shifts in political architecture, ritual, and community inaugurated by Uda's new concept of a royal household within the palace provides one lens through which to understand the equally radical and novel use of poetry matches under his regime.

Uda's choice of physical location for his new household government appears to have intentionally departed from the palace's preexisting continental coordinates. The Seiryōden was oriented around an east-west axis, rather than the north-south one associated with the ruler in Confucian geomancy.[18] The orientation of this placement within the palace suggests an appeal to native conceptions of royal authority based on descent from an ancestral solar deity. Uda's architectural shift in the center of gravity at the palace might also have represented an attempt to appropriate Yoshifusa's strategies for establishing ritual authority within his living quarters. In its choice of materials and overall design, the Seiryōden resembled a Heian aristocrat's mansion more than it did a continental monarch's palace. In its functions, this portion of the palace combined private and public dimensions of Uda's life. It was here that the sovereign slept, ate his meals, and journeyed to the Rear Palace occupied by his concubines. Here too deliberations over promotions for the coming year were now being made.

Two observances were created for Uda's living quarters to mark it as the new ritual hub of government. Known as the *shihōhai* (Prayer in Four Directions) and the *kochōhai (*Lesser Court Blessing), these rites became an integral part of the annual roster of royal rites. The *shihōhai* was a series of prayers directed to heavenly, terrestrial, and ancestral deities. The *kochōhai* was an abbreviated, smaller-scale version of the annual New Year's Day rite of *chōga* (Court Blessing), in which court officials assembled before the sovereign on the first day of the new calendrical year to bless his reign. Whereas the Court Blessing originally involved a substantial portion of the palace's officials coming together in the imposing Great Hall of State (Daigokuden), Uda's new rite gathered a much smaller group within the more intimate confines of the Seiryōden. Participants in the *kochōhai* observance were limited to courtiers of Fifth Rank and above who possessed the privilege to enter the sovereign's living quarters.

Like the architecture of the Seiryōden, these household rites suggest a turn away from continental modes of ritual toward self-consciously native ones. The *kochōhai* departed from the Confucian ritual axis that placed the ruler to the north and the subject to the south. Instead, the attending officials assembled in the eastern courtyard of the Seiryōden facing west toward their sovereign. The *shihōhai* rite was even more overtly associated with Yamato cultural forms by Uda who, in a noteworthy passage from his diary, asserted its legitimacy by appealing to native religious tradition: "Our realm is a divine realm. Thus, every morning, obeisance in the four directions to the greater, median, and lesser deities of Heaven and Earth shall henceforth be celebrated without fail."[20]

In citing his realm's divinely sanctioned distinctiveness, Uda's description of this rite recalls the rhetoric used in the *chōka* for Ninmyō that Yoshifusa had sponsored. Unlike his Fujiwara predecessors, however, Uda's introduction of a new ritual space supplementing the preexisting structures of sovereignty also led to the creation of new modes of social distinction at court. During his reign a new category of male courtier was established who was defined by his right to attend on the sovereign directly in the latter's living quarters.[21] Literally "person who ascends into the hall," the title of *tenjōbito* was reserved for those male officials who were permitted into the entry room known as the Tenjō no Ma (Courtier's Hall) located in the southern eaves of the Seiryōden. Membership in this group was limited to courtiers of Fifth Rank or above, with the exception of officials who attended on the sovereign personally as his members of his Secretariat (*kurōdo*).

As time went by, permission to enter the Seiryōden became increasingly important to defining status at the Heian court. Upper-ranking nobility competed to have their sons serve as "hall pages" (*tenjō no warawa*) in the sovereign's living quarters, and men lamented promotions from the lowly Sixth Rank if it meant giving up a post that might enable such proximity.[22] Even Sei Shōnagon (fl. 1000–1010), the notably status-conscious writer of the *Pillow Book* (*Makura no sōshi*), places these male attendants in her list of "splendid things" (*medetaki mono*) despite their lowly origins:

> Although he is careful to put on a humble manner, he now walks around in the company of young noblemen and the scions of renowned clans. The sight of him attending the royal person in his living quarters at night cannot but arouse feelings of jealousy in them. He serves His Majesty in such intimate proximity for three or four years, despite an uncouth appearance and poor taste in colors. What a waste! When it comes time for him to receive a promotion to the Fifth Rank and lose the right to ascend into the sovereign's living quarters, he is sorrier than if he were to lose his life, and applies vigorously for any opening that comes up in the provincial governorships.[23]

This circumscribed community of men and women surrounding the royal person in Sei Shōnagon's time was first established at Uda's court, where one's position within the sovereign's household provided new means for defining social status. This was especially true for the sovereign's consorts, for whom such titles as *miyasundokoro* (mistress of His Majesty's Bedchamber) and *kōi* (His Majesty's robe changer) pointed to both one's status and one's proximity to the royal person. At the same time as court women were becoming increasingly prominent within the innermost secluded portions of the palace, however, they were also largely marginalized within the general body of officialdom. In this sense, Uda's new household form of government represented the culmination of a process that had been taking place throughout the ninth century. Up until Saga's reign women officials had acted as the intermediaries between the sovereign and his male officials: carrying messages between the two during Council of State deliberations, conveying the ruler's proclamations to his court during the New Year's Day ceremonies, and bringing food and stipends to his courtiers during official banquets.

Over the course of the ninth century, however, women had become increasingly invisible within the court's bureaucracy. Even at their height, they were a minority within the larger body of officialdom. Among the 7,000 or so people who lived and worked in the palace compound and its immediate environs, only one in ten are thought to have been women.[24] In Saga's reign, the term "female official" (*jokan*) was already being used to distinguish them from the general body of court officialdom. By the latter half of the ninth century, documents drafted and circulated by women officials become restricted solely to affairs relating to the inner palace.[25] In 879, stipendiary fields allotted to women officials were abolished and their lands redistributed among their male peers. In keeping with this trend, they were also increasingly excluded from the palace's annual rituals over the course of the early Heian period.[26]

Uda's court witnessed the culmination of women's segregation from the material, political, ritual and social contexts that defined state officials. During his reign, it became customary to call female attendants by the rank of a male relative rather than by their own surnames and posts.[27] Like the hall courtier, these new means for identifying court women became established features of the eleventh-century court in which women such as Murasaki Shikibu and Sei Shōnagon wrote. Yet while women were becoming increasingly invisible within the structures of state officialdom, their visibility within Uda's household increased. As we shall see, female members of the court played a prominent role in the poetry matches that helped define his new household government.

Both the unprecedented nature of Uda's new household regime and its attendant political implications are suggested in the initial rejection of rites associated with it by Uda's successor. In the entry for New Year's Day in Engi 5 (905), Daigo's diary recounts his decision to abolish the *kochōhai* rite (no doubt at his regent Tokihira's prompting) because it lacked any precedent within the official structures of the state ritual: "Today it was decided to suspend the Lesser Court Blessing. We declare that in perusing the written histories of the past, there is nothing private to be found with regards to the sovereign. This is a private rite."[28] Tokihira's attempts to erase Uda's new vision of a court community was rolled back by his brother and successor Fujiwara no Tadahira (880–949), a man who generally appears to have taken a more conciliatory stance toward the former sovereign. In his diary entry for New Year's Day in Engi 19 (919), Tadahira makes special note of his success in reinstating the *kochōhai* rite:

> The official observances were as usual, and the ministers in personal attendance on His Majesty performed a Lesser Court Blessing. It had been suspended by royal command in previous years, but today the ministers all begged earnestly for its revival. When the princes have their own New Year's Day ceremony, why should the ministers be without similar rites? The latter's principles are the same as those guiding the ministers and people.[29]

This diary entry reveals the different meanings that different parties could ascribe to the same social space. Whereas Tokihira and his young ruler might have seen Uda's new rites as a threat to their positions, Tadahira here seems to be suggesting they present an opportunity for him and others to assert their places at court. The shifting fortunes of the Lesser Court Blessing charted in the diaries of Daigo and Tadahira suggest that Uda's household rites attracted considerable attention from the upper echelons of court society. In the period between Daigo's abolition and subsequent reinstatement of these "private" rituals, Uda continued to espouse the form of community they represented outside the palace in the poetry matches he held at his various residences.

Like these annual observances, poetry matches provided Uda with the means to display, affirm, and define his household as a natural extension of his sovereignty over the realm. Both forms of ritual cited Yamato precedents rather than continental ones. Both also took place within the sovereign's living quarters, with their community of inhabitants and regular visitors. In the case of poetry matches, all of the sponsors and participants were men and women who served in proximity to Uda during his time in power.[30] Not until well into the tenth century were poetry matches held across a broader spectrum of court society. The *Kokinshū* anthology exemplifies this tendency by including only poems from matches sponsored by Uda and his immediate family.

Unlike the annual observances mentioned above, however, Uda's poetry matches did not rely exclusively on the palace as their locus. Instead, they elaborated an entirely autonomous complex of symbols, one in which seasonal time, love, and *kana* writing created a topography, temporality, sociality, and language that paralleled the Confucian ideology of state and sovereign while being distinct from it. The palace was replaced by the mansion garden; calendrical observances were replaced by seasonal time; relations between lord and minister were replaced by kinship ties, and the literary Chinese canon were replaced by *kana* script. Within this new household community, moreover, women played a prominent role in coordinating the interests of the imperial clan with those of its aristocratic peers and rivals.

Palace Women, Politics, and Poetry

One particularly noteworthy feature of Uda's matches is their tendency to appear at politically sensitive junctures involving the members of his immediate family. Although the earliest two poetry matches appear to have been held during his father's reign, the next six took place under his sponsorship or that of his brothers, mother, and consorts. Female members of his household seem to have played a particularly important role in this regard. Their poetic activities during Uda's reign culminated in an unprecedented attempt to anthologize one poetry match after Mototsune's death in 891. In fact, the prominent role played by these women continued after his abdication, making their presence in such events one of their signal features.

The period in which the first royal poetry matches took place was marked by a significant shift in the balance of power between Uda and the Northern House. With the death of Mototsune, Uda was able to make his son Atsuhito crown prince in 893. Atsuhito's mother belonged to a branch of the Northern House that was separate from that of Mototsune's line. Her father Fujiwara no Takafuji (838–900) and brother Fujiwara no Kanesuke (877–933) provided vital political support to Atsuhito once he was enthroned as Daigo. As Uda's rivalry with the Northern House intensified after his retirement, so would the frequency with which he held poetry matches. With the ascendancy of Tokihira at Daigo's court, poetry matches at the retired sovereign's numerous mansions increased noticeably. After the latter's death, they reached unprecedented levels of elaborateness in the Teiji Villa Poetry Match (*Teiji-in no uta-awase*) of 913 and the Kyōgoku Consort Hōshi's Poetry Match (*Kyōgoku no miyasundokoro Hōshi no uta-awase*) held in 921.[31]

Such historical details suggest that, like the *uta* exchanges represented in the court's official histories, Uda's poetry matches took place at times of political uncertainty. Two contests held just prior to his abdication were sponsored by Fujiwara no Inshi (d. 896) and Fujiwara no Atsuko (872–907), consorts of Uda's who were from different branches of the Fujiwara clan.[32] The first of these women was Daigo's biological mother, the second was his adoptive one. Atsuko had been married to Uda as part of the settlement he reached with her father Mototsune in the aftermath of the Akō Debate. Despite her kinsmen's hopes, however, she failed to produce a son. Uda's decision to have her become the adoptive mother of his heir by a rival branch of the Fujiwara clan suggests that his assertion of monarchical prerogatives was balanced by a need to maintain ties to the Northern House. It is probably not coincidental that women representing opposing interests were engaging in displays of poetic competition in the year when the competing claims of their families to the succession were being negotiated and formalized.

In addition to the poetry matches themselves, their textual recreations could carry political significances. Some replicated the temporal structure of banquet rituals within the spatial organization of their texts. In 893, Uda's court produced the *Shinsen man'yōshū* (*Newly Selected Collection of a Myriad Leaves*), an anthology that appears to have been originally based on a poetry match.[33] The anthology and the topics used at the match it memorialized were both unprecedented. Two scrolls contain poems on the seasons from the two teams of Left and Right, to which were added poems on "love" (*omoi*) and "longing" (*koi*) which had been composed during the banquet concluding the event.[34] Due to the large number of verses in this match (it consisted of a hundred rounds), most scholars assume it was a "desk match" in which the aim was to arrange poems in complex temporal and spatial arrangements.[35] Regardless, the anthology is often seen as having an influence on both the poetry of the times and the *Kokinshū* in particular, which shares several poems with this earlier text.[36]

The anthology bears a complicated history involving two distinct textual lineages, making it difficult to ascertain its original form. Yamaguchi Hiroshi, who has carefully studied the issue, argues that the *Shinsen man'yōshū* originated in selections from a poetry match held in the apartments of Uda's mother Princess Hanshi (833–900) in the early 880s.[37] In the anthology's original form, poems from the Left team were placed in the first scroll and ones from the Right in the second, with the seasons preceding love in both cases. Later accretions included poems from subsequent poetry matches, as well as *shi*, leading to markedly different versions of the text.[38] The lack of prose prefaces or authors in these versions poses further difficulties to dating them.

The official status of the *Shinsen man'yōshū* is as ambiguous as its textual history. At first sight, it seems plausible that the anthology was compiled at Uda's command by a group of editors, like its successor the *Kokinshū*. Both anthologies share the same basic organization—a two-part division into Seasons and Love. On the other hand, the *Shinsen man'yōshū*'s anonymous preface is addressed to a teacher rather than to the reigning sovereign, suggesting that it was never officially presented at court.[39] Scholarly accounts of the anthology typically debate its subsequent attribution to Uda's chief minister and ally Michizane. An equally intriguing possibility is that its origins are with Uda's mother, who had overseen the poetry match that lay at its core. It is easy to imagine that members of Hanshi's entourage could have compiled the anthology to memorialize their mistress's achievements at a time when she was playing a prominent role in political struggles over the succession to the throne.

The timing of the decision to anthologize Hanshi's poetry match is significant in its own right. In 893, Uda asserted his position at court by promoting three of his followers (including the ill-fated Michizane) to the governing Council of State. Two months later, he made his son Atsuhito crown prince. Although the circumstances surrounding Uda's decision can only be conjectured, it is likely that Hanshi would have backed his choice of heir, especially given her apparent antipathy toward the Northern House.[40] It is suggestive in this regard that Uda's mother, who was herself from the imperial clan, seems to have taken steps to ensure that Tokihira's kin did not marry into the line of succession. She allegedly prevailed on Uda to prevent one of Tokihira's daughters from entering the crown prince's entourage.[41]

Having settled the succession, Uda retired as sovereign in 897 in an attempt to oversee the court from a position whose novelty rivaled that of the regent's. The ex-sovereign created a new title for himself which combined priestly status with that of rulership in the form of a "tonsured sovereign" (*hōkō*). It was the first time a retired sovereign had taken the tonsure, and appears to have been modeled on the example of the Six Dynasties dynasty ruler Liang Wudi (464–549), a vigorous monarch who had extensively patronized both Buddhism and poetry during his reign from 502 to 549. Henceforth, power at the Heian court would ebb and flow between Uda and Tokihira. The latter is assumed to have dominated the court of the young sovereign Daigo, who was only twelve when he ascended the throne. One scholar who has meticulously charted the political balance of power in the period asserts that Tokihira effectively controlled the court from 901 until his death in 909. After that, Daigo and Uda formed the twin poles of power in the capital until the latter's death in 931.[42]

Shifts in the political balance of power which accompanied Uda's abdication and Tokihira's ascendancy would see female compilers supplanted by male ones headed by a Fujiwara aristocrat who, like Mototsune, was eager to assert his place as a minister in a male-oriented Confucian state. When Tokihira assumed power after Uda's abdication, the *Shinsen man'yōshū* associated with the former's court was replaced by a new compilation titled *Shoku man'yōshū* ("Collection of Myriad Leaves Continued"). This title suggests a deliberate attempt to create an imperial anthology that both referenced and surpassed the earlier attempts to memorialize ritual poetic events that had been pursued at Uda's court.

In its incarnation as the *Kokinshū*, this male-authored text became the first officially sponsored anthology of *uta*. Nevertheless, the contribution of palace women to this enterprise left significant traces. Women at Uda's court who recorded and anthologized poetry matches could have inspired the male editors' later use of the same techniques. It is often maintained that the *Kokinshū*'s carefully structured sequencing of poems had no precedent in earlier forms of court poetry. The texts of poetry matches, however, often arrange their poems in complex temporal and spatial arrangements in which shared words created harmonious exchanges between poems.[43] Of particular note in this regard are the maiden-flower poems in the *Shinsen man'yōshū*, which were incorporated from two of Uda's poetry matches on this topic that took place after his abdication and are commonly believed to have been part of the original nucleus of the anthology, which grew to incorporate other poems under Uda's supervision.[44] Both their careful arrangement within the *Shinsen man'yōshū* and the fact that these matches bear close ties to Uda's consorts suggest that this later portion of the anthology could have actively involved women as transcribers and compilers.

During the time in which Tokihira was consolidating power within the palace, Uda's household spread across a network of mansions. He first moved to a residence located just south of the Third Avenue, the Suzaku-in, which had been Saga's center of government after he had officially abdicated. The retired sovereign's financial interests were administered from the eponymous Uda-in estate, which had previously been the residence of his father, mother, and twin brothers Koresada (d. 903) and Koretada (857–922). In 904, Uda moved from Saga's old residence into a new mansion erected for him on the grounds of the Shingon sect temple Ninna-ji where he had taken the tonsure. There, Uda established himself as the imperial clan's patriarch. It was at this residence that Daigo paid his annual visit in the new year in his role as the filial Confucian son.

Uda's connections with Shingon temples, which had played a key role in developing *kana*, might explain his fascination with its script. Just as Yoshifusa's regency bolstered its provisional status with the "provisional names" of *kana*, Uda used the same script to assert his equally contingent title of "tonsured sovereign." His strategic appeal to Shingon Buddhism also allowed the tonsured sovereign to establish some distance from the influence of Tokihira's female kin in his household. On account of Uda's priestly status, and taboos on the presence of women in Buddhist temples, his consorts were ensconced in another mansion named the Teiji-in, with Atsuko at their head. After the death of Tokihira's sister, Uda appears to have taken over the mansion and moved his court there. It was during this period and in this location that his most elaborate poetry matches took place.

Women featured prominently in the poetry matches held by the tonsured sovereign. The years immediately following Uda's abdication were a particularly active period. The "maiden-flower" (*ominaeshi*) appears to have been an especially common topic in Uda's poetry matches at this time, perhaps on account of its association with the women of his extended household. During the brief interval that he resided at the Suzaku-in, Uda held two maiden-flower poetry contests there. Another one was held at his administrative headquarters at the Uda-in mansion. Yet another match at the same mansion involved the composition of *mono no na* or "names of things" poems in which the names of various objects and animals, including the maiden-flower, were concealed in the words of a poem.

Uda's obsession with the maiden-flower in his poetry matches can be seen as a comment on the political prominence of women at court during this particular period. The connection between the maiden-flower and women, already well established in *Man'yōshū* poems, was further intensified in the Heian period.[45] During this time, the flower was first poetically associated with the scented sleeves of women. Usually the scent of a blossom spurred on this sort of association, but in the case of the *ominaeshi*, it was the name of the plant rather than its physical characteristics that endowed it with an appealing feminine scent.[46] The frequency with which the maiden-flower's name is invoked in poems from this period suggests a self-reflexive awareness of the ways in which language could be manipulated in written poems. One example by Tsurayuki from a maiden-flower match held by Uda at his Suzaku-in mansion in 898, preserved in the Names of Things section of the *Kokinshū*, is exemplary of this tendency to deploy the name of the maiden-flower to create multiple meanings.

Mount Ogura,	***O**gura yama*
atop whose peak stamp,	***mi**ne tachi narashi*
in longing cries,	***na**ku shika no*
deer, whose autumns spent thus,	***he**nikemu aki o*
surpass what any might know.	***shi**ru hito zo naki*[47]

Tsurayuki's poem redistributes the letters of her name to create a new text that blends the dual seasonal and sexual connotations of the original word. The autumnal setting in which feminine flowers bloom and a male stag cries for his mate evoke a human corollary in a man longing for a maiden. This coordination of seasonal and sexual rhythms in Tsurayuki's verse work together to represent Uda's household as a site at which Heaven and humanity are harmoniously arranged.

The heightened interest in linguistic play that can be seen in Uda's maiden-flower matches hints at a deliberate equivalence between the rules of prosody and those of politics. Due to their multiple kinship ties as mothers, sisters, aunts, and wives, the women of Uda's household held pivotal roles in determining the relations among competing male interests at court, especially those involving succession to the throne. The *ominaeshi* occupied a similarly pivotal (and thus potentially fluid) semantic position within *uta*. Because the five syllables of this word typically filled an entire line of a verse without any coordinating particles, "her" placement allowed the maiden-flower to be either addressed as a subject in the second person or spoken about as an object in the third person. The result was that both maid and flower were simultaneously represented as tokens of exchange between men who spoke about and desired them, and as figures whose own desires needed to be addressed in order to ensure that ties to kin and political allies would function smoothly.

The fact that these poetry matches were held both before and after Uda's abdication suggests that they staged a consistent claim on his part to power and status at court. The historical record confirms this, insofar as Uda continued to be involved in court politics after his retirement, chiefly through his entourage, whose members often also held posts in Daigo's palace and its administration.[48] These men and women constituted the interface between his household and the outside world, mediating the flow of information, goods, and people to and from his person. By involving these personal attendants in his matches, Uda staged his place at the center of a court which possessed its own retinue, harem, mansions, and sources of wealth and labor. In keeping with this strategy of mimicking the reigning sovereign's court, Uda's household poetry matches also adopted a temporal symbolism that alluded to the Confucian ruler's oversight of the relations between Heaven and humanity.

Seasonal Temporality and Mansion Gardens

One striking feature common to all poetry matches of the early Heian period is their concern with a seasonal temporality rather than the strictly demarcated units of calendrical time. Many of Uda's matches presented poems from all four seasons. Others focused on a single seasonal phenomenon, such as chrysanthemums or maiden-flowers. Significantly, none of the known dates for early poetry matches correspond to those on which annual court observances were held. Even when the matches invoke the months, both the individual poems and the topics tend to emphasize seasonal time as a cyclical movement, one that often overflows the precise divisions of calendrical time.[49] Given the nature of their topics, it seems likely that many matches were held in conjunction with the various seasonal phenomena they mention.

By providing an alternate form of cyclical temporality to that of the calendar, Uda's poetry matches also provided an implicit challenge to the sovereign's monopoly over time. Ordering time was one of the chief means by which the sovereign harmonized human activities with celestial cycles. For this reason, overseeing and establishing the annual calendar was one of the primary duties of a Confucian monarch. Law codes such as the *Engi shiki* aided this undertaking by detailing the schedule for all governmental work and observances down to the provincial level for each day of the calendrical year. Rites such as those for New Year's Day were carefully synchronized so that they were held at the same time in both the palace and provincial capitals, thereby creating an effect of simultaneity across the realm.[50]

The shared time of court and country was set in motion by the ruler's personal perusal of its future unfolding. Every year on the first day of the Eleventh Month, a rite known as the *goryaku no sō* (Presentation of the Royal Calendar) was held in the Shishinden hall. There, the reigning sovereign perused the first draft of the calendar for the ensuing year before it was distributed to governmental offices and the highest-ranking individuals. By viewing the calendar in its totality, the sovereign encompassed the coming year and its human actions within the scope of his gaze, previewing the temporal unfolding of the realm at a glance. As we shall see in the next chapter, the textual structure of the *Kokinshū* enacts a similar form of royal prefiguration.

By representing a seasonal round of natural phenomena succeeding one another, poetry matches at Uda's court created an alternate version of cyclical temporality. In doing so, they reconfigured not only the temporal coordinates of royal cosmology but its spatial ones as well. Whereas calendrical time centered on government offices or its most formal ritual spaces such as the Shishinden hall, seasonal time unfolded in the gardens of aristocrats' residences, palace consorts' apartments, and retired sovereigns' mansions. In place of the single locus of ruler and palace, through which the state declared its claim to the wealth of the realm, seasonal poems provided a multiple constellation of centers from which authority and status could be displayed and asserted by figures such as retired sovereigns or regents. It is no coincidence in this regard that the proliferation of sites at which poetry matches took place mirrored the proliferation of political groupings at the Heian court in the first decade of the tenth century. Tokihira, for example, held a "garden match" (*senzai awase*) on the topic of autumnal flora at his mansion. Even the marginalized retired sovereign Yōzei held a poetry match. In keeping with his historical reputation as an eccentric, it had the unusual topic of summer insects. By contrast, Daigo's first poetry match at the palace took place in the thirteenth year of his reign, about the time his father held one of his most elaborate contests at the Teiji-in.

It is helpful in this regard to compare Heian poetry matches to earlier Fujiwara strategies for supplementing the state's existing structures of meaning and power. Yoshifusa's cherry blossom banquets had first established seasonal time and the personal residence as ritual coordinates for staging authority within the Heian capital. Perhaps in distinction from this Fujiwara springtime setting, Uda's poetry matches tended to focus on autumn flowers, such as chrysanthemums or maidenflowers. This seasonal choice also signified the culmination rather than the incipient potential of the germinating process. Likewise, the position of tonsured sovereign signified a later stage in authority, succeeding and supplementing that of monarch and regent. In both Yoshifusa and Uda's cases, seasonal flowers also marked the reproductive wealth represented by women and the family resources they brought to the imperial clan through marital alliance.

The capacity of poetry matches to rearrange the symbolic geography of a capital city that was ostensibly organized around the palace and royal person can be seen in part as a result of the lengthy associations that had developed in earlier poetry between seasonal time and the exurban periphery. Poems tracking seasonal change can be traced all the way back to the creation of continental-style urban communities in the mid seventh century. Within the geography of the city mapped out by such poetry, the seasons manifested themselves first in the mountains and uncultivated wilderness surrounding the capital before moving into its exurban periphery and from there into the gardens of urban dwellings.[51] The structured movements of seasonal temporality thus elaborated a series of overlapping spatial boundaries between country and city, garden and residence, and aristocratic villa and palace. Within a court-oriented geography, this poetic representation of the seasons and gardens can be seen as privileging the margin over the center as a source of meaning.[52]

At least one scholar has seen the growing prominence of the mansion garden in Heian poetry as part of an attempt to buttress the *ritsuryō* state's increasingly shaky claim to legal ownership of the realm's lands by reestablishing its place at the center of the cosmos.[53] In the reign of an active monarch like Saga, poetic performances of harmony between sovereign and subject in garden settings had indeed asserted the former's right to the realm's resources. As was argued in the previous chapter, the carefully composed harmonies of landscape arrangements and human actions that took place in the Shinsen-en can be seen as a physical manifestation of the virtuous Confucian monarch's ability to harmonize humanity with Heaven. Similarities between Saga's poetic staging of royal virtue at an imperial park, however, and their later incarnations in the mansions of the nobility and former sovereigns point to the redistribution and dispersion of such symbols of authority rather than the reassertion of a royal monopoly on them.

In the tenth century, the state's claim to ownership of the realm's resources was increasingly being undermined by dramatic growth in the number of tax-free estates (*shōen*) owned by the upper nobility, retired sovereigns, and Buddhist temples. If, as Thomas Keirstead has argued, we can see the mansion garden as a site for naturalizing aristocrats' claims to ownership of such estates, then the poetic performances situated in this space can likewise be seen as an extension of such aims.[54] Like Saga's Shinsen-en park, mansion gardens often functioned as stages upon which musicians performed and banqueters composed poetry against the backdrop of carefully composed landscapes.[55] Such tableaux provided a means for their residents to represent themselves as fulcrum points between Heaven and humanity, thereby asserting their rights to ownership of property and its wealth. In this sense, poetry matches, banquets, and other gatherings at which poetry was composed in a garden setting appropriated the "economy of virtue" that had previously naturalized the Confucian monarch's monopoly over the rights to administer resources and redistributed these rights among a larger group. With the growth of poetry matches under Uda and his peers, the flow of energies between society and cosmos were cast on a smaller scale in the aristocrat's management of his private estates. The result of these proliferating legal and symbolic claims was an increasingly multipolar court, fragmented into competing clusters of economic and political interests.

Longing for Community in Poetry Matches

In addition to creating new spatial and temporal frames for community, Uda's poetry matches also created new forms of sociality within them. One distinguishing feature of these events was the frequent connections their poems made between the seasons and love, the latter being a topic that often appeared in the final rounds of the match, or at a banquet held afterward. Although this linkage is often seen as an important contribution to the later poetics associated with the *Kokinshū* and its organizational strategies, the reasons for its appearance at this historical juncture have not received a great deal of scrutiny in most scholarly accounts. A few scholars in Japan, however, have suggested that this association between the seasons and longing is connected to earlier ritual practices that sought to regulate sexuality through seasonal taboos, thereby guaranteeing agricultural bounty and wealth. These rites often elaborated a form of sociality—in the shape of the household—that bore a complex relationship to the state. The occasionally overlapping, occasionally complementary, and often competitive nature of this relationship between household and state in the early Heian period made the latter's symbolic associations a particularly apt means for representing Uda's similarly ambivalent place vis-à-vis the official court.

It is perhaps obvious, but nonetheless important to underscore the fact that the group setting in which these poems appeared endowed their articulations of personal sentiments with public significance. In other words, the public performative nature of these poetic expressions of desire created a sense of community among the participants at such gatherings. There are numerous precursors for such performances, in particular among rituals in which the monarch sought to harmonize relations between the sexes. Such royal rites in turn were often related to the ritual practices of smaller clan communities and households. One example of this phenomenon was the state's sponsorship of *tōka* performances, in which large groups of men and women sang and danced in carefully choreographed public displays of gendered harmony in the capital. Although these dances were continental in origin, they also evoked earlier local customs such as *utagaki* (song fences) in which men and women performed courtship songs.

The specific link between love and the seasons in early poetry matches suggests further ritual associations with annual observances in which erotic language was deployed for incantory effects. Poetic precursors for this link can be found in such topical categories as the "summer exchanges" (*natsu no sōmon*) found in Scrolls 8 and 10 of the *Man'yōshū*. Some scholars have argued that these compound topics reflect a religious incantory tradition in which the seasons were summoned through prayers that incorporated erotic language.[56] According to this account, the expressions of female longing for a male lover that appear in such poems were intended to summon the seasons, in the same manner as the erotic language used by female ritualists and mediums in "shrine songs" (*kagura uta*) were intended to summon deities. The consummation of such visitations was marked by the physical union of human and seasonal objects, typically through the action of plucking foliage and placing it in one's hair in order to incorporate the season's energies within the individual body.

The overlapping poetic connections between sexuality and seasonal rites in the *Man'yōshū* are most suggestively conveyed in its blossom imagery. Picking flowers is often accompanied by the calling out of a lover's name; blossoms are likened to a lover; and the consummation of an encounter is often juxtaposed with their full blooming. This association between blossoms and sexuality was continued at Uda's poetry matches, which show a marked interest in the former as a topic for poetic composition. Flower imagery might also be associated with agricultural cycles. As noted before, the cherry blossom banquets held at

Yoshifusa's mansion often included ritual performances of rice planting that were intended to ensure a bountiful harvest. Uda's marked preference for autumn flowers, which was in part a response to these earlier Fujiwara-sponsored seasonal poetic gatherings, might also have been intended to invoke the harvest season.

The historical record contains scattered hints that such associations between expressions of sexual desire, seasonal poetic imagery, and agricultural cycles had their origins in individual household rites carried out in summer. During such annual observances, young men and women of a family confessed their unrequited longings to the gods. It has been suggested that the intention of these rites was probably to ensure a bountiful harvest by declaring that the household's members had been abstinent during the growing season.[57] Though mentioned only in passing in court histories and ritual codes, these "household rites" (*jintaku no sai*) are known to have been held in the Sixth and Eleventh months, with the former corresponding roughly to the same period in which the *Man'yōshū*'s "summer exchange" poems are set. It is perhaps no coincidence in this regard that the earliest documented poetry match—held at the private residence of Ariwara no Yukihira during the reign of Kōkō—was devoted exclusively to the topics of longing and the summertime *hototogisu* bird. Subsequent matches also combined desire and summertime topics.

Although we have no specific knowledge of the precise format in which the songs of household rites could have been performed, it is possible that they resembled those of other, better-documented forms of ritual singing which in turn influenced poetry matches. *Kagura uta*, for example, are known to have been sung by two choruses arranged to the left and right of the deity, with the latter singing first. The scholar Yamagishi Tokuhei has suggested that these ritual conventions also informed poetry matches, in which the left-hand team presented its poems first.[58] If *jintaku no sai* rites had involved male and female choruses, they could have been sung in alternation, as appears to have been done in *utagaki*. Although poetry matches did not divide teams by gender, the principle of two groups articulating sexual desires through *uta* might have links to these other ritual expressions of longing.

One thing that does seem certain about *jintaku no sai* is that they were defined in part through their similarities to court-sponsored observances. During the same month in which these household rites were held, a large-scale purification rite also took place at the palace. On the twenty-second day of the Sixth Month, male and female court officials gathered before the Suzaku Gate that separated the palace compound from the rest of the city to undergo a *misogi* purification. After this ritual cleansing had been observed, its participants returned to their homes or a nearby river and performed another purification in which they washed away defilements by transferring them onto an object known as a *katami* and setting it afloat. Declarations of desire in verse could have featured prominently in such purification rites. It is worth noting in this regard that the frequent references made to rivers in anonymous *Kokinshū* love poems suggest that they might have been originally sung as part of such ablutions.[59]

This connection between individual household rites of purification and those binding together the larger court community of palace officials attests to the importance placed on regulating sexuality within the ruler's portfolio of ritual responsibilities. Putting such responsibilities into practice entailed the appropriation of local rites that had associated the sexual practices of the clan with its agricultural bounty and resituating these observances with a new urban community presided over by the sovereign in his palace. The purpose behind this appropriative strategy was probably twofold: to naturalize continental concepts of rulership through appeals to preexisting practices, and to subsume these earlier, competing forms of sociality within the larger "household" community of the state centered around the capital and its Confucian pater familias.

In such a context, the articulation of sexual desire was inextricably intertwined with ritual performances of authority and community. From the earliest inception of a permanent urban center, the Yamato state sought to assert the cosmological necessity of its role in managing relations between the sexes within the latter space. A decree found in the *Shoku nihongi* from 706, for example, blames the unregulated and incessant intermingling of men and women for the famines and plagues then sweeping the provinces:

> The rites are the principle twining Heaven and Earth together, and the mold that shapes human relations. The Way, virtue, benevolence, and

> righteousness all spread via the rites. Education in proper behavior and the rectification of popular customs are realized through them. But in recent times, many aspects of the bearing and demeanor of government officials have departed from propriety. Moreover, men and women do not keep separate, but mingle indiscriminately day and night. And so it is reported that pollution is rife both inside and outside the capital.[60]

This declaration appears to imply that, without the proper regulation of relations between men and women, the balance between human society and the larger world will be thrown askew. Its Confucian language draws on continental conceptions of the ruler as the "Son of Heaven" who mediates between the seasonal cycles of the celestial realm and the sexual practices of the social realm.

Similarities between household rites and those sponsored by the court meant that the forms of community each articulated had the potential to compete and clash with one another. Throughout the Nara and early Heian period, edicts resembling the one cited above sought to ban large-scale gatherings of men and women as lewd, illicit, and disruptive to the social order.[61] The antipathy demonstrated toward such gatherings, though cloaked in the language of Confucian moral rectitude, might also have been motivated by the perception that they posed a threat to the state's interests in making the monarch and palace the central axes for defining society. It is therefore possible that the "lewd and illicit gatherings" mentioned in these edicts could be referring to ritual practices that, in a later incarnation, would inform the "individual household rites" of the Heian period.

The *ritsuryō* state's ambivalence toward rituals that privileged the household over the state would help explain why there are so few references to them in those officially sponsored legal codes and histories through which the history of the early Heian period is largely reconstructed. Such silences in themselves comment eloquently on the capacity of these rites to represent concepts of community that did not depend on the state for their articulation. It is easy to imagine that this potential would have led Uda's poetry matches to evoke their conventions, in keeping with his political interests in asserting his household's status as separate but equal to that of the palace. If the seasonal temporality of his poetry matches called into question to the state's monopoly on the ritual management of time, then their frequent yoking to the topic of love could have presented a similar challenge to the state's complementary monopoly on the ritual management of human relations. Insofar as household rites linked its members' sexual practices with its material fortunes, their evocation in Uda's poetry matches allowed him to assert both the links between members within his household and that same household's rights to the realm's bounty.

Poem Slips and Poetry Matches

Perhaps one of the most innovative aspects of Uda's poetry matches was the manner in which they harnessed the performative potential of the written text to represent his household. His contests often treated the poem as a material object, akin to the "things" (*mono*) compared in other forms of matches.[62] Poems written on slips of paper were used to create circuits of exchange between human and celestial registers of the world. Furthermore, the manner in which these texts manipulated *kana* suggests that, for the first time, it was being treated in its own right as a source for citation and thus a means of asserting authority through the manipulation and control of language.

The profusion of topics at poetry matches suggests that *uta* in these events were viewed as something to be inscribed, like *shi* at court banquets. *Waka* in such cases were poems that "harmonized" with the words of a topic by echoing the latter. As noted before, the practice of composing *uta* on lines from literary Chinese originated with the Fujiwara regency.[63] In keeping with his interest in emulating and appropriating Yoshifusa's ritual techniques, Uda appears to have followed this same practice by sponsoring texts in which *uta* were the primary mode of poetic composition. Exemplary of this tendency is the *Kudai waka*, a collection of 110 *uta* by the scholar Ōe no Chisato whose words echoed lines of *shi* taken from the recently imported *Hakushi monjū* (*Bo Juyi's Collected Works*). Insofar as the *Kudai waka* is associated with Uda's court, it can be seen as an attempt to evoke the traditions of topic-based composition at Saga's court, and thereby claim an equivalent form of authority for the former.[64]

Poetry matches, however, tended to involve a different mode of citation from that used in other forms of topic-based composition. Whereas *uta* in Ōe no Chisato's collection and Mototsune's earlier *Nihon shoki* lectures referred to entire passages from texts written in literary Chinese, Uda's matches cited only the individual *kana* letters of a single Japanese word in their poetic reinscriptions. One consequence was that these poetry matches provided a significant impetus to the use of discrete words as topics for *uta* composition.[65] The first four poetry matches sponsored by Uda after his retirement all treated individual words in this manner. Three of these four matches use the word *ominaeshi* (maiden-flower), whose pentasyllabic name was particularly amenable to acrostic variations in the five lines of a 31-syllable *uta*.

Even in the case of poems that were not acrostics, Uda matches appeared to place emphasis on the poems' precise replication of the *kana* letters used in its topic. One noteworthy example of this concern can be glimpsed in a dispute at the Kyōgoku Consort Match. During the sixth round of the contest, Uda criticized one team for "not adhering completely to the principle of words" (*koto no kotowari ni tsukizu*) when it used the word *nobe* instead of *hara* to denote wild uncultivated fields.[66] While another participant pointed out that *nobe* is an "alternative name" (*azana*) for *hara*, the retired sovereign maintained that it contravened the topic and was thus at fault.

Although the "principle of words" that Uda cites in this context is not further elaborated in the text, the marked concern with establishing a precise correspondence between words and their referents seen here resembles the classical Confucian concern with the "rectification of names" in ordering the realm. As noted earlier, Uda's concern with the political effects of language was a defining characteristic of his reign. One aspect of his desire for definitions was the production of new reference works during his reign. In the Shōtai era (898–901) a Buddhist priest at Uda's court produced a character dictionary called the *Shinsen jikyō* (900), in which individual words were organized by character radical rather than by semantic category as was done in "topical dictionaries" (*leishu*) used by *shi* poets. Perhaps even more significant, it was the first reference work in Japan to provide *kana* glosses for words written in literary Chinese.[67]

This development of new schema for organizing and defining lexical items corresponds suggestively with a similar way of treating words which can be detected in Uda's poetry matches. The use of *kana* in the *Shinsen jikyō*'s entries reflected a concern with pronunciation and orthography rather than source-text citations. A similar mode of situating words in poetry matches made them radically different from other earlier forms of composition. Although both the acrostics and topic-based forms of composition found in these matches had their origins with *shi* poetry, the forms of language manipulated in each case were noticeably different. In place of literary Chinese sources, whose individual words all derived their meanings from their relation to a definable set of textual *loci*, the *kana* words of Uda's matches derived their meanings from the relations among their individual letters without any reference to original source citations.

This view of language, in which written letters produced referents only through their multiple shifting relations to other letters, has been linked by Ryūichi Abe to Shingon Buddhist theories of language in which all meaning and significance was contingent rather than absolute. As mentioned before, Abe further suggests that this view posed a profound challenge to the orthodox Confucian concept of an essential correspondence between words and their referents. Uda's connections with a sect that stressed the provisional nature of signification would have suited a sovereign seeking new ways to define his relationship to the palace and its institutions. At the same time, these new Yamato forms of poetic inscription did not replace their continental counterparts. Uda continued to sponsor banquets at which *shi* were composed on topics after his official reign. Rather, as Thomas LaMarre has argued, it was the creation of a harmonious doubled arrangement between continental and Yamato modes that was sought after.[68] Uda's own claims to mediating in both realms can be seen as a reflection of his overall attempts both during and after his reign to define his authority through ritual modes of rulership modeled after those of both the state and the aristocratic household of his Fujiwara rivals.

Written poems also affirmed connections between words and things at matches through their physical attachment to miniaturized landscape dioramas known as *suhama*. These dioramas, which were an integral part of early poetry matches, were largely unprecedented forms of display. Often they were used to literally represent the topography mapped out by seasonal movements. The earliest recorded match at Yukihira's mansion, for example, used miniaturized models of a mountain house and of a hut in a paddy field to represent the different landscapes through which the *hototogisu* bird moved as summer crept from the encircling mountains onto the level fields surrounding the capital's urban perimeter.[69] Like the mansion garden, the diorama miniaturized the larger world in a controlled, harmonious arrangement of forms and movements presided over by its owner.

Uda used such dioramas to display his authority both during and after his reign. The earliest known poetry match from his tenure as sovereign hints at the role played by poem texts in these landscapes. According to the accompanying *kana* record, this event was held in the palace, and took the form of a chrysanthemum match in which the left-hand team made a diorama display and planted nine flowers in it.[70] Poems containing various place-names were then attached to the display on paper slips known as *tansaku*. The act of attaching a slip of paper to an object in this instance quite possibly drew on earlier ritual practices. The ubiquitous presence of mountains in the *suhama* models of early matches, for example, were perhaps inspired by similar shapes associated with the boundary poles used in coronation ceremonies. Such representations appear to have functioned as a medium for manifesting divine spirits, in keeping with the belief that mountains were the point on earth to which gods initially descended from Heaven.[71] In a similar manner, the mountains of Uda's palace *suhama* can be seen as sites at which the spiritual essence of particular locales were manifested and presented to him, perhaps in a miniaturized version of the realm-viewing rite.

Not only the *suhama* but also the poem texts attached to it appear to have played a ritual role. The process by which the slips on which poems were written imbued objects with a divine presence, for example, shares similarities with a genre of *kagura uta* known as "grasped things" (*torimono*), which describe a material object through which divinities entered into the bodies of performers at shrine rituals. This process was paradigmatically expressed in a three-stage move: first negating the secular, commonplace origins of the object; then affixing the name and geographical locus of a deity to it; and finally securing this transformation by citing the object's new status in the form of a refrain.[72] The following *kagura uta* is one example of this means for rhetorically imbuing something with sacral qualities.

This paper slip	*mitegura wa*
does not belong to me.	*waga ni wa arazu*
In Heaven resides	*ame ni imasu*
the Divine Lady of Toyo-oka,	*Toyo-oka Hime no*
whose paper slip it is,	*miya no mitegura wa*
whose paper slip it is!	*miya no mitegura wa*[73]

Like this shrine song's sacred slip of paper, the poem slips attached to the *suhama* of Uda's chrysanthemum match transformed objects by imbuing them with the spiritual charisma of the place-names inscribed on them. The display of these place-names before Uda in his palace match thus allowed him to order and view his realm in miniature by "knowing," and thereby ruling, the *kami* spirits of particular locales. The ritual uses of these written texts would attain their most elaborate form in the poetry matches he held after his retirement.

The Teiji Villa and Kyōgoku Consort Matches

Two poetry matches held by Uda in the second decade of the tenth century capped his attempts to assert the prominence of his household over the palace. Both events offer a rare opportunity to investigate the ritual nature of early Heian poetry matches due to the relatively detailed depictions provided in the *kana* records appended to them.[74] Like the formal records of palace rituals kept in literary Chinese, these accounts provide us with lists of participants, poets, props, and protocol. The fact that similar details are recorded for poetry matches in itself suggests the ritual significance of these events, since this type of record was typically intended to ensure that their owners could replicate particular court observances in the future.[75] As it happens, both *kana* records for these poetry matches fulfilled a similar function by providing models for an even more splendid and elaborate contest held by the female attendants of Uda's grandson Murakami (926–967, r. 946–967) at the Seiryōden in 960.

The details recorded for both poetry matches also suggest the particular political aims involved. Uda's Teiji Villa Match affirmed the cooperative coexistence of two lineages within the imperial family. Its careful negotiation of prerogative and power in judging between his paternal line and the preceding Fujiwara one culminated in a show of musical harmony between the two and the affirmation of the rights of both lineages to his bounty. The Kyōgoku Consort Match, by contrast, marked a new relationship between Uda and the dominant branch of the Fujiwara clan. By journeying to their clan shrine, Uda publicly affirmed his ties to the Northern House and dispensed his bounty to the retinue of an important woman in that family.

The Teiji Villa Match was held in the spring of 913 at the former residence of Uda's Fujiwara consort, which lay at the western end of the capital's Seventh Avenue. Uda had moved to this mansion in 907 after the death of Atsuko, who had been its principal resident prior to that time. In the absence of Mototsune's daughter, it was princesses who headed the teams in the match of 913. The maternal grandfathers of both women—Fujiwara no Arizane (848–914) and Minamoto no Noboru (848–918)—were minor nobility who bore no relation to the Northern House. Although the match was originally held in forty rounds, the record of this match includes twenty rounds on spring and five each on summer and love. The smaller number of rounds on these final two topics might have been the result a lack of time in which to recite their poems. Regardless, the connection they make between summer and longing evoke the *jintaku no sai* household rituals mentioned previously.

The Kyōgoku Consort Match was held eight years later, in the summer of 921, at the residence of Tokihira's daughter Fujiwara no Hōshi. In the fourth month of the previous year she had given birth to Prince Masaakira (920–929). To mark his new ties with the Northern House that this son represented, Uda made a pilgrimage to the Fujiwara clan shrine at Kasuga the following year, accompanied by the infant prince and his mother. There, Uda was received by one of his allies at court, Fujiwara no Tadafusa (d. 928), who was governor of Yamato province at that time. After hosting the tonsured sovereign and his entourage, Tadafusa made an offering of twenty baskets of fruit with a poem slip attached to each. Thirteen were sent to Hōshi's carriage and seven to those of her infant son. Among the twenty poems provided by Tadafusa, eight were composed for him by Mibu no Tadamine (fl. 890–920), a low-ranking courtier who was also involved in compiling the *Kokinshū* anthology.

The contest itself was held upon Uda's return to the capital. Teams of female attendants were headed by his daughter Minamoto no Junshi on the Left and a younger sister of Hōshi on the Right. Both women had intimate ties to the Northern House: the head of the Left team was married to Tokihira's younger brother, and the captain of the Right was the deceased patriarch's seventh daughter. Both captains also represented the next generation of women at court who could represent imperial and Fujiwara clan interests respectively. Team members were selected from the two noblewomen's female attendants. The twenty poems that had been offered up by Tadafusa to Hōshi and her child were treated as topics, with both teams providing compositions that harmonized with the words of the originals. An additional two rounds on the topic of love in summertime were added at the end to mark the season in which the event took place. Tadafusa was summoned to judge how skillfully the opposing teams' poems corresponded with his original compositions.

The details of these matches that both *kana* records often focus on are ones that are also shared with other court rituals, in particular "contests of skill" (*waza kurabe*) such as wrestling matches between youths in the Seventh Month, archery contests between hall courtiers at the Seiryōden, and horse races held on the Double Fifth at the Kamo Shrine. Both poetry matches as well as these other competitions were divided into teams of Left and Right; both had youths tally the results, and both presented the tonsured sovereign with lists of the various team members to a musical accompaniment at the start of the match. Music also played a role at the end of other forms of competition. The members of the winning team in a *waza kurabe* typically concluded the event with a music and dance performance. The goal of such performances appears often to have been to assert social harmony between the competitors. The *kana* record accompanying the Teiji Villa Match notes that both teams performed music, even though only one had won the match.

Other details from the records for these two matches suggest a particularly close connection with *sumō* wrestling matches.[76] Both kinds of competition involved decorated displays, *shime* poles in the case of *sumō* wrestling and *suhama* dioramas for the poetry matches. Both were composed of teams headed by "captains" (*tō*). Courtly *gagaku* music was played to mark the entrance of the *sumō* teams in wrestling matches and the entrance of the *suhama* displays in poetry matches. In both cases the contests typically consisted of twenty rounds. Debates held over opposing team's entries in poetry matches resembled the consultative deliberations held at *sumō* matches when the outcome of a round was unclear. Other connections with *sumō* can be seen in Uda's earliest contests. His chrysanthemum match at the palace, for example, uses the terms *urate* and *hote,* which also are found in wrestling matches, to describe the first and final rounds of the competition.

The chief difference between these other "contests of skill" and Uda's poetry matches had to do with the gender of their participants. In Confucian discourse, events such as archery contests channeled the gentleman's competitive energies through the structures of ritual etiquette (*li*) in such a way as to maintain social harmony between him and his peers. In keeping with this masculine orientation, it was male aristocrats who headed the teams involved in such contests. In all other respects, however, the similarities with poetry matches are more pronounced than the differences. The formal resemblances suggest that both poetry matches and *sumō* contests might have shared symbolic features as well, among them the ways in which teams represented larger social structures oriented around figures of authority.

One of the roles of the annual wrestling matches held at the Heian court was to stage the ritual submission of the provinces and court to their ruler.[77] Wrestlers were usually members of the Inner Palace Guard selected from provinces adjoining the capital and sons of the nobility or princes.[78] Although the composition of *sumō* teams do not appear to have represented the interests of political factions, their organization into groups of nobility and commoners headed by a member of the imperial family did reflect the fundamental axes organizing economic and political interests at the Heian court. Royal kin provided a reservoir of legitimating symbols for nobles and their household followers, allowing the latter to pursue their interests through marital ties, patronage, and household affiliations with members of the imperial family.

Similar social axes organized the teams of poetry matches, and the politics surrounding them can often be inferred from the composition of their teams. One scholar who has provided a detailed analysis of the Teiji Villa Match, for example, has noted that the "allies" (*kataudo*) of each side were affiliated with different imperial lineages.[79] The Left consisted of members with marital relations to Kōkō, Uda, and Daigo, while the Right was composed of courtiers with similar ties to Montoku, Seiwa, and Yōzei. This division between a Fujiwara-dominated lineage and that of Uda suggests his match was in part designed to assert his preeminent position in the imperial household at a time when he lacked a Fujiwara rival of similar stature.

Although the victory of Uda's lineage at the Teiji Villa Match may seem inevitable, the contest was carefully arranged to appear as though there were no losers. Through strategic poetic interventions, the tonsured sovereign played a critical role in establishing harmony between the two teams and their political interests. According to the accompanying *kana* record, two poems by Uda are assigned to the Left team to prevent what would otherwise be a clear triumph by the Right. At the same time, however, the Right is spared what might otherwise have been a humiliating defeat by having them lose by only one round. The close result is acknowledged when both teams perform dance and song at the end. The text of the match itself suggests a somewhat different situation, with poems by the sovereign appearing for each team and the Left winning more rounds outright. Regardless of these apparent inconsistencies, what does seem certain is that Uda took a direct interest in ensuring that competition between the teams was channeled into a harmonious resolution. The strategic filiations of his poems in the match also suggest his role in managing other forms of competition at court. Uda's own awareness of his decisive role comes out in the appended *kana* record. When his poem is entered into the sixth round, the tonsured sovereign jokes (perhaps self-consciously) that it would be impossible to imagine it losing.[80]

The carefully choreographed performance of political harmony between competitive teams in both matches took place against a backdrop symbolizing the sovereign's position as pivot between Heaven and humanity. In these settings, natural imagery blended seamlessly with the court's social hierarchies, especially through arrangements of color which merged Heaven and humanity in the form of seasonal landscapes and court ranks. The robes worn by the team members at the

Teiji Villa Match were associated with seasonal landscapes of cherry and willow respectively. More generally, the *kana* records for both matches note that the Left team was decked out in shades of green while the Right team wore red. The division of teams by these two colors is a staple feature of many court rituals such as dance performances, horse races, and falconry contests. In combination, they were also favored for describing landscapes.[81] Just as the Left was traditionally given precedence in court ceremonial, its associated color in poetry matches marked it as superior to its rival. Red was the color lining the official court robes of the Upper Fifth Rank, while green was reserved for those of Sixth Rank.[82]

Poems played a similar role in mediating between Heaven and humanity at the Teiji Villa Match. Initially, princes presented their teams' poems to the tonsured sovereign, with their team members lined up behind them. Human bodies merged with seasonal objects when the poems were handed over to Uda by these captains on branches of cherry and willow matching the shades of the teams' robes. After their recitation and judgment, the poem slips were placed on each side's *suhama* display. Poems on mist were attached to miniaturized mountains, those on bush warblers to blossoms, and those on *hototogisu* birds to *unohana* blossoms. In their movement to and from Uda, the poem slips thus organized space into the different but complementary registers of Heaven and humanity. When initially presented to the tonsured sovereign, they were organized by kinship and political filiations. Social relationships were then transformed into a landscape when they were subsequently organized by topic and placed on the *suhama* displays. Amid these choreographed movements, Uda appeared in the role of a Confucian monarch harmonizing the relations between the celestial and social spheres.[83]

This coordination of Heaven and humanity was in part made possible through the material nature of the written poem as an entity that could define space through its attachment to other poems or objects. Like the landscaped colors of the courtiers' clothing, poem slips were flexible boundary surfaces whose capacity to enwrap, touch, and join different objects made them a fluid medium for defining both human relations and seasonal registers. Textile surfaces also defined the boundaries between the inner human and an outer world at these poetry matches in similar ways. For example, both clothes and writing merged in the Kyōgoku Consort Match, where *kana* letters appeared on the robes of the Right team. Written out in the "reed hand" (*ashide*) style, these letters in turn merged with the shapes of various flora and fauna depicted on the robes. Textiles also feature prominently in both matches as tokens of royal patronage in a manner similar to their role at court banquets. In the Teiji Villa Match, official court robes (*sokutai*) were bestowed on the princes and aristocratic members of the teams. In the Kyōgoku Consort Match, the participants received a stipend in the form of bolts of cloth.

By distributing wealth and ranks at the event's end, Uda confirmed the status of his male and female attendants as both court officials and members of his entourage, as well as his own continued rights to distribute the realm's bounty. Like Saga's *sechien* banquets, Uda's matches staged him as the virtuous monarch harmonizing Heaven and humanity in order to provide for his subjects. But, whereas the former placed an emphasis on masculine acts of inscription by court officials, the latter emphasized the act of recitation by a female attendant. The recorder of the Teiji Villa Match makes particular mention of the fact that the reciter was a woman. In the case of the Kyōgoku Consort Match, a guard captain on the Right and a minor counselor for the Left recite the poems for their teams, but only after a young girl fails to do so. If there was a distinctly feminine quality to *kana* writing at such events, it seems to have been recognized in the performative mode associated with their vocalization rather than their calligraphic forms.

The teams spared no expense in hiring craftsmen, poets, and musicians to ensure an impressive display. In return, the sovereign who oversaw and judged the results rewarded their members with stipends and ranks. In this regard, the distribution of wealth at poetry matches resembled that from sovereign to subject in other banquets where poems were inscribed. Unlike those banquets, however, the wealth on display in poetry matches was implicitly private and outside the state, closely tied as it was to the symbolism of gardens and estates in which these events took place. A significant portion of the resources expended in poetry matches went to the construction of *suhama* dioramas that, like the mansion garden, formed a tamed and harmonious composition expressing their inhabitant's rights to ownership of property. In

Uda's poetry matches, the garden setting became a stage on which its inhabitant could distribute the wealth from his personal estates to the members of his household. Just as the private estate ultimately depended on the institutional language of the *ritsuryō* state for its legitimacy, Uda's poetry matches drew on the established state performances of royal virtue and generosity to legitimate the political and economic arrangements of his personal household.

Poetic Composition and Composers at Uda's Court

One striking feature of Uda's new poetic regime was its use of proxy compositions. The phenomenon of having lower-ranking courtiers compose poems for their aristocratic peers is a hallmark of formal *hare* poetry as defined by modern scholars. This feature, however, also distinguishes Uda's poetry matches from earlier forms of formal public composition. Whereas poets at court banquets and lectures on the *Nihon shoki* inscribed their *shi* and *uta* at these gatherings, the poets of poetry matches handed in their compositions well in advance of the event and were themselves not direct participants. Nor were poetry matches the only area in which proxy composition was pursued in Uda's reign. As some historians have noted, this form of poetic composition appears to have been ubiquitous at his court both during and after his official reign.[84]

The development of proxy composition in the early Heian period appears to have been accompanied by changes in the meaning of the word used for composition, *yomu*. Unlike in *sechien* banquets, in poetry matches a distinction appears to have been made between two forms of the word: as a voiced reading by a designated "reciter" (*kōshi*) and as the initial act of a composition by a "composer" (*utayomi*). In other words, new distinctions in the range of performative acts associated with poetic production and reception were intimately tied to the creation of new ways for identifying the people involved in these activities. In concluding my account of Uda's new poetic regime, I will assess these developments and their place within the broader history of Japanese poetic practice.

It has often been remarked that the verb *yomu* lies at the heart of modern literary histories of Heian poetry. In the words of the eminent scholar Tsuchihashi Yutaka, "What is at issue is not simply the meaning of a single word, but the entire history of Japanese verse."[85] As another scholar has noted, literary historians have frequently used the word to distinguish Heian poetry from its predecessors.[86] Performative modes, periodization, and poetic genres are all aligned in this scheme, which typically divides *uta* into early "songs" (*kayō*) that are "performed" (*utau*) and later "court poems" (*waka*) that are "composed" (*yomu*).

Despite (or perhaps because of) its importance to modern histories of early Japanese poetry, *yomu* is notoriously difficult to define. The word variously refers to the actions of counting, calendrical prognostication, oracular divination, the interpretive act of assigning meaning to a text, chanting in metronome, reading aloud, and composing in syllabic meter. Among other things, this wide range of meanings ignores modern distinctions between production and reception, orality and textuality, and creation and citation.

Most accounts of *yomu* begin with the earliest extant Japanese texts, in which it can be seen far less frequently than *utau*. The latter verb seems to have encompassed not only singing, but also choreographed physical gestures set to music.[87] Its predominance as a term for poetic performance is often believed to have continued into the eighth century, although there is still debate on this point.[88] By contrast, *yomu* is not a specifically poetic act when it appears in *Man'yōshū* verses, where the word typically refers to the act of counting the beats of a drum or the days and months.[89] In addition, the prose prefaces accompanying *Man'yōshū* poems provide a number of characters such as 詠, 誦, and 読 that could have been pronounced as *yomu*, and which could also mark different nuances in meaning that are no longer discernable. The use of these characters does suggest, however, that *yomu* was related to the manner in which a poem was recited. As a vocalized mode of performance, then, *yomu* appears to fall within the broader semantic boundaries of *utau*.

A more recent approach to the early history of *yomu* provided by the scholar Shin'ya Tomiichi emphasizes its relation to cognate terms from the Heian period which are associated with (presumably) older styles of singing. According to this line of argumentation, it bore a particularly close connection to a style of singing termed *yomi-uta*, which was reserved for the *ōuta* (grand verse) performed on New Year's Day and other formal occasions. Musical scores appended to such songs in the tenth-century *Kinkafu* (*Songs to Koto Accompaniment*) give us a remarkably detailed understanding of this performative style.

In his analysis of these scores, Shin'ya concludes that *yomi-uta* entailed the enunciation of syllables in a metronome voice, marking each one with equal weight and avoiding melodic embellishments.[90] As such, it was closer to counting or keeping beat than it was to singing. According to Shin'ya, *yomu* would originally have possessed a similar emphasis on enunciation and rhythm rather than melody. Like the *yomi-uta* mode of recitation, it would have reduced the melodic and gestural elements of a song performance to the rhythmic enunciation of syllables.

Uta as something "composed" pared the gestures, music, and vocal melodies of "performing a song" (*uta o utau*) down to the physical acts of counting out syllables on fingers or enunciating them in a metronome beat. Such a connection to rhythm is indirectly confirmed in the *Man'yōshū,* where (as noted previously) *yomu* is often used to describe the act of counting drumbeats. The result was to separate words from the other performative elements that made up a verse, making diction a distinct object that could be isolated and analyzed in such early poetics treatises as the *Kakyō hyōshiki* (*A Formulary for Verse Based on the Canons of Poetry,* 772).

The suggestion that *yomu* was related to enunciatory rhythm might also help explain why it was a verb that could be used for *shi* as well as *uta.* Although we cannot reconstruct the precise rhythm associated with *yomu* in the Heian period, we do know something about the general conventions for chanting lines of *shi* and *uta.* Both forms of verse were recited at banquets to the same rhythms, just as they often were accompanied by the same melodies of zither music. Some scholars have speculated that this mode of chanting involved a rhythm of eight beats in quadruple time.[91] Within these eight beats, the pentasyllabic and heptasyllabic units associated with both poetic forms would have been interspersed with pauses (*ma*) that had the effect of making individual lines metrically regular. In such a context, moreover, *uta* would possess a rhythmic symmetry between lines akin to the metrical symmetry of continental poems. In other words, similarities in performative modes between *shi* and *uta* in the Heian period could very well have been more important in many contexts than the linguistic or metrical distinctions between these forms of poetry that we prioritize when we focus on their written texts.

This emphasis on rhythm over melody might also explain why *yomu* was not exclusively associated with poems. A performative mode that emphasized metronomic enunciation would have been well suited to the recitation of a wide range of written texts, such as *norito* prayers, royal *senmyō* proclamations, scriptures from the continental Buddhist and Confucian canons, and the "ancient words" (*furugoto*) concerning local deities and sacred places that were intoned by the royal guild of *kataribe* (bards) at enthronement ceremonies. In keeping with the distinction between the rhythms of daily speech and those of recitation, such texts were typically endowed with a sacral aura. One influential account of *yomu* has argued that this form of speech was originally reserved for an elite group of literate priests and officials who mediated between divinities and mortals in their capacity as "bearers of the sovereign's words" (*mikotomochi*).[92] In poetry this sacral quality often took the form of descriptive epithets preceding place-names, epithets that functioned as metonymic fragments gesturing to some narrative or legend concerning that particular location.[93]

By reciting such texts in a calendrically synchronized manner in various locales such as state-sponsored temples and provincial offices, moreover, the practice of recitation created a temporality that extended beyond the normal bounds of local space to create an effect of simultaneity throughout the realm. The script to be performed, the calendrically prescribed time of its utterance, and the metronomic regularity with which syllables were uttered all made *yomu* a reproducible, precise act that sought to bind the realm together in a regular and regulating rhythm. The importance of precision in such acts is suggested by the fact that recitation was considered an art in its own right, entrusted to particularly skilled practitioners known as *kōshi* at banquets and other formal occasions.

By the end of the ninth century, *yomu* appears to have retreated from its ancient legacy as one of many incantatory modes of singing into the muffled, internalized voice of metrical composition.[94] Because *yomu* had previously involved a relatively restricted form of musicality in comparison to other forms of singing, it was perhaps most amenable to the separation of words from vocalized performance. In keeping with what we know about other premodern cultures, however, such forms of poetic composition were likely to have involved a complex relationship to both oral and textual forms of language.[95] Enduring links between orality and composition can be seen in the influential etymology of *yomu* provided by the eighteenth-century scholar Motoori Norinaga (1730–1801), who claimed that *yomu* involved both the act of composition and oral recitation of syllables. Composition, according to this account, involved first determining the words to be used and then mouthing their syllables to keep metrical count.

The increasing separation between recitation and composition that took place over the course of the Heian period can be traced back more precisely to the period in which Uda's poetry matches flourished. It is significant in this regard that the term *utayomi*, which appears in these settings, referred to someone who produced the words of a poem in isolation from a particular performative context, rather than someone who recited it before a group of people. The appearance of the *utayomi* at Uda's matches thus entailed both a new concept of poetic production (composition) and a new social identity (composer) associated with that act. The articulation of this new identity, however, did not entail a conception of authorship, insofar as the text of a poem was not owned nor even performed by its producer. One apparent paradox of tenth century *uta* is that the category of a specific individual who created poem texts was articulated through a form of poetic practice in which his or her poems were associated with a person other than their creator.

The links among recitation, citation, and composition implied by the semantic range of *yomu* meant that the concept of the author as someone who had a unique relationship to a poem was never a strong one. Despite its focus on the wording of an individual verse, *yomu* did not distinguish between the citation of a preexisting poem and the creation of a new one.[96] The word could refer to not only an individual's act of composition but also the act of reciting it by another person, in some cases even altering words in the original to suit particular circumstances. As David Bialock has argued, individual poems can be seen as variable manifestations of a poetic pattern that was as strictly demarcated in its vocabulary and formal features as any individual canonical text.[97] The extremely intertextual nature of all forms of court poetry meant that it was, on some level, always a recitation of earlier words and poems. Overall, Heian court poetry was chiefly concerned with the ability to arrange preexisting phrases into new patterns.

Even if primary emphasis was not laid on the individual subject's act of creation, however, his or her ability to rework and recite old words in new contexts was given increasing weight at Uda's court. Nor was the recognition of individual poetic skill limited to poetry matches. Historical texts from the time often single out a courtier's facility at composing *uta* as something worthy of comment. Failures to compose correctly, for example, are recounted in Michizane's record of a formal tour of the regions south of the capital by Uda shortly after his abdication. At one point this text provides a vivid description of the trials involved in composing a metrically regular poem when a member of Uda's entourage is ordered to produce a verse: "Captain of the Right Guards Fujiwara no Sukemichi presented his verse and then, turning to face a wall, he counted out his poem on his fingers. After a while he addressed His Majesty, saying: 'I have infringed on the rules for composition, please let me remove three letters,' but His Majesty forbade this. Everyone took note of the occurrence."[98]

The account of Uda's journey preserved in the *Fukurozōshi* (*Book of Folded Pages*, 1157), a medieval miscellany of poetic lore written by Fujiwara no Kiyosuke (1104–1177), describes other sorts of compositional failures as well. At one point two young aristocrats—Minamoto no Noboru and Ariwara no Tomoyuki (a son of Ariwara no Yukihira)—fail to compose acrostic poems on the topics of *yatarakarasu* (giant raven) and *shimo no kamo* (duck in the lower rapids) that Uda had provided. Their chagrin is described at some length:

> Though they paced about and mouthed phrases, Noboru and Tomoyuki were unable to complete a poem. Greatly grieved, they said, "We ought to match Sukemichi and the others in coming up with a verse. Though we know something of the Way of *waka*, being able to tell what is good from what is bad, tonight we must bemoan our poor attempts after exhausting all our faculties and racking our brains to no avail. Sukemichi and the others don't know this Way. How humiliating it is that we should be shown up in front of them! It's as if we have no knowledge of it.[99]

In contrast to these two men, Sosei, who is then summoned to compose a poem at Uda's command, succeeds in creating verses that harmonized with the words his lord had assigned. The retired sovereign praises him as "a gentleman famed for his *waka*" (*waka no meishi*), and appoints him the "head chanter" (*shushō*) for the event. The latter term usually refers to the *shi* poet in a group composition who establishes the rhymes with which subsequent poems must harmonize. With regard to *uta*, the meaning is less clear, but it probably refers to the first person to write a poem in a group context, possibly setting the topic or words to be used by the others in their subsequent compositions. Regardless, the use of the term here suggests that in this particular context, *waka* are conceived of as poems that "harmonize" in a manner similar to that of *shi*.

It was probably the social stakes involved in the ability to successfully harmonize with their sovereign's words at such gatherings that led members of Uda's court to turn to proxy poets with increasing frequency. Proxy compositions first appear in settings where social harmony among the participants is the primary concern, such as *sechien* banquets and poetry matches.[100] Insofar as such events also involved the distribution of wealth among the participants, proxy compositions possibly guaranteed economic benefits for the parties involved, regardless of their actual personal facility at poetic harmony. This is particularly likely in the case of poetry matches whose written *uta*—like the *suhama*, robes, and other props that functioned as tokens for the circulation of political and economic resources—were prepared well before the event. Like these other material objects, poem-texts represented the wealth of the aristocratic members of a household, rather than the property of the skilled individuals who produced them.

In such a context, the phenomenon of specialists in writing poetry did not inevitably lead to the development of a concept of authorship as a socially recognized form of ownership. Even the *Kokinshū*, which pays unusual attention to the identities of poems' authors, rarely marks the act of inscription.[101] It was probably not until the advent of *kana* narratives in the late tenth and early eleventh centuries that the concept of written poetry as an individualized mode of expression first came to the fore. In texts such as the *Kagerō nikki* (*The Gossamer Years*, ca. 977) and *Tale of Genji* poetic epistolary exchanges frequently function as a substitute for direct conversation between individuals. Perhaps one consequence of this increasing emphasis on the written poem as a means of personal expression was that *yomu* was increasingly supplemented by other verbs such as *miru* and *iu.* Whereas *yomu* was an inherently social act requiring a reciter and audience, *miru* could refer to a more solitary and silent mode of reading a romantic tale or letter. *Monogatari* tales also contrast the formal mode of recitation associated with *yomu* with a more conversational mode known as *iu* (to speak), one that relied on the intonation and rhythms of conversational speech to enable communication between two people rather than performances in front of large groups.[102]

Ultimately, different nuances in the relationship of poet to poem at the early Heian court could be said to have entailed different notions of community. Insofar as most of these concepts posited the royal person as the organizing locus for social, cosmological, and political space, the accompanying forms of poetry were mostly *hare.* Another part of what made such gatherings formal was the often implicitly hierarchical nature of the act of *yomu*, which encoded social differences between the composer of a poem and that person's implied audience. In both Uda's poetry matches and Daigo's imperial anthology, *yomu* can be seen as an act of deference to a higher authority. It is revealing in this regard that every poem in the *Kokinshū* has a "composer" (*yomibito*), except for those by immediate members of the imperial line.[103]

At the same time, there are also significant differences between the forms of community represented by poetry matches and those of imperial anthologies, ones which are not discernable within as broad a category as "formal" poetry. The setting in which men and women supplied poems for matches represented a household whose resources included a reservoir of invisible laborers such as the carpenters and craftsmen who made the *suhama* or the musicians who performed at these events. One function of the *utayomi* in such contests was to mark the human capital and wealth of these households by representing the composers as anonymous producers. By contrast, the *yomibito* of the *Kokinshū* was a named author of the poem. As we shall see, this difference in the nature of the composer was in part informed by the very different sort of community created in the anthology, one in which the model of the *sechien* banquet rather than individual household rites was evoked. This difference, in itself, can be seen as a testament to the novelty of Uda's poetry matches, insofar as they asserted a form of sociality that was both parallel to and distinct from that of the palace and its ritual regime.

Chapter Three

Compiling Community in the *Kokinshū*

Making an Imperial Anthology

When most modern scholars describe the *Kokinshū* as a public and imperial anthology, they are referring to its having been compiled by royal command. It is important to keep in mind, however, that the term *chokusenshū* or "imperially ordered collection" dates from well over two centuries after the anthology's compilation, the earliest known instance appearing in the twelfth-century treatise *Fukurozōshi*, where the term *senshū* (commanded collections) is used to refer to royal anthologies in distinction from *kashū* (household collections).[1] In discussing the imperial nature of the *Kokinshū* in this chapter, I will focus not so much on the royal order to produce the text as on the text itself. In particular, I believe the nature of the anthologizing process, the language used within the anthology to describe its participants, the manner of its organization into categories, and the ways in which communities are created through the arrangement of poems can all shed light on the *Kokinshū*'s significance as the first anthology of *uta* designed to represent the court to itself as a collective entity.

This approach is not without difficulties. One such is the extended period over which the *Kokinshū* took shape, which makes its connections with court politics complex and multilayered. Like most *kana* texts from the Heian period, the *Kokinshū* survives in later, occasionally divergent recensions. Complete versions of the anthology are generally divided into five textual lineages: the Gen'ei-bon, Masatsune-bon, Kiyosuke-bon, Shunzei-bon, and Teika-bon texts.[2] The first of these lineages is the only one that possesses manuscripts dating back to the Heian period. The other four are named after their Kamakura-period copyists. Teika's text, the one favored in most modern editions, is arguably the most extensively altered version of the five. This is especially true in the area of orthography, where he seemed to favor alternations between *kanji* and *kana* designed to make reading easier.[3]

One of the earliest sources we have for the textual history of the *Kokinshū* is the *Fukurozōshi*. According to this medieval miscellany of poetic lore, Tsurayuki wrote three versions of the anthology in his own hand.[4] One presented to Daigo was first called the Engi gyohon to mark its official status as an imperial text. It was later given to Princess Teishi (1081–1156) in 1023 on the occasion of her coming-of-age ceremony. Named the Yōmeimon' in-bon after Teishi's posthumous title, this version was kept by her wet nurse's family until this text was lost in a fire in 1141. The second manuscript by Tsurayuki was in the possession of Fujiwara no Kanshi (1021–1102), the chief consort of Go-Reizei (1025–1068, r. 1045–1068). Known as the Ono no kōtaigōgū no gyohon, this text was eventually destroyed by a fire in 1102. The final version mentioned in the *Fukurozōshi* is an edition said to have been copied out by a female relative of Tsurayuki, possibly his wife or daughter, and known to posterity as the Hanazono no safu gyohon.

Textual studies by Nishishita Kyōichi and Kyūsojin Hitaku, which constituted the earliest area of postwar research into the *Kokinshū*, offer contradictory conclusions about the way the anthology evolved. Nishishita's pioneering work divided extant texts into two lineages: ones he believed were closest to the original (such as the Kiyosuke-bon texts) and ones with much later supplements (such as the Gen'ei-bon texts). In the end, however, he sees many texts as combining these two lineages and concludes that none of the extant manuscripts reflects the original version of the anthology.[5] Kyūsojin's later thesis turned the conventional wisdom established by Nishishita on its head. Whereas Nishishita took an orthodox approach that treated individual manuscripts as products of later copyists, Kyūsojin saw differences between texts as the results of different stages in the original compilation process. On the basis of differences in their organization, he divided extant texts into original compilations and revised versions, and then further divided the latter group into three types: private editions, editions for Daigo, and a large number of public editions that he further subdivides into five stages of evolution.[6] Textual studies have largely reached their apogee with Kyūsojin Hitaku's work, but without offering any definitive account of how the anthology took shape.[7]

A large part of the difficulty in tracing the evolution of the anthology is due to the dearth of materials with which we can chart the compilation process. In general, discussion of the issue focuses on the controversies surrounding the Kana Preface date of Engi 5 (905), which were first articulated by the medieval scholar Kiyosuke in his *Fukurozōshi*. Scholars have tended to believe that this was either the year the anthology was first presented or the year that the editors received the order to compile it (or possibly both). The *Fukurozōshi* raises a host of other questions that modern scholars have continued to puzzle over in reading both the Kana Preface and its companion Mana Preface. Why are two different dates given in both prefaces? Why and when were poems that date from later than 905 added on? Why is the Kana Preface's description of the anthology's categories of poetry different from the actual ones found in manuscripts today? If, as some scholars contend, the Mana Preface used the Kana Preface as a draft, why would the dates they provide suggest the opposite? If the prefaces were composed with the assumption they would be attached to the completed anthology, then why is the actual date of completion and presentation never specified? Why wouldn't the prefaces have been amended to reflect the addition of some poems at least eight years after 905? Some scholars have argued that the difference between the Kana Preface's description of the anthology and the anthology's actual form is due to this later process of revision.[8] It is also possible that the Kana Preface reflects a trial attempt at an early stage of compilation, one that led in turn to a reworking of the materials used for the anthology in subsequent versions.

The general consensus at the present time is that the compilation process took place over a period stretching from 905, when the anthology was probably first presented to Daigo, to at least as late as 913, when Uda held the Teiji Villa Match.[9] What began as a project initiated by a Fujiwara regent was completed at a court at least partly under the influence of a rival tonsured sovereign. Debates over whether it was Uda or Daigo who played the most important role in the initial stages of compilation have tended to favor the latter.[10] One scholar who has investigated the issue in detail sees Tokihira as playing the most important role in the initial stage of compilation and Uda in the case of the later additions.[11] Others argue that Daigo's personal interest in these same later additions can be inferred from the prose prefaces and authors mentioned.[12] Regardless, it seems clear that the anthology's current shape reflects the interests of more than one powerful figure at court.

In addition to the leaders of the Heian court, moreover, lower-ranking courtiers also played an important role in shaping the *Kokinshū*'s contours. A few scholars have suggested Tsurayuki's personal investment in the anthology's content. Mezaki Tokue, for example, contends that the Ki are given a prominent place within the anthology centering on the political downfall of Prince Koretaka partly because of Tsurayuki's interest in memorializing his clan's history.[13] Up until this point, anthologies commissioned by sovereigns had always been compiled by aristocrats and princes. By contrast, the *Kokinshū*'s compilers were otherwise absent from the rituals, procedures, and practices that helped constitute the political elite as a community. As a result, the text of the *Kokinshū* is a palimpsest of not only different historical moments but also different social and political groupings. The sometimes shared, sometimes conflicting interests of sovereigns, retired sovereigns, aristocrats, and lower-ranking courtiers are all discernable to varying degrees within its text.

Despite the many difficulties involved in reconstructing the textual history of the *Kokinshū*, we can attempt to tease out a picture of the way different elements in the text were informed by particular historical contexts. The categories, structure, use of prose prefaces, and range of selected material that made this anthology stand out from its predecessors all contributed to a new form of officially sanctioned text that provided a model for representing authority at court for centuries afterward through the enterprise of poetic anthologizing. They also offer important clues to the forces that helped shape the *Kokinshū*. Chief among these was the role played by Tokihira in establishing a new regime at court.

After the Banquet: Preparing and Presenting the *Kokinshū*

While Uda was heavily involved in poetry matches, his successor showed little interest in such gatherings. It was not until thirteen years into Daigo's reign that a poetry match was first held at the palace, probably in competition with Uda's at the Teiji-in. Nor was this lack of interest limited to *uta*, according to the scholar Ki no Haseo (845–

912) who describes the situation at Daigo's court in the following terms in his *Engi igo shi jo* ("Preface to *Shi* Poetry from the Engi Era Onward"):

Thus, from the Engi Era onward,	故予延喜以後
I no longer knew joy in poetic expression.	不知好言詩拋
Elegance was cast away as useless.	風月徒拋拋
Urbane splendor was practically abandoned.	煙華如棄
And though public banquets were held,	雖関公宴
no one dared reveal deep thoughts,	不敢深思
but only thought of censure for formal infractions.	只避格律之責而已[14]

In contrast to Uda, Daigo appears to have been relatively uninterested in sponsoring banquets where *shi* were composed. Annual *sechien* banquets were limited to the *naien* in spring and *chōyō* banquet in autumn. Daigo also favored a more orthodox approach to these gatherings. In contrast to the large number of members in Uda's intimate coterie who had participated in the composition of *shi* at banquets, poets at Daigo's *sechien* were limited to the traditional cast of *monnin* scholars affiliated with the university.[15]

It is surprising that, given the later association between Daigo and the *Kokinshū*, his reign began with such an unpromising attitude toward poetry. While the young sovereign appears to have been relatively unconcerned with verse in the early years of his reign, however, other prominent members of his court were not. Chief among these was the Northern House leader Tokihira, who dominated Daigo's court during the first decade of the tenth century. Tokihira's ascendancy is traditionally dated to 901, when he succeeded in having Uda's chief ally Sugawara no Michizane exiled from court. From his new position of power, Tokihira proceeded to inaugurate one of the court's most active periods of textual production. As Minister of the Left he oversaw the completion in 901 of the sixth (and last) court history, a project initially entrusted to Michizane. It was this history, the *Sandai jitsuroku*, which chronicled Yoshifusa's blossom banquets and the rise of *yamato uta*, a tradition that Tokihira himself consciously emulated and expanded on.

In addition to continuing projects begun under Uda, Tokihira initiated many new ones of his own. He had court scribes collect past government edicts in a vast compendium entitled the *Engi kyaku* ("Supplementary Legislation of the Engi Era," 908) which was completed a year before the Fujiwara minister's death. In 905, the same year in which the order to compile the *Kokinshū* was issued, Daigo's court also began drawing up a new set of ritual and administrative codes, which would become the authoritative version known to posterity as the *Engi shiki*. One year after beginning these projects, Tokihira followed his predecessor's example and held a banquet at which *uta* were written on topics taken from lectures on the *Nihon shoki*. Like Mototsune's event, Tokihira's banquet was probably designed to create solidarity among the court's elite at a time when the regent was seeking to strengthen state institutions.

Given the continuities between Tokihira's policies and those of Mototsune and Yoshifusa, the *Kokinshū* can be seen as one element in a larger Fujiwara-sponsored attempt to formalize their links to the imperial family through the use of *yamato uta* in banquet rituals involving poetic inscription and harmonization with topics.[16] One particularly noteworthy example of the latter practice is a blossom banquet held by Tokihira three years prior to the order to compile the *Kokinshū*. The event took place in the context of Tokihira's attempt to establish a new Fujiwara lineage of rulers. While asserting his role as chief minister of state in the manner of his father, Tokihira had also succeeded in installing his younger sister Fujiwara no Yasuko (885–954) as one of Daigo's consorts. The prominent place of sister and brother at court was formally acknowledged in 902, when Tokihira presided over a wisteria banquet held in Yasuko's living quarters at the palace. Daigo's diary describes the event in detail:

> Today, formal offerings were made beneath the wisteria in the Higyōsha apartment. Minister of the Left [Tokihira] received these, naming Sugane the imperial tribute bearer. He was made chief steward of the imperial consort's estate. Afterward, everyone was seated in rows beneath the wisteria blossoms. After the wine had made its rounds, the Senior Captain of the Right [Sadakuni] was commanded to present a list of poetic topics under the heading "verse harmonizing with the topic of wisteria blossoms at the Higyōsha apartment." The Minister of the Left wrote out the preface with the royal inkstone, and then presented the participants' poems to the sovereign in a

> box. Afterward, he had musicians perform on the flute and zither. The flute used was the renowned instrument of the former Jōwa Sovereign [Ninmyō]. Wine cups were raised, and the spirits of the assembled ministers were all cheered by the performance of song and dance to wind and string instruments. Prince Atsukata commanded the Superintendent of Bizen Province, Tadafusa, to blow on his flute. Afterward, stipends were dispensed to the assembled ministers, each according to their rank.[17]

Tokihira's wisteria banquet not only celebrated Yasuko's installation within the palace but also formalized his place as the sovereign's intermediary with the court nobility through a carefully choreographed circulation of poems. Whereas the composition of *shi* poetry at Saga's blossom banquets had reaffirmed harmony between the ruler and the larger body of state officialdom, *uta* written in *kana* here expressed the elite's acknowledgment of the kinship ties between the sovereign and his Fujiwara relatives. Daigo's uncle Fujiwara no Sadakuni (867–906) handed out topics, and the resulting poems were assembled, compiled, and presented by his new brother-in-law, Tokihira. In the place of "men of letters" overseeing the circulation of written texts in mimicry of state procedures, men of the Northern House here mediated the movement of poetic topics and texts between the sovereign and his courtiers.

Each element in this gathering was laden with political symbolism. Tokihira's pivotal role in the circulation of poetic topics and texts at the banquet was mirrored in the exchange of wealth that opened the event. "Offerings" (*hōken*) of food, wine, and rare objects at banquets had been used to formalize patron-client relationships among the court elite since the ninth century.[18] In this case, Tokihira's gifts to Daigo are exchanged for the right to oversee his sister's estate. The resulting poems in *kana* harmonizing with the topic of blossoming wisteria formalized the nobility's accord with these economic, marital, and political arrangements under the Fujiwara, whose name literally means "wisteria field." The use of *waka* in the title of the text that Tokihira has others compile could indicate both "harmony" with the topic phrase of wisteria blossoms and political acceptance of the Northern House's role in overseeing its distribution. Tokihira's position as the ultimate guarantor of wealth and status at Daigo's court was confirmed at the end of the banquet with the dispensation of stipends.

At the time this banquet was held, Tokihira had already been directly exposed to Uda's new forms of political and poetic theater. The Fujiwara patriarch is known to have participated in at least one maiden-flower match held at the retired sovereign's Teiji Villa four years earlier. The use of *kana* as a medium for marking lineage and kinship at earlier poetry matches may have inspired Tokihira's choice of this script for the poetry composed at his banquet. In Tokihira's new regime, however, Uda's maiden-flowers were replaced with the wisteria as the favored floral symbol of authority. The revival of blossom banquets by the Fujiwara patriarch perhaps also signaled a return to Yoshifusa's ritual staging of the Northern House's privileged place at court.

The following year, Yasuko gave birth to Prince Yasuakira (903–923). One year later, Tokihira's new nephew was made crown prince. In light of these events, it could be argued that the *Kokinshū* (at least initially) took shape in order to commemorate the establishment of a new Fujiwara line within the royal succession. As we will see later, this is especially evident in the Blessings section of the anthology. Perhaps more important, however, the *Kokinshū* was also related to this banquet in its format, its language, and the editorializing process in which Tokihira, again, oversaw the circulation and presentation of poetic topics.

Tokihira's choice of a banquet rather than a poetry match to mark his place at court in 902 would be reflected in the *Kokinshū*'s conceptualization of court society. Whereas poetry matches represented a new form of community in the shape of a household composed of men and women, banquets affirmed the orthodox definition of the court as a Confucian entity in which relations between men were the chief focus.[19] In place of the women who recorded and perhaps even compiled poetry matches, male officials were responsible for compiling the new anthology, just as they were the creators and compilers of texts at banquets. It is in this nexus between *kana* composition and the banquet rituals through which wealth and food were distributed that we can begin to see what made the *Kokinshū* an imperial anthology.

According to the official Mana Preface to the *Kokinshū*, the process by which the anthology took shape proceeded in two distinct stages:

> A royal command was issued to men such as the Grand Scribe Ki no Tomonori, Palace Librarian Ki no Tsurayuki, the Former Assistant to the Governor of Kai Province Ōshikochi no Mitsune, and Sub-Lieutenant of the Right Palace Guard Mibu no Tadamine, bidding each to offer up his household anthologies and old songs from ages past. This was called the "Collection of Myriad Leaves Continued." Then another command was given, and the poems were divided by categories into twenty scrolls. The new anthology was given the name "Collection of Poems Ancient and Modern."[20]

When these two stages in compilation took place is not specified. The change in the text's title and the decision to issue a new command for its reconfiguration suggests an abrupt rupture in the process; one possibly caused by the death of the first editor, Ki no Tomonori. This man, who had ties to both Uda and his father Kōkō, would have been a logical choice on the former sovereign's part. Uda's possible role in first initiating the project of compiling the *Kokinshū* can also be inferred by circumstantial evidence. He is known to have ordered collections of poems from several courtiers, including his minister Sugawara no Michizane. The use of *man'yōshū* in the initial title likewise suggests continuity with Uda's court, at which the similarly titled *Shinsen man'yōshū* anthology had been compiled.

Just as Tokihira continued Uda's earlier projects in the form of the *Sandai jitsuroku*, the continuation of the *Shoku man'yōshū* project could have been intended to signal continuity with past practices in the aftermath of political changes.[21] At the same time, however, Tomonori's death seems to have provided an opportunity for the project to take on a radically new shape under the aegis of his younger relative Ki no Tsurayuki (a man with long-established ties to Tokihira).[22] The categories that organized the new version of this anthology appear to have had their origin with its new editor. When Tsurayuki presented a list of old verse to Daigo for inclusion in the anthology, he prefaced it with a *chōka* in which the anthology's categories of Seasons, Blessings, Longing, Partings, Lamentations, and Miscellaneous Verse were listed.[23]

Rather than simply name the new collection after the *Man'yōshū* in the manner of its predecessors, the title of the *Kokinshū* expressed a bolder ambition to encompass both "new and old" poetry. Both forms of verse were related in different ways to the assertion of Confucian kingship. "New poems" chiefly came from the personal collections of the editors and their contemporaries. The practice of compiling such household anthologies extended back at least as far as the Nara period. These texts typically included verse by the ancestors, kin, and allies of the compiler in addition to that person's own poems. Insofar as these household anthologies represented forms of sociality (such as kinship or friendship) that lay outside the relationship between sovereign and subject, the decision to reorganize these clan collections according to topical categories had political significance. The process has been described by one scholar as one in which the individual courtier and his clan were "dissolved" within the court and its structures.[24] The effect of such a process was not unlike that of Uda's poetry matches, in which poems were initially organized by teams of allies and kin and then rearranged as parts of a larger landscape presided over by the sovereign.

By contrast, the "old poems" of the anthology were already implicated in the practices of state and court. Although there is some uncertainty about what the term *furuki uta* means precisely, it seems likely that it mainly refers to earlier songs. The two editors who are known to have presented such verses to Daigo were involved with offices responsible for the transmission of songs performed at banquets and shrine rituals. Mibu no Tadamine, an otherwise obscure figure, was a palace guard responsible for performing ritual songs such as the *azuma uta*. The chief editor, Ki no Tsurayuki, who was Palace Librarian (*uchi no gosho-dokoro no azukari*) at the time the anthology was presented, would have had access to many earlier collections of songs.[25] He also appears to have been reared in the Naikyōbō office, whose women members sang and danced at palace banquets, and taught male courtiers to perform zither songs.[26] Tsurayuki's dual position as the son of a minor court official and of a female performer would help to explain not only his familiarity with both written poetry and song but also his initial opportunities to meet nobility such as Tokihira who, like many officials at court, had frequent liaisons with the women of the Naikyōbō.

Songs played a significant part in the makeup of the anthology. The *Kokinshū* appears to make a distinction between ones sung for specifically ritual purposes and those performed for entertainment at palace banquets. The former appear in the final scroll of the anthology, which is devoted to songs reserved for enthronement ceremonies and shrine rituals.[27] The latter appear most often as anonymous verse scattered throughout.[28] Nearly all of these anonymous poems appear in groups, making it possible to see each individual scroll of the anthology as a collection itself of "new and old verse" grouped together in alternating sequences.[29] The densest concentrations of such poems, however, appear in the Longing and Miscellaneous Verse sections. It is conceivable that many of the anthology's anonymous love poems were originally erotic verses sung to instrumental music by female performers for the male officials they entertained at banquets. Likewise, a large number of poems in the Miscellaneous Verse section of the *Kokinshū* appear to have originated as banquet songs.[30] In the *Kokinshū*, all of these verses are stripped of the rhythmic phrases and refrains known as *hayashi kotoba* that accompanied transcriptions of song in other Heian texts such as the *Kinkafu*. In the process, the editors created new written poems from older compositions.

The preservation and adaptation of old songs was itself a core feature of Confucian rulership. Such activities, as Akiyama Ken has noted, were inspired by the example of the officials in the Han Dynasty's Music Bureau (Yuefu) who collected popular music and songs and rewrote them as *shi* and other forms of verse.[31] Daigo's order to preserve these songs in a new imperial anthology thus placed him in the role of the continental-style monarch, who ensured social order and harmony through the regulation of music and song. The young sovereign would play the same role in other arenas as well. One year after the *Kokinshū* was first presented to him, Daigo can be seen taking a direct interest in the affairs of the office responsible for the songs from which many of the anthology's poems had been selected. In an entry from 906, the sovereign's diary records him ordering one Ō no Yasumaro to train a successor who could continue to preserve the performance traditions for zither songs overseen by the Bureau of Palace Song (Ōuta-dokoro).[32] The incident suggests that renewed interest in such songs was one consequence of the *Kokinshū* project.

In addition to providing material for the anthology in the form of old songs, banqueting practices also played a central role in the process of compilation. The location of the selection process itself echoed the dual concerns of banqueting and royal concubinage epitomized by Tokihira's earlier wisteria gathering. The preface to poem 795 in the posthumous collection of Tsurayuki's poems known as the *Tsurayuki-shū* ("Tsurayuki Collection") describes the editors making selections of poems for inclusion in the *Kokinshū* while in the eastern part of the Shōkyōden.[33] Located within the Rear Palace where the sovereign's consorts resided, this hall was also the site of the annual *naien* banquet at which *shi* were composed and stipends distributed.[34]

After the initial stages of selection had been completed, the anthology's compilers appear to have moved from the banquet hall to the kitchen. By 907, all three of the surviving editors held jobs involving the gathering, preparation, and presentation of food for the royal table. In this year Tsurayuki was promoted to the post of *naizen no tenzen* (junior officer of the Palace Table Office) responsible for the preparation of the sovereign's meals. Ōshikōchi no Mitsune (fl. 870–928) was assigned to the Palace Kitchen Office (Mizushidokoro), which brought food from the royal kitchens to the palace dining room in the Seiryōden. Mibu no Tadamine held the post of *hinami no niezukai* (daily bearer of offerings), which was responsible for supplying fresh food to the palace. All of these posts were under the supervision of the Kurōdodokoro (Secretariat), headed by Tokihira at the time. As befitted his role as chief editor, Tsurayuki played a particularly vital role in the Palace Table Office, whose duties included ordering, inspecting, and storing cooking implements and foodstuffs brought in from various provinces. Perhaps the most important of his duties was overseeing the preparation and presentation of food for *sechien* banquets such as the one held on New Year's Day, an elaborate affair that included fish, vegetables, charcoal, and firewood assembled from over twelve provinces.[35]

The editors' overlapping roles as suppliers, preparers, and presenters of food for Daigo's table is a striking coincidence, one that has largely gone without comment in scholarly accounts of the editorializing process. As far as can be ascertained, none of these posts bore any relation to the positions these men occupied before or afterward. Since these posts were all held in the period immediately after the likely initial compilation of the anthology, it is possible to see the editors at this point as somehow involved in the process of disseminating its text while under Tokihira's supervision in the palace kitchen. As both suppliers of food and poems, they would have been able to ensure that Tokihira's vision of a new political order was spread to the court's elite in attendance at palace banquets.

The editor's posts in the palace kitchen also offer clues to the performative context in which the text might have first appeared. Despite the prominent place of the *Kokinshū* at the Heian court, we have no account of its initial reception. Given the size of the collection, it is difficult to imagine that it was initially distributed in its entirety to a large number of people. Recitation of particular poems or portions of the text at banquets, on the other hand, would have created an accessible format in which to appreciate it. Banquets had long been the chief setting in which other forms of verse were recited. The intricate structure of the anthology, with its unprecedented concern for organizing and arranging poems into larger units, might also suggest that they were intended for recitation in sequences. Proximity to the banquet spaces of the palace would have enabled the editors to distribute partial copies or recite portions of the text to the nobility attending these events. Such performances could have been staged as propaganda pieces designed to legitimate Tokihira's regime. Many of the more tightly organized sections of the anthology appear to have been created with precisely this purpose in mind.

The editors' dual roles as compilers and kitchen staff can also be seen as a nod to earlier ritual traditions of rulership that associated the presentation of food and song with the submission of the realm's regions to their imperial lord. As the scholar Mitani Kuniaki has argued, such practices suggest that royal power in early Japan was represented in part through a web of interrelated practices revolving around the ruler's ritualized consumption of the realm.[36] "He who consumes the realm" (*osu kuni*) appears frequently as an epithet for kingship in *Man'yōshū* poetry and *senmyō* edicts. Even monarchical acts of seeing and hearing were associated with royal consumption. The suffix *-mesu*, which occurs in verbs reserved for the ruler such as *kikoshimesu* (to hear/to eat/to rule) and *shiroshimesu* (to know/rule), could be glossed with characters denoting either the acts of eating (食) or seeing (見).

Perhaps the paradigmatic example of the way the sovereign ingested his domain was the enthronement rite itself, as this ritual act of "consuming the realm" was reenacted daily in royal meals whose ingredients were provided by the surrounding provinces. During the enthronement rite, two provinces known as the "Province of Libations" (*yuki*) and the "Province of Grain" (*suki*) that represented the eastern and western halves of the realm respectively presented rice, wine, and seafood from their territories. The men and women who offered up local foodstuffs from these regions also presented songs whose lyrics included the names of the locales that produced their offerings.[37] In providing both poems and food, the *Kokinshū*'s editors also evoked two key elements in this ceremony inaugurating the sovereign's consumption of the realm.[38]

Yet another link between food, song, and text is suggested by Daigo's apparent interest in developing new documentary means for enabling his consumption of the realm's material and cultural resources. One directive from the Council of State in Enchō 3/11/14 (925) ordered the compilation and presentation of "provincial gazetteers" (*fudoki*) listing the names, products, legends, and songs of various places.[39] This was the first time since the eighth century that such an undertaking was considered by the Yamato court. Although this project was never completed, the ambitions that lay behind it may well have been inspired by the ways in which the *Kokinshū* had enabled a new mode of "consuming the realm" through verse. Regardless, it seems that the anthologizers were not simply compilers of texts in the manner of their predecessors at Saga's court, but preparers of banquet verses, a role akin to that of the equally humble courtier-performers who sang and danced at such gatherings. This difference in roles also was to lead to a difference in the manner in which the text presented its poems.

Poem Prefaces and Performative Contexts

The language used in the *Kokinshū* affords its own insights into the ways in which banquet practices endowed it with an imperial aura. Earlier *kana* texts such as the *uta* in *Shinsen man'yōshū* or the records of Uda's poetry matches were organized around specific poetic events. In keeping with this tradition, the *Kokinshū* situates its poems within a particular social setting by marking various gradations of hierarchy, time, and mode of address in the prose that surrounds its poems. One result of this recontextualization of earlier poems is that proxy poets, who were anonymous in other settings such as poetry matches, became named authors in this anthology.

Names of authors and topical headings are integral features of the anthology, as important in the reading of a poem as the poem itself. The earliest evidence we have of the *Kokinshū*'s reception suggests that familiarity with both elements was expected in court society. In an often-mentioned passage from the *Pillow Book*, Emperor Murakami tests the knowledge of one of his consorts by asking her to recite particular poems from the *Kokinshū* after he has given her the topic and name of the poet.[40] Almost every poem in the *Kokinshū* falls under one of these two designations. Verse without these features are marked as such with the phrase "composer unknown" (*yomibito shirazu*) or "topic unknown" (*dai shirazu*). The practice of marking both author and topic is probably derived from *sechien* banquets, where poets were named in order of their rank and their poems prefaced by the topics they addressed.

The nature of authorship in the *Kokinshū* is one feature that distinguishes it from other *kana* texts. Both of its immediate predecessors, the *Shinsen man'yōshū* and Uda's poetry matches, neglected to identify the authors of poems in their texts. The *Kokinshū* itself indirectly attests to this norm when it marks many poems from contemporaneous poetry matches as anonymous compositions.[41] In choosing to indicate authorship in its own text, the anthology appears to have drawn on the conventions of *shi* anthologies, which often privileged this category as an organizing principle for arranging poems.[42] At the same time, however, authorship in the *Kokinshū* is subsumed within larger structures, ones that locate its poets within particular performative contexts, such as officials in Travel, for example, or birthday celebrants in Blessings.

This context-specific means for marking authorship in the *Kokinshū* also makes it distinct from earlier imperial anthologies, where a consistent mode of naming is used throughout. The *Ryōunshū*, for example, provides the full rank, title, clan and personal name of each of its authors, and the other two anthologies provide only the names of the authors, with surnames abbreviated to the first character in a continental style of nomenclature. Whereas Saga's anthologies sought to bind the realm together by marking poets as equal parts of a harmonious whole, the *Kokinshū* creates distinctions in rank and hierarchy among its courtiers at the same time as it acknowledges their presence.

Class appears to have been the primary criterion by which authors are differentiated within the text. Courtiers of Fourth Rank or higher, for example, are given the honorific title of "lord" (*ason*) after their clan name and before their personal name. Both male and female officials are marked in this manner, suggesting that authorial gender was not a significant axis of difference within the anthology.[43] Political considerations appear to have been at work in the few cases where exceptions occur. The two verses in the anthology by Uda's former ally Michizane (poems 272 and 420) omit his personal name, possibly because he was being deified in an attempt to pacify his spirit.[44]

Such distinctions in naming drew on the language of official court gatherings, rather than that of generic anthologies. The nomenclature used in calling out individual's names at formal events often differed according to his or her relative rank and the social context in which the utterance was made. The *Ryō no gige* commentary to the state's legal codes, for example, specifies that, at promotion ceremonies, those of Third Rank and above are called by their "individual names" (*imina*) first and then by their "clan names" (*kabane*), while this order was reversed for those of lower rank.[45]

As one scholar has noted, the forms of nomenclature used within the *Kokinshū* resemble those observed at palace banquets, where the name and rank of composers were presented before the sovereign according to similar distinctions in rank.[46] Thus, the anthology is more than simply a collection of poems produced on royal command. Rather, it represents the entirety of its text as a specific poetic event in which verses are inscribed on topics and offered up to the sovereign at a formal banquet.[47] This difference from other forms of anthologizing suggests a possible distinction between the two incarnations of the anthology. Whereas the earlier *Shoku man'yōshū* could have merely been a collection of verse along the lines of earlier anthologies, the *Kokinshū* would have represented an entirely new context for presenting its poets and poems, one in which the text itself becomes an eternally recurring banquet at which both entities take shape.

The *Kokinshū*'s representation of itself as a form of *sechien* banquet at which poets present their names along with verses on specific topics could also explain why the work's title appears to depart from the conventions used for similar anthologies at the time. In particular, the appearance of the word *waka* in its full name suggests that its poems embody the ideal of harmonizing with the lord through topic-based forms of composition. Textual characteristics and contextual practices can be seen as being related to one another in other ways as well. Court banquets often featured anthologizing as their penultimate act. Individual poems submitted within the basket in front of the sovereign were rewritten in a comprehensive clean copy before being presented to him. As if in emulation of this practice, editorial activity surrounding the *Kokinshū* took place within the Shōkyōden, a palace building where *sechien* banquets were often held.

Other features of the language used to identify poets in the anthology suggest a close relation to Tokihira's wisteria banquet in particular. Like that event, the *Kokinshū* seeks to define an imperial lineage in which Fujiwara women are as prominently featured as the male sovereign. One result of this agenda is that the broad range of alliances and kinship relationships staged by Uda in his poetry matches was dramatically narrowed within Daigo's anthology. Honorific language in its text is reserved for the immediate line of succession. Only poems by sovereigns, tonsured sovereigns, crown princes, and their mothers (such as Yōzei's mother Takaiko) are marked as "royal verse" (*ōmu uta*) in their prose prefaces.[48]

Another feature of royal banquets that informs the textual contours of the *Kokinshū* is its use of "topics" (*dai*). The specific significance of this term has tended to be ignored by modern scholars, who typically borrow the much later phrase *kotobagaki* to describe the prose that introduces poems in the anthology.[49] The use of the word *dai* in the *Kokinshū*, by contrast, suggests that the anthology is drawing on established conventions for writing poetry at *sechien* banquets. The prior history of this term suggests a longstanding connection to the practice of poetic inscription. In literary Chinese, 題 (*dai*) often acts as a verb indicating the act of writing out a poem on material surfaces, such as leaves, walls, stone, paper, or wood.[50] In Japan in the ninth century, it referred to the topics provided by the ruler or his regent when either figure commanded poetic compositions from the attendees at annual banquets.[51] In these settings, the physical inscription of topics took the form of written cards in a basket. To compose a poem on a topic was, in effect, to echo the sovereign's words written in literary Chinese. By marking every poem as possessing such topics (whether they are known or not), the *Kokinshū* transformed all of its *uta* into ones that harmonized with the words of the sovereign.

Dai appear to have taken on a slightly different significance in poetry matches. Whereas the participants in calendrical banquets at the palace were defined in terms of the relationship between sovereign and subject, poetry matches privileged kinship ties within the household. And in place of topics drawn from the literary Chinese canon, the *uta* of Uda's matches cited seasonal words, such as summertime *hototogisu* birds and autumnal maiden-flowers, which had no specific locus in the continental classics. At times, the *Kokinshū* appears to use the word *dai* with this practice in mind. The only section of the anthology in which every poem has a *dai* is Names of Things, in which the *kana* letters of an individual word are redistributed across the words within a poem. Many of these verses appear to have been composed on royal command at official gatherings as well as poetry matches. Conversely, the majority of poems without *dai* also have no identifiable author, suggesting they began as banquet songs rather than as written poems.

The use of Japanese in the anthology's prose prefaces allowed them not only to narrate the circumstances behind individual poems but also to mark the speaker and addressee to whom this narration is directed. Unlike the literary Chinese used in previous forms of poem prefaces, the *kana* used in the *Kokinshū* could thus mark the social context in which its poems were being presented and produced through a variety of linguistic markers. One striking example is the anthology's use of the auxiliary verbal suffix *ki,* which is limited to prefaces for poems that the chief editor Tsurayuki offers up directly to Daigo. Rather than mark the isolated actions of a particular speaker, *ki* here invokes a past moment shared by the editor and his sovereign. This usage suggests that Tsurayuki wrote the *Kokinshū*'s poem prefaces with the assumption that they would be read by a reigning sovereign who shares these past poetic memories with his editor.

The act of composing poems on royal command also established the overall temporal coordinates of the anthology. All such poems are preceded by a mention of the reign of the ruler who commanded their composition, the one exception being poems ordered by Daigo.[52] The reigns of deceased sovereigns are named by the location of their burial mounds; those of retired sovereigns who are still living are marked by their era names or residence. For example, Uda is marked in this manner for poems composed at his command when he reigned, and in relation to his mansions (such as Suzaku-in) for poems composed after his retirement. Such distinctions unambiguously situate the anthology in a textual present organized around Daigo's reign.

Other temporal distinctions in the anthology's prose distinguish the immediate community of hall courtiers who attended on the sovereign in the Seiryōden from other nonimperial authors. The prose describing these men uses the same language of era names usually reserved for imperial family members, but chiefly in situations were they command lower-ranking officials to compose *uta* for them. Such formal temporal designations create a distinctive male community in which the hierarchical relationships between sovereign and subject are reproduced in turn between the sovereign's men and their lower-ranking peers. Through such parallelisms, the *Kokinshū* creates a court community in which status corresponds to proximity with the royal person. Since Tsurayuki's adornment of hall courtiers with the language of officialdom took place during a period in which their community and the rites defining it were recent developments, it is possible that one of the anthology's goals was to assert the status of this new social identity.

All of these forms of language within the anthology's prose prefaces to individual poems work together to produce what Katagiri Yōichi has termed a "social setting" (*ba*): a point in time and space occupied by a particular speaker who bears a particular social relationship to his or her audience.[53] The *Kokinshū*'s production of this setting leads to further questions about the context in which this address takes place. Scholars who use the term *ba* define it as either the context in which a poem was composed or that in which it was received.[54]

While it is possible to identify the intended reader of the poem prefaces as Daigo, the manner in which they were conveyed to him is more difficult to determine. Some have hypothesized that they were intended for recitation by Prince Kanemi (d. 932)—a man who appears to have played the role of intermediary between the editors and Daigo, and someone of sufficiently high rank to address the sovereign directly when the anthology was formally presented.[55] This argument hinges on the occasional use of the humilific verb *haberi* in poem prefaces. Typically used to denote the enunciator's lower rank vis-à-vis the addressee, *haberi* commonly appears in letters and in representations of conversation in Heian *monogatari*.[56] Its epistolary usage in particular suggests that Tsurayuki himself may have addressed his comments on poems to Daigo in writing rather than in person.[57]

With regard to their content, the prefaces to individual poems in the *Kokinshū* appear to have no consistent format. The time, place, topic, and social context in which poems were composed are related either in isolation or in a variety of combinations with one another. The sheer diversity of their content could suggest that these prefaces were written piecemeal as responses to individual questions about particular poems. The preface to poem 997 in the anthology provides one example of this practice when it relates that its poem was composed in response to a question from Seiwa about the period in which the *Man'yōshū* was compiled. In some cases, Daigo might have wanted to know what poetry match a poem came from, leading to a brief explanation by Tsurayuki. In other cases, he might have wanted to know what topic had inspired the original poem, or the occasion on which it was first recited. Poem prefaces describing landscapes, for example, were perhaps intended to relate the subject matter of a painting, or the topic for a poem when it was presented at a poetry match.[58] Comments to narrative groups of poems involving famous figures such as Narihira may also have been influenced by the *Shijing* commentarial tradition, in which the primary concern was to identify the historical setting in which a poet's intentions were originally expressed.[59]

Such information would have been useful in providing poetic precedents to aid future compositions using similar language in similar settings. The function of historical information in these prefaces relates to another meaning of *dai*, which the *Kokinshū* also appears to draw on. In literary Chinese, the word could refer to the prose preface describing a poem's origins (*daikyaku*). One possible model for providing such information would have been the canonical *Classic of Poetry*, whose poems feature prefaces mentioning the historical circumstances in which they were composed. If this is the case, then these prefaces also suggest that the anthology was being treated like the *Shijing* at the time of its initial reception, that is, as a classic requiring historical contextualization in the form of prefatory comments.

Tsurayuki's poem prefaces can be seen as inaugurating an exegetical tradition surrounding the *Kokinshū* that would extend over a millennium. Later readers appended additional lore about particular poems in the form of "after comments" (*sachū*).[60] With the increasing corporatization of cultural property under retired sovereigns in the late Heian period and the appearance of a market for its services among the powerful at the end of the twelfth century, an industry of commentary and interpretation quickly sprang up around the anthology. Poetics treatises such as the *Shunrai zuinō* (*Shunrai's Poetic Essentials*, 1111) began to interpret words and phrases from *Kokinshū* poetry; detailed biographies of its poets were compiled in texts like the *Kokin wakashū mokuroku* (1113); the first commentaries to the anthology's prefaces written; and guides to proper pronunciation produced. In establishing the *Kokinshū* as a canonical text, these later writers also marked a widening gulf between the court of their times and that of Tsurayuki's. By returning to Tsurayuki's original commentary to the anthology, however, we can gain insights into the social axes through which the anthology defined itself as the embodiment of an imperial community at the time of its compilation.

Complementary Categories in the *Kokinshū*

One of the oldest areas of scholarship on the *Kokinshū* has involved analysis of its structure in general and its "categorical divisions" (*budate*) in particular. Sporadic interest in such issues can be detected in some of the earliest medieval commentaries. With the elaboration of ever more specific topics for use in the composition of *renga* (linked verse) during the middle ages, sequences of poems within each category became defined accordingly. A commentarial tradition exemplified by the Muromachi-period linked verse poet Sōgi (1421–1502) and the Edo scholar Keichū in his encyclopedic ten-volume study *Kokin yozaishō* ("Personal Notes on the *Kokinshū*," 1691) read *Kokinshū* poetry through the lens of such practices.[61]

This mode of reading became a dominant strain of criticism in the twentieth century, exemplified by the scholar Matsuda Takeo whose minute divisions of the anthology's contents into "themes" (*shudai*) and "sub-themes" (*fuku shudai*) in many cases drew on categories developed in the medieval poetic tradition.[62] Medieval *renga* also provided the paradigm through which Konishi Jin'ichi produced his influential account of the *Kokinshū*'s structure as one in which particular themes were developed through sequences of poems that were bound together by associative links or temporal and spatial progressions.[63]

Another approach to the anthology's structure has been offered by Arai Eizō who organizes each feature into complementary pairs, beginning with its larger categories and extending to the wording of individual poems and the identities of their authors and recipients.[64] Arai's approach is both infinitely flexible in the structures it can find within the anthology, and more historically nuanced than an interpretive scheme that draws on the later practice of linked verse. At the time in which the *Kokinshū* was being compiled, the concept of poetic topics was only beginning to be articulated. By contrast, the principle of complementary pairings had long underpinned concepts of society, cosmos, and language shared by the Yamato court and its continental counterparts. Within this model, meaning was produced through the relations of one entity to another rather than in autonomy. Similarly, the poetic categories used to organize poems within the *Kokinshū* can be seen as gaining significance in distinction from one another, rather than as isolated entities.

Arai's complementary pairs of poetic categories can also tell us much about the imperial nature of the anthology. The largest groupings produced by pairs of categories in the text, for example, invoke the binary poles of Heaven and humanity that underpinned the macrocosmic structures of Yamato kingship. At the most general level, the ritual songs that make up the final scroll of the *Kokinshū* can be seen as forming a complement to all of the preceding nineteen scrolls concerned with human affairs in the rest of the anthology. This division paralleled the most fundamental organizing principle of the *ritsuryō* state, which was divided into a Department of Divinities (Jingikan) that managed shrines and religious matters and a Department of State Affairs (Dajōkan) that oversaw the secular branch of government. In its overarching structure, the *Kokinshū* thus reflects the organizational rubrics of the governmental apparatus with its ritual and administrative branches.

Within the former grouping of nineteen scrolls, a further pairing of heavenly and human spheres is made by the two largest multichapter categories: Seasons (*shiki no uta*) in Scrolls 1 through 6 and Longing (*koi no uta*) in Scrolls 11 through 15. Both categories respectively describe the human subject's relationship to the heavenly cycles of time and the human ones of social intercourse. Such appeals to cosmological principles and categorical pairings could very well have held specific political overtones at the beginning of the tenth century. Insofar as the complementary pairing of these forms of time is derived from the poetry matches of Uda's court, the anthology's integration of them within the larger rubrics through which the state's ritual and administrative branches were defined can be seen as having the further effect of subsuming Uda's household regime within Daigo's palace-centered administration.

Blessings (*ga no uta*) in Scroll 7 and Lamentations (*aishō no uta*) in Scroll 16 provide another complementary temporal pairing, the former consisting of prayers for long life and the latter of elegies for the deceased. Their respective placements before and after Longing situate the latter's brief encounters within the total span of the human life cycle. In all three cases, time is defined in a social context involving two parties: blessings for long life are produced by one party for the benefit of another, love poetry always cites an absent partner, and lamentations are addressed to the deceased by the living or by the nearly deceased to their nearest and dearest in sequences that often seems to replicate the rites of mourning themselves.[65]

Another complementary pair is formed between the Miscellaneous Verse (*zō no uta*) in Scrolls 17 and 18, and those of Partings (*ribetsu no uta*) and Travel (*kiryo no uta*) in Scrolls 8 and 9 respectively. The latter group can be thought of as a chronological unit organized around departures from the capital to the provinces and foreign lands. Partings, which sets this process in motion through poems commemorating separations brought on by the demands of the state, was the more established of the two categories, with precedents in both the *Man'yōshū* and poetic encyclopedias such as the *Geibun ruijū* ("Literary Writings Topically Arranged," 624).[66] Whether the people separating are men and women, male companions, or parents and children, the vast majority of poems in this section of the *Kokinshū* deal with provincial postings. The Travel section proceeds from this point in time to describe the various locations to which these officials could be sent. It is also from this perspective, in a space located outside Heiankyō that the word *miyako* (capital) would come to denote the cultural center of the courtier's life.[67]

At first glance, the category of Miscellaneous Verse would appear to bear little relation to these other two, except for the fact that it also consists of two scrolls. As a category that was already well established in earlier anthologies such as the *Man'yōshū*, Miscellaneous Verse would not have needed any further definition. At the same time, however, these two scrolls display a careful structuring of content that, in turn, suggests a particular valence to the *Kokinshū*'s use of the term. The first scroll of Miscellaneous Verse opens with many poems that appear to have been composed for banquets at which the Confucian relationships of lord and minister, and those between comrades, are celebrated and formalized through prayers, expressions of joy at being promoted, and blessings. This is in keeping with the earlier definition of this category of verse in the *Man'yōshū*, which essentially consists of poems that were recited in public settings, such as *kunimi* rituals, hunts, processions, and banquets. The second scroll, by contrast, has many poems in which the official's alienation from these relationships is foremost, taking the form of religious seclusion, retirement from a government post, and protests addressed to superiors.

Among these four scrolls one can see a host of pairings organized in a manner not unlike that of a literary Chinese quatrain, in which parallel lines form couplets, and couplets form complementary pairs. Just as one line in a couplet might be syntactically more precise than the other, providing the template through which its partner is read, the more precisely demarcated unit of Partings and Travel defines its complementary opposite in Miscellaneous Verse. In this case, the distinction appears to be spatial. Whereas Partings and Travel clearly possess an outward trajectory away from the capital, Miscellaneous Verse is composed of poems that are chiefly located within its environs. Both units are themselves bound together into complementary pairs in the same manner as individual lines of a quatrain form couplets. Partings are the necessary predecessor to Travel, and the celebratory affirmation of ties between members of the court in the first scroll of the Miscellaneous Verse prefigure the cutting of these ties in the second scroll. All of these categories and scrolls taken together thus define courtiers in terms of their potential capacity as public officials.

Miscellaneous Verse completes the categorical pairings through which the *Kokinshū* represents orthodox forms of expression for state officials. This is probably why the Kana Preface does not mention the other two remaining categories of Names of Things (*mono no na*) and Miscellaneous Forms (*zattei no uta*) when it describes the anthology's contents. Both categories appear to be linked on account of their shared interest in language. Names of Things consists of acrostics that were largely composed by scholars who are otherwise absent from the anthology.[68] Perhaps because of their connection to continental learning, Names of Things represents an attempt at organizing *kana* words along the lexical lines that were employed in the case of literary Chinese. It arranges the words used in its poems according to the conventions used in topical encyclopedias of the time, for example, especially in its initial ordering of birds before insects and animals before plants.[69] Through such careful arrangements, this category evokes the scholarly organization of knowledge, things, and language in a manner that evokes the Confucian doctrine of the "rectification of names" which underpinned the social order.

Whereas Names of Things appears to be concerned with ordering words, the corollary category of Miscellaneous Forms transgresses the formal and social norms of poetic language. Many of its poems exceed the metrical standard of thirty-one syllables, including three long *chōka* verses by the editors that directly address the sovereign.[70] A significant number of poems in this section are *haikai* verse that threaten social harmony through their use of erotic and humorous language that partake in an earlier tradition of cursing found in the *gishōka* (jesting verse) of the *Man'yōshū*.[71]

The incantatory nature of such curses could explain why this group is located on the boundary between verses dealing with human affairs and the ritual songs of the anthology's last scroll. Because they do not conform to the definition of *uta* as something that should bless, harmonize, memorialize, or celebrate proper human relationships; *haikai* poems exist outside of the orthodox structures through which courtiers are enjoined to express themselves. Yet at the same time, their relegation to the margins of the anthology suggests that they could not be ignored, and their proximity to the final scroll of ritual songs suggests their magical powers. Such poems remain a significant form of poetic practice and a potential threat to social harmony that had to be acknowledged and contained.

In the broadest sense, then, the categories used to structure the *Kokinshū* can be seen as drawing on the concept of harmony, both as a cosmological principle of complementarity between the macrocosmic elements constituting the world, and as a social practice in which the regulated use of language was intended to ensure the proper relation of individuals to their social peers within the state and its structures. In addition to the approaches of Arai and his predecessor Matsuda, however, we should also acknowledge the possibility that other relations obtain in the arrangements of individual poems within categories. The scholar Okumura Tsuneya, for example, argues for the frequent presence of dialogues formed through such sequences.[72] Such an approach has appealed to scholars seeking to move beyond a static structuralist stance in favor of a more dynamic one that would include issues of reception. Katagiri Yōichi sees the dialogic arrangements identified by Okumura as reflecting the concrete dynamics of the group literary settings in which the anthology was first received, one in which criticism, approval, and narration of a poem's circumstances all accompanied its recitation.[73] In Katagiri's account, such dialogues offer a glimpse of the banquet settings that appear to have played such an important role in the anthology's compilation.

My own approach to the arrangement of poems within the anthology will focus on the categories that Tsurayuki singled out at the time that it was initially offered up to Daigo. At first, the Kana Preface appears to replicate the logic of complementary pairing as a way of defining these. Seasonal poems succeed one another in time as spring, summer, autumn, and winter, and are followed by Longing poetry. At this point, however, the text becomes more selective, mentioning only the categories of Blessings and Travel. All other forms of poetry are relegated to the Miscellaneous Verse category, which is described as poems that are not seasonal. Like the overall structure of the anthology, each of the categories that Tsurayuki singles out for special mention embodies a vision of the court that draws on ritual structures and the language of the state to organize and arrange both individuals and their poems. In the remainder of this chapter, I will focus on each of these categories and the manner in which their internal structures hint at the concerns that were likely to have been at work during the initial period in which the anthology was compiled.

Blessing a New Imperial Line

Complementary pairings of poems produce their own structures within the anthology's individual categories as well as between them.

Two of the smallest sections in the anthology, Blessings and Travel, use this organizational principle to great effect. They do so, moreover, in a manner that suggests they are particularly closely implicated in Tokihira's agenda for establishing a new regime under Daigo, one that would be distinct from the household government of his rival Uda. The care taken in arranging these sections and their prominent place within the anthology's Kana Preface suggest that they bear a particularly close relationship to the editors' vision of an imperial court. Neither category had a precedent in the *Man'yōshū*, and both are singled out in the Kana Preface for special mention at the expense of their partner categories of Lamentations and Partings. In each case, their particular political and historical significances are suggested by their internal structures.

Blessing poems (*ga no uta*) were designed to praise social superiors in a wide range of formal occasions at the Heian court, including coming-of-age ceremonies, promotions, annual observances, and birthdays. Only the last two forms appear within the Blessings category of the *Kokinshū*.[74] Different titles for this scroll and variants in wording of its opening poem have led some scholars to suggest that the oldest poems in Blessings might represent an earlier, more declarative form of incantatory verse rather than the hopeful prayers used in the category's birthday celebrations.[75] Banquets for such birthday celebrations appear to have grown in popularity and elaborateness from Kōkō's reign, perhaps on account of the relative age of this sovereign and his retainers.

In contrast to their broader usage and earlier history, the verses in Blessings seem to be concerned chiefly with legitimizing and commemorating the union of Tokihira's Northern House with the line of succession. Tsurayuki's poem prefaces methodically outline the kinship links between the historical figures that bless and are blessed by one another in this scroll. With the exception of the first four anonymous verses that open Blessings, all of its poems are accompanied by prose prefaces that identify the authors, the recipient of the verse at a birthday celebration, and, in many cases, the imperial family member who hosts the celebration. The relationships between host and celebrant are given particular attention, and appear to follow customary practice at the time insofar as the hosts are generally parents, children, siblings, spouses or maternal relatives of the celebrant.[76] Modern scholars, beginning with Matsuda Takeo, have noted that these figures are all related either to Tokihira's father Mototsune or Daigo's grandfather Kōkō.[77] In stressing the blood ties between these two figures and their kin, Blessings can thus be seen as an attempt to mend a rupture in the succession between Kōkō's non-Fujiwara line and the preceding one, which had been dominated by Mototsune and his kin.

As Arai Eizō has noted, the description of Blessings within the Kana Preface defines the recipients of *ga* verse through the state's core Confucian axis of "lord" (*kimi*) and "subject" (*hito*).[78] As with the other categories it mentions, the Kana Preface also defines Blessings in terms of a paradigmatic relationship between natural imagery and human intentions. Unlike the seasonal categories mentioned in Tsurayuki's description of the *Kokinshū*, however, two parallel human actions are presented for Blessings: praising the sovereign's long reign through felicitous imagery and praying for the long life of his subjects.[79] In keeping with the Kana Preface's description of Blessings, and perfectly replicating the ordering of its prose, this section begins with poems blessing the sovereign, and follows with verse celebrating the birthdays of his subjects. As we shall see, Blessings is composed of poems that either address the sovereign or are by nobility who address one another.

In keeping with his overall approach, Arai proceeds to treat Blessings as a series of poetic pairs. The anthology's organization of this scroll, however, does not permit a neatly symmetrical reading. The final poem, for example, stands alone from the rest in commemorating the birth of an individual. If there is a consistent manner in which to read the relationships between the poems in this section, it is through the relationships obtained between the recipients and celebrants of these blessings, all of whom are identified in Tsurayuki's prefatory comments. Such relationships do not proceed solely through the logic of complementary pairings in which an isolated dyad is produced. Rather, both the poems and the people they circulate among gain definition in relationship to their immediate textual predecessors and to people farther back in the lineage. These complex, overlapping relationships are due in part to the prominent place accorded to women of the Fujiwara clan, who appear prominently throughout the Blessings sections in the multiple roles of daughter, mother, aunt, empress, and imperial handmaid.[80]

In a manner evoking the "old and new verse" of the anthology's title,

Blessings has older verse preceding poems of more recent historical times. The scroll opens with four anonymous verses (343–346) all praying for the ruler's long reign.[81] The formulaic language of these four opening poems, each of which repeats the words a "thousand years" (*chiyo*) and "lord" (*kimi*), echoes the incantatory phrases chanted during the annual New Year's Day Court Blessing rite. The eternally recurring nature of this annual ritual is reproduced within the anthology by marking these verses as anonymous, thus removing them from historical time.

From ageless declarations of harmony between sovereigns and subjects, Blessings turns to the relations among members of the latter group in the ensuing seventeen poems (347–363). This shift in social relationships is accompanied by a shift in time, as Blessings turns from an ahistorical cyclical temporality organized around the court's ritual calendar to a linear, historical one organized around individual subjects' decennial birthdays. Kōkō composes the first poem for the seventieth birthday of his loyal retainer Henjō in 885. The next poem, 348, appears to return the favor, composed as it was by Henjō for one of Kōkō's aunts on her eightieth birthday. The gendered dyad of male and female members from the imperial clan in this pair of poems is balanced by a Fujiwara equivalent in the ensuing couple. Poems 349 and 350 respectively celebrate the fortieth birthdays of Kōkō's chief minister Mototsune and of one of this Fujiwara patriarch's daughters.

The links between Mototsune and Kōkō created in these four poems include further parallels between their female halves. Both women's birthdays were hosted by nephews who were princes at the time, suggesting that these celebrations are intended to mark the women's kinship status as much as their age. Although historians usually focus on the Fujiwara mothers of crown princes in their accounts of the clan's preeminent place at court, Blessings reveals that aunts also played a key role in defining kinship and alliances within the imperial family and its aristocratic partners. Here they tie together the men of the quatrain. Since Kōkō and Mototsune were maternal cousins, it is possible that the aunt of Kōkō's whose birthday is celebrated in poem 348 was a female relative of both men.

Poem 351 then proceeds to form a pair with its predecessor, one in which both female recipients of birthday greetings are related in different ways to both Fujiwara and imperial lineages. Another son of Seiwa hosts a birthday celebration for another female relative of Mototsune. This time, host and recipient are son and mother, rather than nephew and aunt, and the woman in question (Takaiko) is a younger sister of Mototsune rather than his daughter. As though to emphasize that the woman addressed in poem 351 is older than the female relative of Mototsune addressed in poem 350, the birthday celebration which the second poem marks shifts from the fortieth year of the recipient's life to her fiftieth year. This suggestion of a narrative development between the two poems reinforces the impression that Mototsune's household is the organizing locus at this juncture in Blessings. Through the female recipients' ties to Mototsune, poem 351 also forms a unit with the preceding two verses, thereby creating a household of women and their patriarchal head at the same time as the birthday celebrations in question mark the relationship of these women to the imperial clan.

Fujiwara females are supplanted by royal princes with the introduction of three verses (poems 352–354) written for the seventieth birthday of Kōkō's half-brother Motoyasu (d. 901). At the same time, continuity between the two groups is preserved through ritual rather than chronological time, insofar as the fortieth and fiftieth birthdays of Mototsune's daughter and sister are succeeded by the seventieth birthday of this prince. In eschewing the chronological time-frame of dynastic succession in favor of a biographical one oriented around the stages of aging in an individual's life, Blessings also creates linkages between its historical figures that are not exclusively concerned with the relations between subject and sovereign. This shift from the dynasty to the individual perhaps replicates the distinction between dynastic chronicles (*benji*) and biographies (*liezhuan*) deployed in continental historiography. In this case, the relationship takes the form of political alliance between powerful males. Since Motoyasu appears to have often acted as an intermediary between Kōkō and Mototsune, his placement here preserves these two men as the twin poles defining Blessings.[82]

The suggestion of an alliance between senior male members of the Fujiwara and imperial households is amplified and reinforced in the succeeding pair of poems (355 and 356) whose recipients are low-ranking male officials loosely affiliated with these entities. Nothing is known about the first of these men, Fujiwara no Miyoshi. Yoshimine no Tsunenari (d. 897) is given a brief obituary in the *Sandai jitsuroku* which mentions his tenure as governor of Tanba province.[83] As low-ranking officials, these men are peripheral figures within their respective clans.[84] Appropriately enough, they appear at the tail end of a textual lineage that has privileged patriarchal heads of households and their female relatives up until this point.

The next series of seven poems (357–363) concludes the list of birthday celebrations with the year in which the anthology was first officially presented to the reigning sovereign. According to the preface preceding this group, all seven poems were composed for a screen painting offered to Daigo's maternal uncle Sadakuni on his fortieth birthday in 905. The introduction of this sequence into the Blessings section marks a significant break in the scroll's structure. Nowhere else are so many poems reserved for one figure, and their arrangement into a seasonal series beginning in spring and ending in winter creates a miniature, self-contained temporal cycle within the scroll's larger progression. This and other peculiarities such as the inconsistencies in the manner that authors of Sadakuni's birthday poems are named in different versions of the anthology, have led some scholars to posit that the group was added after the anthology's initial presentation.[85]

The nature of Sadakuni's relationship to both the imperial and Fujiwara clans, however, suggests his presence in the section is integral to the scroll's overall structure and political message. Three years before the *Kokinshū* was offered up to Daigo, Sadakuni had appeared at Tokihira's wisteria banquet as an intermediary between the sovereign and the other participants, overseeing the circulation of topics and poems between the two. The prominence accorded Sadakuni both at that event and within Blessings can be attributed to his position as a maternal uncle to the reigning sovereign. Tokihira himself had previously been thwarted from establishing such a tie, which would have placed him in a position of prominence analogous to that of his own father Mototsune. By bringing Sadakuni into both the sequence of the Blessings section, and the wisteria banquet that preceded it, past continuities in avuncular ties between the Fujiwara and imperial clans are cited to legitimate Tokihira's own status as uncle to the crown prince in the "present" moment of Daigo's reign.

After the current relationship between a sovereign and his maternal Fujiwara uncle has been commemorated, the Blessings section ends by foretelling this pairing's future incarnation in Tokihira's relationship to the new crown prince. The poem in question is by the female official Fujiwara no Yoruka, composed to commemorate the birth of Prince Yasuakira in 903. This woman, who as *naishi no suke* was second in command to the Imperial Handmaid, is marked as both a high court official and a Fujiwara clan member, thereby binding aristocratic house to monarchical state in a poem that likewise brings together both the royal emblem of the sun and the Fujiwara clan shrine at Kasuga:

From the lofty peak	*mine takaki*
of Mount Kasuga	*Kasuga no yama ni*
the rising sun,	*izuru hi wa*
forever unclouded,	*kumoru toki naku*
shall shine forth.	*terasu beranari*[86]

Coming as it does at the end of Blessings, this poem creates a point in time around which all the scroll's other social relationships and temporal schemes retroactively take shape. The recipient of prayers has gone from the sovereign in the opening quartet of anonymous verses, to his subjects in the body of the scroll, and then finally to a person whose status as crown prince makes him both subject and future sovereign. As is typical of many scrolls in the anthology, this ending to Blessings suggests a cyclical development rather than a linear one.

This final poem in Blessings thus resonates with its predecessors in a series of backward-looping movements. Its mention of the Fujiwara clan shrine at Kasuga echoes the opening poem of Sadakuni's birthday celebration, linking all eight poems together in a move from present relationships between the Fujiwara Northern House and Daigo to future ones made possible by the birth of a new crown prince. Going even farther back through Blessings, this last poem's evocation of Mount Kasuga resonates with the opening poem's prayers for a reign in which a stone become a rocky crag:

Our lord shall reign	*waga kimi wa*
for thousands and thousands of years,	*chiyo ni yachiyo ni*
for as long as it takes a small pebble	*sazare ishi no*
to become a giant crag,	*iwao to narite*
covered in a carpet of moss.	*koke no musu made*[87]

By the time we have reached the end of Blessings, the pebble of the first poem has become Kasuga's mountain. In this manner the opening verse foretells and foreshadows the last one. The overall effect is to enfold the historical moment encapsulated in the final poem within the cycle of ritual time with which Blessings opened. Prince Yasuakira's birth promises a new round of songs by his subjects hailing him at future New Year's Day assemblies before their sovereign.

In sum, the Blessings section appears to commemorate and comment on events that had taken place only a few short years before the anthology was first presented to Daigo. The desire to naturalize a new linkage between the Northern House and the imperial clan informs not only the motives behind the establishment of Blessings as a topical category within the *Kokinshū* but also the remarkably detailed manner of that scroll's organization. Neither of the two succeeding imperial anthologies of *uta* appear to present such a carefully structured ordering of kinship and clan in their own equivalent sections. Perhaps this happened because the sense of urgency underlying Tokihira's political agenda would lessen as the Fujiwara family's grip on the succession to the throne became more assured.

The forms of time used to create lineage in the Blessings section of the anthology are as unprecedented as its textual organization. The court history *Sandai jitsuroku* that Tokihira oversaw during this same period followed continental conventions for representing chronological time in which continuity between sovereigns provided the underlying narrative thread. Early Heian clan genealogies such as the *Kogo shūi* (*Gleanings from Ancient Stories*, 807) were likewise organized as linear chronologies that linked their histories with that of the imperial clan. By contrast, Blessings substituted a ritual form of time that cross-cut such linear forms of narrative, allowing relationships between members of the court to be defined through their kinship ties with one another as aunts and nephews, fathers and daughters, brothers and sisters, and male cousins. *Uta* written in *kana* allowed such relationships to take shape within the *Kokinshū* in part because they drew on an earlier poetic tradition in which kinship and political alliances were codified through the exchange of verse. With Uda's poetry matches, *kana* poems had become the tokens through which lineage and affiliation within the imperial family could be negotiated and formalized. In Blessings, the Northern House of the Fujiwara can be seen as claiming to define the line of succession to the throne in the same ways, and with the same authority.

Travel to and from the Capital

If lineage defined Tokihira's newly established regime within the confines of the court, travel to the provinces defined its relation to the rest of the realm. As with Blessings, the decision to create and highlight the new poetic category of Travel can be seen as a product of policies being promulgated by Tokihira's regime at the time. During the early 900s, Tokihira issued a host of edicts designed to increase the court's income from public lands. Insofar as governors and other officials from the capital provided conduits through which this wealth would flow to the center, they were a key group to acknowledge at court and recognize in poetic form.

Like Blessings, the Travel section of the *Kokinshū* defines the court's members in relation to the ruling sovereign residing within the palace. The composers of Travel poems are always outside the capital, as their accompanying prose prefaces take pains to note. Place-names in these poems and prefaces map out the spatial coordinates of Daigo's realm through the geomantic categories of land and water and the administrative ones of province and realm. Many mark points at which representatives of the central state oversaw maritime and land traffic at harbors, rivers, and mountain barriers. Regardless of where they are located, however, Travel poems keep the capital as their Pole Star. Movement is defined as either going away from it or back to it.

At once the smallest and most tightly organized of the anthology's categories, Travel presents a carefully composed structure that in turn helps define the particular mode of court masculinity that was suggested in its companion categories of Partings and Miscellaneous Verse. All four scrolls are dominated by banquet poems composed by or for male officials. Travel could have been subsumed under the more-established category of Partings. Instead the editors devote the majority of this scroll to men from their own clans and social classes, perhaps as a way of balancing the Fujiwara and imperial clans that predominate in Blessings.

The only female author in Travel is the daughter of an assistant provincial governor (and thus an adjunct to the male-oriented system of provincial postings). Every other poet in this section is a male official who is either exiled or serving his sovereign away from the court. In the same manner as a relatively unambiguous line from a quatrain can lend definition to the other three in the poem, Travel gives focus and definition to the image of the court official in this quartet of scrolls, defining him as a man locked out of both the highest posts at court and marital relations to the sovereign under the Fujiwara regency. Perhaps for all of these reasons, this scroll provided the template for Tsurayuki's later account of a governor's return to the capital in his *Tosa Diary* (*Tosa nikki*, ca. 935).

As the smallest category within the *Kokinshū*, Travel has spawned a host of structural studies by modern scholars. One divides them into sea journeys, trips by land, and trips within the immediate vicinity of the capital.[88] Each of these sections can be seen as containing an internal structure in which poets are situated in increasing proximity to their sovereign. In a characteristically detailed analysis of Travel, Matsuda Shigeo divides the scroll into journeys from the capital (406–411), journeys to the capital (412–413), journeys to provincial postings (414–416), and royal processions (417–421).[89] Arai Eizō notices that four poems evoking the capital district begin and close Travel, making a cyclical movement to and from the sovereign.[90] A more recent study has sought to read this section in relation to earlier poetic and ritual traditions, noting that prayers for a safe journey begin and end Travel.[91]

Travel's concern with elaborating spatial rather than temporal structures is reflected in the emphasis it places on organizing poems into pairs rather than overlapping sequences. In addition to being the smallest section in the anthology, Travel is also the most symmetrical. Its sixteen poems are divisible into groups of two, four, and eight in the manner of continental verse, thereby evoking the couplets, quatrains, and eight-line regulated-verse forms that can be found in continental poetry. In fact, poems in this section are often tightly bound together into pairs, and pairs of poems in turn often complement and contrast with other pairs, a feature reminiscent of the poetics of the literary Chinese quatrain.[92] Such arrangements exert a centrifugal pull away from extended narrative sequences in favor of static binary relations, a fitting arrangement for a section of the anthology concerned with defining fixed spatial relations between court and country as the grid organizing officials' movements.

In a manner characteristic of the opening poems in other categories such as the Seasons and Blessings, the boundaries of the first Travel poem encompass the verses that follow. In this case, the opening poem is composed by an envoy to the Tang empirum, Abe no Nakamaro (698–770), who views the Yamato realm from afar.

Heaven's high plains	*ama no hara*
I gaze across to see:	*furisake mireba*
In Kasuga,	*Kasuga naru*
over Mount Mikasa,	*Mikasa no yama ni*
this same moon rose over me!	*ideshi tsuki kamo*[93]

Both time and space are collapsed in this powerfully condensed verse. The poem sweeps backward from the present moment to a remembered past. At the same time, Nakamaro's vision of the moon retraces the spatial trajectory of that journey as it sweeps through the skies back to the moment when he set out from that same spot. Here, the outermost boundary radiating from the imperial center is defined as the adjoining continental empire of the Tang. The succeeding poem, in which a member of Saga's court is exiled to the island of Sanuki for refusing the mission that Nakamaro accepted, suggests the punishments awaiting officials who do not obey their sovereign. All other poets in subsequent Travel poems are defined either as loyal officials or ones in exile, the twin positions that classically defined a Confucian official in relation to his ruler.

From the boundaries of the realm, Travel moves in toward the border of the capital region in a pair of anonymous poems whose placenames also mark the boundaries between provinces. The locales evoked in this pair limn the contours of the five Home Provinces (Kinai) surrounding the capital. The Izumi River of poem 408 marks the boundary between the provinces of Yamato and Yamashiro, and the Akashi Bay of poem 409 overlooks the western maritime edge of the Kinai region in the province of Settsu. Both poems evoke waterborne traffic, first by river and then by sea. They thus form a quatrain with the preceding two poems, which also concern waterborne travel. As a couplet, poems 408 and 409 also mark out the geographical boundaries of power and prestige for the capital's inhabitants, who vastly preferred postings to the Home Provinces over spending time in more rebellious and distant regions.

The less attractive alternative to postings in the Home Provinces is presented in the next pair of verses. Poems 410 and 411, which provide the kernel for the well-known "Journey to the Eastlands" (*Azuma kudari*) episode in the *Tales of Ise*, move beyond the home territories into the rebellious and distant eastern frontier. Both form a couplet in which their composer Narihira travels ever further east as he invokes the capital, first at the province of Mikawa and then the Sumida River bordering the provinces of Musashino and Shimotsufusa. A pair of poems (412 and 413) recited on the road back to Heiankyō follows Narihira's wistful glance back at a woman in the capital in poem 411. Together, these four poems create a balanced movement of emotional energy, first outward from, and then back inward to the royal center.

At this point, Travel introduces a quartet of poems describing the movements of male officials away from the capital toward the provinces. Two poems (414 and 415) take us back out from the capital into the vaguely defined border territories of its northwestern boundary. The first poet journeys to the Northland (Koshi no kuni) and the second ventures into the Eastland (Azuma). The vast expanses of these distant regions are then contrasted with places closer to the center and more precisely demarcated. The authors of the following two poems (416 and 417) journey to specific provinces. The first travels to Kai, east of the capital, and the second poet to Tajima, to its west. The axial orientation of this pair echoes the symbolism of the enthronement ceremonies, at which two provinces represented the realm to the east and west of the capital. As a pair, these two poems thus evoke both the language of the administrative state and the rituals by which it asserted its authority over the realm.

Travel then moves from this quartet of poems concerned with provincial postings outside the capital region to a group of four poems composed on the subject of journeys by members of the imperial clan within the Kinai region. In both cases, the journey in question mimics royal processions. The first pair of verses (418 and 419) describes the hunting party of a prince in the Katano fields where Kammu once marked the ritual boundaries of his new capital. Narihira composes the first poem at the command of Prince Koretaka in accordance with the rituals of royal hunts. As if signalling the status of these poems as marginalized texts located outside the bounds of royal authority, however, the second poem is composed only after Koretaka himself is unable to do so. The prince's failure to harmonize in verse, coupled with the fact that Koretaka was passed over as crown prince, makes this sequence of poems a representation of exile from the court and its rituals of rulership.

The succeeding and final pair of poems (420 and 421) continues to evoke monarchical rites, this time by commemorating Uda's procession through the provinces of Yamato and Izumi in 898. This elaborate, twelve-day affair involved falconry, banquets, and numerous compositions of *uta* and *shi* at the tonsured sovereign's command. By placing this event in Travel, the newly retired sovereign is represented as simply another subject of the current sovereign outside the capital. These two poems close the scroll with an offering of prayers to local gods to ensure safety on a journey, thereby evoking Nakamaro's recollection of a similar set of ceremonies at its beginning. Through this process, Travel concludes with a temporal move from the past to recent times.[94] The result is to make the scroll's entire structure fit the anthology's eponymous blend of "old and new."

Through such careful pairings, Travel defines its poetic sphere as one in which courtiers move away from the sovereign while their loyal hearts look back to him in adoration. As Ebersole notes, the longings, fears, and anxieties that typify travel poetry also serve as testaments to the virtue of a ruler who can compel such personal sacrifices for the public good.[95] At the same time, the attention paid to outlining the symbolic and political geography of the realm distinguishes this scroll, especially from the preceding Partings section. In evoking both the temporal coordinates of lineage in Blessings and the spatial ones of the state in Travel, the anthology created poetic sequences that outlined the twin pillars of Daigo's court in its early years. Had any of the scrolls in the anthology been recited as a group at banquets hosted by Tokihira and his sovereign, it is easiest to imagine that these two would have been chosen, both for their comparative brevity and their intimate connections to the political agenda of the most powerful figure at the young ruler's court.

Ritualizing the Seasons

By dividing its two largest sections into the Seasons and Longing, the *Kokinshū* created complementary forms of time evoking respectively the twin realms of Heaven and humanity as they relate to the individual courtier. Both spheres are brought together in the Kana Preface, which describes the seasons in terms of human actions on natural objects: plucking sprigs of plum, listening to *hototogisu* birds, breaking off autumn-tinted branches, and viewing snow.[96] Insofar as the Seasons precede Longing, the former can be said to encompass the households in which love poems circulated and defined human relationships. In a similar manner, the Spring section of the anthology prefigures and contains all of seasonal time within itself. This structuring principle, in which the first element encompasses and prefigures all succeeding ones, appears to draw on continental concepts of imperial texts as entities possessing the same structures as the cosmos.[97]

One of the chief means by which heavenly and human cycles were harmonized was through the annual enactment of royal rituals. Consequently, calendrical time is integral to the anthology's inaugural sequence of poems and the ostensibly seasonal imagery that they portray. The temporal scheme of the Seasons, it is important to note, is not "natural" in a modern sense. The appearance of *uguisu* (warblers) at the very beginning of Spring in the anthology, for example, is unseasonably early, given that these birds usually showed up in the capital only in the Second Month.[98] As I hope to demonstrate in this section, a literal reading of the representation of the seasons in the *Kokinshū* is not always possible. Rather than simply represent natural cycles, the opening sequence of poems in Spring seeks to calibrate their phenomena with the calendrical regimen of state ritual.

Spring holds a prominent place in the *Kokinshū* not only as the opening category of the entire anthology but also as a celebrated season. As was noted in Chapter 1, spring was also a season closely connected to the Fujiwara clan beginning in Yoshifusa's time. During this period, cherry blossom banquets and other seasonal poetic rites had created an alternative form of cyclical ritual time in which the regent could play the role of sovereign, dispensing the realm's bounty to his officials. By contrast, Uda's poetry matches had favored summer and autumn, with their attendant imagery of *hototogisu* and maiden-flowers, as the setting in which his household assumed sovereignty. Both forms of cyclical time lay outside the official lunar calendar of the court. As we shall see, the *Kokinshū* appears to reunite them in order to reintegrate the household with the ritual structures of the state.

This political agenda is suggested in the anthology's inaugural verse, which famously addresses the discrepancies between a solar seasonal cycle and the lunar calendrical one of court ritual:

> Composed on a day when spring arrived within the old calendrical year. Ariwara no Motokata.

Within the year,	*toshi no uchi ni*
spring has come!	*haru wa kinikeri*
Shall we call the year	*hito tose o*
"last year,"	*kozo to ya iwamu*
or "this year"?	*kotoshi to ya iwamu*[99]

The single year of the third line suggests a span of time that is at once precise in its length as a single year and vague in specifying the points in time at which it begins and ends. There are two possible years presented here, depending on whether one counts back from the solar equinox or New Year's Day. With this first poem, the human actions of demarcating and defining time in poetic form are foregrounded. Calendars (*koyomi*) kept track of the days in an action that was literally referred to as "counting the days and months" (*tsuki hi o yomu*) in the *Man'yōshū*. Likewise, the *Kokinshū*'s opening verse is "composed" (*yomu*) in an attempt to "keep count" (*yomu*) of time. Our "reading" (another meaning of *yomu*) reenacts the poem's own backward action of counting the past year from the present point in time. Insofar as it brings together poetics and calendrics in this way, the first poem in the anthology inaugurates not only the temporal flow of Heaven but also a range of human responses to that flow in modes of counting, composition, and interpretation.

Just as the *Kokinshū*'s opening poem provides various points in time from which to count backward, the anthology provides multiple points from which to read preceding poems retroactively. The first opportunity to do so is provided here in the second Spring poem. The fact that this verse belongs to the chief editor of the anthology suggests the compilers' interest in reading poetry through such binary arrangements. Tsurayuki's poem provides a breathtaking tour of the entire seasonal cycle as it passes from summer in the first two lines through to winter in the third and spring in the fourth and fifth. Its compressed verbal flow thus contains the entire temporal span of the seasonal section of the *Kokinshū* that it helps to open:

Composed on the first day of spring. Ki no Tsurayuki.

Soaking sleeves,	*sode hichite*
I'd cupped these waters,	*musubishi mizu no*
since frozen over.	*kōreru o*
With spring's arrival today,	*haru tatsu kyō no*
winds must be melting them.	*kaze ya toku ramu*[100]

This poem is an example of what Suzuki Hideo has identified as the tendency for *Kokinshū* poetry to speculate about and produce relations between events and phenomena near at hand and those of other times and places.[101] In general, natural objects in this poetry do not exist in and of themselves but are rather contingent upon the perceptions of a subject or larger relations of cause and effect.[102] The poems of this anthology, like those of its continental counterparts, represents their human subjects at the moment when they suddenly realize or consider such relations, making them the pivot through which cosmological patterns of correspondence and natural correlative categories are manifested through the human act of creating parallelisms and juxtapositions in poetic structures.[103]

The focus on sensory phenomena in Tsurayuki's poem is often contrasted with the more abstract calendrical reckoning of Motokata's verse. According to the scholar Imai Yutaka, however, both poems also share a ritual element insofar as their imagery can be read as an evocation of the New Year's Day banquet that took place in the inner palace's most formal hall, the Shishinden.[104] We know from details preserved in the *Jōgan shiki* code that these rites were considered an indispensable part of the calendrical roster, so much so that they were held even on those occasions when the reigning sovereign didn't appear before the full court.

The banquet that constituted the penultimate moment in the New Year's Day festivities was preceded by the formal presentation of the new calendar to the sovereign in an observance known as the Presentation of the Royal Calendar (*goryaku no sō*). The opening poem, which is most typically treated as privileging the seasons over the lunar calendar, can thus also be read as describing a calendrical rite which, held as it was in the Eleventh Month, prefigured the arrival of a new year within the old one. Likewise, the image of melting ice in the second poem which, as many scholars have noted, is probably a reference to the description of spring's beginning in the *Record of Rites*, also evokes another major element in the New Year's Day series of rituals. During these observances, a tile shaped from ice was presented in a rite known as the Ice Divination (*hi no tameshi*), its relative thickness being taken as a portent of good fortune.

The ritual narrative that Imai identifies in fact does not end with these two poems. After the first two rites mentioned above, a banquet was held. When the first round of wine had been drunk, Yoshino no Kuzu performers representing the subject peoples of the realm serenaded the banqueters with flute music.[105] Reproducing this order of events, the ice of Tsurayuki's poem is followed by an anonymous song evoking Yoshino's mountains:

Spring haze,	*harugasumi*
where has it risen?	*tateru ya izuko*
On the hills of Yoshino,	*Miyoshino no*
sacred Yoshino,	*Yoshino no yama ni*
snow goes on falling.	*yuki wa furitsutsu*[106]

This anonymous poem (itself perhaps performed at a banquet) replaces temporal order with a spatial one in which Yoshino represents a cold distant land far from the "spring sun" of the court. The name also suggests the ritual topography of the New Year's Day performance by the Yoshino no Kuzu, who sang outside the main gate of the courtyard before the Shishinden ceremonial hall. Their distance from the center of the rite also reproduces the symbolic geography of the Yamato court which, borrowing the continental idiom of empire, was centered around the sovereign and bordered by distinct ethnicities.

The Yoshino poem in Spring pivots between the New Year's Day banquet alluded to in the preceding two poems and the next *sechien* banquet on the seventh day of the new year, an event which is evoked in the two poems that follow. Known as the *aouma no sechie* (White Horse Banquet), this rite marked the official announcement of promotions and appointments for the new year. After the Yoshino no Kuzu had finished performing at the banquet concluding this ceremony, women performers from the Naikyōbō office danced in the courtyard before the Shishinden Hall on a stage demarcated by plum trees festooned with cotton cut in the shape of blossoms. The dancers themselves wore headdresses resembling bush warblers as they moved to a *gagaku* musical piece titled "Springtime Bush Warblers Trilling" (*Shun'ōten*). Spring preserves this ritual order as Yoshino's mountains in the *Kokinshū* give way to the image of warblers crying out from plum trees still covered in snow in the next two poems.

A poem by Her Majesty, the Second Avenue Empress:

Amid the snow	*yuki no uchi ni*
spring has come!	*haru wa kinikeri*
The bush warbler's	*uguisu no*
frozen tears	*kōreru namida*
must now be melting.	*ima ya toku ramu*

Topic unknown. Composer unknown.

On plum branches	*ume ga e ni*
warblers come to perch,	*kiiru uguisu*
on spring's verge,	*haru kakete*
they cry, while still	*nakedomo imada*
snow continues to fall.	*yuki wa furitsutsu*[107]

These two poems on snow, plum, and warblers evoke the tableau of a Fujiwara empress gazing out onto the women dancers at the White Horse Banquet, while a female performer sings for her. As with many anonymous verses in the *Kokinshū*, the second of these two poems describing bush warblers and plum is a *saibara* banquet song whose repetitive phrasing and refrains have been eliminated in order to make thirty-one syllables.[108]

In the next spring poem, a male official petitioning the Fujiwara empress for an appointment replaces the female singer who addressed her. His poem praises the "spring sun" of Yoshifusa's sister Takaiko while simultaneously carrying a plea for her future consideration in a lament for his old age:

> Composed at Her Majesty's command after a summons to appear before her on the third day of the new year when Her Majesty was still Chief Consort to the Crown Prince. By Fun'ya no Yasuhide.

Though I am	*haru no hi no*
bathed in the soft light	*hikari ni ataru*
of spring's sun,	*ware naredo*
my head, to my woe,	*kashira no yuki to*
has turned white as snow!	*naru zo wabishiki*[109]

This is one of the few *Kokinshū* poems with a preface that mentions the calendrical date of an annual court observance. On the third day of the new year, the reigning sovereign paid his respects to his mother and father. Because the Second Avenue Consort's son Yōzei was not yet the ruler, however, this poem both represents a seasonal moment and anticipates a later calendrical one, as Arai Eizō has noted.[110] Like the final poem in Blessings, Fun'ya no Yasuhide's verse cites the timeless protocol of ritual, while it also prefigures the anthology's political present (in which both mother and son were still alive) in its poetic past.

This union of seasonal and calendrical time in Spring transforms *uta* from something originally located "in the intervals between the rites of government" (*matsurigoto no itoma*), as the prefaces to the *Kokinshū* and the *Shinsen man'yōshū* put it, into something that re-creates the annual roster of court observances. By arranging its opening sequence of poems in a ritual narrative, the *Kokinshū* initiates Spring (and all time in the anthology) through a poetic harmonization of Heaven's solar temporality with the lunar one of court observances. Through such harmonies, the anthology's arrangements of poems perform one of the central functions of ritual governance. The organization of poems in this section thus does more than simply call into question the relations between seasonal and calendrical time, as Richard Okada has contended.[111] Rather, it can be seen as attempting to actively integrate and harmonize the two after presenting their disjuncture in the opening poem. Even this apparent disjuncture, when read in light of the *goryaku no sō* rite, appears to follow closely the order of annual observances.

A similar attempt at harmonizing the solar and calendrical cycles can be seen at work in the overall structure of the seasons in the anthology. Although seasonal topics in poetry matches had already been associated with particular months in the calendrical year prior to the *Kokinshū*, none had been associated with a particular annual observance.[112] Significantly, calendrical language is used toward the end of each season in the anthology. Spring draws to a close in the final portion of the Third Month (*Yayoi no tsugomori*), Summer in that of the Sixth Month (*Minatsuki no tsugomori*), Autumn in the final day of the Ninth Month (*Nagatsuki no tsugomori no hi*), and Winter on the last day of the calendrical year (*toshi no hate*). At the same time, both Spring and Autumn open with poems whose prefaces mark the first day of a season rather than the beginning of a calendrical month.[113] Since Spring and Autumn comprised a year in literary Chinese, the shared structure of these two sections of the *Kokinshū* can be read as representing an overarching notion of time that is both calendrical and seasonal.

The importance attributed to spring in the anthology suggests its significance as the penultimate Fujiwara season, an association dating back to Yoshifusa's cherry blossom banquets. This is perhaps one reason why the cherry blossom replaces the plum as the premier symbol of springtime in the *Kokinshū*, with nearly the entire second scroll of Spring being devoted to their blossoms. This focus on one particular natural object in itself can be seen as a comment on the historical context in which the *Kokinshū* was compiled. Whereas Autumn could draw on a variety of poems and poetic topics from Uda's poetry matches,

Spring had fewer recent poetic precedents. The editors thus probably had to create new poems for this section of the anthology as a way of balancing the retired sovereign's poetic legacy with a new one celebrating the role of the Fujiwara at court.

Such editorial concerns were informed by a political context in which both Fujiwara and imperial patriarchs were competing for legal rights to the land's wealth. At the same time as Tokihira launched attempts to expand state income in the form of public land, Uda was seeking to establish his own network of estates. In such a context, the assertion that the Fujiwara season of springtime is most closely aligned with court ritual could suggest a claim that their court, not Uda's, embodied the virtuous rule of a sovereign whose ritual actions were the ultimate guarantor of material bounty. The imagery of the opening Spring sequence thus can be seen as rhetorically structuring both seasons and landscapes in the *Kokinshū* as manifestations of royal virtue, which legitimated the state's claims to economic and ritual power.

Seasonal time in the *Kokinshū* is, in this sense, as much a matter of politics and wealth as of natural phenomena. One especially striking example of this link can be seen in the frequency with which textiles—the stuff of taxation, stipends, and marital alliances—are often interwoven into the anthology's depiction of landscapes. Descriptions of autumn maple leaves as brocade, springtime willow branches as threads, and waterfalls as white cloth abound in *Kokinshū* representations of seasonal tableaux. Many of these textile figures are peculiar to the poetry of the period. The association of Tatsuta with brocade and maple leaves, for example, is not exclusive or fixed in the *Man'yōshū* anthology in the same manner that it is in the *Kokinshū*.[114] These links are often forged through a form of poetic double vision known as *mitate* that posited a visual similarity between brocades and autumn foliage (brocade patterns in fact often depicted the latter).

The act of seeing was itself invested with this historical sense of newfound discovery, as poets begin to favor the more active *miru* (I see it as) in place of the intransitive *miyu* (it looks like) that would predominate among *mitate* in the middle ages when these same visual metaphors had become commonplace.[115] One factor enabling the discovery of these new *mitate* was the ability to see a word written in *kana* as something that "looked like" another word. Thus, the place-name Tatsuta could function as a pivot-word containing the verb *tatsu* (to cut cloth), and through this association, suggest brocade. Such rhetorical moves literally convert the heavenly cycles of seasonal landscapes into human wealth. Their ability to transform one into the other no doubt contributed to the popularity of pivot-words in court poetry of the period.

As we saw in the previous chapter, seasonal poetry as a category first appeared in the poetry matches of Uda's court, where it became a symbolic means for asserting his household as an alternative source of power, wealth, and legitimacy at court. Both the *Kokinshū*'s seasonal poetry and the arrangements it produces between individual poems attempt to resituate the natural cycles outside of the household and in the palace under the aegis of its calendar. In choosing to represent Spring's opening through the syntax of the new year's ritual roster of banquets, the *Kokinshū* editors situated Heaven's bounty within the regime of observances through which the reigning sovereign and his state, rather than an aristocrat or retired sovereign, presided over the dispensation of the realm's bounty.

Longing for the Court

If the Seasons section works to harmonize the relations of the state to Heaven, Longing coordinates the state subject's relationship to "this world of ours" (*yo no naka*) consisting of the social relations between men and women overseen by their sovereign. An intimate relation between Heaven's seasons and human sociality is suggested in the Kana Preface, where Longing is described in the seasonal language of autumn and summer, in reference perhaps to the favored topics of Uda's poetry matches, or perhaps to the earlier household rites the former drew on. With its summertime setting and archaic language, the opening poem of this section can also be seen as alluding to such observances:

Cuckoos	*hototogisu*
cry in the Fifth Month,	*naku ya satsuki no*
sweet-flag's season,	*ayamegusa*
when longings stir within,	*ayame mo shiranu*
blind to all reason!	*koi mo suru kana*[116]

Anonymous poems such as this one are often arranged into lengthy sequences within Longing. The opening poem is a representative example of such verses' rhetorical characteristics. One of their distinguishing features is a tendency to open with a description of a landscape, and follow it with an expression of human sentiment. Frequently, such poems end with a conventional expression such as the above poem's *koi mo suru kana* (longings stir within), which can also be seen in many *Man'yōshū* poems.[117] Equally archaic is the repetition of the syllables *a ya me* in two separate lines as a way of demarcating the realms of Heaven (in the form of sweet-flag flowers) and humanity (in the form of customary practice or passion-restraining reason).

Another way in which Longing's opening poem evokes household rites is in its suggestion of sexual taboos. Disruptive desires need to be ordered, and this poem does so by verbally harmonizing Heaven and humanity through the repetition and transformation of the aforementioned syllables *a ya me*. Longing is represented as an emotion that threatens the "social order" (*ayame*) defining the proper relationships between men and women in the same manner that a textile pattern (another meaning of the same word) creates formal regularities in a robe.[118] This *ayame* in the fourth line is prefaced by the "sweet-flag" (*ayamegusa*) in the third line, a type of iris that featured prominently in observances held on the Double Fifth. As with the Seasons, Longing here is linked to the calendrical rituals of the court while simultaneously evoking an alternate way of organizing time.

One oft-noted way in which this section of the *Kokinshū* controls and orders emotions is to assign an inevitable progression to their development. The poems in Longing are arranged across five scrolls in a narrative that moves from the first stirring of interest in a distant figure to abandonment and estrangement.[119] Poems in Longing thus always concern the courtier's relationship to an absent object of desire, one that inevitably disappears out of sight but not out of mind. The editors appear to have taken great care in constructing this narrative sequence. Many of their own poems appear here as "topic unknown," as though the circumstances of their composition are related to the anthology and to no other context. Probably these poems by the editors were composed to fill in the section and ensure appropriate transitions between poems within Longing's overarching narrative. This narrative provided a far more detailed and ambitious depiction of human desire than previous attempts at Uda's court, so much so that it dominated the language of court poetry and prose for centuries afterward.

Many scholars have argued that there is a gender shift within this narrative from a predominantly male poetic persona in the initial stages to that of an abandoned woman in the final ones.[120] Without this overarching structure, however, there is no way of determining gender in many individual poems. Suzuki Hideo has argued that the disembodied nature of much of Heian poetry, combined with its eschewal of gendered pronouns, enabled poetic expressions of longing to encompass a variety of relationships involving both genders and all social classes.[121] Poems by male officials at banquets seeing one another off to a provincial posting, for example, often contain language that is indistinguishable from poems of parting between lovers. The same was true for verse by the female entertainers who danced and sang for the men at such banquets, as can be seen in the following poem from Partings:

> Composed by Shirome at a party in Yamazaki port bidding farewell to Minamoto no Sane, who was heading out to take the waters at the hot springs in Tsukushi.

If things in life	*inochi dani*
were as our hearts	*kokoro ni kanau*
might desire them to be,	*mono naraba*
how could sorrow ever come	*nani ka wakare no*
at parting company?	*kanashikaramashi*[122]

Shirome is the one identifiable female "entertainer" (*asobi*) in the entire anthology. These women were located at ports such as Yamazaki on the Yodo River, where they entertained men traveling to and from distant provinces. Many are mentioned in the *Man'yōshū*, suggesting that they were a distinct profession whose skills at composing verse in exchanges with men in large group settings could be as sought after as their sexual availability.[123]

The fact that no female entertainers appear in Longing suggests that the world of this section of the *Kokinshū* is specifically that of the capital, not its outlying ports and harbors. Put another way, Longing represents the world of the court and the families of its officials rather than emotions shared by humanity at large. In fact, the majority of authored poems in this section are by the anthology's editors, or men from their social background who occupied low-ranking posts in the government.

Men from the uppermost echelons of court society are also mentioned, such as Mototsune's brother Fujiwara no Kunitsune (827–908), Tokihira's younger brother Fujiwara no Nakahira (875–945), Minister of the Right Minamoto no Yoshiari (845–897), and princes such as Montoku's son Kagenori. Many of the women in the anthology are anonymous correspondents with these noblemen, but a few are named. These include high-ranking palace officials such as the Assistant Imperial Handmaid Fujiwara no Yoruka, and a host of otherwise unknown female attendants such as Hyōe and Inaba, who were named for the posts held by their fathers, in keeping with the patriarchal means for identifying women of the middle echelons that had gained currency at Uda's court.

All of the poets in Longing are thus "subjects" (*hito*) of the "sovereign" (*kimi*), people whose status in society is defined by their position within the court hierarchy. Perhaps this is one reason why these two words appear as the favored terms of address in the poems of this section. In contrast to its *Man'yōshū* precursors, *Kokinshū* poems tended to eschew gendered pronouns, preferring such terms as *hito* (that one) or *kimi* (you my lord, my love) to *agaseko* (my boy) or *wagaimoko* (my girl). In Longing, the word *hito* usually refers either to the object of desire or a third party who constrains the relationship in the form of gossip or familial intervention.

Some scholars have argued that *hito* is used for the indirect expression of resentment or criticism about the object of desire, as opposed to the more positive passionate nuances that could accompany *kimi*.[124] This would be in keeping with Longing's definition of desire as a doomed endeavor, but its diplomatically evasive tone is also ideally suited to poems that could be read by many people other than the intended addressee, including the sovereign himself. This was often the case with epistolary poems in particular, which could be read by people other than the parties concerned when they were subsequently anthologized. Many poems in Longing are taken from collections of such correspondence. The preface to poem 736 gives one example of how love letters could circulate once an affair had ended:

> After the Minister of the Right had stopped living with her, she gathered together all of his old letters and, thinking to return them to him, she composed and sent this. Assistant Imperial Handmaid, the Lady Fujiwara no Yoruka:

I had come to rely on / *tanome koshi*
these word-leaves that now / *koto no ha ima wa*
I will return to you. / *kaeshitemu*
As my body grows aged, / *wagami furureba*
there is nowhere to place them. / *okidokoro nashi*[125]

That a high-ranking Fujiwara woman official at Daigo's court has a poem of this sort included in Longing suggests that many members of the court were eager to have their epistolary verse evaluated by their peers, despite the potential political dangers in revealing a failed love affair with an influential figure at court. By the same token, the anonymity of many poems in Longing might not suggest any impropriety on their writers' parts. Perhaps the female correspondents of lower-ranking men such as Tsurayuki are not named because they are of even lower rank than the daughters of provincial governors. As it happens, there is no equivalent anonymous term for men in the prefaces to these poems. Male courtiers in Longing are all identifiable by name and thus marked as members of public court society. It was rather in prose forms, such as the satirical and scandalous episodes of the *Tales of Ise*, that anonymous men first took center stage.

Even when the object of desire is mentioned and its gender implied in Longing poems, however, it often remains unclear whether this figure is being described or addressed by the poem's speaker. Heian poetic language, and *hito* in particular, did not make clear distinctions between second- and third-person forms of address.[126] Heian *uta* were particularly amenable to this blurring because they omitted the honorific verb forms found in Heian prose and earlier verse forms such as the *chōka* used for royal panegyrics. Given that such forms of social deixis tend to be more prevalent than grammatical person in marking speakers in Japanese, it could be said that their absence in court *uta* is even more radical than the lack of pronouns.[127]

Similar ambiguities of grammatical person and gender can be found in the continental court poetic tradition, especially the erotic verse of the Six Dynasties courts, whose language and rhetoric provided a template for its Heian counterpart. In his analysis of erotic "palace verse" by Liang dynasty court poets which describe female entertainers and palace concubines, Paul Rouzer argues that these confusions of gender and person enabled a conflation of the male poet's desires for court women and his desires to be like them—as skilled practitioners of arts and talents such as song, dance, and poetry which could be used to gain the attention of the ruler, and thus his favors.[128] Desire and anxiety inevitably accompanied struggles to gain favor at court, concerns that were shared by men and women who competed with one another (and with the salons of different patrons) to gain material and political security.

This tradition of writing poetry in the voice of an abandoned court lady was already well established by the time the *Kokinshū* was being compiled. Similar poems on topics such as "boudoir laments," in which such a woman pines away for the emperor, appeared frequently at Saga's court, often as a group exercise in composition by men and women of his entourage who harmonized with topics provided by their sovereign. The personae used, such as that of the legendary Han dynasty imperial consort Lady Ban, shared much with these men and women, who were equally dependent on their ruler's favors. In fact, it is male poets from the mid ninth century such as Narihira and Henjō who appear to have been the first to extensively use this trope in *uta*.[129] In a similar manner, both men and women in the Longing section of the *Kokinshū* deploy the figure and voice of the waiting woman as a persona distinct from that of the author.[130] One example of this shared language can be seen in the following two poems in Longing, one by Ono no Komachi (fl. 833–858), and the other by Uda's favorite male companion Fujiwara no Toshiyuki:

Perhaps it must be so	*utsutsu ni wa*
in the waking world.	*sa mo koso arame*
But what misery it is to see	*yume ni sae*
people's eyes shunned	*hito me o yoku to*
even in dreams!	*miru ga wabishisa*[131]

To Suminoe's shores,	*Suminoe no*
waves draw nigh.	*kishi ni yoru nami*
As night comes,	*yoru sae ya*
are you shunning people's eyes	*yume no kayōiji*
on the path of dreams?	*hito me yoku ramu*[132]

It is impossible to determine definitively whether the speaker in either poem is male or female. The road of dreams that both verses mention could be traveled by either men or women, regardless of the distinctions in gendered mobility that obtained in the "waking world." Nor is there any obvious or necessary relationship between author and gender in either case. Both poems can be read as evocations of the continental trope of the court lady waiting for the favors of a superior with anxious helplessness. At the same time, however, this waiting figure could just as easily be a male official who must negotiate the jealousy and gossip of others in his quest for the ruler's love and favor.

The conflation of both positions was a standard trope in *shi* poetry, and, if we assume that the *Kokinshū*'s "public" nature derives in part from its appeal to continental political norms, then such a conflation is just as likely to be operative here. In other words, the gender of both poet and poetic personae are immaterial insofar as both were equally dependant on the uncertain favors of the same royal male patron. In this sense, the sovereign becomes the ultimate object of desire to which Longing poems in the *Kokinshū* are directed, regardless of the original context in which they were composed. By organizing desire in this manner, the Longing section affirms thereby the courtly orientation of the world that it creates.

The social conditions that spawned this conflation of court lady and male official are as applicable to the *Kokinshū* as they are to the Six Dynasties palace *shi* where this trope flourished. If anything, the political situation at the Heian court in the early tenth century was closer to that of the Liang dynasty (502–557) than it was to that of any earlier Yamato sovereign. As was mentioned in the previous chapter, Uda's decision to take the tonsure was likely to have been in conscious emulation of the Liang emperor Wu, who sought thereby to ensure his place at a multipolar court in which various princes and their salons made competing claims to the same symbolic and material resources. Such competition was arguably most intense in the realm of *uta*, where female attendants could compete with their male peers, such as the editors of the *Kokinshū*, for the patronage and attention of sovereigns, regents, retired sovereigns, and royal consorts.

Despite the potentially open-ended nature of the above verse by Komachi, later readers have tended to read her poems as autobiographical expressions of a specifically private and passionately feminine form of desire. Like Sappho in the West, Komachi is little more than a name attached to certain poems, to which stories and later traditions have been added over subsequent centuries. As one recent study of these traditions has noted, modern scholarship has been primarily concerned with reconstructing her life from poems and commentaries rather than historicizing the social and political conditions in which such narratives arose.[133] Tsurayuki appears to have been especially concerned with portraying Komachi as an ailing palace lady, as can be seen in his Kana Preface to the anthology. A similar impulse to personalize her poetry can be seen as informing the manner in which Komachi's poems are frequently shaped into autobiographical narratives within Longing. Her prominent place in this scroll is rivaled only by that of her male counterpart Narihira. Two poems by her begin the second scroll of Longing, and two by him head the third and fifth scrolls of this same category.

We do know that the Komachi who appears in the *Kokinshū* was active in the mid ninth century, along with her compatriot Narihira. Many of her poems are exchanged with middle-ranking male officials from Montoku and Ninmyō's courts in contests that match her wit and erudition against theirs. The distinctive nature of her personal name suggests a literate female from a lower social background than is the norm for a poet in the *Kokinshū*. Most of the anthology's women poets had fathers who were court officials or high ministers, men who embraced literacy as the sign of their office. Unlike such women, however, Komachi's name does not refer to her father. The word *machi* (ward) is often used in women's names to refer to the area in the capital in which their fathers lived. One famous example is Montoku's consort Ki no Shizuko (d. 866), who was more commonly known as Sanjō no Machi in reference to the Third Avenue where her father Ki no Natora (d. 848) resided. Mezaki Tokue has suggested that the *machi* in Komachi's name, by contrast, could refer to a section of the palace, such as the Naikyōbō no Machi where the palace's female performers resided.[134] He notes that the diminutive *ko* (little) appears frequently in women's names listed in population registers from the period, including those of a sixteen-year-old girl, making it possible to render Komachi's name as something like "the girl from the palace performers' ward."

The unusual nature of Komachi's social position is also suggested in the Kana Preface, where she is placed after scions of the imperial clan such as Henjō and Narihira, but before low-ranking officials such as

Ōtomo no Kuronushi who composed a poem for Daigo's enthronement in 897. In the prefaces to her epistolary poems in the *Kokinshū*, Komachi is often represented as a foil for male officials whose education and intelligence she affirms through exchanges replete with canonical allusions and orthographic ambiguities. One of her most famous poems, which appears near the end of Longing, creates a line with two opposite meanings depending on the pronunciation that the reader provides:

A thing that changes	*iro mie(t/d)e*
color (un)seen	*utsurou mono wa*
can be found in our world,	*yo no naka no*
where lovers, in their hearts,	*hito no kokoro no*
harbor this flower!	*hana ni zo arikeru*[135]

This stunningly powerful poem, with its relentless contraction from exterior world to interior subject, culminates in the discovery of an inner fickleness that lies at the heart of polite society. It is not clear from the opening line of the poem, however, whether this false flower is visible or not. It is possible that *miede* (unseen) could just as well be *miete* (seen) due to the lack of diacritics that distinguished voiced from unvoiced consonants. The result is that the poem's pivot is visual in two senses, a fact that further suggests its textual nature. Komachi also takes the image of the heart as a flower, which connoted spiritual purity in Buddhist scripture, and wittily changes it into something that hides its truth. Her poem thus takes advantage of orthographic ambiguities to alternatively hide and suggest opposite meanings, while also making recondite allusions. Komachi, in this sense, is truly the equal of her literary male peers.

Despite the possibility of viewing them as literary exercises in adopting continental poetic personae in the manner of her male peers, Komachi's Longing poems are given an insistently autobiographical treatment by the *Kokinshū*'s compilers. One way this is achieved is by the arrangement of these poems into tripartite dream sequences, two of which can found in this section of the anthology. In the first of these sequences, the final poem's potential ambiguities of grammatical person and point of view are covered over and enfolded within the less-ambiguous poems that precede it. The two opening poems are enunciated from a first-person point of view, one through negative hypothesis, the other through the verbal auxiliary *ki* used to indicate recollection of a past event by the speaker.

Is it because I was thinking	*omoitsutsu*
of my love while I slept,	*nereba ya hito no*
that I glimpsed that one?	*mietsu ramu*
If I had known it was a dream	*yume to shiriseba*
I would not have opened my eyes.	*samezaramashi o*

Ever since I saw	*utatane ni*
the one I long for	*koishiki hito o*
while tossing and turning	*miteshi yori*
I began to place my trust	*yume chō mono wa*
in what we call "dreams."	*tanomi someteki*

When assailed	*ito semete*
by pangs of longing,	*koishiki toki wa*
in pitch-black	*muba tama no*
of night robes	*yoru no koromo o*
are turned inside out!	*kaeshite zo kiru* [136]

The middle poem in this triptych plays a pivotal role in binding all three together to create the impression of a "passionate poetess." This becomes clear when we consider the possibility that the first poem can be read on its own as the expression of a gender-less, disembodied form of desire.[137] Such a reading becomes difficult to sustain, however, when the poem is read as part of a coherent narrative organized around the author. By the time we have reached the final poem, desire has coalesced into physical form as Komachi turns her robe inside out and waits for a lover.

A similar attempt to affix the poetic voice to the author's gender can be seen in the second triptych of dream verses, whose final poem again uses the auxiliary verbal suffix *ki* as a first-person mode of recollection. The second poem of the sequence includes the verbal auxiliary *ji*, indicating negative personal speculation. Both verses anchor the opening one, which seems to assume a more distanced perspective when read on its own. The triptych begins with Komachi's poem on avoiding people's eyes that was cited earlier in this chapter. Read in sequence with the other two, it emplots a narrative of desire that grows increasingly disempowered. Frustration and anxiety intensify, as the object of desire becomes increasingly hidden from sight:

Perhaps it must be so in the waking world. But what misery it is to see people's eyes shunned even in dreams!	*utsutsu ni wa* *sa mo koso arame* *yume ni sae* *hitome o yoku to* *miru ga wabishisa*
Let the night come while I am still caught up in endless longing! At least on the path of dreams no one will reproach me.	*kagiri naki* *omoi no mama ni* *yoru mo komu* *yumeji o sae ni* *hito wa togameji*
Though I travel back and forth, never resting my feet on the path of dreams, I have never caught a glimpse of my lover in the waking world.	*yumeji ni wa* *ashi mo yasumezu* *kayoedomo* *utsutsu ni hitome* *mishi goto wa arazu*[138]

Komachi's dream sequences constitute one of the most striking features of her poems in Longing. In early texts such as the *Nihon shoki* and *fudoki*, dreams are chiefly oracular messages from the gods presaging future events. In *Man'yōshū* poetry, too, the appearance of a lover in one's dreams is treated as a sign of that person's concern for the one seeing them, and thus a harbinger of their eventual reunion. In Komachi's case, however, dreams provide a space in which neither lover nor beloved are assured of any future meeting. One scholar has argued that this shift represents the influence of Six Dynasties court poetry, in which a woman's dreams of her husband or lover serve to underscore the impossibility of their reunion.[139] The continental gloss provided by such conventions and their manifestation in this tripartite arrangement of poems has the effect of neutralizing agency and rendering desire into a passive form.

The potentially transgressive nature of Komachi's dream poems could have been one reason why the editors appear to have been so invested in domesticating their expressions of desire. A distinctive feature of her verses is the way in which they offer women the same visual mobility as men, thereby enabling a female desiring subject to inhabit a position usually reserved for the male voyeur in the waking world.[140] The above sequence by Komachi is remarkable for its insistent repetition of a gaze that first spies out someone who is hiding from others, but ends up seeing no one. In this sense, the editors' sequencing of Komachi's dream poems not only marks them as personal experiences of their female author, but also suppresses their potential for seeing and desiring in ways that transcended gendered distinctions. In sequence, Komachi's poems reinforce the image of a passive and helpless woman waiting for the visits of another.

The arrangement of these dream-triads represents in miniature the overarching narrative development of poems in Longing as they move inexorably toward the absence of the desired object. It also reveals a concerted attempt on the part of the editors to control the threat posed to the social order (*ayame*) mentioned in the opening Longing poem by reinscribing that desire within a textual "pattern" (*ayame*) in which individual expressions are yoked together into narratives that proclaim love's limits.

Desire is doomed not only to fail but also to have its written traces exposed before the eyes of the sovereign and his court. Personal desires and the webs of relationships that they produced in individual poems are all reproduced within the anthology as voices that defer to and acknowledge the sovereign as their overseer. Like *Man'yōshū* travel poetry, in which officials long for their wives, or *shi* poems in which men and women speak as languid palace beauties, the ultimate object of desire in the Longing section of the *Kokinshū* can be seen as the ruler, whose official demands sacrifice the desire for a lover to the desire for his favors.

The above reading of the *Kokinshū* is intended to suggest that the elaboration of purely formal principles of organization tell us only so much about the modes of representation at work in its text. It is perhaps impossible to exhaust the possibilities for reading political ideology in the anthology, although an attempt to do so might tell us much about its role in producing visions of the Heian court that were to define it for centuries afterward. One of the most striking features of the *Kokinshū* is that its vision of continental-style Confucian kingship circulated at a court that was increasingly unable to control the realm's material and political resources. The interrelated processes of provincial devolution, growth in the number of private estates, and increasing military disturbance that accompanied the Heian court throughout its later history were already noticeable at the beginning of the tenth century. Insofar as it provided a vision of royal authority that could exist apart from these historical forces, this anthology's imperial qualities went well beyond the initial order to compile it.

Chapter Four

Writing Yamato Verse in the Kana Preface

Placing the *Kokinshū's* Prefaces

The Kana Preface (*kana jo*) to the *Kokinshū* is the single most renowned account of Japanese poetics in the tradition. In outlining the genesis, history, rhetoric, and purpose of what it calls "Yamato verse" (*yamato uta*), it provided an account of *uta* whose scope surpassed that of the prefaces to Saga's *shi* anthologies and rivaled that of the canonical Great Preface (*Daxu*) to the *Classic of Poetry*. Equally noteworthy was its use of *kana* script to express its ambitious vision. Literary Chinese had been the preferred language in the prefaces to earlier anthologies of *uta*, such as the *Shinsen man'yōshū* and *Kudai waka*, as well as in other imperially sponsored texts such as the *Engi shiki* and the *Ryō no gige* commentaries on the legal code. In acknowledgment of these precedents, the *Kokinshū* also included a second preface in the court's official language, known as the Mana Preface (*mana jo*).

The relationship of the *Kokinshū*'s two prefaces to one another is a longstanding mystery. Both conclude with the name of the *Kokinshū*'s chief editor Ki no Tsurayuki, and both include dates from the same month in 905, although the Kana Preface does not end its account of the anthology with this date, and appears to refer to later events. Neither date mentioned in either preface necessarily refers to the time in which they were written. The general consensus is that the Kana Preface was presented around the time the order to compile the anthology was issued, whereas the Mana Preface was presented later when the final version had been completed. At least one scholar, however, has argued for the opposite.[1]

There are similar uncertainties about the relative status of the two texts at Daigo's court. Despite modern treatment of the Kana Preface as an authoritative account of poetics, it was largely ignored until the twelfth century. Instead, it was the Mana Preface which was treated as the official account by Heian authorities on poetry such as Fujiwara no Kintō (966–1041) and the priest Nōin (998–1050).[2] It was only beginning with the *Kokinshū jo chū* ("Commentary to the *Kokinshū* Prefaces"), authored by the scholar Fujiwara no Kenshō (ca. 1130–1210), that the two texts were discussed in relation to one another. As we shall see, the relative neglect experienced by the Kana Preface in this period can be explained in part by its unorthodox treatment of the stylistics of *uta*.

It is usually assumed that the Mana Preface was included in the official version of the anthology offered up for the sovereign's perusal (*sōranbon*). This practice was the norm for all texts written on imperial command. Official prefaces followed certain conventions and were typically written in elaborate parallel constructions of literary Chinese.[3] Curiously, however, the *Fukurozōshi* declares that Tsurayuki's version of the anthology intended for Daigo did not include either preface.[4] If anything, the language of the Kana Preface suggests that the work was not intended for official presentation at the time of its writing. No less an authority than the scholar Katagiri Yōichi has argued that the absence of the humilific verb *haberi* in the Kana Preface (in contrast to its frequent appearance in individual poem prefaces in the anthology) indicates that the text was not even addressed to Daigo.[5]

To date, then, textual criticism offers little prospect for tracing the point at which either preface was added to the *Kokinshū*. What does seem likely is that the Kana Preface can be placed at one remove from the Mana Preface, both in time, as a predecessor (or later supplement) to the latter, and in its status, as a text never intended for official presentation at court. Ironically, this secondary status has been radically reversed in the later textual history of the anthology. Whereas the Mana Preface is missing in many versions of the *Kokinshū*, including all three of Tsurayuki's versions mentioned in Kiyosuke's *Fukurozōshi*, the Kana Preface is appended to every extant manuscript.[6]

One clue as to how we might place the Kana Preface within its historical context is offered by another preface in *kana* written by Tsurayuki around the time that the *Kokinshū* was first being disseminated. The *Ōigawa gyōkō waka no jo* ("Preface to Poems for the Royal Procession to the Ōi River") was written on the occasion of official peregrinations made by Uda and Daigo to the capital region's northwestern river in 907. Overall, scholars have neglected this *kana* preface, despite its many striking similarities to its more famous counterpart. Both prefaces are accompanied by similar ones in literary Chinese, both rely on parallel constructions that use poetic epithets to adorn nouns, and both contain a similar structure in which the history informing the composition of a collection of poems is followed by an account of its topics and a plea addressed to the reader. As we shall see, the Ōi River preface and the practices surrounding it offer several insights into the Kana Preface. In particular, the practice of composing poetry on topics, the latent rivalry between Uda and Daigo, and the importance of writing as the medium through which the poet participates in and negotiates his relation to the royal sphere all find significant echoes in the Kana Preface. At some points, in the Kana Preface's description of Hitomaro as the ideal court poet, for example, the relationship to the Ōi River preface appears so strong that it suggests that the latter was written some time shortly after the former.

The procession to the Ōi River for which this preface was written followed the Double Ninth *sechien* banquet of 907. Uda was the first to journey there on the tenth, one day after the court's premier autumn observance. In addition to views of the scenery by the capital's northwest river, the ceremonial elements of this royal procession included compositions of both *shi* and *uta* harmonizing with nine topics describing the riverside scene. Daigo followed Uda's example the next day on the eleventh. Both events are likely to have had political overtones. Uda and his father Kōkō had previously held such royal processions as part of their program to reassert their visibility and authority. Shortly after his abdication in 898, for example, Uda had embarked on a grand tour of the provinces south of the capital in an event whose scope rivaled that of earlier sovereigns such as Kammu, suggesting that he might have been considering an attempt to stake out a new locus of authority in the region at the time.

Coming as they did during the period in which Uda's court existed side by side with that of a young Daigo dominated by Tokihira, the processions of both sovereigns to the Ōi River in 907 point to a rival staging of royal claims to the land. Uda's event in particular, which followed immediately after the autumnal *sechien* banquet of the Double Ninth, suggests it was an extension of that monarchical ceremony, complete with his own topics for *shi* compositions. In enacting the archaic kingly rite of "realm viewing" (*kunimi*) that was part of such peregrinations, Uda's procession presented an alternative claim to ownership of the land and its bounty. As with the tonsured sovereign's poetry matches, the procession to the Ōi River replaced the calendrical time of court banquets with the seasonal one of autumn, while at the same time mimicking the style and import of royal ritual.

Daigo's procession the following day suggests an attempt to match Uda's political claims. In the literary Chinese preface that precedes Tsurayuki's *kana* one, care is taken to designate the processions of both sovereigns with the same character 幸, perhaps in acknowledgment of their rival claims to authority. Later sources, including poetry collections in which poems from the event appear, seem to differ on whether Tsurayuki's verses are for Uda's procession or for Daigo's.[7] Perhaps Daigo sought to stage a similar poetic display of harmonization on the same topics as Uda, while replacing the *shi* of his father with *uta*.

In some ways, the doubled nature of this event recalls the bipartite structure of a poetry match, in which the claims of rival lineages were acknowledged and negotiated through the competitive matching of poems on predetermined topics. In this case, it is easy to imagine that Daigo might have actively sought out Tsurayuki and his compatriots from a desire to counter Uda's initial move with one that carried both literary and symbolic weight. There would have been special significance in having the *Kokinshū*'s editors present *uta* for the young sovereign's own procession. As members of his kitchen staff, they oversaw his consumption of the realm; and as his *utayomi* they ensured a suitably impressive display of the poetic resources at his command. Both poetry and food appear in the literary Chinese preface preceding Tsurayuki's *kana* version, which describes the people who presented poems as "those skilled at fishing on the banks" (漁渚好事者), perhaps in an allusion to the palace kitchens' supplying of fresh fish for the sovereign's table. By gesturing to these rites of royal consumption, the Ōi River procession might have been intended to reassert Daigo's own sovereignty in a manner reminiscent of the anthologizing project he sponsored during the same period.

Two of the *Kokinshū*'s editors are known to have submitted a list of poems with a preface for the procession. This is a departure from the practices of Tang court banquets and Heian *sechien*, where a preface was typically written by the most distinguished member, but not by each participant.[8] Rather, the prefaces submitted by Tsurayuki and Tadamine for the Ōi River procession resemble *chōka* both men had written as prefaces to lists of old poems they had submitted to Daigo during the initial stages of the *Kokinshū*'s compilation.[9] All four texts share similar structural features: they all present a list appended to poems, these poems are all metonymically mentioned through allusion to representative portions of their entire texts, and they all conclude with an appeal for special consideration by the monarch to whom they are addressed.

It is likely that Tsurayuki's preface and poems were submitted in advance of Daigo's procession, as was the case with poetry matches. He cites the topics presented for composition on the occasion of the procession, but his ensuing account of the way these topics are used differs markedly from their treatment by other poets who composed poems for the event. Tadamine's preface makes his own absence from the actual event explicit when he claims that "all these matters were conveyed to me on the wind" (*kakaru koto kaze ni tsutaite uketamawaru*).[10] One scholar has suggested that Tsurayuki wrote his preface solely on the basis of the topic-phrases in literary Chinese that had been used by Uda, without having seen or participated in the event itself.[11]

Judging from what the Ōi River procession can tell us about the norms for composing *kana* prefaces in Tsurayuki's time, it seems that such texts were typically written when poets submitted their personal collections of poems to an important figure. Perhaps in a similar manner, Tsurayuki's Kana Preface originally accompanied only manuscripts of the *Kokinshū* that he had personally compiled and distributed. As Kiyosuke notes, two of the three manuscripts in Tsurayuki's hand possessed a Kana Preface while none had a Mana Preface. The third version, which lacks any prefaces, could have been a preliminary draft submitted to Daigo before the anthology's wider distribution.

The possibility that the Kana Preface was written by Tsurayuki for copies of the *Kokinshū* which were distributed to a broader readership might explain why the scope of *yamato uta* in its text is radically expanded beyond the royal domain. The history of Yamato verse is not limited to human times but begins rather with the cosmos. Nor is the use of this poetry limited to harmonizing with the ruler. Partings between friends and lovers, travel, praising nobility, and blessings on birthdays, for example, are also mentioned as appropriate contexts in which to recite verse.

The Mana Preface, by contrast, was likely to have been appended to a manuscript intended for the palace archives, rather than for distribution among members of the court. Its potential future use as a document that could be referenced in an official court history might explain why this preface, like the court's earlier historical chronicles, emphasizes the royal nature of *uta* as "harmonizing verse" (*waka*) whose primary purpose was to affirm proper relations between subject and sovereign. The account of *uta* provided in the Mana Preface thus stresses a mode of court poetry that is not so much distinct from that of continental *shi* as it is parallel in its antiquity and political purposes.

Perhaps because the Kana Preface accompanied its author's handwritten manuscript of the *Kokinshū*, it appears to attach more importance to the textual nature of poetry than does the Mana Preface. It is in this area that the Kana Preface can be seen to make its most distinctive contribution to poetics. Although the precise historical circumstances, motives, and relative status of the two prefaces to the *Kokinshū* cannot be definitively determined, reading them in conjunction makes it apparent that there was more than one way of defining *uta* in the early tenth century. Despite the conflation of *waka* and *yamato uta* as terms for "Japanese poetry" by later poets and scholars, the two prefaces seem to represent distinct concepts of poetry. Although both draw on continental formulations of language, poetry, and writing, the Kana Preface is not simply a translation or adaptation of the Mana Preface. Whereas the Mana Preface is concerned with a form of "harmonizing verse" whose poetics are rooted in the continental concept of poetry as an outgrowth of music and song, the Kana Preface outlines a distinctly Yamato form of verse that often depends on the visual reception of *kana* writing for its stylistic effects. This emphasis on the written nature of poetry is in keeping with similar distinctions between *waka* and *yamato uta* that can be seen in the *Sandai jitsuroku* and earlier histories. The close association made between *yamato uta* and writing, moreover, entails a further gendered bias in how they are represented. In the Kana Preface, the image of public verse as something composed on royal command in the manner of *shi* poems at *sechien* banquets engenders a further distinction between the female entertainer who sings *uta* and the male official who writes them.

Writing from the Heart

The familiar opening lines of the Kana Preface have often been seen as describing an intensely personal form of lyric expression. Their assertion that Yamato verse has the subject's heart as its source appears at first glance to be a faithful reproduction of classical continental views of poetry as the external manifestation in words of an individual's inner sentiments. Some scholars have questioned whose heart is being invoked in this passage, however, and where it is located. One of them points out that early Japanese verse often represents *kokoro* (mind) as an external emotional force that cannot be controlled by the individual, but rather acts on that person from outside.[12] Another has suggested that the poet's heart in this passage is responding to contact with imperial divinity.[13] There is also a political dimension to this concept of the heart as something that responds to a higher authority. At times, the concept of personhood in the Kana Preface's opening lines appears to shift between a universal notion of the "human subject" and the political one of a "royal subject" defined in relation to his or her sovereign. In fact, some versions of the Kana Preface replace the words *hito no kokoro* (the subject's heart) with *hitotsu kokoro* (a devoted heart), a phrase found in royal *senmyō* proclamations.

This portrayal of the poem as something generated in response to external forces suggests the banquet practices of "the lord intoning and the ministers harmonizing" in which poems were produced in response to the ruler's words. Both the Mana and Kana Prefaces share similar language in this regard. The use of the word *waka* to describe courtly *uta* in the former text, however, makes this view of poetic genesis as political response more overt. In the Mana Preface, as in the official chronicles, *waka* are often portrayed as poems that are produced in response to the demands of a social superior. Their effects are also described in vocal terms, in keeping with the musical valences of "the lord intoning and his ministers harmonizing," suggesting thereby its tonal qualities and their corresponding efficacy in ordering the state. Such views recapitulate the canonical Great Preface to the *Classic of Poetry*, which describes *shi* in the following manner:

> Verse comes from the heart's aims. Aims hidden inside the heart are exposed in words as verse. Feelings stir within and take shape in words. When words do not suffice, we sigh them. When sighs do not suffice, we chant them. When chants do not suffice, our hands and feet move of themselves. Feelings come out in the voice; when the voice gains patterning it is called "tone." The tones of well-ordered ages are as easy and pleasant as their governments are harmonious. The tones of disordered ages are as filled with grievance and anger as their governments are decadent. The tones of a land that has been destroyed are as deeply moving as their people are troubled. Thus, for ordering successes and failures, moving Heaven and Earth, and stirring ghosts and ancestral spirits, nothing comes close to verse.[14]

The concern with sound displayed in this opening passage from the Great Preface depicts the power of poetry in language that echoes canonical continental views of music. In texts such as the classic musicological treatise *Yueji* (*Record of Music*, ca. second century B.C.E.), the things of the world (including the vibrations of music and song) stir the mind, which responds with emotion: "The mind is moved spontaneously by the actions of things upon it. Feeling emotions in response to these things, it is moved and thereby takes shape in the voice. The voice resonates sympathetically with others and gives birth to variations. Variations are perfected through their patterning into tones."[15]

The Mana Preface shares this same concern for song and the vocal properties of *waka* when it mentions "voices" (*sei*) and "songs" (*ei*) in its account:

> *Waka* is rooted in the heart's ground, bursting forth as blossoms within a grove of words. In the world of people, there are none who do not act without intending something. Thoughts and feelings change swiftly, sorrow and joy turn into one another. Feelings are

> born from our desires, and songs take shape in words. And so the voices of those at ease are joyful, while the wailing of those who are frustrated is sorrowful. Through *waka* one can relate things that lie heavy on the breast and give vent to one's dissatisfaction. For moving Heaven and Earth, stirring gods and ghosts, transforming human conduct, and bringing harmony to husband and wife, nothing surpasses *waka*.[16]

Within the continental tradition of thought, music presented the preeminent paradigm for describing numerous dimensions of human cultural production.[17] Music was among the earliest cultural forms to be critically evaluated and discussed in classical continental philosophy. It was also viewed in these sources as a medium of exchange between humans and the supernatural and cosmological forces around them, and thus was considered a vital element in ritual. Beginning in the Han period, scholars and commentators discussed music in terms of acoustics, meter, geography, and calendrics. It was treated as a technology for ordering both the world and the mind through emotive forces that could be manipulated to shape social behavior and sway spirits. Musicology also provided models for the emotive tonalities favored in Six Dynasties poetics, which exerted significant influence on its Heian counterpart.

Such classical continental views of music provided the language and concepts for treating *waka* as a political, social, and ritual technology. The term *ying* (resonance), which was used to describe the relations of one sound to another in musical patterning, also referred to the act of composing poetry in response to the commands or verse of another person. "Harmony" (*he*) also was a musical term used to describe the ideal relationship between two fundamentally different but complementary tones. In the political sphere, this complementary principle in music and song could be applied to regulate and align relations of social difference such as those between lord and minister or husband and wife. Insofar as the Great Preface's account of poetry is modeled on the performance of song and dance to music, it also partakes of their performative power.[18]

Both prefaces to the *Kokinshū* follow the continental conventions for discussing poetry established by the Great Preface when they dutifully record this belief, and when they list the ways in which poetry can affect others. Both *waka* and *yamato uta*, we are told, possess the ability to harmonize the relations between people and society and between society and supernatural forces. At a time when disease and famine were seen as the working of deceased enemies' vengeful spirits, and when warriors on the northeastern frontier were growing increasingly restive, such statements assert the direct relevance of verse to the state. This relevance can be seen further in both prefaces' claim that verse creates accord between men and women. "Harmony" in fact is mentioned only this one time in the Kana Preface, perhaps in acknowledgment of the crucial role verse played in representing community through the coordinated performance of male-female pairings in *utagaki*, *tōka*, and poetry matches.

Although both *waka* and *yamato uta* are endowed with a similar political and suasive force, however, the Kana Preface makes no mention of the musicality which is seen as key to this operation in canonical continental poetics. Rather, sound is conspicuous by virtue of its absence. This silence is a significant departure from earlier Japanese poetics treatises such as the *Kakyō hyōshiki*, which is largely concerned with tonalities and rhyme schemes borrowed from *shi* poetics. In fact, euphony was not taken up in poetics treatises again for another two centuries.[19]

In place of tones, the Kana Preface describes Yamato verse as "leaves of words" (*koto no ha*). One scholar has argued that this phrase is used throughout the *Kokinshū* to refer to the written word rather than to language in general.[20] The main instances in which it appears in the anthology's prose prefaces all seem to refer to the non-poetic language of epistles. In the Mana Preface, by contrast, the botanical metaphor includes a mention of voice. There, *waka* are described as the flowering of a grove of words rooted in the heart's soil. This account of poetic genesis echoes a famous letter by Bo Juyi in which the Heian court's favorite Tang poet likens flowers to the poet's voice: "Poetry is rooted in emotion, sprouts forth in words, flowers in the voice, and comes to fruition in meaning" (詩者根情苗言華声実義).[21] In changing the Mana Preface's flowers to leaves, the Kana Preface appears to replace voice with script.

The Kana Preface's implicit rejection of the continental musical model for poetry is amplified in its ensuing assertion that "When we hear warblers crying in blossoms or the voices of frogs dwelling in the water, who among those living does not compose verse?"[22] Although this passage has often been read as asserting that verse is produced by all living things, an equally plausible case can be made for arguing that Tsurayuki is describing a uniquely human form of expression.[23] This implicit emphasis on the human nature of *yamato uta* departs subtly but significantly from the equivalent passage in the Mana Preface, where human poetry is merely one manifestation of a universal propensity toward song: "Though warblers trilling among springtime flowers and cicadas crying out from autumn treetops lack the complex flourishes of melody, each puts forth song. All the creatures of this world do so as a matter of course."[24] In the Kana Preface, by contrast, chirping birds and croaking frogs become inspiration for human compositions of poetry rather than fellow poet-singers.

The writerly nature of poetry in the Kana Preface is also suggested by the distinctive tripartite structure of its account of poetic genesis, one in which external objects mediate the conversion of emotional energy into language: "Since the people in this world are overgrown with events and deeds, they affix the thoughts in their hearts to things they see and hear and bring forth words."[25] These lines are justly famous for introducing the terms *kokoro* (hearts), *mono* (things), and *kotoba* (words) into Japanese poetics. Within this tripartite structure, the function of the middle term *mono* is particularly striking. Unlike its continental predecessors such as the Great Preface or the *Record of Music*, the Kana Preface's heart is not aroused by external phenomena but is attached to them. The verb *tsukeru* (to affix) used to describe the relation between *mono* and *kokoro* here calls to mind the practice of attaching written poems to representations of natural objects at poetry matches. The scholar Hirasawa Ryūsuke described the poetics of this passage as visual, one in which language mirrors mind and matter.[26] As we shall see, the concept of poetic style that Tsurayuki develops in the Kana Preface often relies on both vision and textuality rather than sound and musicality for its rhetorical effects.

In its account of poetic genesis, as Stephen Owen notes, the Great Preface provides a corollary movement from exterior poem back to interior heart in the act of reception.[27] This classical continental model in turn drew on physiological and cosmological models of *qi* energy as something that traveled back and forth in a series of resonating movements between different spaces. But whereas the Great Preface's notion of poetic influence is based on a musical model in which the receiver hears tones, the complementary corollary to the inscription of Yamato verse entails reading. Taking this one step further, it could be argued that the careful structuring of poems in the *Kokinshū* themselves resonate in a spatial, textual version of the Great Preface's temporal, music-based model of "arousal and response" (*ganying*). For the reader of this imperial anthology, every poem gains meaning through the harmonies its words establish as they repeat and respond to those of other poems adjoining it on the surface of a scroll.

Two Histories, Two Forms of Verse

Through subtle additions to the Mana Preface's account of poetry, the Kana Preface introduces a concern with writing into a preexisting discourse on poetics that was rooted in the performative traditions of music, song, and dance. Such continental paradigms had informed the Yamato court's views of *uta* and its ritual efficacy from well before the Heian period. By contrast, the act of writing poetry in *kana* had begun to develop into a full-fledged ritual practice only during the second half of the ninth century. Until that point, public performance of *uta* had chiefly consisted of song accompanied by music and dance. In order for written poetry to claim a distinctive place at court as a prestigious practice with its own distinct pedigree, it would have required a genealogy of equal antiquity.

Already, during Yoshifusa's regency, a history for Yamato verse was being developed in court chronicles such as the *Shoku nihon kōki*. Both prefaces to the *Kokinshū* were written at a time when the connections between *yamato uta* and history were the subject of renewed scrutiny at court. In 906, Tokihira sponsored the composition of written *uta* on topics derived from the *Nihon shoki* for a banquet commemorating a series of lectures on the court's foundational history. One of the goals of this banquet was to establish a precise chronology for the court through a reappraisal and revision of the history's textual structure. It was during these lectures, for example, that the concept of the first seven generations of deities as a distinct "age of the gods" (*kami no yo*) was probably first articulated.[28]

Both prefaces to the *Kokinshū* appear to follow this new division of the court's canonical history. At the same time, there are significant differences between the two texts in the way that *uta* are positioned vis-à-vis the *Nihon shoki* narrative. The Mana Preface provides a fairly detailed history of *waka*, one that includes early Yamato sovereigns and that explicitly associates this form of *uta* with the "age of mortals" (*hito no yo*). In contrast, the history for Yamato verse outlined in the Kana Preface is broader in its social valences, lengthier in its genealogy, and more pronounced in its emphasis on the history of writing and composition rather than on the enactment of social harmonies between subject and sovereign.

Like its description of the individual poem's genesis, the Kana Preface's account of poetry's historical origins alludes to conceptions of writing. Unlike *waka*, the birth of *yamato uta* coincides with the initial cosmological division of Heaven and Earth in Tsurayuki's account.[29] By associating Yamato verse with the origins of the cosmos, the Kana Preface echoes canonical continental accounts of writing, which represented the genesis of textual signs as something immanent in the patterns of the world, prior to and outside human culture.[30] In these accounts, the evolution of human texts constituted one stage in a larger cosmological movement toward increasing complexity. The preface to the *Wenxuan*, which provided the Heian court with a canonical history of continental literature, viewed writing as a later stage in human development, positing a pure and simple past for people prior to that point.[31] The Mana Preface appears to draw on this convention when it makes similar claims for *waka* as a distinctly human activity happening at a later stage of social complexity and manifesting itself in a profusion of genres. By contrast, the Kana Preface claims cosmological origins for *yamato uta*, and represents its proliferation in the human world in terms of profusion of configurations of scene and sentiment, rather than metrically distinct forms of verse.

Other differences in the histories of poetry provided by the two prefaces are also worthy of attention. In his detailed and careful comparison of both texts, the scholar Ozawa Masao notes that, whereas the Mana Preface specifies individual actors and events in its narration of poetry's historical development, the Kana Preface tends to blur or omit them.[32] If anything, Tsurayuki's text appears to replace temporal order with a spatial one. In his account, the development of Yamato verse reflects the cosmological hierarchy of a superior Heaven and an inferior Earth, rather than the chronology of the *Nihon shoki*. The first instances of *yamato uta* attributed to particular agents place a verse by the goddess Shitateru Hime before one by the god Susanoo no Mikoto, whereas this order is reversed in the court's canonical history. By placing a female deity located in Heaven before a male deity located on Earth, the Kana Preface arranges its account of poetry according to cosmological principles of precedence in which Heaven is exalted and Earth lowly. It does so, moreover, in a manner that echoes the cosmological and genealogical origins of the Yamato dynasty, which is descended from celestial female deities rather than terrestrial male ones.

In the Mana Preface, this cosmological ordering of heavenly female before terrestrial male is reversed in order to preserve the gendered protocol of harmonizing verse in which the male initiates and the female responds. In the Mana Preface's history, *waka* are first used in an exchange of poems between a heavenly male deity and an earthly female one, in an allusion to the *Nihon shoki's* account of the prince Hikohohodemi no Mikoto, who composes a verse praising his wife Toyotama Hime after she leaves him. In keeping with the ideal of poetic harmony, she then replies in kind. In this account, *waka* are not defined metrically but by their function as something exchanged according to protocols of social distinction (in this case, gendered ones). The Mana Preface goes on to list examples of *waka* that vary from thirty-one syllable *hanka* and the parallel 5-7-7-5-7-7 metrical structure of *sedōka* to the infinitely expandable *chōka* form. By contrast, the Kana Preface puts form before function when it defines *yamato uta* as poems with thirty-one "letters" (*moji*). The importance of metrics to the Kana Preface's definition of *uta* is consistent with the compilers' editorial policies. Whereas the earlier *Man'yōshū* anthology allows poems to exceed metrical norms in at least five ways, the *Kokinshū* allows for only one: the addition of an extra vowel.[33]

Both the Kana Preface and the Mana Preface make special note of the first thirty-one-syllable verse in the *Nihon shoki*. But whereas the Mana Preface views this poem as the origin of poetry in general and the *hanka* (envoy verse) in particular, the Kana Preface posits a prior divine stage in which verses were being made. Although this prior stage remains unspecified in his text, Tsurayuki might be referring to the chanted exchange between the divine pair Izanami and Izanagi during their initial, failed attempt at procreation. During this age of the gods, Tsurayuki muses that "it must have been difficult to discern the feelings behind words in such artless expression."[34] The chanted exchange between Izanami and Izanagi in the dynasty's founding myths fails at first because they do not properly distinguish their gendered roles and consequently the "sentiments" (*kokoro*) appropriate to their actions. Until the male initiates and the female responds, the progeny of these two gods are monstrous.

In contrast to Izanami and Izanagi's failed exchanges, the poem composed by their son, Susanoo no Mikoto, is fixed in form, and provides a model for establishing proper relations between men and women. In the *Nihon shoki*, Susanoo's verse concludes a narrative in which this outcast from the imperial line's divine family journeys to the distant land of Izumo and becomes its ruler after rescuing and marrying the daughter of a local deity. Susanoo's sojourn can be seen as a prefiguration (and thus legitimization) of the Yamato dynasty's subsequent strategy of the using of marriage alliances with local clans to extend its political authority over new regions. Perhaps for this reason, both prefaces associate the birth of poetic form with this establishment of a divine ruler on earth in the age of mortals. In Susanoo's poem, moreover, relations between male and female take shape in the creation of a domestic interior within a royal household at the same moment as *uta* becomes fixed in thirty-one syllables:

Eightfold are the clouds that rise	*yakumo tatsu*
in Izumo, where lies an eightfold fence.	*Izumo no yaegaki*
To enclose my woman,	*tsumagome ni*
do I build this eightfold fence.	*yaegaki tsukuru*
Ah that eightfold fence!	*sono yaegaki o*[35]

Through its structure, Susanoo's poem appears to enact the genesis of human society, moving from landscape to the construction of human domestic interiors. This movement is then affirmed through the citation of its own words in the final line. The poem's incantatory repetition of the word *ya* (eightfold) creates a citational effect, invoking and affirming the proper composition of male, female, superior and inferior, divine and mortal. Structurally, it can be seen as a polyvocal poem, in which the first two lines evoke the scene of Izumo from outside the enclosure (*mono*), whereas the next two lines express the first-person desire of the god to enclose his wife (*kokoro*).[36] These two divisions are then enfolded within a citational act that also suggests a shift from the age of the gods to that of mortals. The "that" (*sono*) of his poem's final line creates a break between the present moment of enunciation and the past event to which it refers. Through such citations, the mythic origins of the social order are recounted and then affirmed in a manner that evokes the ways in which *yamato uta* at Daigo's court were used to cite the Yamato dynasty's history at *Nihon shoki* lectures.

This link in the prefaces to the *Kokinshū* between the establishment of political and poetic order was not new. It echoed mythical narratives and beliefs in incantatory language that had taken shape at the Yamato court two centuries earlier. Texts such as the *Hitachi fudoki* (*Hitachi Province Gazetteer*, ca. 713), *norito* (ritual prayers), and the *Nihon shoki* all describe a primeval chaos in which trees and plants spoke and earthly deities buzzed around like flies. Only with the descent of Ameterasu's descendants to earth were these spirits first subdued and rendered silent. The muting of the landscape in the Yamato dynasty myths provides the implicit precondition for a poetics in the *Kokinshū* in which entities from the natural world are objects manipulated by human agents rather than subjects who speak and act for themselves.

Although both the Mana and Kana Prefaces take Susanoo's verse as the point of departure for a history of human poetry, their subsequent chronologies differ in ways that suggest different definitions for *waka* and *yamato uta*. The Mana Preface's founding pair of human verses seem to define *waka* as poems that respond to the suasive powers of kingly virtue. One poem is composed in offering to the mythical Emperor Nintoku at his palace in Naniwazu.[37] Its partner poem is provided by a beggar in response to the kindly intervention (and poem) of Prince Regent Shōtoku Taishi. Taken together, the Mana Preface joins two male poles of the royal patriline in a harmonious balancing of complementary actions: providing unsolicited advice that addresses the ruler's actions in a political context, and responding to the benevolence of a superior.

In place of ruler and crown prince, the Kana Preface presents us with a gendered dyad in the form of a sovereign at Naniwazu and a female performer at Asakayama. Although the Asakayama poem has been identified as poem 3807 in the *Man'yōshū*, the identity of the first poem has been the subject of debate for centuries.[38] The very first commentary to the Kana Preface—embedded in most modern recensions of the text and usually attributed to the poet and theorist Fujiwara no Kintō—sees the Naniwazu poem as the same one offered up to Nintoku in the Mana Preface. This commentary claims the poem was composed by an immigrant scholar named Wani as a way of remonstrating with Nintoku, urging him to ascend the throne at a time when he is deferring to his brother. It is equally possible, however, that the Kana Preface is drawing here on the *Nihon shoki*'s chronology, in which a poem by Nintoku is the first thirty-one syllable *uta* composed by a Yamato sovereign. In other words, it is concerned with the first such poem produced by a reigning sovereign rather than the first one addressed to him.

Like its previous divine pair of poems by Shitateru Hime and Susanoo no Mikoto, the Kana Preface's human pair is defined in terms that are both geographical and gendered. Naniwazu refers to the location of Nintoku's palace at the center of the Yamato realm. Its partner is a song by a serving woman at a banquet in the realm's northernmost border in Michinoku province. The female half of the Kana Preface's earlier divine poetic couple also appears to be associated with the northern, foreign fringes of the realm. Shitateru's verse in the *Nihon shoki* is described as being in a "rustic mode" (*hina-buri*),[39] something that the interpolated commentary to the Kana Preface glosses as "Ebisu verse" (*ebisu uta*), in a possible reference to the indigenous people located on the Heian imperium's frontiers. In fact, as becomes evident by the time we reach the critique of six poets, female figures are consistently associated with the court's periphery throughout the Kana Preface.

This dyadic pairing of genders with social spaces also constitutes the matrix from which all Yamato verses are first reproduced by the literate courtier. The Naniwazu and Asakayama poems, we are told by the Kana Preface, are respectively "the father and mother of verse" (*uta no chichi haha*), that is, the first ones practiced by those learning the ABCs of *kana* brushwork. There is evidence to suggest that this claim reflected common practice at the time.[40] As with his account of poetic genesis,

Tsurayuki's first pair of human poems also draws attention to the textuality of *uta*. The verses associated with male ruler and female entertainer create the possibility for generating future written poems, thereby reenacting the history of verse within the individual developmental history of each literate member of the court. Gender, geography, and the imperial world order shaping them are thus inscribed in the body of each courtier as his or her hands are trained in poetic composition.

Past Perfection in the Prefaces

The subsequent account of human verse in both prefaces follows the tripartite conceit favored by classical continental histories, in which the present moment is contrasted with an idealized antiquity and a degraded recent past. Both prefaces locate poetry's past perfection in *sechien* banquets at which the abilities of poets to compose appropriate verse on the spot were tested. The antiquity imagined here harkens back to a tradition of banquet verse that can be seen in both the *Man'yōshū* and the historical chronicles. Composing impromptu *uta* in the banquet ending a formal *sechien* affair had been a feature of court poetic practice for at least a century by the time that the *Kokinshū* was compiled. The anthology's claims for *uta*'s antiquity were also made possible by the existence of an antiquity in texts such as the *Nihon shoki* which could rival that of the Zhou rulers who represented past cultural perfection in classical continental history.

In ancient times, we are told in both prefaces, *uta* by the ruler's ministers and officials enabled him to ascertain and evaluate their inner qualities. This scenario draws on Confucian visions of the monarch, which stressed the ruler's need to gauge his ministers' actions through their words as they sat in attendance.[41] In some respects, this vision is a fantasy conjured up by the writers of the *Kokinshū* prefaces. Although examples of *waka* being offered up at royal command exist in the *Man'yōshū* and in the official court histories, in none of these instances does the sovereign peruse his subject's written poems.[42] As was noted in Chapter 1, *uta* may have been recited at official banquets, but they do not appear in formal compositional rites until the end of the ninth century.

When it comes to the scope of *uta* in this idealized antiquity, however, the two prefaces differ significantly. Whereas the Mana Preface is primarily concerned with "harmonizing verse" in a royal context, the Kana Preface provides a broader vision of *uta*'s contributions to a variety of communities at court. *Waka* are poems exchanged between the sexes or between sovereign and official in order to produce social propriety and gendered hierarchies. *Yamato uta*, by contrast, are used in a variety of social situations, including lamentations at growing old, requests for patronage, declarations of friendship, praising a host at a banquet, or responses to changes in the seasons. All these poems in the Kana Preface are "spoken" (*iu*) in an intelligible manner as communicative acts rather than "recited" (*yomu*) in a highly formalized and monotone mode of enunciation. The distinction here appears to be between performative modes appropriate to different social settings (informal versus royal) rather than a poem's linguistic status (textual versus oral).

Both prefaces associate *uta*'s fall from grace at the Yamato court with a turn toward fickle concerns. The descent from past perfection to present degradation was a convention in representing histories of poetry in both Six Dynasties China and Heian Japan. *Uta*'s history had already been couched in these terms in the preface to the *Shinsen man'yōshū* anthology and in the historical annals of the *Shoku nihon kōki*. In continental literary histories, poetry was often portrayed as an object of ostentatious play and erotic frivolity in the recent past, serving no social purpose and thus falling short of the ethical and social standards for poetic expression that the Great Preface to the *Classic of Poetry* enjoined. Similarly, both *waka* and *yamato uta*'s fall from grace is represented as a fall away from the ideal Confucian relations between sovereign and subject.

In the Mana Preface, *waka* become the province of commoners seeking material gain after its decline. The "blossom and bird envoys" (*kachō no tsukai*) it mentions likely refer to the female performers who sang erotic verse at banquets held outside of the court for private household entertainments.[43] Their male counterparts are beggars who continue the incantatory tradition of *waka* as itinerants who go from house to house chanting formulas and magical verses in return for food.[44] Although priests are credited with preserving the incantatory traditions of *uta* in the *Shoku nihon kōki* chronicle, their role in society appears to be viewed more critically in the Mana Preface. Mendicant monks chanting *darani* and *uta* were a common sight in the early Heian capital, where they were subject to state regulation. From the official point of view, such incantatory powers constituted a threat to public order and could even be used as a form of blackmail.[45]

The Kana Preface's description of *yamato uta*'s fall from grace differs in its implicit focus on the intended purpose of written poetry as something to be anthologized. This poetry's recent past, in which it belonged to "houses of the amorous" (*irogonomi no ie*), is perhaps referring to mid-ninth-century poets such as Komachi and Narihira and the epistolary verse exchanged between men and women at that time. Alternately, these "houses" could refer to the female entertainers mentioned in the Mana Preface who sold their sexuality at aristocrat mansions and in other venues.[46] In any case, the Kana Preface criticizes such poetry because it is hidden from public view rather than because it is erotic. Buried like a sunken log, its sentiments will blossom fleetingly but never achieve fruition in a lasting form. The blossoms and fruit imagery used here suggests the transitory nature of private verse in contrast to official anthologies that seek to preserve the contours of a court community in written form. Unless they are written and preserved, the Kana Preface declares, these poems will remain "evanescent words" (*hakanaki koto*) forever lost to posterity.

Insofar as the regulation of relations between men and women was a Confucian monarch's prerogative, the Kana Preface implies that state-sanctioned forms of verse, such as anthologies and *sechien* banquets are preferable to private performances held by urban households or informal epistolary exchanges. Female entertainers, who represent a debased form of verse in the Mana Preface, appear in the Kana Preface as a respected lineage of palace officials whose activities complement and parallel those of ruler and male bureaucrat. Tsurayuki's own childhood in the palace office for female performers could explain why he gives them such a prominent place within his vision of court poetry. At the same time, as we shall see, this vision of the female poet as entertainer in the Kana Preface is clearly distinguished from that of the male official as composer and inscriber of verse.

Envisioning the Court Poet in the Kana Preface

The ideal court poet in the Kana Preface is represented in terms that allow Tsurayuki and the editors to claim membership in a tradition of royal panegyric poetry extending back to the late seventh-century bard Kakinomoto no Hitomaro. The Kana Preface's fictive vision of this court poet is maintained through complex textual maneuvers which overlay the times, places, and people of earlier courts with the present moment of the editors. Although both prefaces hold up the eighth-century royal poet Yamabe no Akahito as Hitomaro's peer, the Kana Preface presents an extensive and rhetorically elaborate treatment of the latter as the ideal court bard who forms a complementary pair with his sovereign. In its description of Hitomaro and his Nara sovereign, the Kana Preface appears to create a historical "double-vision" or *mitate*, overlaying the image of an ancient court bard accompanying his sovereign on royal processions with an image of the *Kokinshū*'s editors composing verse on topics commemorating the processions of their own sovereigns. This retroactive fantasy is nowhere present in the Mana Preface, which gives Hitomaro only passing mention in a history that stretches back to Emperor Tenchi's court at Ōmi.

In the Mana Preface, Hitomaro is specifically associated with Emperor Heizei, who the text claims was responsible for ordering the compilation of the *Man'yōshū*. In the Kana Preface, Hitomaro is represented as a contemporary of a "Nara sovereign" whom he accompanies on royal processions to view autumn leaves and cherry blossoms:

> In observing what has been transmitted from antiquity, it is clear that this Way first spread in the time of the Nara sovereign. His Majesty must have ruled wisely, secure in his knowledge of the feelings of his subjects that they expressed in verse. In that era, one Kakinomoto no Hitomaro of Senior Third Rank was the immortal of poetry. His name tells of a time when sovereign and subject were as one. It is said that at autumn dusk, His Majesty's eyes saw russet foliage floating down the Tatsuta River as royal brocade, and on spring mornings Hitomaro's heart was unable to think of the cherry blossoms on Mount Yoshino as anything else but clouds.[47]

The many anachronisms of this passage make it one of the most puzzling sections in the Kana Preface. Not only is the seventh-century poet associated with a much later sovereign, but also no poem exists in his corpus likening cherry blossoms to clouds. Furthermore, the lowly Hitomaro is here given the extraordinarily exalted rank of Senior Third, one typically commensurate with the post of grand counselor (*dainagon*). From the eighteenth century onward, scholars have sought to reconcile a literal reading of this passage with historical fact. In his study *Kokin wakashū uchigiki* (1789), the famed classicist Kamo no Mabuchi (1697–1769) even went so far as to speculate that these inconsistencies were the product of a later writer.

It is possible, however, as one scholar has recently demonstrated, to read this passage as alluding to the *Kokinshū*'s time rather than that of Hitomaro.[48] The two eras are likened to one another through an elaborate form of wordplay that uses the rhetoric of acrostic verse favored in so many *kana* poems. The full name and title given the ancient poet, (*ōkimi*)*tsu no kurai Kakinomoto no* (*Hito*)*maro*, contains the opening syllables of the names of each of the three surviving editors in its first three syllables: (Ō)shikahachi no Mitsune, (Ki) no Tsurayuki, and (Mi)bu no Tadamine. These *kana* letters used to write out his rank and name also contain the words *kimi* (sovereign) and *hito* (subject). In what might be seen as a characteristically witty move on Tsurayuki's part, the declaration that "sovereign and subject were as one" (*kimi mo hito mo mi o awasu*) points to this wordplay, at the same time as it suggests an image of ruler and poet merging as one self with a shared vision of the world.

In a similar fashion, Hitomaro's association with the distinctly Heian visual conceit of likening cherry blossoms to clouds also points to the *Kokinshū*'s two senior editors. The link between Yoshino's mountains and clouds that is attributed to Hitomaro in the Kana Preface also appears in a pair of Spring poems (59 and 60) in the anthology. The first of these, by Tsurayuki, likens cherry blossoms to clouds. The second, by his editorial predecessor Tomonori, mentions Yoshino's mountains. Tsurayuki's poem from this pair was offered up at Daigo's command, making it implicitly part of the royal bardic tradition that Hitomaro exemplifies.

While the figure of Hitomaro appears to overlap with the *Kokinshū*'s editors in the Kana Preface, the identity of the Nara sovereign is far murkier. In the *Kokinshū* poem prefaces, deceased rulers are typically referred to by the location of their burial mounds. According to this convention, the sovereign mentioned here is likely to be Heizei, who died and was buried in the old capital after his failed rebellion against

Saga. As the sovereign to whom the ordering of the compilation of the *Man'yōshū* is attributed, Heizei's coexistence with Hitomaro in the Kana Preface perhaps suggests the former's role in preserving the latter's poetry in a later anthology. As with the Kana Preface's prior history of verse, temporal chronology in this instance is readily sacrificed to other considerations.

Another possibility, in keeping with the implied parallel between Hitomaro and the editors, is that the Nara sovereign here could represent Uda, whose post-retirement peregrinations frequently took him to Yamato province. It has often been noted that the visual metaphor of autumn foliage as brocade mentioned in this poem does not appear in any earlier verse by an identifiable ruler.[49] It does appear, however, in the list of topics given to Tsurayuki and the other editors during the royal processions of Uda and Daigo to the Ōi River. Like Heizei, Uda presented an alternate locus of authority to that of his successor, just as Nara represented an alternate and earlier capital to that of Heiankyō. An awareness of the tense relations between Daigo's and Uda's courts which dominated the years surrounding the *Kokinshū*'s compilation can be seen in Tsurayuki's care to mention both sovereigns in his preface for the Ōi River procession. Perhaps similar political tensions can be detected beneath the Kana Preface's idealized image of ruler and courtier joining in perfect harmony.

Other similarities exist between the royal processions of Hitomaro's sovereign in the Kana Preface and those by Uda and Daigo to the Ōi River. In both cases, landscapes are represented as a monarchical vision of complementary elements. Most of the poetic topics commanded by Uda and Daigo for their processions involved visual likenesses between a river landscape and either human or celestial phenomena: boats on the water as floating leaves, autumn mountains as brocade, chrysanthemums on the riverbanks as stars, geese flying high above as the shapes of letters, and so on. In each case, the sovereign's vision of his lands affirms cosmological patterns linking the triad of Heaven, Earth, and humanity. By harmonizing with the lines of literary Chinese, the poet cited the sovereign's vision of his realm, thereby reinforcing these assertions of a unified cosmos.

In the Kana Preface, complementary poetic pairings cluster around sovereign and subject in a manner that replaces linear historical time with the overlapping cycles of seasonal and calendrical time. Hitomaro's vision of cherry blossoms on Yoshino complements the Nara sovereign's vision of the Tatsuta River. Autumn and spring encompass seasonal temporality, and the closeup view of the Tatsuta River complements the distant one of Yoshino's mountains. "Water" and "mountains" themselves comprised the compound phrase used in continental texts to denote landscape (*shansui*). In accordance with the structural poetics of the *Kokinshū*, seasonal time and calendrical time are interwoven in these depictions. In seeing the Tatsuta River as brocade, the Kana Preface's Nara sovereign transforms this seasonal landscape into the formal tableau of the palace's New Year's Day rites. The production of brocade was a strict monopoly of the palace, and robes from this labor-intensive cloth were chiefly reserved for imperial mausoleums and the captains of the palace guard. The latter wore them only during the court's most formal rites, such as the New Year's Day court assembly and enthronement ceremonies.[50] Both rites were variants on the archaic kingly ritual of *kunimi*, replacing the landscape viewed from a mountaintop with a "people-scape" of courtiers viewed from the palace throne above the courtyard in which they assembled.[51]

Perhaps Uda had these royal and ritual connotations in mind when he provided brocade as a topic for his own procession to view the realm west of the capital in 907. At a time when he and his son were presenting rival claims to ownership of the state's wealth, the appearance of this visual conceit in poetry commemorating their royal progressions must have resonated politically. In both instances, possession of the land and its wealth are represented as a consequence of the sovereign's virtue, which possesses the power to favorably influence and transform both Heaven and humanity. The association of seasonal splendor with court ritual in Uda's topics, it could be argued, contained his claim to imperial virtue as the generating force and legitimizing rationale behind his ownership of the realm's resources. Whether the Kana Preface acknowledges Uda's present authority through these references to the Ōi River processions and brocaded landscapes, or whether it relegates him to an honorable past evoked by the former capital at Nara remains, perhaps purposefully, ambiguous.

Like the names of Hitomaro and his sovereign, the names of the places they view within the Kana Preface appear to allude to other times and places. The Tatsuta River that appears in this text is arguably as much an opportunity to introduce the word for "cutting cloth" (*tatsu*) into Tsurayuki's vision of brocaded foliage as it is the designation of a particular geographical location. This rhetorical amplification of the image of brocade could be designed to strengthen the suggestion of a New Year's Day assembly of officials. Another link to this rite is provided by the succeeding mention of Yoshino, which could allude to the Yoshino no Kuzu performers who played music at the banquet that followed the formal New Year's Day assembly. In this poetic vision, sovereign and subject represent ritual center and performative periphery within the rites of kingship, thereby also hinting at the physical distance of the court poet from formal observances in which only high-ranking officials were permitted to participate.

Other distinctions between ruler and poet can be seen in the manner in which their respective poetic visions are constructed. The rites of viewing the realm enacted in royal processions are also echoed in the Kana Preface's depiction of the different ways subject and sovereign perceive their respective landscapes. Both see one thing as another, but the Nara sovereign actively transforms the landscape into brocade through the honorific transitive verb *mitamau* (His Majesty sees it as). By contrast, Hitomaro's vision of clouds and cherry blossoms is passive, one registered within his heart as something that "comes to mind" (*oboekeru*). As one scholar has noted, such distinctions could be drawn from the conventions used in commemorative verse composed for royal processions found in the *Man'yōshū*.[52] In accordance with such conventions, the poet in this portion of the Kana Preface responds to a vision that has already been established by his sovereign rather than possessing a gaze that is an active transforming force.

The following statement—that sovereign and poet share one self—counterbalances distinctions between them in this passage. The phrase might allude to the role of the court poet as a mouthpiece for his sovereign. The rank of Senior Third that Tsurayuki bestows upon Hitomaro was usually accorded to grand counselors (*dainagon*) who were responsible for conveying the words of the ruler to other ministers and officials. In this sense, the Kana Preface's ideal court poet is an intermediary, someone whose words make manifest his sovereign's will.[53] The *Ryō no gige* commentary to the state's legal codes, for example, describes the holder of the post of grand counselor as the "throat and tongue of the monarch," through which the sovereign's word and will are conveyed to the court.[54] In the Kana Preface, however, Hitomaro becomes the imperial eye rather than the imperial tongue.

Ultimately, the conditions under which the poet harmonizes his vision with that of his ruler underscore distance rather than intimacy between the two parties. The fantasy of a union between the two men presented in the Kana Preface's account of Hitomaro is purely textual. An official of Tsurayuki's low rank did not usually have an opportunity to see his sovereign, nor did his sovereign usually see him. Put more specifically in terms of the practices to which this passage alludes, Tsurayuki and his fellow editors did not accompany their sovereign on the royal processions for which they wrote poems, nor would they have been high enough in rank to participate in the New Year's Day assembly held in Daigo's household quarters in the Seiryōden. Writing, in the form of topics handed down to the poet, both creates the possibility for editors and sovereign to share a harmonious vision of royal virtue and simultaneously underscores their physical separation at court. What circulated in the place of visible bodies was written texts, which provided these men with their only opportunity to be seen by the superiors for whom they compiled the anthology.

Engendering Six Styles of Court Poet

The stakes involved in authorial visibility are suggested in the prefaces' subsequent critique of six named poets. This portion of the Kana Preface is particularly noteworthy for its similarity to the corresponding section of the Mana Preface. Modern scholars often discuss the use of *sama* (style) here in terms of the rhetorical concerns associated with the latter text's six principles of poetry. There has been less commentary on the ways the concept of style in both prefaces creates the first model of authorship for court *uta*. This new model was perhaps in part a result of the increased interest in the status of the composer of poetry that had developed at Uda's court, where the term *utayomi* first appeared at poetry matches to describe specialists in poetic composition, and where the ability to come up with a proper poem had become subject to royal scrutiny and critical appraisal.

Immortality and visibility before the sovereign appear as the implied goal of poetry in both prefaces. The ability of writing to ensure the poet's longevity finds its ideal form in the ancient bard Hitomaro, whose future fame was guaranteed by his inclusion in the earlier *Man'yōshū* anthology. Similarly, the six poets named in both prefaces are granted a claim to posterity by virtue of their inclusion in the *Kokinshū*. The Kana Preface in particular alludes to the importance of maintaining a written legacy when it uses botanical language to describe the six poets as people whose possession of a superior knowledge of style enables them to stand out from a dense textual thicket of word-leaves. By virtue of their inclusion in the anthology and the wide array of social classes and genders they embody, the six represent a possibility for having named authorship in an imperial anthology that appears to be open to all members of the court.

Despite this opportunity, however, none of the six attains the poetic heights of Hitomaro, whose person is described as being perfectly matched with that of the sovereign. Both prefaces imply that stylistic shortcomings in the poetry of its six authors condemn them to eternal exile from the royal center. Insofar as the figure of Hitomaro in the Kana Preface overlaps with that of the *Kokinshū*'s editors, they and other lower-ranking male officials at Daigo's court are capable of attaining the same status. At the same time, they are also vulnerable to the same fate as the six poets who are criticized. Probably the incentive for poetic excellence in this instance is the promise of future inclusion in court anthologies by virtue of one's skill at composing on topics. The ability to successfully harmonize with the ruler's selected words in poetry would be one way in which sovereign and subject become as one. In a period when the competitive courts of Uda and Daigo were increasingly embracing the practice of topic-based composition, the need to cultivate royal patronage through skill at such poetic practices would have been felt keenly by Tsurayuki's readership.

With the reference to the male poet Hitomaro as its ideal, and through the language it uses to criticize the six poets, the Kana Preface suggests that its implied reader is a male official-courtier who might read and use the anthology as a template for his own topic-based poetry.[55] Just as all authors except for the sovereign are identifiable by name and rank within the *Kokinshū*, all the members of court other than the ruler are subject to being evaluated and ranked within a hierarchy of poetic and personal qualities. The Kana Preface suggests that the highest nobility might be exempt from evaluation when Tsurayuki declares that he has omitted any mention of them for fear of appearing to treat them lightly. The ambiguity of this statement, however, leaves open the possibility that they too might be subject to critical scrutiny in the realm of poetic composition under other circumstances.

In presenting a sustained argument for authorship and individuality in the poetic realm, the prefaces raise the stakes for the individual courtier. The written legacy of a poet is presented as a double-edged sword, offering the promise of eternity on the one hand and public humiliation on the other. In declaring that poetry reveals an individual's qualities, both prefaces create a condition of free-floating anxiety for its readership. Whereas Tsurayuki provides examples for his six styles of poetry, none is offered for his six poets. Just as scholars have sought for centuries to determine the basis upon which each of the six poets is evaluated, readers of Tsurayuki's preface in his own time must have wondered—and worried—about the basis for their potential evaluation in the absence of any clear examples of what was to be avoided. Such concerns would no doubt have provided an incentive for turning to the *Kokinshū* as a template for one's own poetry.

Both prefaces to the anthology imply that the poem is somehow an expression of its author's inner nature. Its externality can in fact be said to be one of the distinguishing features of *sama* in this part of the Kana Preface.[56] This view of poetic style was in keeping with the prefaces' shared vision of poetry's proper place at court as a tool to help the ruler evaluate his courtiers. Both texts use language that draws on established continental conventions for poetry criticism, which maintained that various character types could be recognized and judged by the ways they manipulated language. The format of such criticism, which typically consisted of pithy two-sentence epigrams balancing an individual's strengths and weaknesses, had been developed in continental texts such as Cao Pi's *Discourse on Literature*, in which the princely patron is represented as evaluating and awarding poets at a competitive court.[57] By the late fifth and early sixth centuries, such forms of criticism had become widespread in continental poetics.

In continental criticism, the concept of emotions as a form of *qi* energy generated internally and manifested externally through material traces in bearing, physiognomy, or writing style was a crucial element in the analysis of character types through language. Underlying Cao Pi's role as the princely evaluator, for example, is the assumption that a writer's emotional state is reflected in the "style" (*ti*) of his or her works. This word, which also appears in the Mana Preface, typically denoted normative characteristics that could inhere in bodies or words, but was not particular to any single body or text. Expressive styles thus were not "individual" in a modern sense, but rather "types" that were shared with other people. As an outer manifestation of inner qualities, style enabled the reader/ruler to evaluate and apprehend the poet as a recognizable character type with set traits. During the Six Dynasties, when poetic and political patronage were closely linked, the evaluation of courtiers could take place along both axes simultaneously. The use of grades and ranks from officialdom in texts such as the *Shipin* (*Gradings of Poets*), made the connections between bureaucratic and poetic evaluation explicit. Elaborate modes of rankings and descriptive terminologies were developed to evaluate the court poet, providing a science of human psychology that was put into practice in the arena of competitive topic-based poetic composition. In such settings, the composer was expected to embody certain norms associated with the topic on which his poem was composed.[58]

Both prefaces to the *Kokinshū* associate poetry with personality in a manner that appears to draw on this continental mode for evaluating topic-based composition. Poetic harmony in Tsurayuki's time—as it was enacted through the skillful citation and reworking of topics provided by the sovereign—found its Confucian ideological correlate in the political and social harmonies engendered by the courtier's faithful reception of his lord's commands. Skillful poetic harmony thus manifested the emotional tenor of the male official's loyalty and love for his sovereign, making it a form of poetic and political display that could have held considerable weight in a competitive environment in which there was more than one patron at court.

Given the links between physiognomy and poetics in continental criticism, style could be seen as both a physical trait and a discursive one. The word *ti* had a wide range of corporeal connotations, denoting everything from physical shape to mannerisms, deportment, and behavior, as well as the embodiment of some principle in physical form.[59]

A similar melding of the corporeal and political dimensions of style can be seen in the Kana Preface's depiction of Hitomaro's physical and poetic union with his sovereign. Conversely, some of the six poets are described in language that represents stylistic failure as an inability to inhabit the body of a male official. In both prefaces, the failed poet often displays a style that is likened to the physical appearance of women and commoners.

This association between the body and expressive style was more than merely metaphorical. One paradigm for theorizing their connection to one another was provided by Six Dynasties critical literature on calligraphy, which saw the written sign as the physical trace of the writer's body and emotion. Brush strokes were conceived of as the materialization of pulsing lines of *qi* energy from the writer's body on surfaces of silk or paper.[60] Both *Kokinshū* prefaces appear at times to draw on this paradigm in their treatment of poetic style. One scholar has noted that their tendency to evaluate the six poets through language describing human bodies and dispositions rather than natural objects could very well derive from calligraphic treatises such as the *Gujin shuping* ("Critiques of Old and New Calligraphers"), a critical evaluation of twenty-five calligraphers compiled at the command of Emperor Wu of the Liang dynasty.[61]

Because the brush was a preeminently male instrument within the Confucian conceptualization of officialdom, stylistic failure in the calligraphic arena could be described in terms of a physiognomy inappropriate to the writer's gender and class. The *Gujin shuping*, for example, describes one writer's style as being "like the maid of a great house who has become its lady. Though possessing rank, her deportment is nervous and ill at ease. Ultimately, this does not resemble the writer's true self." The writing of another is described as being "like a rustic fellow moved into a new mansion. At first he appears to be someone from Yangzhou, but when you talk with him his accent gives him away." In a strikingly similar manner, poetic style is represented in the *Kokinshū* prefaces as the outermost surface of the writer's body, which in turn embodies normative traits or "styles" (*ti*) particular to different social classes and genders. Feminine appearance and duplicity are linked in the characterization of Henjō's style as resembling a painting of a woman that arouses the male viewer in vain. An accusation of rusticity is directed at the royal bard Ōtomo no Kuronushi, who is compared to a woodcutter resting under blossoms, and intimations of social climbing are directed at the scholar Fun'ya no Yasuhide, who is likened to a merchant dressing above his station. As woman, rustic woodcutter, and merchant, each of these figures provides a negative example for the male official.

The concept of writing as the visible trace of its authors' physical and psychological traits can be detected also in the visual nature of the metaphors used to describe the remaining three poets. The words of the otherwise anonymous Kisen are described as indistinct, perhaps because so few of his poems survive (as Tsurayuki notes in the Kana Preface), or perhaps because they stretch the limits of intelligibility. The verses of Ariwara no Narihira are likened to a faded flower in the language of emotional resonance used to describe the evocative *xing* mode of *shi* poetics. Like many verses in the *Classic of Poetry* that were associated with this form of rhetoric, Narihira's poems would inspire a commentarial tradition that sought to link them to the historical circumstances of their time. The poetry of Komachi is likened to a palace concubine pining away in her inner chamber, invisible to her ruler and cut off from his favor. Perhaps an added implication is that her poems would not have survived or become visible to the current sovereign had they not been selected for inclusion in the *Kokinshū* by its male editors.

Throughout the accounts of the six poets in both prefaces, the male courtier appears to be the implied reader to whom stylistic concerns are addressed, just as the ideal for the court poet provided in the form of Hitomaro is a man whose body can be matched to that of his sovereign. This implicit concern with the male courtier poet is perhaps most apparent in the manner in which the single female poet among the six is treated. If anything, the Kana Preface reveals an even more pronounced gender bias in its account. In contrast to her male peers, Tsurayuki sees Komachi's stylistic shortcomings as appropriate and fitting to her gender. Unlike Henjō—whose femininity is conceived of as a fictive persona through the metaphor of a painting—that of Komachi inheres in both her physical body and her verse. Her poetry is described in terms of a frailty that is at once corporeal and emotional. In the Mana Preface, these features are overtly eroticized with the word *en* (alluring). The Kana Preface expands on this description of eroticized frailty to declare that such traits embody a distinctly female form of poetry with its own history.

Tsurayuki's peculiar treatment of Komachi takes the image of her in the Mana Preface as a languorous court lady, who composes poetry to gain the ruler's favors in the same manner as her male peers, and transforms her into a female entertainer whose physical and musical charms provide a gendered form of eroticism that is particular to *sechien* banquets. In a noteworthy departure from the Mana Preface, Komachi is the only one of the six poets who is associated with a performance tradition. The ancestral mother of her lineage, Princess Sotōri, is described in the *Nihon shoki* as a beauty whose radiance shone through her gauze robes.[62] Like Komachi, Princess Sotōri is defined by her appearance and her physical attractiveness for men. One scholar has suggested that Princess Sotōri's lineage represents the tradition of female performers who had entertained male officials and nobility since the Nara period.[63] This association appears to have been shared by other roughly contemporaneous texts, such as the *Kakyō hyōshiki*, which notes her expertise at zither music and song.[64]

By associating Komachi with a tradition of female entertainers, the Kana Preface places her in a lineage extending all the way back to the provincial, anonymous woman in Asakayama who composed the marginalized mother of all *uta*, and perhaps even further back to the female deity Shitateru Hime, who provides the first female verse in the Kana Preface's history. Tsurayuki's use of the term "women's verse" (*omuna no uta*) to describe this lineage distinguishes it from an implicitly male norm.[65] The implications of this association have influenced accounts of gender in Japanese poetry from Tsurayuki's time to the present day. Komachi continued to be associated with female performers in the middle ages, in tandem with a growing tendency to domesticate her and other literate court women through Buddhist moralizing discourses. The tradition of creating a distinctly feminine brand of poetry also carried over into modern times, perhaps most notably with Origuchi Shinobu's influential formulation of "women's poetry" (*onna no uta*) as a category of archaic verse grounded in daily life and ritual, in contrast to "men's poetry" (*otoko no uta*) which he saw as a more self-consciously literary endeavor.[66]

Unlike the other five poets who are male officials, Komachi's authorial status is ambiguous. Her written poetry and its claims to a distinct name are presented as a generic tradition of song and dance transmitted through guilds of female performers. From the mother of poetry down to its ailing daughters, women poets in the Kana Preface are represented as being on the outskirts of court and capital, just out of the sovereign's sight. In fact, female entertainers played a prominent role at court in Tsurayuki's day. The women of the Naikyōbō represented a tradition of palace song whose eroticism complemented the male literati composing poetry in literary Chinese. It was these women who danced and sang before male courtiers when the latter anxiously tested their brushes against the topics provided by their sovereign at *sechien* banquets.

The Kana Preface's representation of Komachi thus hints at the larger setting in which Tsurayuki imagines his form of court poetry to take place. It is a masculine arena, one in which officials strive to embody their sovereign's will and words. Like the language of the *Kokinshū*'s poem prefaces, that of the Kana Preface envisages a banquet setting as the performative paradigm for court poetry. In order to define *uta* as the product of a Confucian imperium in which the actions of male and female are harmoniously coordinated, a female form of poetry is provided to complement that of the male official. At the same time, however, it is important to remember that both prefaces' vision of male authorship was far from representative of poetic practice in the early tenth century. The right to append one's name to an *uta* and accrue merit accordingly was not automatically granted to men such as Tsurayuki. This was especially true of the poetry matches Uda was sponsoring at his court. In these settings, both men and women strove for resources, wealth, and patronage through anonymous poems.

Tensions between the realities that circumscribed lower-ranking male poets' visibility in the arena of poetic composition and the Kana Preface's idealized vision of men who embody and unite with their male sovereign appear to accumulate around Komachi, who occupies a peculiarly ambivalent place within the *Kokinshū*'s social hierarchies. She is associated with both the songs of female performers and the written poems of the mid ninth century. Her name denotes a relatively low status, while at the same time her facility with letters makes her a worthy epistolary partner for male officials. Her poems themselves often seem to transgress gender norms when read individually, and to reinforce them when read in narrative sequences. She is at once an author whose name will last along with those of her male peers, and simply one representative of a collective, anonymous performance tradition. Such ambivalences perhaps ultimately can be seen as resonating with Tsurayuki's own background and position at court. He is likely to have been raised among the same female entertainers with whom he associates Komachi, and thus probably had at least some of his poetic training originate in their performance traditions. Like Komachi, his name as it appears in the *Kokinshū* denotes both a low rank at court and a claim to authorship of written poems that places him in an arena of social discourse with his superiors.

With the compilation of the *Kokinshū*, authorship of *uta* was marked in a distinctive new manner that drew on the language and practices of the *sechien* banquet for its legitimacy. This idealized vision of the courtier as a writer of poetry entailed a gendered pairing in which the female entertainer wielded her voice and sleeves while the male official wielded his eyes and brush. Although the *Kokinshū* includes poems by named female authors, the prefaces portray them as singers rather than writers. Ultimately, it is the male editors who guarantee authorship in the anthology, and who are responsible for (re)composing *yamato uta* as they transcribe, amend, and rewrite both songs and written poems. Their vision of court-sanctioned poetry as an exclusively male enterprise was to inform the practice of compiling imperial anthologies for centuries to come. As an anonymous woman in the critical work *Mumyōzōshi* (ca. 1200) would later note, "the fact that we still have no anthology compiled by women is truly lamentable" (*onna no imada shū nado erabu koto naki koso ito kuchioshikere*).[67]

Six Styles of Court Poetry

The visual and textual aspects of Yamato verse mentioned thus far appear to be most fully fleshed out in Tsurayuki's account of six poetic styles. One of the more significant differences between the Mana Preface and the Kana Preface can be found in the latter's description of these six forms of verse. Whereas the Mana Preface simply provides a perfunctory listing of six principles of poetry taken from the Great Preface to the *Classic of Poetry*, Tsurayuki goes into much greater detail in elaborating his six styles. In addition to providing occasional comments, he includes examples of verse for each one, many of which appear to function simultaneously as implicit evaluations of their relative merits. In this sense, Tsurayuki's example poems can be seen as providing a template for reading and evaluating poetry as much as for composition.

Although Tsurayuki's six styles often appear to be derived from continental poetics and Japanese texts such as the *Nihon shoki* or *Kakyō hyōshiki*, they frequently provide unique interpretations of the terms they borrow. The novelty of the Kana Preface's concept of style is suggested by the word selected to describe it. Variously used to mean "direction," "aura," "method," "appearance," and "bearing," *sama* had no prior connection with poetry.[68] As we shall observe, the strong visual connotations of the term can be seen at work in several of the styles provided by the Kana Preface, which often appears to capitalize on similarities between words that are based on orthography rather than pronunciation.

Part of the radical nature of Tsurayuki's six *sama* lies in his suggestion that they are applicable to poetry in any language. Some scholars have contrasted the Kana Preface with the Mana Preface on this basis, claiming that the styles of the former are the particular product of Yamato culture, whereas the six principles are viewed as universal to all poetry.[69] It can also be argued, however, that both are represented as sharing equally weighty claims to universality by virtue of their cosmological origins. The choice of the number six, for example, is informed by the cosmological coordinates of the "six cardinal directions" (*liuhe*)—North, South, East, West, Heaven and Earth. On account of its links to the fundamental structures of the universe, six was often used to delineate formal divisions within structured forms of human cultural activity (*wen*), such as the six notes of the Confucian musical scale or the six styles of painting and calligraphy. Tsurayuki appears to be claiming the potentially universal character of his six *sama* in the Kana Preface when he suggests that "no doubt these can be found in Tang poetry as well" (*Kara no uta ni mo kaku zo aru beki*).[70]

In addition to claiming a universality rivaling that of the Great Preface's six principles, the Kana Preface's six styles could assert connections to an equally ancient history. Each of the example poems Tsurayuki provides for his six styles is of considerable antiquity.[71] One is associated with the mythical ruler Nintoku, while the others appear to be anonymous versions of banquet songs that were themselves probably redactions of much earlier verses. The provenance of these example poems suggests a lineage for *yamato uta* whose antiquity rivaled that of the ancient Zhou dynasty's songs and hymns preserved in the *Classic of Poetry*. Insofar as the latter provided the basis for the six principles of poetry described in that text's Great Preface, such claims to antiquity in the Kana Preface suggest an ambitious attempt to claim equal relevance and cultural prestige for its six styles.

Given the assertion of an antiquity equivalent to that of *shi*, it is easy to see the six styles as fulfilling functions similar to those of the six principles of classical continental poetics. Scholars have long debated the relative emphasis placed on pragmatic versus aesthetic concerns in contrasting the six styles with their continental equivalents. Typically the Kana Preface has been seen as being concerned solely with the aesthetic and expressive challenges involved in balancing affect and language (*kokoro* and *kotoba* being the primary critical terms used in this section of the text), in contrast to the supposedly more political and didactic concerns of the Mana Preface. Such divisions, however, were only sporadically maintained in classical poetics. The critical tradition associated with the Great Preface tended not to differentiate between the pragmatic aspects of poetry (political, ritual, and didactic) and formal aspects, such as metrics and types of metaphor.[72] Orthodox definitions of the six principles in the Heian state curriculum, for example, drew on a commentary to the Great Preface named the *Maoshi zhengyi* ("On the Correct Meaning of Mao's Version of the *Classic of Poetry*," 642), written by the scholar Kong Yingda (574–648), in which both aspects have equal weight.[73]

One of the more novel accounts of Tsurayuki's six styles introduces another element to the discussion by treating them as a different combinations of scene and sentiment. According to Takeoka Masao, each example poem can be read as a configuration of the two elements of *mono* and *kokoro*, in keeping with the Kana Preface's opening description of poetry as a combination of things seen and heard with thoughts in the heart.[74] Tsurayuki's interest in the ways in which scene and sentiment related to one another could have been inspired by a fundamental shift in emphasis taking place in the poetry of his time. Whereas earlier poetry tended to have greater variation in its descriptions of landscape, especially in the elaboration of place-names and their epithets, Heian poetry, including Heian variants of earlier songs, tended to favor a diversity of words for expressing human sentiment and a more limited repertoire of expressions for describing landscape.[75] There are fewer place-names in the *Kokinshū* than the *Man'yōshū*, for example, and those that do appear in the former often seem to be chosen on the basis of their potential for poetic wordplay.[76] In showing the different ways that *mono* and *kokoro* could be brought together, the Kana Preface provided a new dimension to distinctions between different kinds of *uta*, while at the same time suggesting how these configurations could be correlated with the six principles of the Mana Preface.

In the first of Tsurayuki's styles, that of "allegorical verse" (*soe uta*), natural scenes function as analogies for human affairs. The example poem appears to be simply a description of a landscape devoid of any human presence, were it not for Tsurayuki's supplemental comment that it refers to Nintoku's court. Spring's budding blossoms thus become a manifestation of the new ruler's vigor and virtue:[77]

In Naniwazu	***Naniwazu ni***
bloom these tree blossoms!	***saku ya ko no hana***
From winter's shroud,	***fuyugomori***
now burst in spring,	***ima wa harube to***
bloom these tree blossoms!	***saku ya ko no hana***[78]

The Naniwazu verse occupies first place among the six styles partly because Naniwazu is given such an illustrious lineage in the *Kokinshū*'s history of *uta*, and partly because it exemplifies the style of political commentary embodied in the Great Preface's first and foremost poetic principle, that of the "airs" (*feng*). Natural images in poems from the *Classic of Poetry* were often viewed by Confucian commentators as coded political messages. The mode of analogy embodied by this principle is at once rhetorical and pragmatic. Landscape depictions could signal human concerns in an oblique mode, thereby allowing people to address one another in a manner that observed the proprieties of social hierarchy or the exigencies of diplomatic discourse. Through such songs, according to the Great Preface, ministers can criticize their lords, and the ways of the people can be influenced and transformed. In keeping with the royal nature of the *Kokinshū*, the Kana Preface's example of allegorical verse praises the sovereign rather than censures him.

Like *feng*, the suasive and communicative powers of *soe uta* are endowed with a special status among the six styles. No other style has an additional gloss provided by Tsurayuki, who goes out of his way to specify the poem's historical significance in the manner of commentators to the *Classic of Poetry*. At the same time, the word used to describe allegorical verse in the Kana Preface has a history that is unique to the Yamato court and is as old as that represented in the continental classics. The term *soe uta* appears in the *Nihon shoki*'s account of the enthronement of the mythical first sovereign, Jimmu, where it is associated with the martial "Kume verse" (*Kume uta*) and performed along with "inverted language" (*sakashima-goto*) as a means for dispelling malign influences.[79] Possibly these songs were coded messages used in battle, making them an appropriate ancestor for a mode of communication that uses descriptions of landscape to signal political intentions.

The Kana Preface's second style of verse provides another mix of Yamato particularity and continental orthodoxy. The phrase "enumerative verse" (*kazoe uta*) used to describe this second style recalls one meaning of *fu* (the second of the Great Preface's six principles) as the action of counting or enumeration. Tsurayuki's example poem is a *mono no na* (names of things) verse that lists the names of various birds within a love poem. I have loosely translated the names of these birds as "dove," "rob[in]," and "raven" to take advantage of similar orthographic possibilities in English:

On blooming flowers	**saku hana ni**
*fixate***d ove***r is this self,*	*omoi tsu(ku/***gu**)**mi no**
rob*bed of its senses,*	**aji***ki* *nasa*
by a **raven***ous fever,*	*mi ni i***tazu***ki no*
pierced unawares.	*iru mo shirade*[80]

This style of verse depends on certain peculiarities of Heian *kana* script for its effects. The insertion of bird names into the poem is made possible by the orthographic conventions of the time, which made no distinction between voiced and unvoiced consonants. As one scholar has noted, such conventions also made it possible for words with the same orthography but radically different pronunciation to overlap in written poetry.[81] Connections to writing are also suggested in this style's Mana Preface corollary *fu*. As a verb, *fu* could refer to the act of writing, as well as to that of levying taxes, narrating events in a plain style devoid of metaphor, or enumerating objects.[82] As we have seen, a similar connection between counting and composition in Heian poetics was already present in the verb *yomu* (to compose); both practices were increasingly becoming associated with *kana* writing in the late ninth century. Whereas enumeration in literary Chinese could involve line after line of thickly descriptive imagery and objects piled one on top of the other, the Kana Preface condenses this effect within the thirty-one syllables of orthodox *yamato uta* through the visual ambiguities of *kana* writing.

In reserving a place for *mono no na* poems within his six styles, Tsurayuki suggests the importance of written *uta* within his poetics. Acrostic verses are granted not only the status of a particular style within the Kana Preface but also an entire category within the accompanying anthology. The category itself appears to have been particularly closely associated with literacy and learning. Most of the poets who provided poems for the Names of Things section of the *Kokinshū* were scholars, and the editors' arrangement of this category suggests a strong association with lexicography. Overall, poems in Names of Things are organized by the semantic categories used in Chinese-character dictionaries from the Heian period.[83]

Perhaps as important as their writerly quality are the configurations of scene and sentiment that Names of Things enable. Within the *Kokinshū* they occupy a space between Seasons and Longing, suggesting a correspondingly pivotal place between the complementary entities of Heaven and humanity. The Kana Preface's example of enumerative verse, whose scene of various birds is intertwined with the sentiments of a suffering lover, suggests the complex interweaving of the two realms that writing could produce. It is often in such complexity and semantic enrichment of the line that Tsurayuki appears to have found the most meaningful configurations of poetic form.

The distinction between the next two styles, "likeness verse" (*nazurae uta*) and "comparison verse" (*tatoe uta*), also appear to depend on the visual reception of written poems. Scholars have long been hard-pressed to pinpoint the difference between these two styles. Their Mana Preface counterparts share an equally ambiguous history in the continental tradition, where definitions vary enormously. The two characters were often treated as a compound *bixing*, which described analogical relations between natural imagery and human emotion in *shi* poetry, and had been used in the *Shoku nihon kōki* in this manner to describe *yamato uta*. According to the *Maoshi zhengyi* commentary to the Great Preface (a text upon the Mana Preface draws at several points), *bi* refers to an overt likeness between tangible objects (often marked by the character 如) and *xing* to an implicit likeness between a plant or animal and a human situation produced through simple juxtaposition of the two elements.[84] Within the continental poetic tradition such relations were viewed as manifestations of fundamental analogical correspondences embedded in cosmological structures, rather than arbitrary products of human imagination.[85]

The first of these two styles, *nazurae uta*, appears to rely on the written effects of *kana* writing to produce its forms of likeness. The example Tsurayuki provides draws on the rhetoric of pivot-words to overlay a scene of fading morning frost with the sentiments of a lover's life-threatening despair:

My lord, if on this morning,	*kimi ni kesa*
while frost still lingers,	**ashita no shimo no**
lying there, rising, *you are to leave,*	***okite*** *inaba*
with each pang of longing,	*koishiki goto ni*
this fading would go on!	***kie ya wataramu***[86]

This poem presents a complicated interweaving of scene and sentiment in the arrangement of its words. It begins with the speaker addressing a lover in the morning, and then shifts to a description of frost on the ground as that same lover prepares to depart. The shift from scene to sentiment here moves seamlessly across a single cluster of syllables *o ki te*, which refers to both the frost "laid" (置きて) on the ground and a lover "rising" (起きて) to leave. The poem then proceeds to shift from the departing lover's actions to the emotional state of the speaker. Both interior effect and exterior scene are finally fused in the last line, whose "fading" (*kie*) refers both the melting of frost and the dissipation of the dejected speaker's life force.

The majority of scholars who have written about this poem hold that the basis for similarity between scene and sentiment here is implicitly visual, with the sight of evaporating morning frost being a metaphorical manifestation of the lover's spirits as they expire from longing.[87] The verb *nazuraeru* itself typically denotes the visual likening of one thing to another.[88] It could also be argued, however, that another visual similarity between the two elements is sustained through orthography, with the two separate words for "rising" and "leaving" appearing as one cluster of letters. As will be argued in the next section of this chapter, the visual dimension of pivot-words is an important aspect of their rhetoric that has often been overlooked, in particular within medieval redactions of this example poem.

In contrast to *nazurae uta*, the fourth style of *tatoe uta* embodies an older rhetorical means for pairing scene and sentiment in *uta*. In Tsurayuki's example poem, invisible emotion and visible landscape are likened to one another literally on the basis of their magnitude, and formally on the basis of their placement parallel to one another as separate hemistiches within the poem, almost as though they were complementary lines in a couplet:

My longings	*waga koi wa*
are beyond counting,	*yomu tomo tsukiji*
though the storm-lashed	**ariso umi no**
shore's fine-grained sands	**hama no masago wa**
be fully counted.	**yomi tsukusu tomo**[89]

The poem Tsurayuki provides as an example of *tatoe uta* echoes an earlier established form of rhetoric, one found most prominently in the *Kokinshū*'s anonymous love poems. In this poetic style, scene and sentiment are juxtaposed as discrete elements rather than being grammatically intertwined. An equivalent form can be found in the *Man'yōshū* category of verse in which "thoughts are related with natural objects" (*kibutsu chinshi*). In the Kana Preface poem, the boundary between human longing and the seashore is rhetorically maintained through the repetition of the action of "counting" (*yomu*). Such repetitions themselves were also a hallmark of earlier verse forms.

At the same time as it implies a parallel between scene and sentiment, the content of Tsurayuki's example poem suggests that the former is not equal to the latter when it declares that the invisible world of human emotion cannot be encompassed by or enumerated in words. Neither the counting of sand nor the counting of syllables in poetic form can necessarily encapsulate the magnitude of the speaker's longing. There are suggestive similarities here between this archaic style of *uta* and that of *xing* (arising) in the Great Preface, which typically takes the form of a simple juxtaposition of natural imagery and human emotion. In Six Dynasties criticism, this rhetorical form was often viewed as one in which a surplus of meaning or sentiment lingered suggestively in the reader/listener's mind. A similar aesthetic of omission can be seen in the Kana Preface's critique of Narihira's poetic style.

The absolute separation between scene and sentiment in Tsurayuki's comparison verse, enforced by the repetition of words in both parts of the example poem, suggests a gap between *mono* and *kokoro*. In this regard, the poem can be read as an indirect critique of the style it represents, insofar as the former cannot encompass the latter. Likeness verse, by contrast, closes the gap between scene and sentiment, encompassing both within the same *kana* letters. This distinction between *tatoe uta* and *nazurae uta* also implies a contrast between earlier forms of rhetoric that depended on verbal repetition to link scene and sentiment, and a more "modern" one in which *kana* letters could condense this repetitive element into a single pivot-word.

The Kana Preface's interest in achieving a rhetorical fusion between scene and sentiment is also suggested by the negative value it ascribes to poems that describe human feelings without any recourse to imagery. The fifth style of "plain verse" (*tada uta*) contains no scenic elements. Even the "leaves" of the example are written words produced by people:

If falsehood	*itsuwari no*
was not the way of the world,	*naki yo nariseba*
how great would be	*ika bakari*

the happiness brought	*hito no koto no ha*
by the leaves of people's words!	*ureshikaramashi*[90]

The lack of any scene in this poem does not mean that its sentiments are manifest in a transparent, straightforward manner. As with the example poem for comparison verse, the one provided for plain verse seems to critique the style it embodies, this time by suggesting that people's words can produce "falsehood" (*itsuwari*). In sum, both example poems appear to allude self-consciously to poetic practice by declaring the potential shortcomings of counting (composition) in the first case and that of word-leaves (epistolary poems) in the second.

Like its analogical opposite *soe uta*, *tada uta* already possessed an established history in poetics by Tsurayuki's time.[91] Unlike *soe uta*, however, Tsurayuki's category appears to depart from the Great Preface's correlate. The example poem's entreaty for honesty might allude to the Great Preface's corresponding poetic category of *ya*, a form of poetry associated with the rectification of proper social relationships based on trustworthiness and observance of correct behavior. The poems usually associated with this category in the *Classic of Poetry* were banquet songs from the Zhou dynasty. The Kana Preface's example poem appears to claim a similar provenance for the category it represents insofar as it is an anonymous verse that could possibly have been derived from a *saibara* sung at a feast. Both continental and Yamato forms of song could thus be invested with political overtones. Whereas *ya* could carry the further connotation of being forthright, however, *tada uta* are implicitly criticized in the Kana Preface as potentially deceitful.

Similarities between the six styles and the six principles are perhaps most pronounced in the Kana Preface's final category of "incantatory verse" (*iwai uta*), which is directed to deities in the same manner as its continental counterpart of "temple hymns" (*song*). In Tsurayuki's example poem, the hymn appears to be praising a sovereign whose virtuous reign ensures material bounty:

This lord's lordly hall	***kono tono wa***
is bounteous indeed!	***mube mo tomikeri***
With lucky three-stemmed grass,	***saki kusa no***

thatched in three and four layers,	***mitsuba yotsuba ni***
has my lord's lordly hall been built!	***tonozukuri seri***[92]

Incantatory verse seem to be distinct from the preceding five styles, insofar as it foregrounds a pragmatic dimension to verse as a ritual speech-act, rather than treating it as a formal arrangement of words. Some scholars have suggested that the Kana Preface marks a historical shift in the meaning of the verb *iwau* from incantatory speech uttered by the gods which influences people and the world, to prayers through which people seek to affect deities and spirits.[93] By extension, the lord addressed in the Kana Preface's poem would have had connections to divinity as either a ruler or aristocrat who could trace his lineage back through the deities of the *Nihon shoki*.

At the same time as it seems to be primarily defined in terms of its function, however, incantatory verse also can be seen as representing a particular configuration of scene and sentiment. The example provided, like that of the preceding two poems, appears to contain a self-reflexive reference to poetics. Once again, leaves are mentioned, and thus, perhaps, written poetry implied. Unlike the hall created in Susanoo's verse, interior and exterior in this song are one and the same. The leaves of Tsurayuki's example poem provide a perfect union of scene and sentiment in the form of a "lordly residence" (*tono*) and the "lord" (again *tono)* who occupies its interior. Whereas the repetition of words marked the boundary between *mono* and *kokoro* in comparison verse, incantatory verse claims a union of the two, one in which the bounty represented by the exterior of the hall and the leaves that thatch it are a direct extension and manifestation of its lordly inhabitant's virtue.

The repetition of words and phrases found here was a characteristic feature of Heian song. Tsurayuki's own example verse in this case is derived from a *saibara* that praises and blesses a lordly figure by alluding to his wealth in the luxuriant thatching of his hall:

My lord's lordly hall	*kono tono wa*
indeed is so!	*mube mo*
Bounteous indeed!	*mube mo tomikeri*
With lucky three-stemmed grass,	*saki kusa no*

aware,	*aware*
with lucky three-stemmed grass,	*saki kusa no*
hare,	*hare*
thatched in three and four layers,	*mitsuba yotsuba no naka ni*
has my lord's lordly hall been built!	*tonozukuri seri ya*[94]

The Kana Preface pares away the rhythmic refrains of this song to render it into a *yamato uta*. Such actions were also an essential part of the process of compilation, as the editors collected, transcribed, and transformed banquet songs for inclusion in the anthology. Once again, the content of an example poem suggests a further comment on poetic practice. The act of shaping a hall whose roof is luxuriantly thatched with lucky leaves in this poem suggests a similar form of construction taking place in the making of the *Kokinshū*. Just as stalks of plants are cut off and used to thatch the roof, the lyrics of songs are cut back and arranged to fill in the anthology's structure. In this sense, Tsurayuki's final poem in his account of Yamato verse's six styles can also be read as a blessing of the *Kokinshū* and of its lord Daigo whose virtue, like that of the lord in the song, is made manifest through the structures constructed at his commands.

Sound and Vision in Verse

From the very start, the Kana Preface appears to associate Yamato verse with written poetry rather than song. Although it frequently borrows preexisting terms and concepts in its definition of the six styles, its distinctions often appear to depend on the visual properties of *kana* writing, particularly in the case of the categories of *kazoe uta* and *nazurae uta*. In this area, it would appear that the Kana Preface makes a contribution to poetics which is truly original, rather than simply being based on a patchwork of clichés derived from Chinese texts.[95]

Tsurayuki's departure from the song-based norms of continental poetics is arguably one of the more noteworthy aspects of his treatise, but did it have any lasting effects? Placing the Kana Preface in a larger historical perspective would entail placing its emphasis on the visual within the broader historical development of the institutions and practices surrounding Japanese court poetry. In this regard, it is important to note that interest in sound did not come to the fore in mainstream poetics until roughly two centuries after the Kana Preface was written. Once this emphasis was articulated, it became orthodox up through modern times. One result has been that the majority of scholars to date have privileged sound over vision in their accounts of Heian poetics.[96] Conventional wisdom holds that *kana* writing was intended solely for the purpose of transcribing sound. In fact, this mode of transcription allowed for more ambiguities than modern methods, providing the courtier-writer with a correspondingly greater arsenal of poetic ambiguities.

One obvious example of textual ambiguity in Heian *kana* is the lack of the diacritical marks known as *dakuten*, which are used to distinguish voiced from unvoiced consonants.[97] Such omissions could lead to significant differences in the meaning of a verse, as for example in Komachi's renowned complaint about the fickleness of the human heart. As already mentioned, the flower representing emotion in that poem changes hue either visibly or not depending on how the letters are read aloud (her use of visuality is thus doubly apt). Rather than seeing such ambiguities as a deficiency, the Kana Preface appears to embrace the possibilities they presented for enriching the semantic texture of *yamato uta*. Tsurayuki's example of an enumerative verse, in which three objects are listed within a lover's tormented plea, provides another instance. The rhetorical form of this *mono no na* poem could be likened to a textile pattern in which the embroidery of damask or brocade creates a figure that stands out from a plainer background. Just as the value of textiles can be gauged in part by the intensity of labor required to create their complex patterns, a poem's value could be determined by the intensity of craft needed to weave multiple visual semantic strands within a swatch of text.

Another feature of *kana* that is more frequently overlooked in accounts of Heian court poetry is its lack of pitch-accent markings. Shifts in the relative pitch at which syllables are enunciated, whether rising, descending, or level, provide crucial distinctions between similar words in both premodern and modern forms of spoken Japanese. The absence of any clear indication of pitch in the *Kokinshū*'s poems was eventually seen as an impediment to interpreting them. In the twelfth century, versions of the anthology known as "voice-marked texts" (*shōtenbon*) were produced with diacritical markings denoting the relative pitch accent of individual syllables.[98] The use of such marks in *Kokinshū* poems appears to have originated with the poet-scholar Fujiwara no Kenshō (ca. 1130–1210) in the 1190s and continued into the fifteenth century. They were developed more systematically and precisely by his rival Fujiwara no Teika (1162–1241), who attempted a partial pitch-based orthography in which, for example, the letter を represents a higher pitch than the letter お. Because medieval scholarship on *uta* was increasingly intended to instruct newcomers from the linguistically distinct eastern regions of Japan in the western court's poetic traditions, such texts might have been designed to address differences in dialect between instructors and pupils.

The distinctions in pitch accent provided by voice-marked texts also offer insights into the nature of pivot-words, arguably the most distinctive aspect of Heian poetry. In many cases, these diacritics could specify one meaning at the expense of another. Some voice-marked texts apply this distinction to the Kana Preface's example of *nazurae uta* by marking the letters おきて with the diacritics 上上平 to denote the inflection for "rising to go" rather than that for "lying on the ground."[99] Modern scholars of *uta* tend to characterize pivot-words as "homophones" (*dōon igi*) or a form of pun in which a particular combination of sounds carries multiple meanings.[100] Given the distinctions made in voice-marked texts, however, *kakekotoba* such as the *okite* of the Kana Preface's poem might be more appropriately termed a form of "homograph" (*dōji igi*) in which the same combination of letters can signify different words when read aloud. This rhetoric in turn can be seen as a peculiarly textual form of the visual likenesses between separate objects that permeated Heian poetry at the time.[101]

Pivot-words did not depend exclusively on the visual effects of letters to erase distinctions in sound. A similar wealth of potentially ambiguous poetic meanings could be produced through the act of recitation. Intoning syllables in the metronomic manner associated with *yomu* removed changes in pitch accent that were used to distinguish words in daily speech. Whether or not the practice of recitation led to an awareness of orthographic ambiguity or vice versa is impossible to determine. Insofar as Tsurayuki uses the word *moji* to refer to both syllables and letters, textuality and recitation appear to have been related practices for him. The fact that the mid–ninth-century proliferation of *kana* was accompanied by an expansion in the meaning and scope of both *yomu* and pivot-words suggests that both writing and recitation were considered similar phenomena, insofar as they distinguished poetic language from the rhythms and shifts in pitch accent that were essential elements of daily speech.

One thing that does appear certain is that the diffusion of *kana* writing enabled the proliferation of a larger repertoire of pivot-words than had been available to earlier poets.[102] Although pivot-words are present in *Man'yōshū* poetry, their number had increased radically in Tsurayuki's time.[103] Their proliferation in Heian poetry was accompanied by changes in the structural norms of *uta*. Earlier forms of verse often contained a bipartite structure in which the expressions of sentiment were prefaced by a recitation of "ancient words" (*furugoto*) evoking a particular geographical location laden with mythical and religious significance. In the terminology of later times, these descriptions of landscape are "prefatory phrases" (*jokotoba*) which precede the part of the poem devoted to human intentions or actions. Scholars identify three categories of linkage between the prefatory phrase and the *kokoro* portion of early verse: metaphorical equivalence, word repetition, and pivot-words.[104] Generally speaking, Heian poetry witnessed a shift from the first two forms to the third, as the Kana Preface indirectly attests to when it contrasts the older *tatoe uta* form of rhetoric with that of *nazurae uta*.

Pivot-words thus condensed the rhetorics of repetition and harmony that were hallmarks of prefatory phrases in earlier verse.[105] Heian poetry also witnessed an increase in pivot-words that, while semantically related to the main sentence structure of a poem, were not necessarily related to it in a syntactic sense. In practice, the two portions of a poem brought together in this manner frequently reflected the fundamental cosmological categories of Heaven and humanity. The majority of pivot-words, including such common examples as *matsu* (pine tree/pine away), *miotsukushi* (buoy/exhaust oneself), *kai* (shell/purpose), and *mirume* (sea-pine/glimpse), tend to combine a natural object with a human action or emotion. This same division can be characterized also grammatically, as one that combines "things seen and heard" in the form of nouns with feelings and actions in the form of adjectives and verbs.[106] Syntactic and semantic pivots of these sorts enabled a poem to create connections between Heaven and humanity in a manner that evoked the juxtaposed parallelisms of *shi* poetry within the brief space of thirty-one syllables.[107] *Kana* orthography thus provided a new technology for configuring the two elements in a sleeker form that was also more versatile in its application.

The attempt to bridge a gap between letter and sound in voice-marked versions of the *Kokinshū* suggests the extent to which early Heian texts represented a form of linguistic alterity for twelfth-century Japanese readers. This perception was in part the product of a pedagogical industry erected around *uta* at a time when knowledge about poetics had become a tangible form of wealth that could be produced and exchanged in the form of edited texts and treatises. Claims to "correct" interpretations of poems with pivot-words carried with them claims to correct and exclusive knowledge of the poetic tradition, knowledge that could be traded as a form of intellectual capital.

Whereas modern literacy criticism tends to revel in the ambiguities that pivot-words enable, the opposite appears to have been true of its medieval counterpart. One scholar has argued that voice-marked versions of the *Kokinshū* display a tendency to favor "straightforward" readings of pivot-words in which the most commonsense interpretation of a poem was preferred over ones that might threaten its semantic coherence by producing tangential meanings.[108] This tendency to shy away from indeterminacy might also explain why *kakekotoba* were never identified or articulated as a distinctive object of knowledge in medieval poetic criticism. Tsurayuki's category of "likeness verse" appears to have been the only attempt to define and categorize this form of rhetoric for centuries to come, and it appears to have been largely ignored by later commentators.

The industry of interpretation and pedagogy that began to surround the *Kokinshū* with commentaries and guides to pronunciation in the twelfth century also displayed an increasing interest in poetic euphony. In this regard, the period can be seen as marking a significant divide between Heian and medieval poetics, one in which specificities of sound replaced the rich visual world of earlier *kana* poetry. Whereas Tsurayuki emphasized the written word in his account of *yamato uta*, later poets and scholars turned their attention to its musical qualities.[109]

A growing interest in sound also led to an increased interest in metrics during this same period, which first produced terms such as *onritsu* to refer to a poetic meter based solely on the enunciation of syllables.[110]

In his account of the six styles, Tsurayuki appears to have been aware of *kana*'s potential for creating new relations between scene and sentiment in poetry through vision rather than sound.[111] His categories of *kazoe uta* and *tatoe uta* in particular depended on the peculiar ability of this script to deform speech in order to create distinctive harmonies between the human and natural spheres. Judging from the interpolated commentary to the Kana Preface, which takes issue with every single example of the six styles that Tsurayuki provides, the original significance of his approach appears to have already been lost by the mid-Heian period. Nevertheless, the text's account of *yamato uta* possesses a sophistication and ambition in its vision of *kana*'s distinctive contribution to poetry that is noteworthy in its own right. Far from being representative of a tradition that it helped establish, it could be argued that the Kana Preface was, at least in this regard, highly unorthodox both in its time and later.

Chapter Five

Screen Poetry and Reflections of Power

Placing Screen Poetry in Historical Perspective

Regardless of its later history, the visual poetics outlined in the Kana Preface must have resonated with the forms of composition prevalent at Daigo's court. There is perhaps no better example of the attention paid to the visual and material aspects of written poetry in the early tenth century than the phenomenon of inscribing *uta* on folding screens depicting landscapes. Known as "screen poetry" (*byōbu uta*), this new form of verse flourished during the same period in which the *Kokinshū* and Tsurayuki's preface were being distributed at Daigo's court. This chapter will provide an appraisal of the history, practices and forms of rhetoric associated with screen poetry, concluding with an evaluation of the role it played in Tsurayuki's development of a distinct and richly complex poetics in which reflective surfaces refracted and multiplied space. Like the one envisaged in the Kana Preface, this was a distinctly visual poetic that marked the place of the otherwise invisible poet at court.

Like poetry matches, screen poetry was one of the paradigmatic forms of poetic practice associated with the *utayomi* (composer). The editors of the *Kokinshū*, along with other poets from their social background, were frequently employed by aristocrats at Daigo's court to compose poems for screen paintings. Among these screen poets, Tsurayuki has attracted the most critical interest among modern scholars, and not just on account of his fame as the author of the Kana Preface. Information surrounding his screen poetry far exceeds that of any of his contemporaries in scope and detail. More than five hundred poems, comprising the first four of nine scrolls in his posthumous poetry collection *Tsurayuki-shū*, were composed for screen paintings.[1] They are arranged in roughly chronological order, making it possible to trace the poet's activities over the four decades from 905 up through to 945, the final year at which both his poetry and life can be dated.

The abundance of screen poems preserved in the *Tsurayuki-shū* offers a uniquely rich resource for understanding one of the signal poetic practices of the early Heian period. The composition of *uta* poems for screen paintings in the late ninth and early tenth centuries, like poetry matches, was an unprecedented development in court culture. The stylistic features of screen poetry are often seen as a formative influence in the establishment of a "*Kokinshū* style" of formal poetry deemed suitable for an imperial anthology, as well as the development of fictional prose. One succinct formulation of this style by the scholar Fujioka Tadaharu describes it as conceptually mannered and highly subjective in its representation of the natural world—features that are attributed to the practice of imaginatively associating with a painted human figure in screen poetry.[2] Another scholar sees the "public" nature of formal court poetry in its emphasis on the forms of visual metaphor associated with screen poetry.[3] He has also argued that the miniature scale of many of the settings depicted in screen poetry and *Kokinshū* poems were inspired by the carefully ordered landscapes of the aristocrats' villas gardens.[4] As we will see, both poetry and painting were intimately connected to garden design in this period.

The challenges posed to providing a detailed evaluation of screen poetry are similar to those faced in the study of early poetry matches. Although screen poetry clearly played an important role within the spectrum of poetic practices of the early Heian court, there remains little in the way of a detailed record from the tenth century with which to reconstruct or appraise the phenomenon. Almost no accounts exist of the manner in which screen poems were produced or appreciated. Moreover, we have those paintings from the early Heian period, and those that do survive are not accompanied by screen poems written specifically for them. Most of our information about screen poetry comes from prefaces to the poems as they appear in later collections, and these are usually terse annotations that briefly note the date of composition, individual scenes depicted in the painting, and the identity of the sponsor and recipient of the screen.

Screen poetry, like so much of the poetry from this period, sought to bring Heaven and humanity together in new configurations. In this case, the combination can be thought of as one between social setting and landscape scenes. Following the practice of modern Japanese scholars, I use the term "social setting" here to describe the social relations obtaining at particular formal gatherings (what Katagiri among others has referred to as the poem's *ba*), such as annual observances, birthday celebrations, and banquets. By contrast, "scene" will refer to the individual landscape depictions in screen paintings (described as *tokoro* in the prose prefaces to such poems). The screen poetry of Tsurayuki and his peers often merged both forms of space by creating forms of perspective that could be simultaneously located both inside and outside the painting on a screen. Through this blurring, written *uta* provided a sophisticated technique for staging power and authority at palace banquets and birthday celebrations.

Equations between different scenes and settings held significance for not only the patrons of these events but also the poets who produced them. The blurring of perspective that screen poetry made possible enabled Tsurayuki to develop a complex visual and spatial poetics that commented on his own place within the court as a lower-ranking male official who composed screen poems at a distance from the actual social settings in which they were put to work. In this sense, his poetics offers insights into how the *utayomi* figured within the larger ritual and political configurations of the early Heian court. The practices surrounding screen poetry rarely seem to have involved the poet gazing on the scene depicted in a painting. Rather, the composition of such poems typically required that the low-ranking courtier work from a written topic handed down by a social superior in the same manner as was done with other forms of harmonizing verse. It is through this lens that I will approach screen poetry, rather than in terms of its supposed links to a native Japanese form of painting.

Gender, Genre, and Yamato Style

The ways in which the history of screen poetry at the Heian court is discussed in modern accounts tend to associate it with distinctly indigenous styles of painting that are either implicitly or explicitly gendered as feminine. Such assumptions, however, are not necessarily informative or accurate in assessing the impact of screen poetry during its initial period of efflorescence in the early tenth century. Practices linking

Chinese styles of poetry and painting were established features of the Heian court from Saga's time onward. Accounts that limit themselves to *uta*, on the other hand, typically begin in Montoku's reign (851–858) with a poem by his attendant Sanjō no Machi on a waterfall composed for the reigning sovereign, and one by Sosei on the Tatsuta River composed for Seiwa's Fujiwara consort Takaiko. The prefaces to these poems in the *Kokinshū* go out of their way to note that these *uta* are inspired by paintings, but remain unclear as to whether these poems were actually attached to screens.

Both poems have been linked by modern scholars to the development of a native genre of painting known as *yamato-e* (Yamato paintings). Sosei's poem in fact appears to be the earliest one describing a painting with a specifically Japanese locale. Whether the depiction of the landscape that inspires Sosei's poem is stylistically distinct from a Chinese one, however, is less clear. The term *yamato-e* first appears nearly a century later in the *Gonki* diary of the famed Heian calligrapher Fujiwara no Yukinari (972–1027).[5] By contrast, the category of Tang painting appears to have an older history. The term *kara zu* (Tang composition) can be traced back to Uda's court, where it appears in the *Kurōdo shiki* ("Procedures for the Secretariat," 890). The articulation of categories such as *yamato-e* (Yamato paintings) or *onna-e* (women's paintings) with which screen poems are often associated could very well have been an eleventh-century phenomenon, part of the larger fascination with elaborating differences in Yamato and Tang styles that can be seen in the *monogatari* tale literature of that period. In the context in which Tsurayuki and his peers composed screen poems, however, this sort of reflexive self-awareness of their compositions as distinctly "Yamato" ones is purely speculative.

In modern usage, the term *yamato-e* is not defined simply by the content of the painting but by its style as well. Such definitions of a specifically "Japanese" form of landscape painting, moreover, often spill over into more questionable characterizations. One scholar, for example, detects a softness and intimacy in Yamato paintings that he sees as contrasting with the allegedly suprahuman and transcendental qualities of their Tang counterparts.[6] Such distinctions in style are often gendered by scholars who see *yamato-e* as embodying a uniquely feminine sensibility, in part perhaps because court women often played a prominent role in producing and commissioning paintings.[7] One frequently cited example is Sanjō no Machi's poem in the *Kokinshū*, which describes a waterfall on a miniaturized scale and with an emotional intensity that is often ascribed to *uta* on paintings.

> Composed by Sanjō no Machi when she was an attendant of our deceased sovereign Montoku. His Majesty was perusing a landscape scene on a folding screen at the palace when, entranced by the spot where water was splashing down from a cascading fall, he commanded those in attendance to compose verse on this as a topic.

Does this waterfall	*omoiseku*
come from thoughts dammed up	*kokoro no uchi no*
deep inside the heart?	*taki nare ya*
Its sharp descent is seen,	*otsu to wa miredo*
but no sound is heard.	*oto no kikoenu*[8]

Sanjō no Machi's poem creates a seamless pivot between interior sentiment and exterior scene out of a situation in which there is no preexisting visual similarity between the two. Both the waterfall and the feelings she describes share a mute, downward trajectory. Silence in this poem is both a condition of the painting and of being an attendant whose fortunes depend on her sovereign's favors. The poem thus gestures both to the landscape scene depicted in the painting and to the social setting in which it is being viewed and commented on. As we shall see, this sort of dual perspective is itself a hallmark of many poems about paintings, particularly those attached to them.

Leaving its particular rhetorical qualities aside, there is nothing in Sanjō no Machi's *uta* which implies that the landscape she views is a distinctly Yamato one. In tone and conceit, her words echo a poem by Saga, which also describes the muteness of a painted waterfall. It is possible that her verse is inspired by a line in Saga's poem, or by some similar poem written in literary Chinese that could have been provided as a topic. One prominent art historian has argued that the waterfall mentioned in Sanjō no Machi's *uta* could very well have been the same one depicted in the painting that Saga gazed on when he composed his *shi* poem.[9] In her capacity as an attendant to Montoku in his living quarters, it is very likely that Sanjō no Machi would have seen this painting, which was placed in the room at the Seiryōden containing the sovereign's dining table.

The case of Sanjō no Machi's poem is one reminder that, despite the variety of assumptions posited by modern scholars in their accounts of screen poetry, the historical record offers no evidence that there was ever any fixed association among genres of painting, genres of poetry, and gendered sensibilities at the early Heian court. As this example suggests, both *uta* and *shi* could be composed for the same painting. If anything, it seems most likely that many of the screen *uta* of the tenth century were composed for paintings whose depictions of various scenes were informed by continental conventions. As Watanabe Hideo has noted in an exhaustive survey of Tsurayuki's screen poetry, many of the topics on which these poems were composed closely resemble established themes in Tang-dynasty painting, making it likely that the screens in question were painted in a similar style.[10] In such a situation, the only sign that a generic painted landscape might be a "Yamato" one would have been the poetic inscription of Japanese place-names on its surface. In other words, it is entirely possible that poems on paintings did not passively reflect a landscape already inscribed with a particular meaning. Rather, they actively constructed such meanings. As will be discussed later in this chapter, the language of poems often played a central role in endowing generic depictions of landscapes with particular spatial and temporal significances.

Perhaps one reason why the association between a purportedly feminine style and screen poetry is so strong in the modern reconstructions of the latter's history is because women were actively involved in this arena. To some degree, associations among women, paintings, and poems appear to be especially pronounced at Uda's court at the end of the ninth century. During the same period in which this sovereign was negotiating the royal succession with the Fujiwara Northern House (in part through poetry matches), the number of *uta* composed for screen paintings begins to grow markedly. The prefaces to these poems in the household collections of the poets from whom they were commissioned reveal a wide range of subject matter and an intimate connection with the female relatives of Tokihira in particular. Examples include one poem composed for a painting depicting cherry blossom viewing which was presented by Uda to Takaiko on her fiftieth birthday, four poems written on a screen in the palace, one poem for a screen painting in Atsuko's apartments depicting women divers, and yet another for a painting in her living quarters that depicted mountainside paddies.[11]

Atsuko appears to have been a particularly avid sponsor of screen poetry. As Tokihira's sister and the adoptive mother of Daigo, she represented the Northern House's interests within the palace at a transitional juncture in the succession to the throne. Given this political context and Atsuko's particular position within it, it is possible to see the development of screen poetry at Uda's court as a Fujiwara strategy, paralleling that of poetry matches being pursued by Uda's female kin. Perhaps for this reason, Atsuko appears to provide the earliest example of a female salon supported by male relatives, a phenomenon that contributed significantly to Heian cultural production in painting, poetry, and prose in the next century. This salon and Lady Ise in particular, who was one of its most active members, seems to have played a part in the development of the earliest pictorial narratives written in *kana* depicting fictional romances.[12] The most noteworthy example of this innovative practice can be found in the opening group of thirty-three poems in the *Ise-shū* (*Ise Collection*), which trace a series of encounters between anonymous men and women and are likely to have been first written down between 893 and 896.[13]

The potential for screen poetry to develop such fictional narratives had much to do with its capacity to multiply meanings and narrative possibilities in a painted scene. Poems could function as pivots between landscape scenes and these narrative sequences, with surprising juxtapositions between the two often providing a source of entertainment and aesthetic interest. Through the strategic deployment of a pivot-word, such poems were able to add human sentiment to a landscape scene.[14] A poem using the letters かり, for example, could invest a painted scene depicting a hawking expedition with the suggestion that a romantic interlude is taking place just beyond the pictorial frame. This was effected by activating the doubled meaning of *kari* as both "hunting" and "temporary lodgings" being sought from a woman in the vicinity. Because pivot-words often flattened out distinctions in pitch accent between spoken words, they were ideally suited for a situation in which one might silently read a poem while simultaneously viewing a painted scene. It is important to keep in mind that both actions were included in the semantic range of the verb *miru* (to see) as it was used in Heian times.

Although pictorial romances are often seen as quintessential feminine pursuits, however, we should remember that both men and women participated in their production and reception in the tenth century. This was certainly the case by the 930s, when prose poems for many screen paintings begin to form extended narratives, including a sequence of poems in the *Tsurayuki-shū* depicting a series of exchanges between anonymous men and women.[15] One scholar has argued that it was the landscape rather than a consistent set of protagonists that provided the central organizing rubric for such sequences.[16] This characterization offers potential insights into the nature of early Heian *monogatari* such as *Tales of Ise* and *Tales of Yamato*, which were written a few decades later, and which both feature place-names prominently in their titles.

Regardless of the influence they might have exerted on later tales, however, these poem-narratives do not attest to any specific relationship between gender and genre in the case of screen poetry. In fact, many of the screen poems from the period were composed for aristocratic men and women with similar ritual purposes in mind. Rather than showing any consistent links among gender, genre, and native culture, screen poetry in the early tenth century comments on a broader connection between poetry and power at the Heian court. In my approach to its history, I shall focus on function rather than form. Instead of depicting the development of a particularly "Japanese" form of painting, the early history of *byōbu uta* suggests an attempt to adapt the techniques for staging authority and ownership that early Heian rulers had developed in royal processions outside the palace, resituating such rituals within its architectural spaces.

Painting, Poetry, and Power at the Early Heian Court

The practice of composing poetry that describes painted scenes can be traced back to the Nara period (710–794), when paintings belonging to the palace, temples, and the houses of the aristocracy are first mentioned.[17] One early example from the *Man'yōshū* by Prince Osakabe (d. 705) describes the portrait of a Daoist immortal:

It must be for eternity	*tokoshie ni*
that summer and winter have left,	*natsu fuyu yuke ya*
for neither fur robe	*kawa koromo*
nor fan is cast off	*ōgi hanatanu*
by this mountain hermit.	*yama ni sumu hito*[18]

This poem's evocation of an eternal springtime Elysium draws on a continental poetic tradition in which paintings were praised for their ability to create an unchanging world. Six Dynasties *shi* poetry describing painted scenes, for example, observed a formal protocol that began with praise of the artist, followed with a contrastive emphasis between the lack of motion and sound in the painting and its presence in the real world, and concluded with a paean to the eternal beauty of the painted scene.[19]

While the temporal distinction between eternal landscapes within a painting and the more mutable world outside it appears to have been stressed in poetry, however, spatial distinctions between the two settings were not emphasized. We should keep in mind that differences between the two-dimensional representation of landscape in a painting and its three-dimensional counterpart in a garden, which may seem commonsensical to modern eyes, were not necessarily so to Heian ones. Both gardens and paintings could create an effect of depth by dividing visual space into parallel planes rather than through perspective.[20]

Because the structural principles for representing landscape in both media were similar, painters were often landscape gardeners, and vice versa. One of the best-known examples was Kose no Kanaoka (fl. 840–860), who was both a painter and the landscaper responsible for arranging the rocks in the grounds of the Shinsen-en. Other noted painters who designed gardens include Kudara no Kawanari (782–853), Kose no Hirotaka, and En'en. The formal similarities between gardens and paintings are also reflected in the language of Heian poetry in which, as some scholars have noted, depictions of actual and painted landscapes are often essentially indistinguishable.[21]

Gardens and paintings were likely to have shared similarities in function as well as form. The landscapes depicted in both media organized an ostensibly "natural" scene into harmonious arrangements that were viewed (and thus mastered) by the landowning classes who commissioned them. This link between landscape depictions and proprietorship is suggested by similarities in the conventions used to indicate landscapes in paintings and those used to mark landscapes in maps that were intended to designate ownership of property.[22] Unlike modern maps, which reduce elements of geography to abstract signs, those of early Japan often displayed a harmoniously composed and richly bountiful landscape in representing ownership of its wealth. Maps such as one from 756 belonging to the Tōdai-ji temple, and one depicting the environs of Ōzu in Awa Province (known to scholars as the *Awazu kuni no Ōzu shozu*), provide representations of landscape that include elements which would be found in a landscape painting, including everything from the shapes of mountains and rivers, to the details of individual trees and birds.[23]

These links between the pictorial representation of landscapes and the assertion of ownership over the lands they represented is perhaps most readily apparent in practices related to the sovereign and his palace. From at least the early Heian period, painted screens depicting landscapes were a staple of court rituals in which royal power and authority were displayed. They were used within the palace as backdrops to a variety of calendrical rites such as *sechien* banquets, the sovereign's annual visit to his parents in the First Month, and *sumō* wrestling matches. Many of these screens were devoted to specific ceremonies, and were stored away in the Jijūden hall of the palace when not in use.[24] When they were displayed on such occasions, these painted screens were typically set up around the sovereign. Surrounding him lay the depiction of the lands he ruled over and in front of him were the courtiers engaged in choreographed ritual actions. The result was to represent the Heian ruler presiding over the harmonious union of court and country as he bestowed its bounty upon his subjects at official banquets.

The history of these royal practices associated with paintings at the Heian capital can be traced back with some degree of precision to Saga's reign. During the Kōnin era (810–823), the Heian court witnessed a boom in the production of paintings and poems on landscape within the palace. Among the paintings commissioned in Saga's reign was the *Konmei-chi no shōji* (Kunming Pond Screen). Located to the southwest of the imperial Han capital of Chang'an, this pond was made famous in the *Xijing fu* ("Western Capital Rhapsody") in the *Wenxuan* anthology—a locus classicus for all things continental at the early Heian court—as a preeminent stage for royal activities, a place where the sovereign sailed in his royal barge or hunted on horseback.[25] The choice of subject matter for Saga's painting suggests a desire to see the new urban landscape of Heiankyō as a modern capital equivalent to those of other neighboring realms.

These attempts to project the landscapes of a continental-style empire onto his own realm were also at work in poetic depictions of scenery during Saga's reign. In *shi* from his court, the Shinsen-en Park was likened to the Kunming Pond located in the suburbs of the Han capital, and Heiankyō came to possess a similar history to its continental counterpart as the later incarnation of an earlier capital. During this period "Rakuyō" (Luoyang) became an alternate name for the Heian capital, signifying its status as the successor to an earlier eastern capital at Nara in much the same manner as its continental namesake was a successor to the earlier capital of the Han dynasty at Chang'an.[26] Within his new capital, the sovereign tested his ministers' knowledge of *shi* poetry and its conventions for representing landscapes by assigning them topics for praising painted scenes. One oft-cited example is a poem from the fourteenth scroll in the *Keikokushū,* in which Saga praises a mural at the Seiryōden depicting a Daoist recluse in a mountainous landscape. Following his example, the ministers in attendance then proceed to produce verses that cited his.

Such poetic harmonizations with the ruler's words by his courtiers as they all gazed on a painting bear more than a passing resemblance to the format of a royal progression to the Shinsen-en Park. In both cases, sovereign and subject shared a vision of natural perfection that attested to the former's virtue. Screen paintings could thus bring the parkland stage or the destination of a royal procession into the palace, allowing Saga to enact the same performance without going to the actual location. In other words, paintings and the poetic performances associated with them enabled the sovereign seated in front of these landscape depictions to travel around the realm without moving, and to be the visible center of ritual spectacle without being seen by the fully assembled court. Later sovereigns—who made the Seiryōden the new symbolic center of their regimes, and who did not pursue imperial processions with the same frequency or on the same scale as the first three Heian rulers—used palace screen paintings for similar purposes with increasing frequency.

Uda's royal father appears to have been the first sovereign after Saga to develop techniques for staging power through painting in new ways within the Seiryōden. In 885, Kōkō ordered his chief minister and Fujiwara counterpart Mototsune to provide written descriptions of the court's annual observances on a screen located in the Seiryōden's eastern section.[28] This action would have been consistent with Kōkō's stated policy of preserving the ritual legacy of his own father Ninmyō. As was noted in Chapter 2, such ostensible acts of filial piety were likely to have been informed by a desire to reestablish monarchical authority and visibility inside the palace after they had languished under the previous three sovereigns, who had all been sequestered in the houses of their maternal Fujiwara relatives. Like Saga's mural, Kōkō's screen transformed the sovereign's living quarters into a stage on which he presided over the ritual cycle of calendrical events that ensured harmony between Heaven and humanity.

In keeping with his overall policy of expanding on the ritual prerogatives asserted by his father, Uda in turn preserved and developed the new form of depicting calendrical rites that Kōkō had initiated. One of the earliest known *uta* written to accompany a screen painting appears to have been inspired by Kōkō's screen of annual observances. According to its preface in the third imperial anthology, *Shūi wakashū* (*Collection of Gleanings*, ca. 1006), the poem was composed for a section of a painting that depicted women bathing in a river during the *misogi* purification rites of the Sixth Month.[29] There is some debate over whether this screen poem can be dated to Uda's reign, however. At least one scholar maintains that it was composed when the palace screen depicting annual observances moved with Uda to the tonsured sovereign's administrative headquarters at the Ninna-ji temple after his abdication.[30]

If we turn to the *Kokinshū*, the case for tracing the development of screen *uta* back to Uda's court becomes stronger. The earliest such poem in the anthology that is specifically described as being written for a painting can be dated back to that sovereign's reign. The anthology's prefatory comment to this poem uses the phrase "composed and written" (*yomite kakikeru*) to describe the verse, implicitly distinguishing it from other *Kokinshū* poems that are composed *about* paintings but not *on* them.[31] This wording is perhaps also used to distinguish the act of producing a clean copy of the poem intended for the screen from the more general act of composing the verse.[32]

Like the *uta* of Uda's poetry matches, then, screen poems were specifically written texts designed to be physically affixed to representations of landscapes. The similarity in the intended functions of both forms of poetry is suggested by the fact that the same poem could be used for either setting. One poem by the *Kokinshū*'s editor Tadamine, for example, is linked with Prince Koresada's poetry match in the imperial anthology, whereas in the poet's household anthology it is associated with a screen painting.[33] Like the garden settings of Uda's network of mansions in the capital, or the *suhama* used at his poetry matches, screen paintings provided a microcosmic stage on which poetry could represent the macrocosmic place of the ruler at the center of the world in novel ways.

Screen Poetry at Daigo's Court

The new forms of interplay between paintings depicting ritual calendrical cycles under Kōkō and poems inscribed on them in Uda's reign reached its apogee with the screen poetry composed at Daigo's court. In keeping with his apparent antipathy toward poetry matches, Uda's successor appears to have preferred screen poems as a means for displaying authority. During his reign, such poems seem to have rapidly proliferated both inside and outside the confines of the palace. In addition to anniversary celebrations of a new decade in the nobility's lives, screen poems from this period were increasingly used in aristocratic society for coming-of-age ceremonies. In the case of imperial princesses, for example, ritual formularies specify that three sets of folding screens were to be used.[34] While the part that poems and paintings played in such rituals can be dated back to Kōkō's reign, it was under his grandson Daigo that the practice seems to have become widespread at court, and to have fully assumed its peculiarly textual characteristic as poetry inscribed on a screen painting, rather than simply poetry that used the painting as a topic for composition.

Screen poetry expanded dramatically in quantity during the first decade of Daigo's reign. Twenty-two poems were composed in 902 for a screen in Empress Yasuko's residence. Another 13 by six poets were composed for the fortieth birthday of Fujiwara no Sadakuni in 905. Tsurayuki composed 20 poems in 906 for a series of screens depicting annual observances within the palace, and another 14 in 908 for a screen in the Shōkyōden Hall. The large number of screen poems composed in this period also reflected a noteworthy increase in the size of the screen ensembles for which they were commissioned. While four sets of screen panels seem to have been the norm, there are many cases in this period where six, eight, and even twelve panels were produced.[35]

Daigo's court showed a pronounced interest in organizing these large ensembles of poems and screens into seasonal cycles spanning the entire year. Some scholars have suggested that this new mode of organizing screen poetry was inspired by the development of a seasonal temporal cycle in the *Kokinshū*.[36] Even before the anthology was commissioned, however, paintings were being organized into cycles that merged seasonal time with that of the calendar. Yasuko, for example, possessed a screen painting depicting the court's calendar of annual observances as early as 901. Quite possibly this was the same series at the palace for which Tsurayuki composed poems five years later.[37]

In addition to paintings within the palace, depictions of landscapes associated with the *ritsuryō* state's offices also had screen poems composed for them. In the years following the completion of the *Kokinshū*, its editors made numerous *byōbu uta* for paintings of specific regions in the realm, drafts of which were preserved in these men's personal collections. Often these poems mention the names of various places in a particular province to which a man or woman was officially posted. In 916, Tsurayuki's colleague and fellow compiler Mitsune composed a series of ten *uta* to accompany a screen depicting scenes in Ise for the newly appointed priestess of the royal shrine there.[38] Similarly, Tadamine composed poems in 920 to accompany a screen depicting scenes from Settsu for that province's governor Fujiwara no Tadafusa.[39]

Overall, this tendency to organize paintings and poems into large schemes can be seen as reflecting an interest in projecting power and authority in a manner similar to the ritual forms of display used by Saga and earlier Heian sovereigns within the palace. Such combinations of painting and poetry were used to represent authority over the land by male and female members of Daigo's court in a variety of different official capacities, providing propaganda for a regime seeking to fortify the central state's claims to ownership of the realm's wealth in the face of an increasing trend in the early tenth century toward dividing this wealth among aristocratic households and temples.

No doubt, the inscription of place-names in screen poems played a pivotal role in transforming generic depictions of landscapes into named places in such instances, much in the same manner as they could transform *suhama* at poetry matches into specific locales. Through this assigning of names, the landscape painting came to mark authority over a locale in the same manner as a map. In cases where the post of governor did not involve actual journey to that location, screen paintings depicting its landscape could have functioned as a symbol of office within the confines of the capital.

While officials of the state used painted landscapes to represent their authority over the regions they were assigned, Fujiwara aristocrats at Daigo's court used them to stage their households' claims to property within the personal mansions of their owners. It is probably not coincidental that the proliferation of screen poems on landscape paintings took place at the same time as a proliferation of rights to ownership of the realm's lands and wealth in the form of *shōen* estates. The connections between landscape depictions and economic interests among the court's elite might have also informed a new interest in depicting human activity within such scenes that also began to develop at this time. Judging from the content of screen poems composed during the latter half of the tenth century, the activities of commoners engaged in agriculture or festivals became increasingly frequent subject matter in both poems and paintings.[40] The owners of these folding screens thus placed themselves between human and heavenly cycles in mimicry of royal virtue and custodianship over the land, laying claim to the human labor and wealth of such places in the process.

These new forms of screen poetry eventually were incorporated into the Heian court's enthronement rites as well. Beginning in 946 with the accession of Daigo's son Murakami, both *shi* and *uta* were composed to accompany screens depicting landscapes.[41] Here, too, inscription played a key role in the performance of political and ritual authority. Place-names in these poems were chosen for their auspicious nature, often including characters such as 高 (exalted), 大 (grand), and 千 (a thousand). Depictions of local regions combined with seasonal cycles and ritual activities to represent the harmonious triad of Heaven, Earth, and humanity over which a Confucian monarch presided.[42] Because many of the ritual aspects of enthronement ceremonies foregrounded the sovereign's "consumption of the realm" through the presentation of songs, people, and products from representative provinces, it is possible to see the screen paintings and poems presented at these later ceremonies as a variant of this symbolic practice.

This interest in merging the human and heavenly realms for ritual purposes in painted representations of landscapes appears to have informed several characteristics of screen poetry at the time. The screens typically consisted of four separate "sets" (*chō*) arranged in a square around a human figure, thereby placing that person at the center of an unbroken cycle of scenes and times. An average of twelve poems was selected for the four screens from a larger number of entries submitted by several poets. Each set of screens consisted of six segmented "panels" (*sen*) that were joined together by cords, making for an average of one poem for every two panels.[43] The earliest surviving landscape screen painting, belonging to Tōji temple, has squares of paper known as *shikishi* pasted to the upper left and right edges of the screen, suggesting that the poems, which were typically written out on such squares and then attached to the screen, occupied a space distinct from, but adjacent to, the painted scene.

The landscape scenes on each panel appear to have often been seasonally ambiguous, perhaps in order to make it possible for them to be arranged differently to suit different occasions. Individual panels of Heian screens were not attached by hinges, as is typically done today, but rather by cloth strips looped through holes in their edges. This arrangement meant that panels could be separated and reorganized into a variety of different sequences.[44] Like the individual poems of the

Kokinshū's opening Spring section, painted panels were semantically flexible representations of seasonal landscapes, ones that gained particular and potentially different significances as discrete episodes in the ritual narratives of calendrical observances by virtue of their placement within a larger ensemble. The metonymic constructions of meaning created through the spatial arrangements of poems on painted screens or in anthologies could thus operate in very similar ways.

One particularly detailed example of the complex visual and spatial regimes produced in the screen poetry of Daigo's court can be found in a sequence of twenty poems in the *Tsurayuki-shū* that were originally composed in 906 for eight screens in Daigo's household.[45] The scenes described in Tsurayuki's poems cover both seasonal and calendrical phenomena within the span of an entire year. Topics mentioned in their prefaces include a house celebrating the first Day of the Rat, a pilgrimage to the Inari shrine on the first Day of the Horse in the Second Month, a Third Month archery meet, paddies being turned over in the Third Month, a torch-lit hunt in the Fifth Month, cormorant fishing in the Sixth Month, the Weavermaid festivities of the Double Seventh, the presentation of steeds in the Eighth Month, and the chanting of Buddha's name in the Eleventh Month.

When the prefaces to these poems are read in sequence, one can envisage spaces that are discrete in the poetic register overlapping in the painted one. Poems 11 to 13 are particularly suggestive in this regard. The first verse is set in summer, during the purification rites of the Sixth Month, when sins were transferred onto wooden and paper fetishes and floated downstream. The succeeding poem describes an autumnal rite in which robes are tossed into the river on the Double Seventh as offerings to the Weavermaid. Both poems create specific calendrical moments out of a painted scene that could allow for several different interpretations. Perhaps the painting for which the poems were intended included two separate human figures leaning over a river. Alternately, the scene could have involved only one human figure. By adding temporal specificity to such scenes, screen poems potentially could have played an important role in distinguishing different times within the same space.

A similar form of pictorial ambiguity can be inferred from reading the first and last poems in Tsurayuki's series, which depict the Day of the Rat festivities in the new year and a Buddha's Name Gathering at the end of the calendrical year respectively. Both annual rites were associated with individual households in the period, making it likely that the painting for which they were used depicted a private dwelling. One scholar has argued that similarities in the scenes depicted in these two poems suggest that the screens they accompanied were arranged in a circle around the sovereign to literally create an unbroken temporal cycle.[46] Alternatively, the social settings described in both poems could have referred to the same scene in the painting, given that pictorial depictions of snowy landscapes in early spring and late winter could very well have been virtually identical.

As was noted in Chapter 2, seasonal poetry in the early Heian period was often temporally ambiguous, tending to emphasize overlapping phenomena shared between adjacent seasons rather than establishing the sort of clear-cut calendrical demarcations that were marked through human ritual. This temporal ambiguity in the language of *uta* could have found its visual equivalent in painted scenes that depicted liminal points of transition between the seasons. At the same time, the regular geometric divisions of visual space into panels and screens might have been intended to represent the numerically precise divisions of calendrical time. Whether assembled in sets of four or eight, the six-paneled screen paintings commissioned at Daigo's court were all potentially divisible into the twelve months of the year. Through the placement of these screens in a circle around the sovereign, cyclical calendrical divisions could be represented spatially, literally placing his person at the center of a world in which seasonal and ritual time flowed together in a smooth, unbroken continuum.

Pivot-words, Ritual, and Screen Poetry

At the same time as Daigo's palace witnessed a dramatic growth in the production of screen paintings at the palace that were designed to affirm his authority, similar practices were proliferating among his Fujiwara colleagues inside their private mansions. Like poetry matches, much of the screen poetry at Daigo's court was intended to affirm kinship ties among its elite members in formal public settings. In particular, many screen poems were composed for ceremonies celebrating major turning points in the lives of the aristocracy, such as birthday prayers for the continued long life of the celebrant. Typically, a close relative of the person whose birthday was being celebrated would commission both painting and poems.

Tokihira's family appears to have been particularly interested in developing screen poetry as a means of displaying its place at court in these birthday celebrations. The likelihood that the Northern House patriarch was also involved in the compilation of the *Kokinshū* suggests another possible connection between that anthology and contemporaneous screen poetry. While Daigo probably employed Tsurayuki to compose poems for his royal screen paintings on account of the writer's skill in arranging poetic sequences for the Seasons section in the *Kokinshū*, the men and women of the Northern House might very well have turned to this same poet on account of his involvement in arranging its Blessings section, which gave particular prominence to its members.

Screen poems for birthday celebrations first appear during the reign of Uda's father Kōkō. The elderly sovereign and his equally aged coterie turned physical frailty into Confucian sagacity through elaborate *ga* ceremonies blessing the fortieth, fiftieth, sixtieth, and seventieth birthdays of an individual.[47] In the same year that Mototsune wrote out the text accompanying Kōkō's screen of annual observances, the Fujiwara patriarch's own fiftieth birthday celebration was celebrated by his sovereign at the palace. No less a figure than the literatus Michizane composed five *shi* poems for the painted screens that were placed behind the banquet seats at this event.[48] That same year, according to the *Sandai jitsuroku*, another celebration was held at the palace to mark the seventieth birthday of Kōkō's loyal former official Henjō with an intimate *kyokuen* banquet.[49] Although a poem by Kōkō from this event is included in the Blessings section of the *Kokinshū*, however, it is unclear whether the editors regarded it as a screen poem that was directly attached to one of the paintings.[50]

Like the poetry matches of Uda's court and the screen paintings commissioned for state rituals at Daigo's palace, the birthday celebrations of Tokihira's family involved an elaborate choreography in which the celebrant was placed between humanity (in the form of the assembled celebrants) and Heaven (in the form of the landscape painting surrounding the person whose birthday was being celebrated). Screen poems facilitated harmony between the two at birthday celebrations in part by endowing the landscape scenes of paintings with ritual significance. In an inversion of the Kana Preface's poetics of supplementation—in which natural elements were "attached" to human sentiment—screen poetry often attached a human ritual element to the painting's depiction of a seasonal landscape.

Screen poems for these celebrations, like the individual scenes they depicted, were connected through temporal rather than geographical contiguity. This means of connection in itself possibly hints at the logics for representing power and authority that informed these practices. As was noted in Chapters 2 and 3, the sovereign's authority over his realm was often enacted through the coordinated observance of ritual practices that took place simultaneously in separate locales across the realm, thereby "binding" it together. By representing Heaven's blessings and their owner's virtue, seasonal cycles in screen poetry bound together individual landscapes scattered geographically across the realm, in the same manner that their Fujiwara patrons bound together disparate *shōen* estates scattered across the provinces through their legal ownership of these entities. For Tokihira's family in particular, this form of seasonal temporality had an established history of ritual usage dating back to Yoshifusa's regency, when it was deployed in blossom banquets to create a vision of Confucian virtue complementing that of the sovereign presiding over the calendar in his palace.

The manner in which screen poems and paintings performed their magic at birthday celebrations remain speculative. In the introduction to their annotated edition of the *Tsurayuki-shū*, Tanaka Kimiharu and Tanaka Kyōko argue that the words of the poem invested the painted scene with an incantatory power, which in turn enveloped the recipient of the birthday blessing.[51] Surrounded by these screens, the persons being celebrated would have been literally enfolded within a static picture frame, placing them at the center of an eternally revolving temporal cycle manifested through the spatial arrangement of the surrounding screens. Because the poems associated with such events often amounted to prayers for eternal life, the birthday rituals in which they appeared could have attempted to create the desired effect of such prayers, removing the recipients of these blessings from the ravages of time by literally placing them outside of it.

Poems often appear to play a key role in creating this effect of temporal stasis. One example is the opening verse in the *Tsurayuki-shū*, which was composed in 905 to accompany a screen painting commissioned for the fortieth birthday of Daigo's maternal uncle Fujiwara no Sadakuni:

Is it because summer mountains	*natsu yama no*
are cast in such thick shade	*kage o shigemi ya*
that folk traveling on the road,	*tama hoko no*
lined with jeweled halberds,	*michi yuku hito mo*
now halt in their tracks?	*tachitomaru ran*[52]

This poem's evocation of luxuriant foliage shading a mountainside contains a prayer that Sadakuni's years will be as numerous as the leaves in its language. The image of mountain shadows that appears in the verse also borrows the iconography of monarchical benevolence seen in the Kana Preface, where Daigo's protection of his people is likened to the sheltering shade of Mount Tsukuba. Sadakuni is portrayed here in a similar light as protector of the people under him. The patriarch's beneficiaries could also take the shape of trees or grasses in Tsurayuki's screen poems, echoing the Confucian trope of lesser men bowing before their superior's virtue.[53] It is also possible to read the poem's roadside travelers as Sadakuni's followers, family, and others who benefited from his patronage as members of his household. The poem's final line describing people halted in their tracks makes this scene a manifestation of the eternal life and security that it prays for.

Although paintings often contained felicitous objects such as lush vegetation, thick snow, pines, bamboo, cranes, and tortoises that connoted longevity, not every scene within the ensemble of screens necessarily possessed such symbols. In cases where they were otherwise lacking, screen poems could provide the requisite felicitous elements by embedding pivot-words within landscape descriptions. One example is a poem composed by Tsurayuki in 917 for a screen depiction of the Day of the Rat (*ne no hi*).

Because springtime haze	*harugasumi*
in long strands trails, tugging	*tana(bi/hi)ku matsu no*

at pine trees this year,	*toshi nareba*
in what spring would it ever	*izure no haru ka*
fail to extend across the fields?	*nobe ni kozaran*[54]

The word *tanabiku* (to trail in strands) in the second line refers to the haze-shrouded scene of the painting, but the *kana* letters with which it is written (たなひく) also contain the word *hiku* (to drag up by the roots), which refers to the custom of pulling out pine saplings on this day in order to ensure long life. This link between landscape scene and human ritual activity is amplified by the word *nobe*, which pivots between the noun "fields" and verb "extend [life]." Both of these poetic pivots between *mono* (in the form of elements in a landscape) and *kokoro* (in the form of human actions and situations) merge on a visual rather than an aural level. This reliance on a visual register is particularly evident in the former example, which depends on an orthographic convention that ignores distinctions between voiced and unvoiced consonants in order to link the poem's trailing clouds with pine saplings.

Pivot-words merging Heaven and humanity could be deployed for a variety of ritual effects. In the case of the poems that Tsurayuki provided for Daigo's screen painting, the intention was probably to create harmonious resonances between calendrical rituals and seasonal cycles. One noteworthy example of this fusion can be found in the fifth poem in the series, which inserts a seasonal scene into the ritual setting of an annual archery meet.

When catalpa bows drawn taut	*azusa yumi*
spring in mountain swards,	*haru no yamabe ni*
plunging deep,	*iru toki wa*
it is only the wreaths	*kazashi ni nomi zo*
of blossoms that scatter!	*hana wa chirikeru*[55]

Tsurayuki's poem creates a seamless overlap between a scene of distant springtime mountains and the social setting of an archery contest through his skillful use of not one, but two pivot-words. Both *haru* and *iru* refer simultaneously to "spring" (*haru* 春) "entering" (*iru* 入る) distant mountains and a bow being "drawn taut" (*haru* 張る) and then "loosed" (*iru* 射る). This interweaving of separate scenes could well have been rendered even more complex by the calligraphic style in which the poem was written. Poems might appear on squares of paper, but they could also be written in the *ashide* or "reed hand" style in which individual letters were directly incorporated into the plants and animals in the painted landscape.[56]

Tsurayuki's poem also transforms a timeless depiction of court ritual into a particular historical moment. Its springtime setting of blossoming mountains quite likely refers to the specific year in which the screen poem was composed. Although the court's annual archery meet referred to here was typically held in the First Month of the year, it was put off until the Third Month in 906, making it easy to picture cherry blossoms at the event.[57] Quite possibly, the inscription of this poem onto the screen was designed to smooth over any discrepancy between the ideal and actual forms of the rite, in the same manner as the Spring section of the *Kokinshū* sought to create harmonies between seasonal and calendrical time.

This poem also suggests that pivot-words could work in concert with other objects employed in rituals to represent landscapes, thereby creating a backdrop of the realm against which the benevolent ruler presides over the court and its rites. The overlap between Heaven and humanity provided by the pivot-words in Tsurayuki's poem was also created in the actual archery contest's material props. Behind the target used at this event, an indigo cloth was hung up to catch stray arrows. The cloth was hung between two triangular frames known as *yamagata*, which were made from evergreen saplings bound together in the shapes of mountains.[58] Perhaps these human constructs are the "mountain swards" of Tsurayuki's poem. Similarly, the *kazashi* (wreaths) of the poem might refer to branches placed in the quivers of the archers in order to make them look like bird nests. It is perhaps not coincidental in this regard that the pivot-word used to describe these objects in Tsurayuki's poem created similar visual overlaps between social settings and landscape scenes.

Because it is highly probable that most poets never saw the painting for which their poems were composed, and because the painting in question was as likely to depict a generic landscape as a specific ritual occasion, screen poems needed to accommodate and anticipate multiple spaces and times within their words. It is impossible to tell from the language of Tsurayuki's poem whether the painting that it accompanied depicted springtime mountains or a courtyard occupied by archers. By using *kana* letters to signify more than one thing simultaneously, Tsurayuki's poem pivots between social setting and landscape scene, making it possible to accommodate a visual representation of either space. His particular skill at blending these two registers in this example poem makes it easy to see why he was called on so frequently to compose screen poems.

One scholar identifies such multilayered depictions of landscapes as a rhetorical trait characteristic of much of screen poetry.[59] The poems themselves often appear to add additional imagery to the descriptions of a landscape scene provided by their prefaces in individual anthologies. Although we cannot reconstruct the details of particular paintings in such cases, the very fact that the poems themselves often appear to create more than one space or scenario marks them as being specifically designed to supplement pictorial representations. This doubling of a landscape scene could be achieved through the visual likenesses of *mitate* (such as seeing blossoms in a painting as snow), or through speculation about what might lie beyond the frame of the painting. There were more than aesthetic pleasures at work in this gap between poem and picture, however, something that becomes apparent when we turn our attention to the manner in which screen poems were composed. The procedures involved, like other forms of poetic "harmonization" in which a lower-ranking courtier echoed the words of a topic handed down by a social superior, were as laden with social meaning as the practices associated with their reception.

The Politics of Poetic Inscription

The inscription of a poem onto a painted scene, like the attachment of poems to dioramas at poetry matches, transformed generic landscape spaces into places laden with particular meaning. At the same time that these poems provided new possibilities for representing social settings, they also enabled a variety of people—including composers, reciters, and readers—to identify with the positions from which that poem was viewed and heard in the world around it. This was not a utopian form of free play and fantasy, however. The practices of composing and inscribing poems onto screen paintings often appear to have marked the agents of those actions as subordinate and subservient to others. They also suggest that screen poets, like the *utayomi* of Uda's poetry matches, were rarely privy to the settings in which their poems circulated.

Although we can infer a good deal about the subject matter and arrangement of screen poems from Daigo's court, detailed information about the procedures involved in producing them does not appear until the end of the century, when aristocrats begin to mention screen poetry in their diaries. These sources reveal, among other things, the frequent absence of the poet from the ritual event at which his poems were inscribed and read. In this regard, poems for screens resembled poems for matches, insofar as they were produced almost exclusively by the lower ranks of court society. Like the *utayomi* of poetry matches, the composer of screen poems was marked implicitly through this practice as an extension of the human capital and resources available to the household that commissioned his or her work.

One episode from the end of the tenth century offers particularly suggestive insights about the context in which screen poems were composed. In 999 the powerful nobleman Fujiwara no Michinaga (966–1027) commemorated the entrance into the palace of his daughter Shōshi (988–1074) by commissioning a screen painting and *uta* to accompany it. Michinaga's own diary mentions the events surrounding this undertaking only in passing. The entry for the 21st day of the month simply notes his order that *uta* be composed. Six days later, another entry briefly mentions the arrival of the poems at his place.[60] By contrast, the diary of Michinaga's political rival Fujiwara no Sanesuke (957–1046) gives a much more detailed, at times even impassioned, impression of what transpired between these two events. Two days after Michinaga issued his order, Sanesuke's diary recounts that a messenger from the former came bearing the topics for the poems:

> Minamoto no Toshikata came over as Michinaga's emissary and presented me with topics for some screen *waka*. I found it difficult to respond to Michinaga's request, but managed to get out of it by offering some excuse. Apparently many of the upper nobility have al-

> ready been allotted topics. They have also been sent to people below the rank of Counselor who are skilled at verse. Can aristocrats really be expected to carry out such a task?[61]

The reason for Sanesuke's reluctance to provide poems at Michinaga's command is suggested by his final outburst, when he declares that the composition of poetry at someone else's behest is the province of low-ranking officials and retainers. It appears, however, that Sanesuke was the only aristocrat to refuse Michinaga's wishes. On the 28th day of the same month, *uta* were selected for the screen paintings from among poems submitted by the upper echelons of court society, including such luminaries as the retired sovereign Kazan'in (968–1008), and Sanesuke's own cousin, Fujiwara no Kintō. Sanesuke's expression of disgust upon hearing that these men were involved in producing screen poems is particularly vivid:

> That the uppermost nobility would be ordered by a Minister of the Right to present *waka* in this way is something unheard of in the past. How much more so when one of those poems is by a retired sovereign! Michinaga provided his own verse, I am told. This evening I received a letter requesting that I present poems. I had someone say that I was unable to take on such a task. It was, without any doubt, a most unpleasant state of affairs. My heart was unable to acquiesce in the affair. What is more, Kintō is a commander of the Royal Constabulary, not some commoner. In recent times, his bearing has come to resemble that of a lackey. How can our house carry on in such a manner? It pains me to think about it.[62]

Two days later, the poems were written out in a clean copy on paper squares by the renowned calligrapher Fujiwara no Yukinari. Once again, Sanesuke expresses outrage over the manner in which Michinaga extracts service from his peers at court. This time, however, names are literally at stake: "Everyone's name was written on the text of their poem, thereby ensuring his loss of face for all of posterity. The one exception was Kazan's composition, which was marked 'composer unknown.' Michinaga wrote down his rank as Minister of the Left. The whole affair was quite bizarre."[63]

Sanesuke's account suggests that every stage in the process of commissioning screen poetry could be laden with political symbolism. The act of soliciting screen poems simultaneously displayed the commissioner's authority and the subservient position of those who composed poems for her or him. In the case of Sanesuke, whose Ononomiya branch of the Fujiwara clan had been superseded by Michinaga's Kujō line, the acts of composing and inscribing screen poems are tantamount to a declaration of fealty on the part of the inscriber, insofar as they echoed words provided by a social superior. In this sense, screen poems can be seen as yet another form of topic-based harmonizing verse in which the word *waka* (which is used consistently by Sanesuke in his diary) primarily denoted the formal acknowledgement of political hierarchies.

The politics of poetic inscription appear to have held different significances for different social groups at court. Whereas a lower-ranking courtier such as Tsurayuki went out of his way to attach his name to his poems in the *Kokinshū*, a more-exalted member of the court such as Kazan might strive to render his poem anonymous in an attempt to mitigate his poetic submission to a rival. The conditions for claiming or refusing authorship in such cases perhaps were also contingent on the genre of poetry involved, in addition to being dependent on the particular social setting in which one's name was inscribed. While ministers and officials formalized their harmonious accord with the words of their sovereign by inscribing their names on the *shi* poems composed at *sechien* banquets, there is no evidence that Tsurayuki's *uta* were ever composed in situ, or that they ever carried his name when they were circulated at poetry matches, royal processions, or birthday celebrations.

The prominent place of "topics" (*dai*) in diary accounts of screen poetry suggests that they were the primary medium through which these poems were produced. One scholar has even argued that the poets probably never saw the actual paintings for which their poems were intended, relying instead on written descriptions of their scenes.[64] This conclusion seems to be supported by the earliest detailed account of a screen poem composition, found in the *Kagerō nikki*. The episode in question dates from 969, when the author—an aristocratic woman known to posterity as the "Mother of Michitsuna" (Michitsuna no haha)—was requested by a cousin of her husband, Fujiwara no Kaneie (929–990), to compose poems for a painting celebrating the fiftieth birthday of the former man's own uncle, Moromasa (920–969):

> The Eighth Month arrived. During that time a great fuss was being made over the birthday celebration for the Koichijō Minister of the Left. I heard that the Captain of the Left Guards was preparing a screen painting for the celebration. Using an emissary who is hard to refuse, he pressed me to contribute some poems. Various scenes in the painting were outlined for this purpose. The situation was extremely unappealing, and I sent this emissary back many times, but he insisted, leaving me with no choice. And so, as I gazed on the evening moon, thoughts came to me, and I did one or two.[65]

Like her aristocratic male peers, Michitsuna's mother appears to have viewed the composition of screen poetry as something that a person of her status did not normally engage in. Like them also, she appears to have received topics outlining the content of the paintings to aid her in composing her poems. The meaning of the phrase *uta no tokorodokoro kaki idashitaru nari* in this passage has occasioned some controversy among scholars. Because the verb *kaku* can refer to the acts of either writing or drawing, it is possible that the outlines of painted scenes mentioned here are sketches rather than written descriptions.[66] One advantage to relying on written topics, however, might have been the fact that it would have taken less time than that required for sketching out all the scenes, a task made all the more time-consuming by the fact that more than one poet was being asked to contribute *uta*. If we keep in mind Sanesuke's implicit equation between the act of producing screen poetry on topics and that of political submission to a social superior, it appears likely that screen poems, like other forms of poetic harmonization, would have treated words as the preferred means for conveying the superior's vision of a landscape to the poet.

Regardless of the medium through which the painting's content was conveyed to a poet, it is doubtful that the sponsors of a new screen would have risked damaging it by bringing it over to each individual's house. Nor does Michitsuna's mother mention going out to see it herself. In all likelihood the conditions for composing screen poetry in Tsurayuki's time were similar to those experienced by these later aristocrats. In the mid-Heian tale collection *Konjaku monogatari-shū* (*Tales of Times Now Past*), for example, his contemporary Lady Ise is depicted using a messenger to send over a screen poem she has composed at Daigo's command.[67] Perhaps the descriptions of specific scenes that appear in the prefaces to screen poems in the *Tsurayuki-shū* and in the anthologies of his contemporaries were themselves based on the topics sent to screen poets. Like the *dai* of the Ōi River Procession, such written descriptions would have functioned in lieu of the actual landscape scene.

Based on what we can infer about the practices surrounding the production and reception of screen poetry, it seems likely that what was visible and to whom, as with so many aspects of court society, was largely dependent on the viewer's social position. In the case of the poet writing a screen poem, the actual scene depicted in a painting was largely immaterial to the process of composition. While it is something of a convention in scholarship on screen poetry to bemoan the loss of the paintings to which the poems were attached, it could also be argued that our current dependence on the topics found in later poetry collections enables us to see the painting through the poet's eyes, and not through those of the aristocrats who viewed it at ceremonial gatherings. The differing relations that could obtain among poems, topics, paintings, composers, and readers in such a context also suggests that the poetic point of view inscribed in a screen poem was equally variable. This would help explain the marked ambiguity of perspective within screen poetry, a feature that has occasioned some controversy among those modern scholars who have attempted to distinguish it from other forms of verse at the Heian court.

Placing Perspective in Screen Poetry

Despite the evidence suggesting that poets rarely saw the painted scene for which they composed poems, most definitions of screen poetry have envisaged the poet viewing the screen in the act of composition. Tamagami Takuya provided the most influential of such accounts when he defined screen poetry as verse that was composed by the poet in the voice of a character within the painting as he or she gazed on that figure and imaginatively identified with them. On this basis, Tamagami distinguishes "screen poems" (*byōbu uta*) from "poems about screen paintings" (*byōbu e uta*) that are composed in the voice of the poet gazing on the scene as a detached observer located outside the picture frame.[68] The first account of this sort of scenario is made in the late twelfth century by Kenshō in his *Shūishō chū* ("Commentary to the *Shūishō* Anthology," 1190) when he states that "in composing poems for screens, the poet first inhabits the sentiments of a figure depicted in the painting" (*byōbu shoji no e ni yomu wa yagate e ni kakeru hito no kokoro ni narite yomu nari*).[69]

Identification between poet and painted figure based on the former seeing the latter, however, is not the only possible way of describing what took place in the composition of screen poetry. For one thing, Kenshō's text does not specify whether or not the poet must have visual access to the actual painted figure for the identification it describes to take place. Furthermore, Tamagami's distinction between screen poems in which the poet identifies with a painted figure and poems about screen paintings in which the poet speaks as an outside viewer has been challenged by other scholars who have noted that the speaker's perspective within a poem is rarely specified in its accompanying prose.[70] Prefaces to screen poems prefer to make distinctions on the basis of whether a poem was attached to the painting, rather than whether its perspective is located inside or outside of the picture frame. For example, the *Tsurayuki-shū* places poem 780—which is described in its prose preface as being about a scene "in a painting" (*e naru*)—in the Miscellaneous Verse section, rather than in the first four scrolls devoted to screen poems, because it was not inscribed on a screen.[71]

Although the poet's own point of view cannot be inferred from the contextual information surrounding screen poems, some scholars have sought it out on the basis of distinctions in content. Tokuhara Shigemi, a scholarly authority on screen poetry, has argued that poems whose content is limited to landscapes locate their speaker outside the picture frame as a distanced onlooker.[72] As an example, Tokuhara provides the following poem from the *Tsurayuki-shū*, which formed part of the series designed for Daigo's palace screens:

Fishermen's torches	*kagaribi no*
spread light everywhere,	*kage shirukereba*
setting fire to the waters	*ubatama no*
in the river depths,	*yokawa no soko wa*
in the pitch black of night!	*mizu mo moekeri*[73]

Despite Tokuhara's assertion that the poem's point of view here is that of an external onlooker, there is nothing in its language that unambiguously locates its speaker outside the picture frame. The verbal suffix *keri*—which is the only linguistic element in the poem marking its speaker—does not specify the location from which the scene is seen. The poem's onlooker could be located either within the painting (as someone on the riverbank, for example) or outside it as an external viewer. In fact, *keri* could be seen to admit both possibilities simultaneously. Typically, it is used in poetry to mark the speaker's sudden realization of something that has been occurring right before his or her gaze. Accordingly, it could be used here to suggest the perspective of someone within the painting who has just noticed that the fishermen's torches he or she sees look like they are setting the waters alight. Alternately, however, *keri* is often used in *monogatari* to mark the narrator's distance in time from the actual events of the tale he or she is relating. Because screen poetry often uses *keri*, and because both phenomena have historical links to fictional narrative, it is equally plausible to claim that the above poem marks its onlooker as an actual person located outside the temporal and spatial context presented by the fictional depiction of a scene in a painting.

I would argue that it is precisely the ability of screen poetry to blur the spaces inside and outside of the scene that it depicts which endows such verse with its peculiar power. Screen poems often seem to refuse privileging one form of onlooker over another, and it is precisely this multivalency that could allow a screen poet—who likely never saw the painted scene in the first place—to construct multiple viewpoints from which to view a landscape. Important exceptions to this general rule would have been screen poems with aural elements or ones that specified the atemporal nature of the scene they described. A poem whose speaker was claiming to hear a bush warbler trilling, for example, would have to be located within the painted scene. Conversely a poem praising the eternal quality of a painting would unambiguously locate its viewer outside the frame. Outside these two extremes, however, a purely visual depiction of a landscape in a poem could merge the spaces inside and outside the picture frame, along with the distinction between an actual landscape and the depiction of one, or between fiction and reality.

Such blurrings of perspective could have played an important part in the rituals at which screen poems were displayed. Poems composed for birthday celebrations in particular often present the images in a painted scene in a manner that envelops the external world as well. One example is a poem that Tsurayuki composed in 915 for a screen to commemorate the fiftieth birthday of Tokihira's principal wife:

In my mansion grounds,	*waga yado no*
the cranes roosting	*matsu no kozue ni*
on pine branches	*sumu tatsu no*
bring to mind	*chiyo no yuki ka to*
a millennium of snow.	*omou beranari*[74]

This verse is filled with the ritual language and symbolism typical of screen poetry composed for birthdays. Indeed the poem's distinguishing feature could well be that it contains nothing *but* such language, as it appears to pile one auspicious convention on top of the next. The images of cranes roosting on pine trees are conventional felicitious symbols of longevity which likely appeared on the screen painting as well. Tsurayuki amplifies these propitious connotations with the further felicitious image of snow, one that the poem's speaker claims to see within the vision of cranes on the pine branches. As if the images were not propitious enough in themselves, the snow is further linked to the incantory phrase "a millennium" (*chiyo*), invoked here as a prayer for the long life of Tokihira's wife.

The use of the ritual phrase *chiyo* here hints at one reason why screen poems for birthday celebrations were so sought after by the Northern House aristocrats of Daigo's court. In employing a word closely associated with the recitation of blessings directed at the sovereign by his assembled courtiers during the New Year's Day *chōga* rite, this birthday poem endowed the recipient with a similar authority in a miniature version of the court calendar's inaugural moment. In place of officials assembled before their sovereign, the Northern House aristocrat's family gathered around a senior member. In place of a rite designed to begin the new calendrical year with a guarantee of future years overseen by the sovereign who dispensed the realm's bounty to its officials, we have a birthday celebration designed to begin the new year of an individual's life with a prayer for many future ones guaranteeing the material well-being of her family. And in place of the assembled courtiers' multivocal recitation of blessings, the birthday celebration provides mute but eternally reproducible incantations in the form of a written poem. By mimicking the forms of court ritual, birthday celebrations represented aristocrats as people whose physical health was an expression of an overall harmony with heavenly cycles and a guarantee of well-being for the community under their patronage, just as the reigning sovereign's physical well-being was often tied to the general well-being of the realm and the people under his rule.

In this regard it is significant that the poem marks the setting as a mansion garden, the preferred stage upon which aristocrats enacted their authority. The poem's opening reference to "my mansion grounds" (*waga yado*), which marks both the speaker and the locale, is ambiguous with regard to whether these two are located in the painting or outside it. Some scholars read the above poem from the perspective of an external onlooker who is commenting on an absolute separation between the evanescent world of mortals and the world of a figure located within the eternal scene of the painting.[75] However, it could just as conceivably have been the ability of this poem to merge these two spaces that enabled it to work its ritual magic. Given the intimate and long standing connections between painting and gardens, it is possible to see the owner of the mansion grounds in this poem as either a figure within the painting looking at a garden within its painted frame, or a person outside it viewing a depiction of cranes in a painting as though it was set in that person's own mansion grounds.

Like screen poetry, the physical paintings they were inscribed on often worked to blur distinctions between interior and exterior spaces. Because paintings closely resembled gardens in their formal features, they functioned in a similar manner to resituate larger landscapes within smaller-scale domestic spaces. Screens played a variety of roles in organizing the spatial contours of the Heian mansion. They were at once representations of the external world, with its mountains and rivers, and a means for dividing space within the interior world of the mansion's rooms. Paintings brought the outside world into the most private inner spaces of individual residences, turning them into public stages. In such settings cloistered but influential aristocratic women could be displayed before their family, attendants, and peers as though they were appearing outdoors, much in the same manner as a sovereign would have done when he participated in public palace rites or embarked on royal processions.

In sum, the ambiguity of perspective in so many screen poems enabled them to accommodate a variety of subjects and settings both inside and outside the painted frame. At the same time as screen poetry was semantically open-ended in this regard, however, particular social settings restricted the range of perspectives that could take shape in any given poem's language. Although the above verse may be describing either the garden of a figure in a painting or that of Tokihira's mansion, it leaves no room for the *utayomi* who composes it to speak in the first person as if he were looking out over the scene he describes. Ultimately, Tsurayuki's absence from the social setting in which the screen poem performed its magic provided a practical limitation on what he could envisage, imaginatively or otherwise. As I will argue in the final section of this chapter, the social hierarchies that structured the production of both screen poetry and perspective within it were addressed by this low-ranking courtier in ways that often appear to be quite self-reflexive, subtly introducing his own perspective on the different spaces that were brought together in screen poetry.

Reflections in Tsurayuki's Poetry

Tsurayuki's expertise at screen poetry was often manifested in his skillful use of reflective surfaces as a way of adding different landscape scenes and social settings to the verbal descriptions of paintings on which he and other poets appear to have relied. His poems can be breathtakingly complex in their evocation of multiple spaces that intersect and bounce off of one another. Given the syllabic brevity that he mandated for *yamato uta* in the Kana Preface and in his *Tosa Diary*, Tsurayuki's achievements in this regard are all the more noteworthy. One spectacular example of his skill at embedding multiple social settings within landscape scenes which has attracted extensive commentary by modern scholars can be found in a poem composed for Daigo's screen of annual observances. The poem in question describes the rite of "Steed Greeting" (*koma-mukae*), held on the twenty-third day of the Eighth Month, in which officials from the court journeyed to Ausaka on the capital's eastern borders to meet horses sent in tribute from the fields of the realm's eastern provinces. Rather than depict the scene of the Steed Greeting directly, Tsurayuki's poem presents it at one remove through a reflection:

In springwater at the barrier	*Ausaka no*
of Meeting Slope	*seki no shimizu ni*
a roan horse's reflection is revealed.	*kage miete*
They must be bringing over	*ima ya hiku ran*
the Harvest Moon steeds.	*Mochizuki no koma*[76]

The poem creates two spaces through its simultaneous depiction of the setting of "Meeting Slope" (Ausaka) and a distant scene of steeds being brought over to this point of entry into the capital from the eastern provinces. In its final line, Tsurayuki's verse also appears to join different times as well as different spaces. "Mochizuki" (Harvest Moon) could be the name of a stable in the province of Shinano, whose steeds were part of the tribute presented to the Heian court in the Steed Greeting rite. The word could also, as in the translation above, refer to the Harvest Moon midway through the lunar month, thereby placing the poem at a time prior to the official calendrical date assigned for this Steed Greeting, which was usually held on the twenty-third day of the Eighth Month.[77] The "harvest moon" of this poem thus creates an overlap between seasonal and calendrical time by referring to both the natural phenomena of the moon at its height and the calendrical date of a particular ritual, a possibility that suggests the interest—which seems to have been characteristic of Daigo's court—in harmonizing the two forms of time.

All of these complex overlappings of time and space in Tsurayuki's poem appear to pivot around the third line "a reflection is revealed" (*kage miete*), which is itself placed exactly midway in the composition between the two separate halves depicting Ausaka and eastern steeds respectively. The poem's onlooker here, marked by the verbal auxiliary *ran*, infers something about a far-off scene based on something else seen closer at hand in a manner typical of many Heian *uta*. Insofar as both onlooker and scene are manifested in the poem's language through the action of gazing at a watery reflection, Tsurayuki's entire verse can be said to coalesce around this moment.

Given this reflection's central role in the poem, it is all the more significant that it was probably a purely poetic conceit rather than a painterly one. Extant paintings from the Heian and Kamakura periods rarely if ever depict reflections on water.[78] In fact, the word for "reflection" here appears to contain the image it displays within in its own words. The letters かけ in the third line can be read as both "reflection" (*kage* 影) and "roan horse" (*kage* 鹿毛), thus making the poem's vision of steeds dependent on pivot-words rather than any depiction of them in a painting.

In addition to operating like a pivot-word, the line "a reflection is revealed" (*kage miete*) also appears to be deliberately intertextual, thereby further strengthening the implication that language itself is being represented as a reflecting medium. The phrase quite possibly alludes to a similar *Man'yōshū* poem in which the onlooker, like the one in Tsurayuki's verse, speculates about a distant scene while gazing on a reflection of it:

Frogs cry out	*kawazu naku*
in the hallowed river	*kamunabi kawa ni*
where a reflection is revealed.	*kage miete*
They must be blooming now,	*ima ka saku ramu*
those mountain-breeze blossoms.	*yamabuki no hana*[79]

Scholars from Keichū onward have noted that many of Tsurayuki's poems bear a strong resemblance to earlier ones found in the *Man'yōshū*. Some have gone so far as to assert that he had access to an actual manuscript of the anthology.[80] It is in fact possible that he would have been able to consult a copy while he was posted at the Palace Library during his tenure as chief editor of the *Kokinshū*.[81] Unlike the earlier *Man'yōshū* poem, however, the "reflection" in the Harvest Moon poem also uses a pivot-word to create its overlap between different spaces. In this way, Tsurayuki's reflection reflects in turn on the intensely textual nature of his poetic style, which often relies on both allusions to earlier written poems and pivot-words derived from *kana* writing to create its effects.

In addition to the *Man'yōshū* poem cited above, Tsurayuki could be drawing on continental sources of inspiration here. At least one scholar has argued that the association of the harvest moon with Meeting Slope's barrier is derived from a Tang *yuefu* ballad titled "Moon over Barrier Mountain" (*Guanshan yue*), a song whose melodies often accompanied *saibara* sung at court banquets.[82] The same phrase was also frequently used as a topic for *shi* composed on the theme of a woman waiting for her husband to return from a far-off mountain garrison fort. Given Tsurayuki's likely exposure to continental poetry, he could conceivably be aware of these associations.[83] Many of Tsurayuki's poems in fact appear to cite earlier written poetry, both *shi* and *uta*, to create their visual likenesses. His *mitate*, for example, are often marked by the verb *beranari*, which was common to screen poetry and particular to the early tenth century. One scholar who has studied this verb extensively argues that it often marks an inference by the poem's speaker based on an allusion to an earlier text or body of texts.[84]

The image of a reflection chosen by Tsurayuki in the poem above can be seen as particularly ambiguous visually. By the tenth century, the word *kage* had come to possess a long and semantically rich history. In addition to reflections, it could denote shadows, light, and the phantom double of a body. All these meanings drew on the concept of *kage* as a fleeting, flickering presence, located at the cusp of visibility between darkness and light.[85] As phantom projections, they could be detached from the body, journeying elsewhere to be seen by people from afar. Portraits of human figures were often referred to as *kage*, insofar as they represented the projection of an absent person onto the painted surface of a screen. In a similar manner, the reflective waters of this poem, like a portrait or a mirror, create a phantom double of some original object.

The many connotations of *kage* make it important to keep in mind that the reflection of Tsurayuki's poem provides a surface onto which it is possible to imagine the projection of human figures as well as landscape scenes. *Kage* here, in addition to the textual associations outlined above, could also denote the reflection or phantasmatic double of the poem's speaker being made visible to them in the water's surface. Set against the backdrop of a distant landscape in which steeds are being brought over the barrier pass, this reflected double of the onlooker could also suggest the position of Daigo seated before a painted depiction of the Steed Greeting rite. But whereas the ruler relied on his material wealth and political authority to create the effect of a human figure framed by a landscape, Tsurayuki's poem relies on its own pivot-words to create a background against which its onlooker can see himself.

Given the wealth of meanings and significances that can be inferred from the different ways that the word *kage* is deployed in Tsurayuki's Steed Greeting poem, it is significant that the poetic motif of reflections appears to have been particularly favored by him. One scholar has gone so far as to argue that the frequency with which Tsurayuki used reflected images makes this a distinct stylistic trait of his poetry.[86] In many of these poems, reflections are the medium through which a visual likeness is established between two separate objects. This trope would be ideally suited to a visual conceit such as *mitate*, which tended to rely on similarities of color or shading between objects.[87]

What makes Tsurayuki's *mitate* particularly noteworthy is the manner in which they use reflections to blur the distinctions between reality and fiction on which such likenesses tended to rely for their rhetorical effect.[88] As Konishi Jin'ichi points out in his landmark essay on *Kokinshū* poetry and its *shi* antecedents, visual analogies in Six Dynasties *shi* poetry tended to mark the fictive nature of these tropes in an overt fashion. In the words of these poems, something is often "suspected" (*yi*) or "mistaken" (*wu*) for something else.[89] By contrast, as one scholar has noted, the reflections of Tsurayuki's poem do not specify which image is actual and which is imaginary.[90] One of the subtlest examples of this sort of visual indeterminacy can be found in the following poem originally composed for the Teiji Villa Match and later placed in the Spring section of the *Kokinshū*:

In the wake	*sakurabana*
of winds scattering	*chirinuru kaze no*

cherry blossoms, — *nagori ni wa*
waves now rise — *mizu naki sora ni*
in water-less skies! — *nami zo tachikeru*[91]

This poem's likening of cherry blossoms to waves is enabled through a complex visual oscillation in which a series of reflections bounce images from one space to another and then back again. One way of reading the poem is to see its scattered cherry blossoms as being viewed against the backdrop of the sky, an arrangement that makes their swirling white patterns resemble waves on the surface of water. Consequently the sky is said to have waves, even though common sense would dictate that it does not. In an alternate reading, however, these cherry blossoms might first be seen on the water's surface, which would reflect the sky and its clouds there as well, forming a backdrop to the scattered petals.

In this manner, the water of Tsurayuki's poem works to blur any clear-cut distinction between the spaces that lie beneath and above its reflective surface. Ultimately, it is impossible to tell whether the blossoms of this poem are still tumbling from the sky or floating in swirls on the water. The result is a scenario in which there is no actual locale from which the onlooker within this poem can anchor his or her perspective in the "real world" and determine thereby which image is a reflection of which.

The phrase "water-less sky" in this verse represents another characteristic of Tsurayuki's poetics. Visual likenesses in his poems often depended on a predication phrased in either negative or concessive terms.[92] In the above verse, both rhetorical constructions are used simultaneously. The reflecting medium of a watery surface is first presented and then erased in the phrase "water-less sky" (*mizu naki sora*). At the same time as the poem concedes that the sky lacks water, it asserts that, nevertheless, waves can be seen on its azure surface. The manner in which the poem's language presents and then negates its reflecting medium suggests a parallel with the lower-ranking poet who creates the poem's vision of a scene but is himself absent from the locale in which the poem was joined to the actual painted scene.

Given the consistent interest in articulating a poetics for *uta* written in *kana* that is evident in Tsurayuki's other writings, it is possible to see such stylistic hallmarks in his poems as a form of critical meta-commentary on the conditions for producing much of court *uta*. If nothing else, it could be argued that the reflective surfaces so characteristic of Tsurayuki's poetry represent a sensibility that was informed, at least in part, by the tripartite social, spatial, and visual divisions created through the practices associated with screen poems. Like screen poems themselves, the reflective surfaces in Tsurayuki's poetry conflated separate locales by collapsing spatial distinctions. Just as screen paintings separated the recipient of a birthday celebration from the party gathered around him or her, reflective surfaces demarcated two separate spaces "beneath" (*soko*) and "above" (*ue*) the water. In the context of producing screen poetry, this third term can be thought of as the topic-phrase whose written words mediated between the poet's vision of a landscape and the actual one depicted on the screen. Similarly, the pivot-words that are deployed so frequently in Tsurayuki's screen poetry themselves appear to reflect different spaces: the interior world of human affect and intention, and the external world of "things seen and heard" (*miru mono kiku mono*) in the parlance of the Kana Preface.

The result of these implicit equivalences is what could be termed a "screen poetics" in which rhetorical emphasis is laid upon a material surface onto which different visual spaces can be projected. On a metacritical level, this poetics can perhaps best be characterized as one that draws attention to those places where the mediated nature of representation, that is, the manner in which words and material objects enable the portrayal of one thing as another, is itself made visible. The reflections of Tsurayuki's "screen poetics" refer simultaneously to written texts, screen paintings, and the conjunctions between Heaven and humanity which these material props created. Although Tsurayuki was probably never privy to the actual social settings in which screen paintings were used, his deployment of pivot-words and reflective surfaces played a role analogous to that of the painted screen in both demarcating and binding together different spaces through physical placement and perspectival ambiguity.

By drawing attention to the role played by language in constructing similarities between different landscape scenes and social settings, Tsurayuki's "screen poetics" also hints at his own place within the larger social schemes in which not only screen poetry, but also most other forms of what is termed "formal court poetry" (*hare no uta*) were produced. The reflexive foregrounding of language as a mediating third term between different spaces in this poetics can be read as a reflection on the broader phenomena of topic-based proxy compositions, which relied on the "professional poet" as an intermediary party in order to create ritual harmonies in verse between the patron who commissioned the poem and his or her social peers or superiors at poetry matches, birthday celebrations, and banquets.

The reliance Tsurayuki places on concession and negation in constructing his visual likenesses can perhaps also be appreciated through this lens. Both forms of rhetoric, which simultaneously present and efface something, leaving behind a trace of what has been negated, creates a situation not unlike that of the court poet who is first present and then rendered invisible within the social contexts in which his or her poetry circulated. The only thing remaining after Tsurayuki is erased from these networks of production and social exchange is his trace in the words he has produced.

Insofar as it was people other than Tsurayuki who ultimately chose which of his poems would appear in a given setting, and insofar as it was people other than him who appreciated it there, his poetic visions were ultimately subject to the judgments of the people among whom they circulated, as is suggested in the following exchange between Tsurayuki and the priest Shungen.

> His Eminent Virtue the priest Shungen wrapped some cherry blossoms in light paper and sent this poem.

This shower of cherry petals,	*sora shiranu*
which I hear someone	*yuki ka to hito no*
has claimed to be snow	*iu to kiku*
that is unknown to sky,	*sakura no furu wa*
harbors nothing but the wind!	*kaze nizarikeru*

> To which there was this response:

When cherry blossoms	*fuku kaze ni*
billow in waves	*sakura no nami no*
on gusts of wind,	*yoru toki wa*

I think the departing spring to be	*kureyuku haru o*
as illusory as the empty sky.	*sora ka to zo omou*[93]

Shungen's verse appears to challenge a previous assertion of similitude between blossoms and snow made by court poet. It has been suggested that the priest is, in fact, alluding to an earlier poem by Tsurayuki that uses similar language, including the phrase "unknown to the sky" (*sora ni shirarenu*).[94] The poem in question, which was composed for Uda's Teiji Villa Match, presents Tsurayuki's trademark use of negative phrases to sustain its visual equivalences between distinct objects and times:

Breezes beneath the trees	*sakura chiru*
scattering cherry blossoms	*ko no shitakaze wa*
hold no chill at all	*samukarade*
as, unknown to the sky,	*sora ni shirarenu*
I see this snow fall!	*yuki zo furikeru*[95]

In a move that is characteristic of Tsurayuki's poetry, the double negations of this verse (no chill, unknown to the sky) qualify the onlooker's assertion that the cherry blossoms appear to be snow. The negation of atmospheric temperature in particular points to the fact that these two seasonally discrete phenomena can be seen as similar only in an atemporal visual register.

By sending blossoms wrapped in paper, however, Shungen challenges the conditions that enable this similitude. One scholar has read the priest's response as a criticism of Tsurayuki's earlier poem, perhaps even poking fun at the poet in the process.[96] It is interesting to note in light of this reading that Shungen's critique is made not only in words but also through the material to which his poem is attached. By wrapping the blossoms in paper, he makes the invisible wind visible and tangible. His poem thus literalizes Tsurayuki's fanciful metaphor: scattering cherry blossoms don't reveal snow but the wind that drives them, something that (the gesture implies) Tsurayuki perhaps needs to actually *see* in order to understand. The further implication is that Tsurayuki's words in themselves mean little unless they are attached to things seen and heard in the exterior world. In this manner, Shungen's poem reads and reinterprets Tsurayuki's earlier verse, supplementing its words with a material representation of the scenario that they describe, much in the same way that a painting would lend specificity to the visions of the screen poet.

Tsurayuki's response takes up Shungen's challenge and with it, the words of the priest's poem by describing the wind that has scattered its blossoms. Interestingly, his poem's switch to a new visual metaphor likening the wind-blown blossoms to waves in the sky is perhaps a reference to his Spring verse in the *Kokinshū* describing a water-less sky. The negative phrase "water-less sky" used in that poem is also referenced in the final line's multiply resonant word *sora*, which can be taken to mean "sky," "emptiness," or "fiction." The reader is left to wonder which of these connotations Tsurayuki intends. Is he admitting that his previous image of snow falling from the sky is a fiction? Or is he insinuating that the description in Shungen's poem is false? On the surface Tsurayuki appears to be declaring that the scene of blossoms in the sky of late spring, regardless of how it is seen, is ultimately an expression of the Buddhist tenet that all phenomena are empty and impermanent. Such an assertion would appear to be diplomatic, a way of claiming that in an ultimate sense it doesn't matter how one sees a world that is itself insubstantial. Even here, however, one can detect a riposte that jabs at its addressee. Does a priest need to be reminded of the fundamental tenets of Buddhist doctrine?

Tsurayuki's barbed reply suggests the perception of an equally barbed challenge on Shungen's part. While this debate over poetic conceits accompanied by the beautiful token of blossoms wrapped in paper can be taken as an example of the wit and elegance that is often seen as permeating both Heian poetry and the court society that produced it, the tenor of both men's poems suggests that real tensions lurk beneath the surface levity. If the exchange indicates that Tsurayuki's poems enjoyed widespread familiarity among his peers, it also suggests that his status as a poet did not go unquestioned or unchallenged. The fact that earlier poems written by him are being referenced by both men further suggests that what is at stake here is not mere poetic fancies, but the reputation of a courtier who depends on the acceptance of his verse in order to make his way among his social superiors.

The exchange between Tsurayuki and Shungen thus shows how assertions of equivalences in poetic language could be contested within the social arena. Seeing two separate things as the same could be potentially disruptive in a world organized around strict hierarchical distinctions. Social harmony ultimately required more than the exchange and reflection of other peoples' words to be recognized and affirmed, and poetic skill in itself was not enough to ensure that the poet's perspective coincided with that of the aristocrats who viewed his poems inside their palaces and mansions. Driving these activities lay a desire for material security that was ultimately dependent on political and social forces outside the poetic domain. Perhaps in recognition of this fact, the visual likenesses that appear in so many of Tsurayuki's poems were often only sustained through the language of concession and negation, a tentative way of addressing the world that would be eminently suited to a social dependent.

The tensions and attempts at social harmony witnessed in this exchange between Tsurayuki and Shungen, although not subject to the formal strictures accompanying the public arena in which Kammu's poetic harmonization took place, recall the presence of such fractures in that earlier instance. This book's investigation of early Heian poetry comes full circle through this lens, suggesting two separate ends of the spectrum of social practices constituting court poetry over the course of the intervening century. In place of a court banquet where both parties are present, we have an exchange between individuals mediated through letters that travel from one household to the other. In place of ancient songs that are cited, we have written poems by a living poet being referenced. In place of metaphors that suggest the sexual and political ties between Kammu and his chief female official, we have ones that seem to point to a purely natural setting external to two male peers. What does remain the same, however, is the pursuit of harmony driving such poetic exchanges, a pursuit that ends up revealing the lack of accord between two parties at the same time as it strives for this goal.

Epilogue

Yamato Verse and Yamato Japan

Before the tenth century had reached its midpoint, the Heian court was subjected to a series of external shocks as the territories on its boundaries threatened to break away. In the east, a warrior named Taira no Masakado (d. 940) claimed the title of "new sovereign" (*shinkō*) in 939. In the west, another rebel known as Fujiwara no Sumitomo (d. 941) dominated the Inner Sea, even sailing up the Yodo River at one point to look on the capital. Although both rebellions were crushed within the space of two years, they represented a profound challenge to the authority of the Heian court. It is perhaps significant in this regard that the sovereign's prerogative to rule ritually through the calendar seems to have been ignored by these rebels. Although Masakado possessed military and economic resources to back up his claim to the status of sovereign, he does not appear to have employed the "doctors of calendrics" (*reki hakase*) that would have been required to provide his new realm with its own era name or annual calendar. In this sense, his title of "new sovereign" implied not so much an usurpation as a wholesale displacement of the concept of ritual rulership that underpinned the Heian state.

These external crises provided an opportunity for the Fujiwara regency to extend and deepen its authority under the aegis of Tokihira's brother Tadahira, during the reign of the two sovereigns who succeeded Daigo. Although his historical reputation is far more benign than that of Tokihira, Tadahira accomplished much more in establishing the regency as a ritual and political institution.[1] In 941 when he accepted the title of "chancellor" (*kanpaku*), he became essentially a regent who continued to play the same role vis-à-vis an adult sovereign.

By this time, privileges such as the right to see all documents addressed to the sovereign (*nairan*), an office within the palace at the Jikiro, and the right to determine appointments in the court bureaucracy had become formally acknowledged prerogatives of his position. At the same time, meetings of the high aristocracy belonging to the Council of State shifted from morning assemblies to nighttime ones.[2]

During this period, members of the Northern House also began to chronicle their achievements in a variety of new textual genres such as personal diaries and household poetry collections. The new imperial Fujiwara order was also expressed through elaborate poetry matches held in the palace. In 960, a contest known as the *Tentoku dairi uta-awase* (Tentoku Era Palace Poetry Match), set new standards for material splendor and elaborate ritual in such events. Only months after this poetry match, however, the palace's core buildings—including the Seiryōden, the Shishinden, and the Naiki-dokoro office where palace records were kept—were all consumed by fire. Within the space of twenty years, then, the structures of the Heian state had suffered profound assaults at both its extremities and its core.

Historians often see these events as heralding the end of the *ritsuryō* state and the inauguration of a new era at the Heian court. By the end of the tenth century, the early years were already being viewed with nostalgia. Daigo's reign was hailed as a golden age in texts ranging from the *Tale of Genji* to the petitions and poems of prominent scholar-officials such as Minamoto no Shitagō (911–983) and Ōe no Masahira (952–1012). For people writing after the regency had become an institutional reality endowed with its own administrative and ritual prerogatives, such nostalgia must have had a political edge. This would have been especially true for the lower grades of officialdom whose numbers continued to shrink and whose livelihood increasingly depended on service to an aristocratic household rather than to the sovereign of a centralized government. For such people, the imperial anthology and the past it represented came to be seen as the products of the sovereign's direct rule, in contrast to the Fujiwara-dominated regime of their own time.

The sense of historical difference between the reigns of Uda and Daigo and those of their successors has contributed to our modern view of the period as well. Conventional histories tend to use three divisions when discussing Heian Japan. The first is an "early Heian period" (*Heian shoki*) in which the central state was the dominant power (794–970). It is followed by a "mid-Heian period" (*Heian chūki*) in which the Fujiwara regents held political power from roughly 970 to 1070. Finally, there is a "late Heian period" (*Heian kōki*) from about 1070 to 1185 in which first retired sovereigns and then warriors of the Taira clan dominated the court through their household governments. Each of these periodizations—which essentially are derived from the predominant political institutions of the time—overlaps to some extent with changes in the cultural history of *Kokinshū* poetry. In the early Heian period, the anthology was a means for affirming a Confucian state grounded in a continental cosmology. In the mid-Heian period, it provided models for poetic practice and a source of allusions in the fictional tales and epistolary correspondences between men and women at a Fujiwara-dominated court. By the end of the late Heian period, it became part of a pedagogical industry that converted knowledge about this text and the allegedly arcane language in which it was written into a form of cultural capital amassed by powerful households.

The prominence of the *Kokinshū* in each of these periods can be seen as a testament to the continuing importance of *uta* in defining Heian court culture. In the mid-Heian period, there is perhaps no more marked testament to its influence than the *Tale of Genji*, which not only alludes to individual poems throughout its narrative but also draws on entire scrolls such as Partings and Lamentations to organize its "Suma" and "Maboroshi" chapters respectively.[3] Another example is provided by the *Pillow Book*, which offers us the first detailed insights into the ways in which members of the court absorbed the anthology's poems. In tandem with the growing status of the *Kokinshū* was a growth in the status of the people who compiled imperial anthologies. Beginning with the *Shūi wakashū* and its editor Fujiwara no Kintō, the task of composing and compiling *uta* was entrusted to upper-ranking courtiers with close familial ties to powerful aristocrats. In the process, the practices associated with Japanese court poetry increasingly became a household affair.

In the late Heian period, the importance of the *Kokinshū* extended into the realm of formal pedagogy as it became one of the core canonical texts representing a "classical" tradition that required explication and conferred authority upon the people who produced studies of it. A tradition of commentary, developed by particular houses specializing in poetic lore, came to cover a wide array of approaches to the text, including everything from pragmatic tips on successful composition to philological investigations of obscure terms, explication of the historical background informing particular poems, and religious allegorical interpretations.[4] The construction of a Heian poetic past in the twelfth century and beyond in itself underscores the relevance of using the term "medieval" in referring to this period. During this time, the *Kokinshū* can be seen to have played a significant role in defining a historical concept of the ninth and tenth centuries as "early" in the sense that it was seen to represent a linguistic antiquity. Conversely, the construction of this antiquity enabled what could be called a "medieval" mind-set that perceived itself in relation to a past that was replete, idealized, and accessible only through the language of texts.

To say that the *Kokinshū* and early Heian poetry constituted a core component of Japanese court culture, however, begs the questions of when and how *waka* came to be seen as a general term for all forms of Japanese court poetry rather than for only one mode of poetic praxis among a host of others associated with *uta*. By outlining some of the practices and texts that preceded and surrounded the *Kokinshū*, this book has sought to decouple the poetry of the period from this later concept of *waka*. As a form of practice (poetic harmonization) rather than linguistic genre (Japanese poetry), *waka* in the early Heian period constituted only one dimension of *uta*, which included a variety of forms that could be inscribed at banquets, sung as accompaniments to dance performances, recited at poetry contests, or chanted to the accompaniment of stringed instruments. Insofar as *waka* were chiefly concerned with affirming social hierarchies of difference, its character could be described as performative, pragmatic, and social.

If Yamato verse is not simply an alternate designation for *waka*, then what are we to make of the former term? The choice of definition itself would appear to be a question of what was being emphasized in any given case. The *Nihongi kyōen waka* at which *yamato uta* were composed, for example, can also be seen as an instance of "harmonizing verse" through topic-based composition in a public setting before a figure of authority. In both this instance and the *chōka* offered up to

Ninmyō, however, *yamato uta* were not produced on the ruler's command but by the order of his Fujiwara representative. In other instances, the regent could order verse that would "harmonize" with his words, as we saw after Ninmyō's death, but in that case the explicit substitution of the regent for the deceased sovereign might have at least partially informed the choice of wording. As was argued in Chapter 4, the term *waka* in the Mana Preface is primarily associated with the ruler rather than with the broader ensemble of poetic practices that occupied members of the court.

Insofar as it cited the *Nihon shoki* or appealed to "word spirits" (*kotodama*) embedded in traditional phrases and narratives, *yamato uta* appears to have been primarily defined in terms of a distinctively Japanese history and language within the court's official histories. At the same time, the word seems to have been used only rarely in the early Heian period.[5] It was this lack of an extensive prior history perhaps that enabled Tsurayuki to define *yamato uta* in such novel and ambitious ways in the Kana Preface. If a common feature is shared by his vision of *yamato uta* and the one presented in the court histories, it is the emphasis that both place on the act of inscribing poems in *kana*. Despite its relative unimportance in the early Heian period, however, *yamato uta* can be seen as having enormous significance for the later cultural history of the era, insofar as it inaugurated a diffusion of things Yamato, such as Yamato paintings, Yamato objects, and a Yamato language. For this reason alone, an understanding of the place of "Yamato" in early Heian poetic discourse can contribute to our overall understanding of the period, particularly vis-à-vis the tendency to describe its court society in aesthetic and gendered terms.

One way to locate *yamato uta* is in relation to the binary system in which all things Heian were assigned a value as indigenous or continental. Thomas LaMarre has argued eloquently for Heian Japan's lack of linguistic homogeneity, ethnic purity, and discrete territoriality, on account of this way of viewing the world.[6] It is important to remember, however, that the binary terms through which the court represented itself also entailed a concept of society and polity which was coercive and exclusive. Such terms lay at the heart of conceptions of power and authority which can be traced back to the earliest forms of rulership in Japan.[7] Insofar as court poetry used a language of complementary opposites that was intended to represent a self-enclosed and all-encompassing vision of the world, it can be said to have excluded alternative forms of community and identity that might have challenged the court's view of its centrality to meaning and cultural significance. There was no space in this neatly demarcated view of community, for example, in which to acknowledge the multiple permutations and combinations entailed by the existence of hybrid cultures in Northeast Asia which were being forged by the movement of peoples from different linguistic and cultural backgrounds across its maritime zones as traders, pirates, priests, and immigrants.[8]

In addition to providing a framework through which to control and exclude difference, such binaries also doubled the internal meaning of the terms used by Heian Japanese to describe their own identity. As early as the seventh century, the word "Nihon" was used by Yamato dynasty rulers in a dual capacity, to represent themselves in diplomatic discourse with the Tang empirium as a subsidiary realm to the east of that entity, as well as the center of a smaller version of it, complete with barbarians and tributary satellite kingdoms of its own. Similar divisions were also internalized to create two Japans: a Heian court located east of the Tang, and another region to the northeast of this capital whose status fluctuated among that of a semibarbarian frontier, a tributary kingdom, and an independent polity.[9]

The question of how Yamato poetry constructed power and authority in the early Heian period is related to the question of where the term "Yamato" fit within this bifurcated world view. By the middle of the tenth century, the appropriateness of using the word "Nihon" to describe the Heian polity was being called into question on account of its potentially derogatory implications in the same lectures on the *Nihon shoki* in which *yamato uta* were being inscribed.[10] Whereas "Yamato" referred to a region steeped in dynastic myth, "Nihon" signaled its orientation east of the Tang's central kingdom, a direction associated with barbarians in the latter's world view. The turn toward Yamato as a preferred word for describing the Heian court was thus accompanied by a renewed interest in a Yamato poetry that could cite the realm's unique history and proclaim its distinctive rather than derivative place within a larger world.

This predominantly discursive element in the definition of Yamato—one that tied it to the citation of texts that claimed to represent a distinct language embedded in ancient narratives—became pluralized in the eleventh century, when "Yamato" and its complement "Kara" proliferated in styles of painting, ceramics, clothing, and other material objects in tandem with a shift in the modes of court-sanctioned cultural exchange with the mainland from monarchical diplomacy to mercantile trade. This turn away from an exclusive concern with poetic language in defining "Yamato" can perhaps be seen as a corollary to the move away from an exclusive dependence on Confucian ideology to articulate concepts of power, insofar as that ideology saw the state's ability to define and control language as one of its central concerns. In this sense, one can also see the efflorescence of Yamato cultural forms as marking the transition from an early Heian period in which this Confucian ideology remained the dominant reference point, to a mid-Heian era in which the articulation of power and authority was more diffused and diverse.

The influential historian Amino Yoshihiko has viewed the move from Nihon to Yamato in the tenth century as a turn away from the political project of constructing an empire toward the cultural one of creating a sense of communal identity in the private sphere of daily life.[11] Such distinctions between the political and private spheres, however, can lead us to overlook the ways in which a notion of empire informed Yamato modes of court culture in the Heian period. Although the Heian polity may have been territorially conservative after its initial years of conquest and expansion, in court rituals it maintained the language of what could be termed an "empire," insofar as it continued to represent itself as a state with dominion over culturally and ethnically distinct entities on its periphery, making it (to use the term prevalent in continental East Asia) a "central kingdom" with its own tributaries and barbarians.[12] During the ninth and tenth centuries, at least, poetry was repeatedly used to represent, codify, and enact the hierarchical social harmonies between center and periphery, and ruler and ruled, which supported this imaginary geography.

One of my intentions in reading the structure of the *Kokinshū* as an embodiment of the state has been to suggest how fundamental these perceptions were to an understanding of the anthology during the initial period in which it circulated. This connection between poetry and polity perhaps is brought home most forcefully by the boundaries of the text, which ends with an "eastern verse" (*azuma uta*) composed by Fujiwara no Toshiyuki for a newly established wintertime observance at the Kamo Shrine:

Awesome in its splendor	*chihayaburu*
is the shrine of Kamo,	*Kamo no yashiro no*
whose slender princess pine	*hime komatsu*
may pass a myriad reigns,	*yorozu yo fu tomo*
but will never change color.	*iro wa kawaraji*[13]

Toshiyuki's poem is a good illustration of the ways in which Uda's court sought to construct new, more self-consciously indigenous forms of ritual and culture. Both the Kamo festival and the "Eastland song" composed for it were the products of his regime. In fact, nothing in the language of this poem would seem to explicitly associate it with an earlier cultural tradition originating in the eastern portion of the Heian imperium. An alternate version of this verse, which includes *hayashi kotoba* refrains, appears as an *azuma asobi no uta* (song to Eastland music) within a later collection of court songs. There, it is called a *motomego uta* (child-seeking song), a designation that seemingly bears no relation to its lyrics. In his commentary to this verse, the scholar Tsuchihashi Yutaka speculates that Toshiyuki perhaps preserved the melody and musical accompaniment of a song that originated in the east, while supplying new words that praised the deity of the Kamo Shrine.[14] One reason why Toshiyuki's verse might have been associated with the Eastland could be the geographical and geomantic position of the Kamo Shrine, which had been established by Saga as the capital's northeastern ritual boundary. In this manner, spatial connections between the capital's boundaries and those of the empire, between a shrine on the outskirts of Heiankyō and a distant northeastern frontier, are created, affirmed, and legitimated.

By transforming an eastern song into a form of metrically regular poetry intended for court ritual, Toshiyuki thus also transforms regional cultural forms into ones that reflected the spatial organization of a polity oriented around a capital and a palace. Local variations in dialect, cultural tradition, geography, and nomenclature (variations that did not fit within a reductive cultural model of binary opposites) are erased through this operation and replaced with the mutually complementary terms of center and periphery, terms that in turn represent the capital and its environs as a microcosmic analogue for the macrocosmic categories of a civilized realm and a barbarian frontier. Such categories in their turn helped define an "empire" analogous to that of the Tang empirium, which represented itself as the universal center of meaning and value in relation to various ethnic Others.

As with other seriate arrangements of verse in the *Kokinshū*, the significance of this last poem lies in the ways in which it organizes all the poems that precede it. As one scholar notes, the placement of this song suggests that it is intended as a prayer for the eternal glory of both the sovereign and his anthology.[15] In its overall structure, the scroll in which this final poem appears replicates the order in which songs were performed for the enthronement rites.[16] Toshiyuki's verse thus also anticipates a new round of the ritual cycle with which the anthology opened, insofar as the enthronement rites themselves were a variant on the New Year's Day rites that are evoked in the seriate arrangement of poems that open Spring. In this manner, the *Kokinshū* limns a self-contained spatial and temporal universe as we begin with springtime rituals at the court's center and end with wintertime rituals on its northeastern perimeter, with performances of an ethnic Other occupying the human portion of both moments in the cycle. The result is to establish the ritual structures of empire at the very center of the court's representation of itself in this anthology.

Rather than invoke the coercive structures of a culturally hegemonic empire, discussion of the Yamato style cultivated by the Northern House of the Fujiwara has usually entailed an appraisal of the place of women and "femininity" within its court culture. As Mimi Hall Yiengpruksawan has noted, the predominant place accorded the Fujiwara regency in political history, and the prominent role played by women in sustaining it, have led to Heian court society being described in feminine, cultural, and aesthetic terms.[17] Such terms have been used to describe the entire period as well. Beginning in the eighteenth century, historians came to see decadent effeminacy and poor government as the result of this supposed feminine element.[18] To this day, histories of the Heian period tend to lavish attention on its cultural and aesthetic achievements, while treating them as incidental products of, rather than integral to, the governance of the realm.

This modern linkage between Heian culture and the feminine began with the *Kokinshū*, which the eighteenth-century scholar Kamo no Mabuchi famously characterized as a work that embodied a "weak feminine style" (*taoyame-buri*).[19] As with many later scholars, Mabuchi drew a contrast between the anthology and its *Man'yōshū* predecessor, in this case by claiming that a more "forceful manly style" (*masurao-buri*) existed in the latter. One can perhaps detect here the seeds of the modern critical distinction between a positive, direct, and forceful mode of expression in the earlier anthology and a more negative, indirect, and disembodied style in its Heian successor. Just as Heian aristocratic culture is often seen as aesthetically obsessed and disengaged from action or the direct application of power, the implicitly negative quality of detachment associated with its poetry evokes the figure of the cloistered noblewoman, cut off from the public sphere and the direct wielding of political power. Such gendered qualities are anachronistic, of course, much like the ones associated with *yamato-e* I discussed in Chapter 5. If anything, the project of compiling the *Kokinshū* was an exclusively masculine undertaking, perhaps deliberately so in part to contrast it with the poetry matches undertaken by Uda's court.

In contemporary histories of Heian *uta*, women poets have often been seen as the anonymous bearers of a tradition that bridged the divide between the *Man'yōshū* and *Kokinshū*. Nakanishi Susumu, for example, sees poems by women in the late *Man'yōshū* period as constituting a distinct tradition, one that continued as an underground stream in anonymous "women's verse" (*onna no uta*) in the *Kokinshū* before blossoming into the women's literature of the Heian period.[20] Like many current accounts of the history of Heian poetry, the genealogy of this association between female poets and a tradition of informal or anonymous verse can be traced back to the Kana Preface to the *Kokinshū*. As I argued in Chapter 4, however, the Kana Preface is best seen as an anomalous text. Its representation of female poets as performers is the obverse side of Tsurayuki's desire to represent the male-courtier poet as a figure whose self merges with that of his male sovereign.

Such an association, however, was at best tenuous given Tsurayuki's limited access to his sovereign, in contrast to that of the female attendants who served in the Seiryōden and participated in poetry matches. Moreover, the performance of such songs was not the exclusive province of women. Tsurayuki himself, along with many male aristocrats, often assiduously studied these arts under the tutelage of female entertainers, in order to carry out their own ritual and social duties singing at banquets or in shrine rituals. It could in fact be argued that it was precisely the advantage women had over men in gaining access to the royal person which informed Tsurayuki's efforts to displace them from his vision of court poetry.

Another reason why *yamato uta* are associated with a "feminine" cultural sphere is on account of their ubiquitous use in exchanges between men and women in Heian vernacular prose. This phenomenon is often attributed to the social constraints placed upon women who, it is assumed, were too rarely educated in literary Chinese to be able to use any other medium in written exchanges. The literatus Ōe no Asatsuna (886–957) provided perhaps the best-known characterization of them in this regard when he writes in his "Rhapsody on the Union of Men and Women" (*Danjo kon'in fu*) about the use of *yamato uta* as one stage in a man's courtship of a woman.[21] A similar view is suggested in the Mana Preface's account of *waka*'s decline. Certainly, the role played by *uta* in the song-fence (*utagaki*) traditions of earlier times might partly explain why their written forms played a similar role in coordinating gendered exchanges in the Heian period. Asatsuna's characterization, however, is far from telling the whole story. It is important to remember that *yamato uta* could also be used to define the Confucian community of male officialdom in rites such as the *Nihongi kyōen waka*, a practice that continued into the period during which Asatsuna lived. Even in cases where women are prominent, such as poetry matches and birthday celebrations, it is not courtship so much as kinship that was given the most emphasis. Uncles, aunts, or siblings—rather than prospective future partners—appear to have often played the most significant role in such settings.

Perhaps more fundamentally, the difficulty in discussing or specifying a "feminine" element in our accounts of Heian poetry has to do with the mutability of its language, a mutability that in turn reflects the variety of contexts in which any given poem could play a role. Given the importance of proxy compositions to the period's poetic practices, it is probably no coincidence that the voice of a poem could be associated with a variety of people regardless of their gender or rank. Precisely because context was so constitutive of any given poem's social significance, we can find a gendered dimension to *uta* only in particular performative settings rather than in any fixed form of style or voice. If we are to tease out such associations, we need to do so with precise attention to the particular contexts in which they obtained.

If there is one way in which we can perhaps speak of a gendered element in the language of Heian court poetry, it is the ubiquity with which both men and women adopted a female persona within it. This example is, however, illustrative of the ways in which the modern generic distinctions between Yamato and Kara or public and private that tend to accompany discussions of gender are themselves of limited use. The trope of the waiting woman was as frequently deployed in *uta* as in *shi*. Moreover, far from signaling a private realm of affect, it can be said to have constituted the preeminent example of a form of personhood that was forumlated in public terms: as a royal subject defined in relation to political authority. Although we have a modern tendency (again in part a product of the Kana Preface) to associate the feminine social sphere with a private realm of experience and emotion, one could argue that the very "femininity" that is present in so many early Heian poems, particularly those expressing longing and desire, often signaled their public courtly nature rather than their status as something "buried away" in the houses of amorous aristocrats.

I would argue that it was changes in axes of social difference other than gender which drove the development of Japanese court poetry in the early Heian period. Such changes, which involved both genders and all ranks, can be charted through the development of the personal residence as a site for imagining community at court. *Uta* poetry provided the household's (often multiple) physical sites and their gardens with their own temporality, creating a stage on which different members of the court could assert their right to the realm's resources. To complement this exterior stage, landscape scenes on screens produced an interior stage on which birthday celebrations and other rites affirming kinship ties within a household were performed. In the *Kokinshū*, the genealogical linkages of the Blessings section can be seen as another attempt to limn a form of social identity through the household, one which was not precisely congruent with that of the state.

When and how the household became the predominant locus of social identity at court depends largely on the feature of it that is being emphasized. Sublineages within a clan were increasingly referred to as "gates" (*kado*) or "houses" (*ie*) during the Heian period, but in vernacular texts up to the eleventh century the term *ie* primarily referred to the physical locale where a mansion was built.[22] As the wealth accrued from private estates increased from the mid tenth century onward, these mansions themselves grew in size and became widespread among a wide stratum of the aristocracy.[23] Already in the early Heian period, however, members of the court were defining themselves through practices that formally declared their filiations with particular families. By Tsurayuki's time, it had become customary for officials to submit a "name-card" (*myōbu*), which included one's rank, family name, and date of submission, to an aristocrat as a formal token of entrance into his personal service.[24]

Such relationships increasingly came to define community at court as the lower ranks of officialdom shrank, and ownership of the rights to income from private estates became the chief measure of wealth among its members. The fact that such forms of filiation—ones in which the members of a "household" included both kin and retainers—were being developed at the same time as their humbler members were being assigned the identities of composers at poetry matches whose production and display of verse represented the household as a locus of authority suggests that poetic practice in the early tenth century was closely tied to the development of these new forms of community at the Heian court. In this sense, perhaps, we can also speak of the period under question as a transitional one, uneasily situated between concepts of polity that privileged the palace as the sole locus of authority in the early Heian period, and one in which a plurality of households came to increasing prominence over the course of the mid-Heian period.

Indeed, it was precisely the transitional nature of the period that appears to have spurred on such a profusion of new poetic forms, most of which were designed to respond to changing configurations of power and authority at court. Any attempt at historical periodization is, of course, contingent upon the phenomena one chooses to emphasize as significant. Our (necessarily) retrospective view makes it all too easy to see Heian court poetry as a mode of social discourse primarily employed by aristocrats in the pursuit of private household interests whose relationship to the palace and other symbols of the central state was tentative and oblique. I have sought here to provide a corrective to this later view of that poetry by focusing on the historical moment in which its earliest forms were produced in the ninth and tenth centuries, as well as the ways in which that poetry was often directly involved in the production of monarchical authority. Consequently, my use of the term "early Heian" to describe the poetry of this period is intended in part as an expedient means for emphasizing the ways in which it drew on earlier conceptions of rulership that grounded the social order in a Confucian cosmos.

At the end of the twelfth century and over the course of what is conventionally termed Japan's "middle ages," the household became the primary site at which political, economic, and cultural interests at court were organized. During this same period, the use of words denoting Japan, such as Nihon, Yamato, and Wa, spread among priests, warriors, and commoners, as literacy extended to more classes and both genders in various regions throughout the archipelago. At the same time, the Kana Preface's claim for a distinctively Yamato form of poetry whose transmission and anthologizing were vital to the well-being of the realm was repeated and amplified in the prefaces to succeeding imperial anthologies such as the *Shin kokin wakashū* (*New Collection of Poems Ancient and Modern*, 1205), *Shoku kokin wakashū* (*Collection of Poems Ancient and Modern Continued*, 1265), and *Shinshoku kokin wakashū* (*New Collection of Poems Ancient and Modern Continued*, 1439).[25]

These new linkages among language, writing, and community in medieval times have yet to be accounted for in telling the story of *waka* poetry, which continues to focus on the world of the capital with its scholars and poetic factions. To what extent, and when, did such texts as the *Kokinshū* spread to the population outside the court, especially among wealthy warriors in the eastern regions and the mercantile and urban communities that were growing with such rapidity from the thirteenth century onward? At what point did *waka* come to exclusively mean "Japanese poetry"? Such questions might help us understand some of the ways in which the *Kokinshū* and early Heian court poetry figure within a larger cultural history, one in which the concept of a distinctively Japanese poetic form was developed and deployed by different parties to different ends.

The twelfth-century court and its medieval successors represented a decisive break with its tenth-century predecessor in a more fundamental sense as well. There is no way of crossing the divide from one period to the other in any clear-cut manner. Strictly speaking, the Heian Japan we have access to is itself largely a medieval construct pieced together from selective fragments. What is perceived as significant in our accounts of early Heian culture and history has already been determined to be so by scholars who selectively transcribed, catalogued, excerpted, and amended its written legacy in medieval times. Our knowledge of early Heian rituals, court culture, and poetry is largely derived from treatises such as the *Fukurozōshi*, poetic anthologies produced and preserved by different households, fragmentary citations of historical documents, collections of anecdotes, diaries, and compendia of ritual lore (*yūsoku kojitsu*).

The construction of this Heian past in medieval times raises issues with the potential to profoundly complicate our own attempts to reconstruct a less-idealized and better-rounded picture of the ninth and tenth centuries. It has become commonplace among scholars to emphasize the fact that our access to the past is always already mediated through our awareness of our own present and that of those intermediary figures who have conveyed the past to us. My own focus on ritual practices in analyzing Heian court poetry can in itself be seen as a product of a later history, insofar as the medieval transmitters of its court culture privileged such matters to the exclusion of much else. A more diverse and richer world of early Heian poetry—one that encompassed satirical, dramatic, and popular elements, for example—must once have existed to a far greater extent than we can currently imagine, even if it is retrievable now only in marginalia and suggestive hints in the historical record. With such limitations in mind, this book has sought to piece the surviving fragments together in such a way as to create new readings that can contribute to a larger ongoing conversation about Heian poetry that has been taking place now for more than a millennium.

APPENDIXES

Appendix A

Preface to the *Ryōunshū*

Your Majesty's minister Minemori wishes to make the following statement. Emperor Wen of Wei[1] once said: "Writing literary compositions is a great undertaking in binding together the realm, and a thing that flourishes without fading. Our lives have their appointed time before running out; glory and pleasure end with one's bodily self. Believe this!" In my humble opinion, Your Majesty firmly grasps his royal calling within the palace, and rules over all beneath the skies. Ascending the pavilion in spring, you give yourself over to feelings of joy.[2] Cutting through the rank grasses of autumn, you trim away the excessively complicated. Your wisdom and sagacity are Heaven's bequest, and your talents at literary form are a gift from the gods. Moreover, you study in order to aid your sagely powers and expands bounty through inquiry.

The age we live in has blessed us with peace and serenity; days are spent strumming the zither and plying the brush. Lamenting the swift passing of days and months, Your Majesty is loath to see the writings of his day sink into oblivion. And so, you have commanded your ministers to compile a collection of recent literary pieces. Though lacking in talent, we humbly received Your Majesty's command and accepted the order issued. If we were to take the place of skilled craftsmen in carving, it would only be expected that our hands would be cut.[3] Flaws and blemishes have been covered over and extraordinary and startling points brought forward in the collection that we have assembled; and yet it is not easy to find a single poem that is completely perfect. Those who have succeeded in their careers are not placed above, nor are those out of favor placed below. Neither is there any distinction between the dead and the living. Everyone is placed in the anthology in order of court rank.

As for the poems of Your Majesty and the Crown Prince, they are so elevated in repute as to be beyond the visible world of images, and their tones transcend the earthly realm. How are the likes of us to debate their merits? Nonetheless, we have received a special royal command to do so, and have thus ventured to make selections among them. In this we are like the river god praising the vast ocean, or a frog extolling the view from his well.[4] We cannot attain the brilliance of the rising sun, nor the superior man's transformative powers in enlightening the people in the same manner as the wind moves the grass.[5]

Though I am confused and at a loss as to how to carry out this task, I have sought to broaden myself through learning.[6] In the end, I have been unable to give up this duty which has been assigned to me, although I have often wished to do so. Though ashamed of this anthology, I hope the writings it contains will bring forth illumination, just as pearls submerged in a river will provide sparkling clarity to its waters, or jewels sunk in the depths will give luster to the riverbanks.[7]

The anthology begins in the first year of Enryaku (782) and ends in the fifth year of Kōnin (814). There are twenty-three authors in total and ninety-odd poems in all, presented in a single scroll that has been called the "Collection Soaring Above the Clouds." This anthology is not simply the result of your minister's personal judgments. Poems were evaluated and their relative merits debated two or three times with Lords Sugawara no Kiyoyoshi and Isayama no Fumitsugu, among others. Controversial cases were submitted to Your Majesty for inspection. Lord Kaya no Toyotoshi, the genius of our age, has been unable to attend court on account of illness. Nonetheless, your minister has consulted him over the manuscript, and made decisions accordingly. Respectfully submitted by Your Majesty's minister Minemori. (*GR*, 8: 449–450)

Appendix B

Preface to the *Bunka shūreishū*

Your Majesty's minister Nakao wishes to make the following statement. The *Ryōunshū* was compiled by Michinoku Governor Ono no Minemori and others. It covered the period from the first year of Enryaku through to the fifth year of Kōnin and consisted of ninety-two poems in all. Since then, fine literary pieces have appeared one after the other, and though little over four years have elapsed, they have come to fill more than a hundred scrolls.[1]

Not a single month has passed without literary compositions being crafted. Talents at court and gifted men from all over the realm unceasingly express themselves in duckweed-trailing filigrees of fine writing. Some are increasingly lofty in their vitality and essential ideas, which conform to the tones and structures of the ancient *feng* and *sao* poems. Others have gradually allowed their clarity and lightness to increase, and their richness to reflect the gaudy extravagance of amorous poetry.[2] It could be said that plain carts have been transformed into imperial carriages by adorning them with flowers, or that waters have given birth to ice by increasing their stern dignity.[3] A fine reputation ensures their posterity, and praise-filled evaluations bring them to the fore. Precious jade and plum fruits shine with the same luster, the colors of weeds and fragrant herbs are intermingled; pale yellow and red are no different in actuality, the writing chest and cupboard drawer are alike.

Lord Fujiwara no Fuyutsugu bore His Majesty's command to us. Your humble minister debated the merits of each poem with Sugawara no Kiyoyoshi, Isayama no Fumitsugu, Shigeno no Sadanushi, and Kuwahara no Haraaka, distinguishing the good from the bad and setting standards. If there were any lingering doubts, the poem in question was submitted to Your Majesty for judgment. Poems left out of the *Ryōunshū* were perused and placed in this collection. All of the verses have been classified by topic to facilitate consultation. In all there are twenty-six authors, and one hundred and forty-eight poems divided among three scrolls. It has been titled "Collection of Masterpieces of Literary Flowers."

A separate command was issued regarding Your Majesty's works and those of the Crown Prince. Though they appear in the same collection with the others, Heaven is exalted and Earth lowly, the lord intones and his ministers harmonize with him. Consequently, the number of authors was cut back during the editorial stage. I have been foolhardy in daring to take on the task of compiling such an anthology, given my meager talents. After receiving another command, I have humbly composed this preface. Respectfully submitted by Your Majesty's minister Nakao. (NKBT, 69: 192–195)

Appendix C

Preface to the *Keikokushū*

Your Majesty's minister has heard that Heaven initiated written signs, and that the Strider constellation rules over literary composition. In antiquity an office was set up to collect songs, so that the ruler would know his successes and failures at governing the realm.[1] Thus, literary composition is the means by which images of Heaven above and Earth below are made evident, and the way by which the order governing human relations is illuminated. It fully comprehends the principle and nature of all things, and through it, the ideal essence of each and every one is known. Only when form and content are mutually balanced is the gentleman made.[2] One can compare it to the patterned silk gauze that a court robe possesses, or the wings that belong to a goose soaring overhead.

From the Chu and Han onward, poets have carried on in the tradition of their forebears, a current that has flowed especially strong at the confluence of the Luo and Huang and to the east of the Jiang.[3] Yang Xiong's *Model Sayings* was ill informed, and was thus at fault in destroying the Way.[4] The wisdom expressed by Wen of Wei's *Discourses* is of limitless use in ordering the realm.[5] Great was his knowledge of writing's applicability to the times! However, during the Qi and Liang dynasties suasive power and forceful argumentation in literature had already perished. In the days of the Northern Zhou and Sui dynasties, the rules for composition were lost.[6] Yet writing became clear again while passing through muddy currents, and renewal was achieved by emulating antiquity. No doubt the reason why these compositions were no different from those they imitated was because they accorded in spirit with the writings of antiquity.

The poor live in fear of hunger and cold, while the rich give themselves over to idle pursuits. They end up losing themselves in the task immediately before them, forgetting about their legacy a thousand years hence. Therefore, the authors of antiquity placed their selves in their writing, making their intentions known through their poetry and other works. Not entrusting themselves to the fleeting moment of their glory, they sought to pass their names on to posterity. If they were rulers, their writings embodied the grandeur of Heaven's starry patterns. If they were ministers, they served as fine intermediaries and supporters of their sovereign. In what age is talent not rare? When is talent not put to use? The spirit of peace and tranquility once found in the Prince of Liang's gardens now resides in the fine glory of the poet's brush.[7] The talented among courtiers and the people alike employ figurative expressions that are startling and outstanding. Some are strong in their knowledge of antiquity. Others surpass their associates in the civil service examinations. Some contain within them the magical and marvelous. Others capture the spirit of ancient works.

In my humble opinion, the moral influence of Your Majesty is profound in its simplicity, and culture flourishes under your guidance. Yet that which is transmitted to the ears does not come close to that which is seen with the eyes, and discourses on antiquity do not surpass present examples. Thus, an imperial order was given to Lord Yoshimine no Yasuyo, Middle Counselor of Senior Third Rank, Captain of the Right Inner Palace Guards, and Gentleman-in-Waiting to the Crown Prince, bidding him and your other ministers search out and collect fine writings. The words herein are both fine and coarse, and one ought to distinguish those with real ability from those who pretend to it. Their form is not of one sort, and truly perfect writings are mixed with others. If there is no radiance from precious jewels, no luster to the rounded gems herein, then they may at least assume the fine detail of a single dragon scale or unicorn hair.

The former sovereign Saga has already passed on his imperial seal to our wise sovereign Junna, who accepts its bright glory, exalting his virtue. Together, Your Majesties have encourage the increased illumination of accumulated learning, and view extensive erudition as an essential aid to the Way of governing the realm. Your Majesties both strive in your wisdom, and Heaven has endowed both of you with great talents. The elegant writings and soaring compositions of your writings rise high like twin beams of light from two dragons; the inspiration that lodges in your works and your control of style is like the paired illumination from two suns. Their firm and sturdy diction stands out for the exceptional way in which it embodies physical things with its descriptive detail, and their clear and outstanding force is even loftier in expressing human feelings.

When Your Majesties' precious compositions with the brush are being executed, there is no contest between the eight styles of calligraphy. Upon opening the jade-green writing box, there is no ranking of the six sorts of characters. Our latter-day Yao has displayed his concern over the proper ordering of government in ceding the throne. Our latter-day Shun displays deep wisdom and intellectual curiosity.[8] Both sage kings possess the same method of governance. Though our previous sovereign has departed from this world, his writings still remain, and the two splendid suns of this reign wax all the more in their glory. No record of a time such as this can be found in any of the histories.

Yet though Your Majesty's minister would not dare venture to evaluate royal works of writing, your command has descended from on high, bidding me to compare and judge them. One cannot measure their brilliance by the standard of the sun or moon. Nevertheless, my meager knowledge must serve at this time. There is no mistaking the seasons when we have recourse to the shifting balance between *yin* and *yang*. In the end, we have made dragon and snake share the same cave, and caused turtle and fish to cohabit in the calm depths. Some shine with the polish of Mount Jing's jade, others are muted with the latent quality of Master He's stone.[9]

The anthology extends from the fourth year of Keiun through to the fourth year of Tenchō. The authors number one hundred and seventy-eight; there are seventeen *fu* rhapsodies, nine hundred and seventeen *shi* poems, fifty-one prefaces, and thirty-eight examination essays in two scrolls. The total consists of twenty scrolls. It has been titled "Collection for Governing the Country." We earnestly pray that it will last as long as the sun and moon shine, and that it will possess the ineffable depths of spirits and gods. Those poems already included in the *Bunka shūreishū* belong to a treasured book that is not to be tampered with. However, poems that have been left out of that anthology have been used in this one. Authors are divided by rank, and their writings are grouped by topic. However, some are older than others, some still live and others are dead. We have not been comprehensive in our approach, and we expect shortcomings to surface later.

With humility, Counselor and Assistant to the Board of Rites Lord Minabuchi no Hirosada, Junior Fourth Rank Upper Grade; Head of the Academy, Doctor of Letters, and Vice-governor of Harima province Lord Sugawara no Kiyoyoshi, Junior Fourth Rank Upper Grade; Tutor to the Crown Prince Lord Yasuno no Fumitsugu, Junior Fourth Rank Lower Grade;[10] and Assistant in the Central Affairs Ministry Lord Abe no Yoshihito, Senior Fifth Rank Lower Grade have all made clear their judgments in this collection, and have nothing to conceal. Your Majesty's ministers are not satisfied with our learning, nor do we feel our knowledge to be as infinite as the sands. We have felt pressed to our limits by the demands of this task. Though I sought to retire from this project, I was not permitted to do so, and have served as adviser. Respectfully submitted on Tenchō 4/5/14. (*GR*, 8: 490–491)

Appendix D

Chōka for Ninmyō's Fortieth Birthday Celebration

The 26th day [of the Third Month in Kajō 2]: Eminent priests from the Kōfukuji temple and others offered up a blessing in celebration of His Majesty's fortieth birthday. Forty sacred images were crafted and forty scrolls of the "Scripture of Incantations for Adamantine Longevity" were copied out.[1] Following this, passages selected from forty-eight thousand scrolls of sacred scripture were chanted. Afterward, images were made of heavenly beings who neither picked up mustard seeds nor brushed their celestial robes against stones.[2] They fluttered aloft, bearing offerings of medicine for His Majesty and inquiring humbly after his health. The images presented[3] included such scenes as that of Urashimako ascending into the Milky Way, where he gained long life.[4] Another scene depicted the Maid from Yoshino passing through the Heavens.[5] A long poem was also presented to His Majesty.[6] The words of this verse were as follows:

Source of the sun,	*hi no moto no*
this realm of Yamato,	*yamato no kuni o*
by Sukunabiko,[7]	*kamiroki no*
a mighty god,	*Sukunabiko ga*
was planted with thriving	*ashi suga o*
reeds and sedge,	*uehaeshitsutsu*
and made into	*kuni katame*
a firm realm.	*tsukurikemu yori*
Since then, spring has come,	*okitsu nami*
rising with each year,	*okitsu toshi no ha ni*
as waves from the offing.	*haru wa aredo*

Yet this year in particular
each and every thing
grows lush and flourishes.
Pleased are the gods
of Heaven and Earth,
and lovely are the sights and sounds
of sea and mountain.
Plum and willow,
now more than ever before,
spread and flourish,
blooming in fulsome smiles.
Bush warblers too
renew their trilling calls.
Thus in manifold variety
wondrous things abound.
Long ago, a sagely prince
from the palace of the sun,
gleaming in Heaven's realm
with ruddy rays of light,
did tread across
the steps of Heaven's stairs
in the far-off firmament,
and descended here
to our many great isles,
to found the heavenly sun-lineage.[8]
Upon that high throne,
blessed with a myriad ages,
now sits one in his fortieth year
on this spring day!
The sage lord
of our realm
in exalted glory
reigns supreme!
Godly sovereign
of the sun's palace,
he reigns supreme
over all beneath Heaven.

kotoshi no haru wa
monogoto ni
shigemisakaete
ame tsuchi no
kami mo yorokobi
umi yama mo
iro koe kawashi
ume yanagi
tsune yori koto ni
shikisakae
emai hirakite
uguisu mo
koe aratemete
yachigusa ni
kusushiki koto wa
akanesashi
amateru kuni no
hi no miya no
hijiri no miko zo
hisakata no
ama no hashidate
fumi ayumi
amorimashishi
ōyashima
amatsu hitsugi no
takamikura
yorozuyo iwau
yosotose no
haru ni arikeri
waga kuni no
hijiri no kimi wa
tōtoku mo
ōmashimasu ka
hi no miya no
hijiri no miko no
ame no shita ni
ōmashimashite

In reign after reign,	*miyo miyo ni*
succeeding one another,	*aiuketsugite*
each of our lords	*kimigoto ni*
is transformed	*yo no hito kami to*
from mortal into god,	*naritamai*
and reigns supreme.	*ōmashimaseba*
How can the lords whose realms	*yomo no kuni*
adjoin ours in every direction	*tonari no kimi wa*
ever equal him,	*momotsugi ni*
though hundredfold be	*tsugu to iu tomo*
their dynastic lineages?	*ikade ka hitoshiku aramu*
For this reason it is	*soko yue ni*
that gods follow his will,	*kami mo shitagai*
and even buddhas	*hotoke sae*
pay him reverence.	*uyamaitamau*
More so than ever before,	*masu masu ni*
is this true of our present lord.	*ima waga kimi wa*
Surely none such ruled supreme	*mukashi ni mo*
even in the distant past,	*ōmashimasaji*
and of the future,	*yukusue mo*
what are we to say?	*ikani mōsamu*
Sakyamuni's Law[9]	*shaka no nori*
he spreads far and wide.	*Hirometamaite*
For household leavers,	*suke no hito*
the fellowship of the Buddha's Law,	*nori no yakara o*
he shows forgiveness,	*tsumi aredo*
though they be filled with sin;	*yurushitamaitsu*
and shows them lenience,	*toga aredo*
though they have committed crimes.	*Nazametamaitsu*
Without peer	*tatoe naki*
is the blessing of his grace,	*ōmimegumi no*
broad in its bounds,	*geni hiroku*
as he reigns supreme.	*ōmashimaseba*
And so, household leavers,	*suke no hito*
the fellowship of the Buddha's Law,	*nori no yakara wa*
are cherished always	*ōmiyo o*
in this sovereign's reign.	*tsune ni oshimu to*

Thus we pray	*toshi tsuki o*
in earnest entreaty	*sekaetodomete*
that his reign may be blessed	*sugusazute*
with years and months	*iwamu to koso*
whose course is barred	*koinegai*
from passing onward.	*inorimōse*
Yet though this be so,	*shikaredomo*
it is the way of the world	*yo no kotowari to*
for joy to fill us	*yorokobi no*
on a spring such as this!	*haru ni arikeri*
We think to make offerings	*ikani shite*
so that, in some way,	*kimi no miyo*
our lord's reign	*yorozu yo ni*
will be adorned in layer upon layer	*kasanekazarite*
of age upon age,	*sakaeshime*
and thus made to thrive.	*tatematsuramu to*
In branches of mulberry	*kuwa no e no*
we sought signs;	*yoshi motomureba*
and the Buddha himself	*hotoke koso*
fulfilled our prayers,	*negai nashitabe*
displaying the marks	*hijiri no mi*
of his holy body.	*shirushi wa imase*
For this reason,	*kono yue ni*
to bless our lord,	*kimi wo iwau ni darani*
incantations	*shirushimasu*
filled with magic power	*darani no minori*
in forty scrolls	*yoso maki wo*
have we copied and arrayed.	*utsushitotonoe*
Images of holy ones	*mamori nasu*
providing protection	*hijiri no mikata*
into forty figures	*yoso hashira*
have we made and offered up.	*tsukurimatsurite*
Forty priestly teachers	*yoso no shi no*
opened to enlightenment	*satori hirakete*
perform sacred rites,	*okonau*
rectifying people,	*hito o totonoete*
and attaining perfect truth.	*makoto o itashi*

Forty and eight	*yoyorozu ni*
thousand are the scrolls,	*yachi maki soete*
which with earnest entreaties	*koinegai*
we recite in offering.	*omitatematsuri*
Adorned with prayers	*kazarinoriare*
are the blessings we intone.	*iwaimōseri*
How shall we	*okonaeru*
humbly speak of	*kore no shiwaza o*
these actions	*ikani shite*
we have carried out?	*nobekikoemu to*
All through the day's light,	*akane sasu*
gleaming ruddy,	*hinemosugara ni*
and into the depths of night,	*nubatama no*
pitch black,	*sayo tōsu made*
time passes onward	*toki hi hete*
with our feelings,	*omoitsukuru ni*
as an onrushing flow	*tagi tsu se no*
that cannot be dammed.	*sekae mo kanete*
And so we adorn ourselves	*yo no naka no*
with all the deeds	*isu ga shiwaza wo*
of this world,	*soekazari*
and make offerings of words.	*mōshi zo ageru*
Among these deeds	*sono naka ni*
are those of the one who,	*Ōmi no*
parting the white-topped waves,	*shiranami sakite*
made a home for himself	*Tokoyo shima*
on Tokoyo the Eternal Isle,	*kuni nashitatete*
where he came to dwell.	*itarisumi*
Those who see and hear of this	*kikimiru hito wa*
have lives extended	*yorozuyo no*
for a myriad ages to come.	*inochi o nobetsu*
In ancient words	*furugoto ni*
has it come down to us,	*iitsugikitaru*
that in Ōmi's	*Ōmi no*
calm depths did fish	*fuchi ni tsuri seshi*
a humble subject of our lord,	*kimi no tami*
one Urashimako,	*Urashimako ga*

who hooked	*ama tsu me no*
a heavenly maiden,	*tsurarekitarite*
trailing clouds	*murasaki no*
of purple hue.	*kumo tanabikite*
For a brief time	*kata toki ni*
she stayed, then flew off.	*ite tobiyukite*
This here is	*kore zo kono*
that Eternal Isle of Tokoyo,	*Tokoyo no kuni to*
told of in tales.	*kataraite*
After seven days had passed,	*nanuka heshi kara*
he had gained a life	*kagiri naku*
boundless in length	*inochi arishi wa*
on account of his being	*kono shima ni koso*
on this island, it is said.	*arikerashi*
In sacred Yoshino	*Miyoshino ni*
was one Umashine,	*arishi Umashine*
whom a heavenly maiden	*ama tsu me no*
came to visit,	*kitarikayōite*
after which time,	*sono nochi wa*
pressed by her fate,	*semekagafurite*
she donned shawl and robe	*hire koromo*
and flew away, it is said.	*kite tobiniki to iu*
This image before you	*kore mo mata*
is the same person	*kore no shimane no*
who is said to have lived	*hito ni koso*
in that time!	*ariki to iu nare*
Resplendent with clouds,	*itsukusa no*
bedecked in the five treasures,	*takara no kumo wa*
is the Compassionate One,	*daihisa no*
whose thousandfold hands	*chigusa no mite no*
bring a myriad ages	*hito no yo o*
to the lives of mortals.	*yorozuyo noburu*
This image have we	*hitogusa o*
adorned with special care.	*koto ni kazarite*
With a myriad ages	*yorozuyo ni*
has Kannon blessed our lord.	*kimi o iwaeri*
As for the verdant pine	*isonoe no*

on the rocky shore,	*midori no matsu wa*
of the hundredfold sorts	*momokusa no*
of vines twined round it,	*kazura ni koto ni*
it is wisteria blossoms	*fuji no hana*
that bloom and thrive.	*hirakisakaete*
With a myriad ages	*yorozu yo ni*
have they blessed our lord.	*kimi o iwaeri*
Bush warblers	*uguisu wa*
flitting through branches	*e ni asobite*
soar and swoop	*tobimaite*
as they sing melodically.	*saezuri utai*
For a myriad ages	*yorozu yo ni*
have they blessed our lord.	*kimi o iwaeri*
In the salt marsh, cranes	*sawa no tsuru*
that lengthen life	*inochi wo nagami*
appear on beaches,	*hama ni dete*
dancing joyfully	*yorokobi maite*
by the tide that flows	*mitsu shio no*
without ceasing.	*tayuru toki naku*
For a myriad ages	*yorozu yo ni*
have they blessed our lord.	*kimi wo iwaeri*
Filled with the powers	*kusu nori no*
of medicinal lore,	*chikara o hiromi*
enwrapped in the protection	*daihisa no*
of the Compassionate One,	*mamori o atsumi*
for a myriad ages	*yorozuyo ni*
will his reign last.	*ōmiyo naseba*
And so the heavenly being	*yaso sato nasu*
who gathers poppy seeds in a fortress	*ki ni keshi hirou*
eighty miles around	*amabito wa*
raises her hands	*te udakite*
and leaves them ungathered.	*hirowazu narinu*
And the one who brushes	*yamomo sato nasu*
the edges of her shawl and robe	*iwagane wo*
lightly on the top	*hire koromo*
of a firm-rooted boulder	*suso taretobashi*
eight hundred miles around	*harau hito*

leaves it untouched.
Thus do we come before
our sovereign lord,
bearing offerings
of medicines
made with herbal lore.
Our blessings
of this sort
are all
simple and unpolished,
and are all
of little consequence.
Yet they are offerings
made with deep respect
by buddhas and holy men
of the slopes
of Kasuga, where lodged
our traveling company.
The words with which
we have addressed
both gods
and buddhas,
praying for a myriad ages
in our lord's reign,
are drawn from
the original words
of this realm.
We have not borrowed the
words of the Tang
nor employed scholars
to write them down.
In this realm
has it been said of old:
that the realm of Yamato,
source of the sun,
is a realm where flourish
the spirits of words.

harawazu narite
ōkimi no
kusu nori no
kusu o
sasagemochi
kitarisamorau
kaku no goto
iwaeru koto wa
kotogoto ni
ojinakeredomo
monogoto ni
kazu ni aranedo
tabibito ni
yado Kasuga naru
yamagiwa no
hotoke hijiri no
tatematsuri
tamō nari
ōmiyo o
yorozu yo inori
hotoke ni mo
kami ni mo
mōshi ageru
koto no kotoba wa
kono kuni no
moto tsu kotoba ni
oiyorite
Kara no
kotoba o karazu
kakishirusu
hakase yatowazu
kono kuni no
iitsutōraku
hi no moto no
Yamato no kuni wa
kotodama no
sakiwau kuni to zo

In the words of antiquity	*furugoto ni*
they flow down to us.	*nagarekitareru*
In the words of the gods	*kamigoto ni*
they are conveyed to us.	*tsutaekitareru*
Under the sway of these words	*tsutaekoshi*
conveyed thus to us,	*koto no mani mani*
we revisit the affairs	*moto tsu yo no*
of the world at its origins.	*koto tazunureba*
And so each word of song	*utagoto ni*
is sung over and over again.	*utaikaeshite*
We have come to use them	*kamigoto ni*
in matters concerning the gods.	*mochiikitareri*
We have come to use them	*kimigoto ni*
in matters concerning our lord.	*mochii kitareri*
Thus drawing for our guidance	*moto no yo ni*
on the world at its origins,	*yorishitagaite*
we humbly address these words	*hotoke ni mo*
both to gods	*kami ni mo mōshi*
and to buddhas.	*agenobete*
May our earnest prayers	*inorishi makoto wa*
be heard with kind intentions	*nemukoro to*
in this sovereign's reign.	*kikoshimeshitemu*
Our words are simple	*midorigo no*
like those of a young child.	*osanaki koto ni*
They have no clear beginning or end,	*oribashi no*
like wood folded into a chopstick.	*moto sue shirazu*
They are in disarray,	*midare ito no*
like tangled threads.	*midarete aredo*
Yet still, below the palace,	*kokonoe no*
girded in walls ninefold,	*migaki no shita ni*
we line up in procession,	*tokoyo kari*
like geese from the Eternal Isle,	*hikiitsuranete*
and bend our knees,	*saoshika no*
like stags kneeling,	*hiji orikaeshi*
to offer up these words	*samorai*
in service to our lord.	*kikoe so mōsu*
How shall they be heard?	*ikani kikoemu*

Like the tide's flow,	*shio nagashi*
is our trembling trepidation.	*oji kashikomaru*
What shall be heard?	*nani ni kikoemu*

Now as for the form of Yamato verse, it puts implicit and explicit metaphor first, from which it then proceeds to move people's feelings. This is what it is most accomplished at. As the state of affairs in the world falls into decline, this Way has also fallen from usage, reaching a state where now it can be found only among a few priests who have some knowledge of the old words. One could say in this case that when rites are lost at court they should be sought out in rustic surroundings. Therefore this verse has been selected for inclusion in the historical record. The eminent priests and others were lodged in the house of the Minister of the Right [Yoshifusa]. Junior Captain for the Right Palace Guard Lord Tachibana no Sanenao was dispatched with a royal proclamation to recompense the priests for their efforts.[10] Over thirty menservants were given out along with bolts of cloth, each in accordance with the recipient's rank. (*KST*, 3: 3: 223–225)

Appendix E

Kana Record of the Teiji Villa Poetry Match

The Head of the Left Team was the Sixth Princess.[1] The princes on her side were her elder brothers the Fourth and Fifth Princes. Other members of the team included Middle Counselor Lord Fujiwara no Sadakata and Captain of the Left Palace Guards Lord Arizane. Their poets included Fujiwara no Okikaze and Oshikōchi no Mitsune.[2] Muneyuki and Yoshikaze were also on their side.[3] The Head of the Right Team was the Seventh Princess.[4] The princes on her side were her elder brothers the Eighth Prince of Kōzuke and Seiwa Prince Sadakazu. Team members included Middle Counselor Lord Minamoto no Noboru and Captain of the Right Palace Guards Lord Kiyotsura. Their poets included Korenori and Tsurayuki. Prince Kanemi and Lord Kiyomichi were also on their side.

His Majesty Uda wore robes dyed the shade of cypress bark, with trousers of yellow chrysanthemum, a shade favored by his forebear Ninmyō. The men and women of the Left wore red in layers of cherry; those of the Right wore green in layers of willow. The youth in charge of keeping score for the Left wore red with breeches of dark scarlet twill. The one for the Right wore green with breeches of golden green twill. The princes and lords in attendance all wore green and red.

The Left were the first to present their poems and topics on a scroll to His Majesty, doing so at ten o'clock in the morning when the magnificently attired lords of their team also presented their *suhama* display. Four courtiers of Fifth Rank bore it on their shoulders. The *saibara* song "Ise Sea" was played to the Golden Bells melody.[5] The *suhama* display for the Right was presented at noon. It was carried by four strapping youths whose hair was bound up in loops and whose feet were shod in woven sandals. The *saibara* song "Bamboo River" was played very softly to the Sō melody by the princes of that team as they approached His Majesty.[6] The Left's poems were attached to a branch of cherry and brought to His Majesty by the Nakatsukasa Prince. The Right's were attached to a willow branch and presented by the Kōzuke Prince.[7]

The verses were placed all together in a small rosewood box. The lords then seated themselves to His Majesty's left and right at the front of the mansion just above the steps leading up to it. Four lady-chamberlains were also in attendance to the left and right of His Majesty.[8] It was women who served as the reciters.[9] Just as they were about to recite the poems, His Majesty's blinds were rolled up a foot and he spoke, saying, "Who will judge these poems? Is Tadafusa here?" When His Majesty was told that he was not, he looked most regretful. Although the Right won, two of the poems by His Majesty won as well, so that in the end the Right lost by one round. Nonetheless, both teams danced to music afterward in deference to one another.

As for the poems, those on mist were attached to mountains; those on bush warblers, to blossoms; and those on cuckoo birds, to hare-flower shrubs. The remaining ones were placed in the brazier of a miniature cormorant-fishing boat displayed in one of the *suhama*. The Right presented two large basins of silver filled with aloe wood incense to the princes of the Left. Court robes were presented to the women and men of both teams. The topics were from the Second, Third, and Fourth Months. (*SNKBZ*, 11: 491–493)

Appendix F

Kana Record of the Kyōgoku Consort Poetry Match

On the seventh day of the Third Month in the year Engi 21, the Kyōgoku Consort residing at the Teiji Villa went on a pilgrimage to her clan shrine at Kasuga in the company of her royal sovereign.[1] At that time, a man named Fujiwara no Tadafusa was governor of Yamato province.[2] The reception he provided was as one might expect, but he also had baskets crafted in a lovely manner and filled with fruit for their Majesties. No less than twenty such baskets were placed in the royal carriage, each of which was also accompanied by a poem written out on a slip of paper. In the rush to return there was no time to compose suitable responses. And so, when the royal party had come back to their villa, the retinue was divided into teams of Left and Right and commanded to compose poems that His Majesty then matched against one another.[3] The Left was led by a royal consort from the Minamoto clan.[4] The Right was led by the Kyōgoku Consort's elder sister. Each woman led her own attendants.

The Left wore Tang robes of red with layers of indigo. The Right wore Tang robes of green with layers of leafy autumn yellow. Poems were written out in the reed hand in curving lines on skirts of gray that grew darker at the edges. All the princes and noblemen affiliated with the teams at the event were also decked out in shades of red and green: red for the Left and green for the Right. Girl pages, three from each team, handed poems to the reciter. Those of the Left wore red gauze with indigo overcoats and damask breeches. The page in charge of keeping score for them wore robes of russet red with layers of indigo, inner robes of green damask, and breeches of finely patterned cloth.

The pages for the Right wore upper robes of green, inner robes of cherry and scarlet, and breeches of finely patterned cloth. Their scorekeeper wore outer robes of green, inner robes of kerria yellow damask, and breeches of gray damask adorned with miniature paintings. The sight of children on the threshold of adulthood in such outfits made for a splendid spectacle, as did the arrangements of different damasks in sundry colors.

The Left was the first team to bring forth their *suhama*. Four men of Fifth Rank preceded it and four guardsmen carried it on their shoulders. Music was played as it was brought before His Majesty. Its poems were placed in a silver basket, which an older woman brought out and placed on the *suhama* display. The *suhama* of the Right was carried on the shoulders of four women. Although it possessed merit, it fell short of the interest generated by the *suhama* of the Left. Poems for the Right had been written out on silver lotus leaves. Although many people had composed poems, His Majesty summoned Tadafusa to judge them. Because the girl pages were not able to recite the poems proficiently, they were read aloud by Middle Captain Korehira for the Left, and Minor Counselor Ki no Yoshimitsu for the Right.[5] Afterward stipends were distributed to each member of both teams. (*NKBT* 74:67–68)

Appendix G

Preface to Poems for the Royal Procession to the Ōi River

The morning after the Double Ninth banquet, Tonsured Sovereign Uda went on a procession to the Ōi River to view the expanses of the Tonase Rapids there.[1] Our reigning sovereign Daigo also made a procession there. A royal command had been issued, summoning skilled fishermen to present poems on thoughts in autumn. Sixty-three poems harmonizing with these words were composed by royal command, along with this preface. Submitted by Junior Palace Table Officer Ki no Tsurayuki, Senior Sixth Rank Upper Grade.

Behold, His Majesty revived lingering chrysanthemums at the annual banquet of the Double Ninth yesterday![2] Loathe to see them pass with autumn, he set forth on the royal barge from springtime's Plum Ford that lies on this side of the moon's cassia, the Katsura River. He summoned ferrymen and proceeded with his entourage north to the shores of the Ōi River, whose waters rush beneath the flanks of Mount Ogura that lie dim beneath the twilight moon.[3] At that time, there was not a single cloud trailing across the far-off skies, nor was there any sediment to be seen in the depths of the onward-rushing waters that awaited his arrival. All was as His Majesty wished.

Now we have received a royal decree, bidding us to see leaves floating on autumn waters as brocade on autumn mountains bereft of weaver folk; to hear the rustle of autumn leaves scattering on Storm Mountain as the sound of rain falling from a cloudless day; to be startled by the resemblance of lingering chrysanthemum blossoms on the shore to stars in the sky; to wonder if frost-white cranes standing in the river are clouds descending from the heavens; to let fall tears at hearing the cries of monkeys from the gorge; to see traveling geese lost on the cloud path as letter-bearing messengers; to see gulls grown accustomed to men frolicking on the waters where they live; and to wonder at how many ages an old pine on the banks of a creek has lasted.[4]

Such were the words we were commanded to compose verses for. Our timid hearts wavered this way and that as our clumsy word-leaves scattered into the sky, borne along on gusts of wind. All the while, tears of joy mingled with the dew that lay on blades of grass as we returned to the task again and again with each wave that lapped against the rocks. If these word-leaves reach beyond the branch-tips of this age, then who among those who hear of this day henceforth will not repeat them over and over again as fishnets are hauled in hand over hand, or fail to cherish them as grasses of longing? (*mana* and *kana* texts as cited in Ceadel, "The Ōi River Poems and Preface," 79 and 81)

Appendix H

Mana Preface to the *Kokinshū*

Waka is rooted in the heart's ground, bursting forth as blossoms within a grove of words.[1] In the world of people, there are none who do not act without intending something. Thoughts and feelings change swiftly, sorrow and joy turn into one another. Feelings are born from our desires, and songs take shape in words. And so the voices of those at ease are joyful, while the wailing of those who are frustrated are sorrowful. Through *waka* one can relate things that lie heavy on the breast and give vent to one's dissatisfaction.[2] For moving Heaven and Earth, stirring gods and ghosts, transforming human conduct, and bringing harmony to husband and wife, nothing surpasses *waka*. *Waka* are of six sorts. The first are the airs that express the people's concerns, the second is plain narration, the third is explicit metaphor, the fourth is implicit metaphor, the fifth is banquet songs praising the ruler, and the sixth is sacred hymns conveying praise to gods and ancestors.[3]

Though warblers trilling among springtime flowers and cicadas crying out from autumn treetops lack the complex flourishes of melody, each puts forth song.[4] All the creatures of this world do so as a matter of course. But in the first seven generations of the age of gods, times were simple and people direct. Feelings and desires were not distinguished from one another, and *waka* were not yet crafted.[5] Not until Susanoo no Mikoto reached the land of Izumo was the first song in thirty-one syllables made. Nowadays his poem would be considered an envoy verse.[6] Afterward, whether it be the grandson of the Heavenly Deity or the daughter of the Sea God, there was not a single divine being that did not use *waka* to convey his or her feelings.[7]

In our current age of mortals this custom flourished.[8] There arose the categories of long verse, short verse, head-twirling verse, and confused verse.[9] Styles streamed forth in luxuriant growth, like a tree brushing the clouds which sprang from a wisp of a tiny seedling, or like ocean waves floating up to Heaven that swelled from a single drop of dew. And so, whether it is the verse of Naniwazu Bay produced at the court of Nintoku, or the verse of the Tomi-no-ogawa River responding to Prince Shōtoku, poetry is either concerned with divine and marvelous matters or it is profound and beyond the ken of ordinary mortals.[10] Yet, in viewing the songs of high antiquity, one sees that many possess words of archaic simplicity. They were not yet intended to entertain the ear and eye, but rather were used only to teach and admonish. When the Sons of Heaven in ancient times presided over beautiful locations at the height of the season, they would command their ministers seated in attendance to present verses that harmonized with their words. In this way, the feelings of sovereign and subject were revealed, and the natures of wise men and fools distinguished. By this means, the Son of Heaven followed the desires of the people and selected men of talent.

History tells us that *shi* and *fu* were first crafted at Prince Ōtsu's court.[11] Wordsmiths and gentlemen of talent yearned after this style and followed established forms. Shifting to the letters of the distant Han, the customs of our sunrise realm were transformed. Once the practices of the people had been altered, *waka* fell into decline. Nonetheless, there still remained great masters such as Lord Hitomaro, who lifted up exalted thoughts touched by divine inspiration. He towers astride past and present. There was another man named Yamabe no Akahito. Together they are the immortals of *waka*. Many others took *waka* as their calling throughout the ages. But eventually the times turned to decadence, and people came to esteem greed and lust. Wisps of words floated up in clouds, and seductive streams bubbled forth from springs. Substantial fruits all fell to ground, leaving only decorative flowers to thrive. In the houses of the amorous it was used by love's envoys, and among mendicants it was used to ensure a livelihood. And so it became a means for courting women, making it difficult to present before great lords.

In the recent past those who know the ancient ways are no more than six in number.[12] Their strengths and weaknesses are not alike, making it important to discuss what distinguishes one from another. The Bishop of Kazan is a master of poetic form but the flowery appearance of his words bear few substantial fruits, like a painting of a lovely lady that stirs one's feelings to no purpose.[13] The verse of the Ariwara Middle Captain possesses too much sentiment and too few words, like withered blossoms whose luster has faded while their scent lingers. Bunrin is skilled at observing things in his poems but their form approaches vulgarity, like a merchant decked out in gorgeous robes.[14] As for Kisen, the priest of Mount Uji, the flower of his words are lovely but their beginning and end are out of joint, as though one were encountering dawn clouds while still gazing on the autumn moon. The poems of Ono no Komachi are in the tradition of Princess Sotōri of old.[15] They are alluring but lack vigor, like the rouged features of an ailing palace lady. The poems of Ōtomo no Kuronushi follow after those of Lord Sarumaru of old.[16] Though they have an air of ease about them, his style is extremely rustic, like a field hand taking his rest beneath blossoms.

The clan names and court titles of countless others have flowed down to us from past ages, but the majority of these take alluring beauty as their standard and remain ignorant of poetry's fundamental principles. Vulgar people compete with one another for glory and profit and do not compose *waka*. What a shame this is! Though nobility enjoy the titles of minister and general and the wealthy amass gold and coin, their names leave the world behind even before the flesh has sloughed off their bones lying in the dirt. Only those who compose *waka* remain known to later generations. This is because their words are familiar in people's ears and their spirits converse with the gods.

In the past, Emperor Heizei commanded his ministers to compile the *Man'yōshū*. *Waka* were then abandoned over the course of the ensuing ten reigns and one hundred years.[17] Though the urbane elegance of Consultant Ono no Takamura and the light ease of Middle Counselor Ariwara no Yukihira can be found in this period, such men made a name for themselves through talents other than this Way.[18] Now in this, the ninth year of His Majesty's reign, our sovereign's benevolence flows out beyond the shores of our isles of Akitsushima, and his favors lie thick as the sheltering shade of Mount Tsukuba. Voices of discontent at the sudden turn of calm depths into agitated rapids have ceased, and songs of praise now fill our ears, wishing him a life as long as it would take grains of sand to rise into tall crags.

His Majesty thinks of reviving customs that have fallen from use, and desires to restore ways that had been discarded in earlier reigns.[19] A royal command was issued to men such as the Grand Scribe Ki no Tomonori, Palace Librarian Ki no Tsurayuki, the Former Assistant to the Governor of Kai Province Ōshikochi no Mitsune, and Sub-Lieutenant of the Right Palace Guard Mibu no Tadamine, bidding each to offer up his household anthologies and old songs from ages past. This was called the "Collection of Myriad Leaves Continued." Then another command was given, and the poems were divided by categories into twenty scrolls. The new anthology was given the name "Collection of Poems Ancient and Modern."

Though the words we have offered up lack the allure of springtime blossoms, our names have usurped the longevity of autumn nights. How galling it is on the one hand to fear the mockery of one's peers, and on the other to be ashamed of one's lack of talent and skill! Yet how great is our joy to have lived at a time when *waka* is reborn and its Way flourishes once again! Indeed, though Hitomaro has passed away, his *waka* remain![20] On the Eighteenth Day of the Fourth Month of the Fifth Year of the Engi Era, Tsurayuki and the others humbly present this preface.[21] (*SNKBZ*, 11: 422–429)

Appendix I

Kana Preface to the *Kokinshū*

Yamato verse takes the subject's devoted heart as its seed and becomes a myriad word-leaves.[1] Since the people in this world are overgrown with events and deeds, they affix the thoughts in their hearts to things they see and hear and bring forth words. When we hear warblers crying in blossoms or the voices of frogs dwelling in the water, who among those living does not compose *uta*? Without effort, it moves Heaven and Earth, causes gods and ghosts invisible to the eye to feel pity, creates harmony between men and women, and soothes the hearts of fierce warriors.

Verse is said to have first appeared when Heaven and Earth separated from one another. But according to what has been transmitted by the people of our age, it began in the far-off heavens with the goddess Shitateru Hime, and arose on the ore-scattered earth with the god Susanoo no Mikoto.[2] It must have been difficult to discern the feelings behind words in such artless expression. When the age of mortals ensued, Susanoo no Mikoto is said to have been the first to compose a poem with thirty-one letters.[3] And so it was that words expressing sentiments grew and multiplied, describing such things as being bewitched by blossoms, feeling resentment toward birds, being moved by mist, or saddened by dew. Their development could be likened to the months and years spent in a journey across distant lands, or to a speck in the mire at the base of a tall mountain that rises up to reach the trailing clouds of Heaven.[4] The Naniwazu poem inaugurates a sovereign's reign at court.[5] The words of the Asakayama song are by a waiting woman from the countryside.[6] These two poems are as the father and mother of verse. In fact, they are the first ones done by people learning to write *kana* letters.

There are six forms of verse. No doubt these can be found in Tang poetry as well. The first of these is allegorical verse. The following poem addresses Emperor Nintoku allegorically:

In Naniwazu
bloom these tree blossoms!
From winter's shroud,
now burst in spring,
bloom these tree blossoms!

Naniwazu ni
saku ya ko no hana
fuyugomori
ima wa harube to
saku ya ko no hana[7]

The second is enumerative verse. One could say the following is an example:

On blooming flowers
*fixate***d over** *is this self,*
rob*bed of its senses,*
by a **raven***ous fever,*
pierced unawares.

saku hana ni
omoi tsu(*ku*/**gu**)**mi no**
aji*ki nasa*
*mi ni i***tazuki** *no*
iru mo shirade

The third is likeness verse. One could say the following is an example:

My lord, if on this morning,
while frost still lingers,
lying there, rising, *you are to leave,*
with each pang of longing,
this fading would go on!

kimi ni kesa
ashita no shimo no
okite *inaba*
koishiki goto ni
kie ya wataramu

The fourth is comparison verse. One could say the following is an example:

My longings
are beyond counting,
though the storm-lashed
shore's fine-grained sands
be fully counted.

waga koi wa
yomu tomo tsukiji
ariso umi no
hama no masago wa
yomitsukusu tomo

The fifth is plain verse. One could say the following is an example:

If falsehood / *itsuwari no*
was not the way of the world, / *naki yo nariseba*
how great would be / *ika bakari*
the happiness brought / *hito no koto no ha*
by the leaves of people's words! / *ureshikaramashi*[8]

The sixth is incantatory verse. One could say the following is an example:

This lord's lordly hall / ***kono tono wa***
is bounteous indeed! / ***mube mo tomikeri***
With lucky three-stemmed grass, / ***saki kusa no***
thatched in three and four layers, / ***mitsuba yotsuba ni***
has my lord's lordly hall been built! / ***tonozukuri seri***[9]

Since present-day society is drawn to allurements and people's hearts have turned into fickle flowers, nothing but insubstantial verse in fleeting words appears. Poetry is something unknown to most people. It is a buried log in the houses of the amorous, rather than something that could be presented proud as pampas plumes in serious places. But when we consider its beginnings, we realize it wasn't always so. On mornings filled with springtime blossoms and nights when autumn's moon hung in the sky, the sovereigns of antiquity would summon those in attendance on them and bid them present poems about the scene at hand. Some wandered astray in thinking to use blossoms to express their feelings, while others would stumble in fathomless gloom as they thought of the moon in their hearts.[10] On viewing their poems, the sovereign would have known who was talented and who was foolish, and ruled accordingly.

Nor was this all.[11] People would pray that their sovereign's reign last as long as it would take for a pebble to grow into a crag, or they would entreat their lord's favor by referring to the sheltering shade of Mount Tsukuba.[12] They would sing when joy could not be contained at favors bestowed upon them, and when hearts were filled to bursting with pleasant anticipation of the banquet following rites worshiping a deity.[13] Their unrequited longings smoldered with Fuji's smoke and they pined for friends on hearing pine crickets crying in autumn.[14] They would imagine the long-lived pine trees of Takasago and Suminoe twined together,[15] and in recalling the peak of manhood or regretting the maiden-flower's fleeting moment, they would express their feelings and take solace in verse.[16] They would also do so when they saw blossoms scatter on a spring morning or leaves fall in the autumn dusk.[17] Some bewailed snowy hair and waves of wrinkles that grew more visible in the mirror with each passing year; others were startled into realizing the brevity of this mortal coil on seeing dew on the grass or foam on the water.[18] Some, having lost the prosperity they had reveled in only the day before, would suffer the fate of seeing those who were once close now grown distant.[19] Some would set waves against the uppermost tip of Pine Mountain to plight their troth, while others would draw the waters of Nonaka to revive a long-dead affair.[20] Some would gaze sorrowfully on the lower leaves of autumn bush clover as they slept alone, while others would count the beats of a snipe's wings under the dawn moon as they waited for a lover.[21] Some would speak of mottled bamboo to indicate the sorrowful junctures encountered as we make our way in the world, while others would draw on the fickle rapids of the Yoshino River to complain about the manner in which love affairs come to an end.[22] Only verse can now assuage the hearts of those who hear that Nagara Bridge was made long ago and that wisps of smoke have ceased to rise from Mount Fuji.[23]

In observing what has been transmitted from antiquity, it is clear that this Way first spread in the time of the Nara Sovereign. His Majesty must have ruled wisely, secure in his knowledge of the feelings of his subject that they expressed in verse. In that era, one Kakinomoto no Hitomaro of Senior Third Rank was the immortal of poetry. His name tells of a time when sovereign and subject were as one. It is said that at autumn dusk, His Majesty's eyes saw russet foliage floating down the Tatsuta River as royal brocade, and on spring mornings Hitomaro's heart was unable to think of the cherry blossoms on Mount Yoshino as anything else but clouds. There was also another person by the name of Yamabe no Akahito. His poems are startlingly impressive and finely detailed. Indeed, it is difficult to place either poet above the other. Many others excelled at verse, people whose names have been heard through the ages, countless as the knots of mottled bamboo, never-ending as a skein of thread. Poetry from these times and earlier ones have been collected in an anthology called the *Man'yōshū*.

In more recent times there are only one or two people who come to mind as having had some knowledge of the old phrases and sentiments appropriate to verse. Even among these, each is lacking in certain respects. From that time until now, a hundred years have passed and ten reigns have come about. During this period, those who composed with a full understanding of ancient words have been few in number. Of course, I am not speaking of people of high rank, whose exalted positions prohibit saying anything here that might tarnish their reputations. As far as other people are concerned, there are six poets from the recent past who are worthy of mention. Bishop Henjō is proficient in poetic form but is lacking in sincerity, his style is like a painting of a woman that moves the viewer's heart in vain. The poems of Ariwara no Narihira have too much sentiment and too few words, like a withered blossom whose fragrance lingers after its colors have faded. The poems of Fun'ya no Yasuhide use words with an artisan's skill but possess a form incommensurate with his person, as if a merchant were decked out in court finery. Those of Kisen, the priest of Mount Uji, are faint and have no discernible beginning or end, giving the impression of encountering clouds at dawn while still viewing the autumn moon at night. One doesn't come across many poems by him, and he is not well known. Ono no Komachi belongs to the tradition of Princess Sotōri of antiquity. Her poems are moving in their form but lacking in strength. This must be because they belong to a woman. As for the poems of Ōtomo no Kuronushi, their form is common, like a mountain woodsman shouldering brushwood who has paused to rest in the shade of blossoms. There are many others whose names can still be heard, spreading outward as tendrils of vines across the moors, and lying thick as the leafy boughs of a grove. But though they are great in number, the only thing that appears to concern these people is coming up with a poem. They have no true knowledge of form.

Now we are in the ninth turn of the seasons under our current sovereign's reign. His benevolent mercy reaches out in waves that travel far beyond the shores of our many isles, and the broad reach of his favor lies thick as the sheltering shade at the base of Mount Tsukuba. In the intervals between the rites of government, intending not to cast aside any matter, His Majesty desires to revive antiquity in the hope that people will not forget ancient affairs. Thinking to survey the present and transmit its knowledge to later eras, he has commanded Grand Scribe Ki no Tomonori, Palace Librarian Ki no Tsurayuki, Former Assistant to the Governor of Kai Province Ōshikochi no Mitsune, and Sub-Lieutenant of the Right Palace Guard Mibu no Tadamine to present old poems that were not included in the *Man'yōshū* along with ones of their own. The anthology's poems were selected from among these submissions, beginning with springtime garlands of plum branches, followed by the summertime cries of the *hototogisu* bird, continuing with the breaking off of scarlet foliage in autumn, and ending in a vision of winter snow. There are also poems in which people attach cranes and tortoise to thoughts of their lord and pray for the long life of his subjects. There are poems that gaze on autumn bush clover and long for others in summer grasses. There are poems about journeying to Meeting Slope and making offerings for safe passage to the god of Mount Tamuke. Numerous other poems have been selected in addition to these. There are a thousand verses in all, in twenty scrolls called "Collection of Poems Ancient and Modern."

Poems have piled up like fine sands on the beach, flowing in an endless stream like a river at the foot of a mountain. We have no regrets about the fickleness of Asuka River's rapids, but instead feel joy at seeing how a small pebble has turned into a mighty crag. Although the words that pillow our expressions are as insubstantial as the scent of springtime blossoms, our trifling names have dared to claim the longevity of autumn nights. Some of these poems might grate upon people's ears; others might bring shame with the sentiments they express. I, Tsurayuki, along with my fellow editors, all abase ourselves, restless as wavering clouds, lying prostrate like stags crying out for their mates. We are overjoyed at having been born in an age when we could encounter a time such as this. Though Hitomaro has passed away, the words of his poems remain! Although the seasons change one after another, things pass from our world, and sorrow follows joy, the words of the poems in this anthology will remain unchanged. They will last as long as threads of pale green willow bending to the ground and not scatter away as pine needles from the tree branch. They will stretch through the ages as vines across the moors, remaining forever in the bird tracks from which writing came. Surely all people who wish to gain an understanding of the forms of verse and the sentiments embedded in their words will, as when we gaze upon the moon in the vast sky, look up to the past and long for a present time such as ours. (*SNKBZ*, 11: 17–30)

Appendix J

Diagrams of Palace and Residence

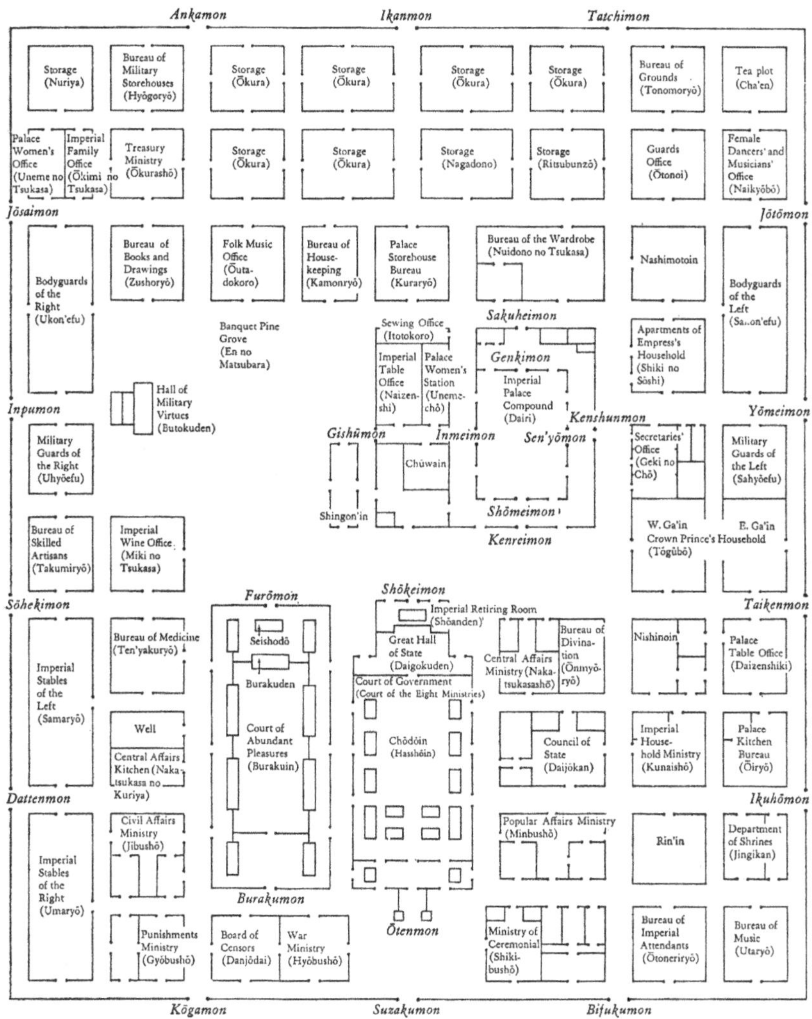

Figure 1. The Greater Imperial Palace. Names in italics are of gates.

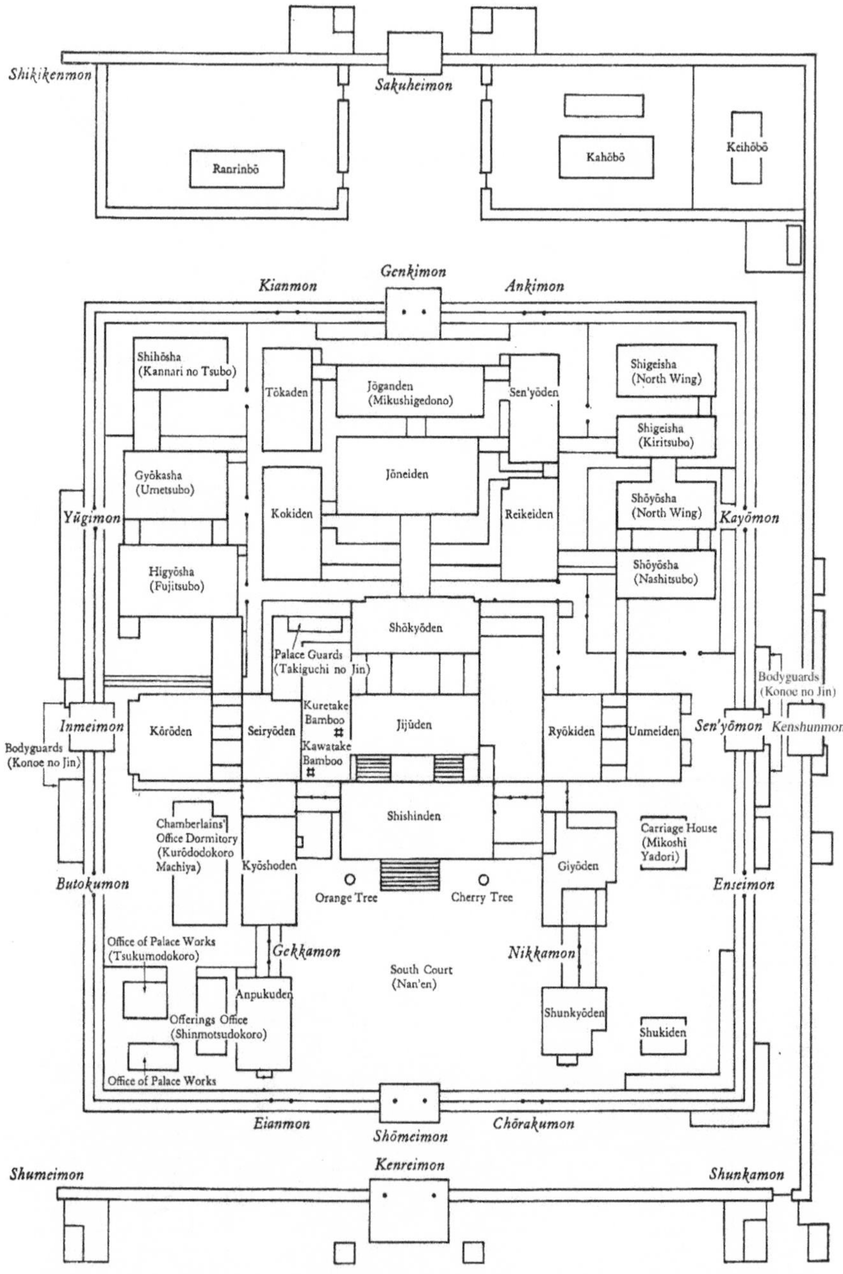

Figure 2. The Emperor's Residential Compound (Dairi). Names in italics are of gates.

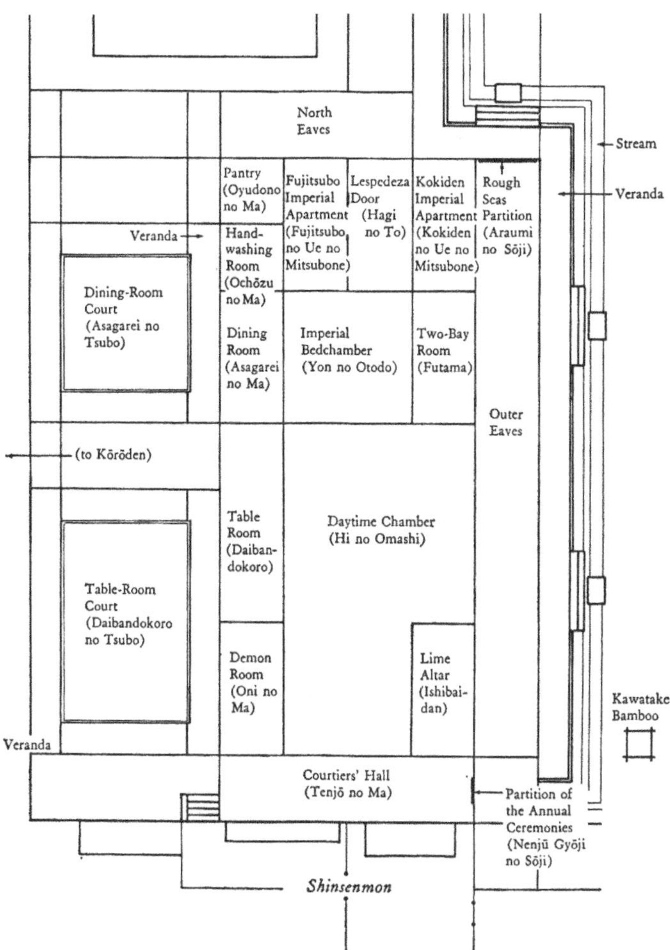

Figure 3. The Emperor's Residence (Seiryōden).

NOTES

A Note to the Reader / pages ix–xi

1. Hiroaki Sato, "Lineation of Tanka in English Translation," 349–350.

2. Earl Miner, "*Waka*: Features of Its Constitution and Development," 679.

3. The terms "head line" (*zuko*) and "end line" (*machiko*) also appear in the *Man'yōshū* anthology.

4. Mark Morris, "*Waka* and Form, *Waka* and History," 571.

5. Fujii Sadakazu, "Kōzō, yu, kokoro to kotoba," 50.

6. For the standard account of this linguistic structure, see Tokieda Motoki, *Kokugogaku genron*, 311–320.

Introduction / pages 1–29

1. The *Kokin wakashū* is more commonly known by the abbreviated title *Kokinshū*, which will be used subsequently throughout this book.

2. Pierre Bourdieu, *The Field of Cultural Production*, 161–175.

3. One account of poetic practice that I have found helpful is provided by Kamitani Kaoru, whose voluminous study *Kana bungaku no bunshōshiteki kenkyū* offers a detailed overview of the way terms such as reading, composing, and writing were articulated in the Heian period. Fujii Sadakazu's *Monogatari bungaku seiritsushi* provides a more phenomenological approach to poetic practice, one that emphasizes its corporeal dimensions in early Japanese texts. I have also found Shin'ya Tomiichi's work in this area particularly helpful, as discussed in Chapter 2.

4. One notable exception is Kurahayashi Shōji's magisterial study *Kyōen no kenkyū*, a work upon which I have drawn extensively in order to reconstruct the performative contexts of banquet rituals. Another scholar to whom I frequently refer, Imai Yutaka, has emphasized the ties between early Heian poetry and a host of rituals in his book *Kokin-fū no kigen to honshitsu* through a detailed and often innovative use of a variety of historical materials. The fact that his work has been largely ignored in mainstream scholarship suggests a general lack of interest in this sort of approach.

5. One illustrative example of this view is provided by Masuda Shigeo, who argues that the chief purpose of the imperial anthology is to replace individual expression with communal harmony through a strategy of abstraction and generalization that is achieved by limiting the range of imagery associated with particular words ("*Kokinshū* no chokusensei," 39–44). In a similar vein, Shimada Ryōji sees the degree of conceptualization and abstraction effected by the codification of seasonal imagery in the anthology as the primary indication of its "public" character ("*Kokinshū* no kōteki seikaku ni tsuite," 12).

6. Kubota Utsubo, *Kokin wakashū hyōshaku*, 1: 28–33.

7. Nomura Seiichi, "*Kokinshū* uta no shisō," 62–63.

8. One exception to this tendency is the literary historian Akiyama Ken, who has urged a reconsideration of the conventional view that the development of poetry in the *rokkasen* period owed more to politically marginalized figures than to those in power. See his article "Rokkasen jidai to wa nani ka," 31.

9. For more on this mode of reading *Tales of Ise*, see Michele Marra, *The Aesthetics of Discontent*, 35–53.

10. For an overview of this branch of scholarship, see Tomiko Yoda, *Gender and National Literature*, 116–120.

11. Hashimoto Fumio devotes more attention to these rituals than the other two scholars mentioned above, although his approach to this topic remains somewhat cursory. Generally, I have found Yamaguchi's work to be the most helpful overall on account of the sheer volume of detail he provides.

12. Similarities between anonymous verses in both anthologies were first noted by the early modern scholar Keichū (1640–1701) in his voluminous commentary *Man'yō daishōki* (ca. 1688–1690).

13. Ozawa Masao, *Kokinshū no sekai*, 91–104 and 130–151.

14. Ueno Osamu, "Heianchō wakashi ni okeru ke to hare," 79–82. A similar view that focuses on the use of prefatory phrases in love poems can be found in Shimada Ryōji, *Kokinshū to sono shūhen*, 29–52.

15. Such studies are too numerous to mention in detail. Some examples that have exerted significant influence on later scholars would include Katagiri Yōichi's account of the formation of poetic toponyms in his article, "Utamakura no seiritsu"; and Suzuki Hideo's ambitious attempt to chart out the changing relations between landscape and affect in his landmark essay "Kodai waka ni okeru shinbutsu taiō kōzō." One variant on Suzuki's work which related it to *Kokinshū* poetry in particular can be seen in Masuda Shigeo's article "*Kokinshū* no hyōgen."

16. For a concise overview of this branch of scholarship, see Inomata Tokiwa, "Jusei," 41–42. The term *jusei* (incantatory) was first developed by Furuhashi Nobuyoshi in his study *Kodai waka no hassei*. Other scholars writing in this area include Mori Asao and Satō Kazuyoshi.

17. See, for example, Masuda Shigeo, "*Kokinshū* to kizoku bunka," 1: 3.

18. Chino Kaori, "Gender in Japanese Art," 24.

19. For an overview of these approaches, see Tanaka Kazuo, "*Kokin wakashū* to chūgoku bungaku," *IKKW*, 483.

20. Perhaps the most painstaking work in this area has been done by Kojima Noriyuki, whose research into the connections between *shi* poetry and the *Kokinshū* culminated in a book titled *Kokinshū izen: shi to uta no kōryū*. Other examples of this approach include Katagiri Yōichi, "Kanshi no sekai, waka no sekai"; and Watanabe Hideo, *Heianchō bungaku to kanbun sekai*. One germinal account of continental influences on rhetorical techniques used in *uta* has been provided by Konishi Jin'ichi, who emphasizes the role played by the "indirection" used in Six Dynasties poetry on *Kokinshū* poetry. See, for example, his article "The Genesis of the *Kokinshū* Style." There is continuing controversy over whether Six Dynasties court poetry was more influential than the works of the late Tang poet Bo Juyi (772–846) in the early Heian period.

21. One exception is Mark Morris, who briefly notes that *waka* in the *Man'yōshū* refers to poems that were composed in response to others ("*Waka* and Form, *Waka* and History," 598). He implies, however, that by the Heian period, *wa* had come to signify "Japan." For a treatment of *wa* in the *Man'yōshū* which sees this practice as one in which the "harmonizer" asserts their subordinate status vis-à-vis the addressee, see Haga Tsunao, "*Man'yōshū* ni okeru 'hō' to 'wa' no mondai," 37 and 49.

22. A similarly idiosyncratic approach was taken toward Tang dynasty poetic canons, one which, as Wiebke Denecke has argued, was designed to create a distinctive vision of "Japan as China" ("Chinese Antiquity and Court Spectacle in Early *Kanshi*," 101).

23. I use the term "Confucian" as a convenient (if somewhat simplistic and anachronistic) shorthand for this body of thought in order to stress the political and ritual elements of rulership articulated within it, although the equally provisional term "Daoist" could be used if one were to emphasize its cosmological aspects. For a definition of Confucianism and its ritual concerns that treats these as expressions of a secular philosophy of government, see Charles Holcombe, "*Ritsuryō* Confucianism," 550–552.

24. *Liji*, 47; *SKT*, 29: 941–945.

25. My use of the term "cosmology" here is intended to reflect premodern East Asian notions of the world that did not posit an absolute division between the human subject and an external "Nature," as in the modern European tradition. For more on this distinction, see Nathan Sivin, "State, Cosmos, and Body in the Last Three Centuries B.C.," 5. More recently, Angela Zito has described the relation between human subject and cosmos articulated in Han and Tang thought as a "dispersal of being," through the circulation of *qi* energy in a series of boundary surfaces and shifting centers of focus (*Of Body & Brush*, 97–103 and 211).

26. *Analects*, 1: 12; *SKT*, 1: 30–31.

27. *Kenpō jūshichi jō*; Ienaga Saburō et al., eds., *Shōtoku Taishi shū*, *Nihon shisō taikei*, 2: 13–15.

28. Informative accounts of the development of topic-based composition in the early Heian period include Fujihira Haruo, "Dai'ei seiritsu zenshi," and Yoshikawa Eiji, " 'Dai shirazu' to iu go ni tsuite."

29. Gary Ebersole, *Ritual Poetry and the Politics of Death in Early Japan*, 23.

30. The tenth century has often been seen as a key turning point away from the structures of the *ritsuryō* state, a view articulated most famously by the historian Ishimoda Shō in his essay "Kodai no tenkanki toshite no jūseiki."

31. Catherine Bell, *Ritual Theory, Ritual Practice*, 98.

32. Maurice Bloch, *Ritual, History and Power*, 14.

33. Yamanaka Yutaka's work in this area remains a classic source for reconstructing Heian rituals, the most detailed study being his *Heianchō no nenjū gyōji*. Other studies of their historical development which I have found particularly useful include Obinata Katsumi, *Kodai kokka to nenjū gyōji*; and Okada Shōji, *Heian jidai no kokka to saishi*.

34. John L. Austin, *How to Do Things with Words*.

35. Jacques Derrida, "Signature, Event, Context," in *Limited Inc*, 13–19.

36. Kondō Miyuki, "*Kokinshū* no 'kotoba' no kata," 2–10.

37. Tani Barlow, "Theorizing Woman," 259.

38. For a concise overview of correlative cosmology and the ways in which it connected different categories through their resonance with one another, see John S. Major, *Heaven and Earth in Early Han Thought*, 28–32.

39. Michel Foucault, "What Is an Author?" 147.

40. Roger Chartier, *The Order of Books*, 27–59.

41. In this regard, the Heian context appears to have been somewhat different from the classical Chinese poetic tradition, in which authorship was a remarkably stable attribute of texts and one whose history as a cultural concept dated back at least to the Han Dynasty (206 B.C.E.–220 C.E.). See Stephen Owen, *The Making of Early Chinese Classical Poetry*, 214–216.

42. I have treated this phenomenon in relation to one text from the period in my article "Writing Like a Man," 25–28.

43. Takeuchi Michiko, *Heian jidai wabun no kenkyū*, 399.

44. The primary examples in this regard are Thomas LaMarre, *Uncovering Heian Japan*; and Ryūichi Abe, *The Weaving of Mantra*.

45. Tokieda Motoki, *Kokugogaku genron*, 527–539.

46. Amagasaki Akira, "Waka no retorikku," 140.

47. For earlier translations of these two prefaces, the reader is referred to Laurel Rasplica Rodd and Mary Katherine Henkenius, *Kokinshū*, 35–47 and 379–385; and Helen Craig McCullough, *Kokin Wakashū*, 3–8 and 256–259.

Chapter One / Heian Histories of Poetic Harmony

1. See Watanabe Mio, "Saga Tennō kōki-den (jō)," 22.

2. Ronald Toby, "Why Leave Nara?" 342–343.

3. Kojima Noriyuki, *Kokufū ankoku jidai no bungaku*, 2: 3, 1112.

4. There are 128 *uta* in the *Nihon shoki* (*Chronicle of Japan*, 720); seven in the *Shoku nihongi* (*Chronicle of Japan Continued*, 798); thirteen in the *Nihon kōki* (*Later Chronicle of Japan*, 840); four in the *Shoku nihon kōki* (*Later Chronicle of Japan Continued*, 869);

none in the *Montoku jitsuroku* (*Veritable Records of Emperor Montoku*, 879); and one in the *Sandai jitsuroku* (*Veritable Records of Three Reigns*, 901).

5. The preface to poem 20: 4493 in the *Man'yōshū* anthology (*SNKBZ*, 9: 450–451), for example, relates how Emperor Shōmu commanded princes and nobility to compose both *uta* and *shi* at a banquet held in the Inner Palace in Tenpyō hōji 2/1/3 (758).

6. Mezaki, "Nihon bunkashi ni okeru waka," 27.

7. Hashimoto Fumio emphasizes this aspect of the banquet in his analysis. See *Ōchō wakashi no kenkyū*, 3–13.

8. *Ruijū kokushi*, 75 (*Saijibu* 6); *KST*, 5: 388.

9. *Kokinshū*, Kana Preface; *SNKBZ*, 11: 24.

10. Kondō Nobuyoshi, "*Shoku nihongi* ikō no kayō," 42.

11. *Laozi*, 42; *SKT*, 7: 79.

12. *Ruijū kokushi*, 32 (*Teiōbu* 12); *KST*, 5: 194–195.

13. Amino Yoshihiko has extensively documented this association between the emperor and non-agrarian economies from Heian times through the medieval period. A summary of his argument is provided in *"Nihon" to wa nani ka*, 131.

14. Ebersole, *Ritual Poetry and the Politics of Death in Early Japan*, 111.

15. For a detailed account of the structure and stages of imperial hunting expeditions, see Enokimura Hiroyuki, "No no miyuki no seiritsu," 116–120.

16. For a detailed account of *kunimi* rites in early *Man'yōshū* poetry, see Ebersole, *Ritual Poetry and the Politics of Death in Early Japan*, 23–29.

17. Mezaki Tokue, *Heian bunka shiron*, 22–29.

18. *Ruijū kokushi*, 31 (*Teiōbu* 11); *KST*, 5: 171.

19. Ōmuro Mikio, *Gekijō toshi*, 57–61.

20. *Ruijū kokushi*, 31 (*Teiōbu* 11); *KST*, 5: 172.

21. *Analects*, 12: 19; *SKT*, 1: 274.

22. Abe Takeshi, ed., *Nihon kodai kanshoku jiten*, 207–209.

23. Takinami Sadako, *Heian kento*, 118–122.

24. A version of the original park in the form of a small garden with a pond can be found just south of the Nijō Castle in modern Kyoto.

25. Kammu engaged in processions to the Shinsen-en with increasing frequency after the palace had been established. In the final five years of his reign he led twenty-eight processions there. His son Saga made it the capital's premier site for displaying royal virtue, with a grand total of forty-three visits.

26. Andrew Pekarik, "Poetics and the Place of Japanese Poetry in Court Society through the Early Heian Period," 98–99.

27. Gotō Akio, "Montoku-chō izen to igo," 57.

28. *Hōjōki*; *SNKBZ*, 44: 19.

29. *Nihon kōki*, Kōnin 3/5/21; *KST*, 3: 1: 114.

30. See, for example, the entry for Jōwa 14/10/26 in the *Shoku nihon kōki*, where it is asserted that literary writings are a manifestation of the state (*KST*, 3: 2: 201).

31. Ronald Miao, "Literary Criticism at the End of the Eastern Han," 1013–1014.

32. Kojima Noriyuki, *Kokufū ankoku jidai no bungaku*, 753–770.

33. Helen McCullough, *Brocade by Night*, 197.

34. Christopher Connery, *The Empire of the Text*, 157–169.

35. Suzuki Hideo, *Kodai waka shiron*, 307–326.

36. Owen, "The Formation of the Tang Estate Poem," 44.

37. Hatooka Akira, *Jōdai kanshibun to chūgoku bungaku*, 253–288.

38. See Appendix A. This connection between authorial ascription and politics can be compared with the tale of Taira no Tadanori (1144–1184), whose one verse in the imperial anthology *Senzai wakashū* (*Collection of a Thousand Years*, 1187) is rendered anonymous after his clan's defeat (poem 66; *SNKBT*, 10: 30).

39. Satō Shin'ichi, "*Keikokushū* no hyōgen ni tsuite," 46.

40. For translations of the prefaces to the first three imperial anthologies, see Appendixes A–C.

41. Christopher Connery has argued that literary Chinese was inherently intertextual, insofar as the meanings of individual written words were always embedded in earlier textual contexts (*The Empire of the Text*, 36).

42. For an overview of Saga's contributions to court ritual, see Yamanaka, *Heianchō no nenjū gyōji*, 43–52.

43. It has been estimated that the number of courtiers below Fifth Rank nearly doubled in size between the end of the Nara period and Saga's reign. See Furuse Natsuko, "Kyakushiki, gishiki no hensan," 357–362.

44. The following description of the procedures for *sechien* banquets draws on the painstaking reconstruction provided by Kurahayashi Shōji in *Kyōen no kenkyū*, 558–583.

45. Ono Yasuo, "Heianchō no kōenshi ni okeru jukkai ni tsuite," 22.

46. Ozawa, *Kokinshū no sekai*, 45–47.

47. *Tōka* in particular had a long and complex history of gendered associations. In the court histories they are often treated as a continental-style performance involving both genders in the manner of *utagaki*. By the tenth century, however, separate male and female traditions were established as annual court rites. See Mine Yōko, "Kodai nihon ni okeru tōka no igi to sono tenkai," 24.

48. Stipends appear to have been handed out to all participants regardless of their success at composing *shi* poems.

49. Royal proclamations, for example, were passed to the sovereign through his ministers and then back to them. For a detailed description of the procedures through which these texts were created, see Tsuda Hiroyuki, "Ōken no kotoba," 74–77.

50. Ozawa, *Kodai kagaku no keisei*, 29–30. Ozawa's study of the Kana Preface is among the most thorough in its comparisons of this text with classical continental poetics and other early Japanese treatises such as the *Kakyō hyōshiki*, *Kisen shiki*, and *Shinsen zuinō waka*.

51. *Bunka shūreishū*, preface; *NKBT*, 69: 194.

52. *Engi shiki*, preface; *KST*, 26: 3: 3.

53. Ozawa, *Kokinshū no sekai*, 284–298. Ozawa notes that this practice differed

slightly from that of Six Dynasties *shi*, in which individual lines of a poem were distributed among the poets present.

54. See Gotō Akio, "Montoku chō izen to igo," 56.

55. Owen, "*Traditional Chinese Poetry and Poetics*," 94.

56. François Cheng, "Some Reflections on Chinese Poetic Language and Its Relation to Chinese Cosmology," 33 and 42–44.

57. *Ruijū kokushi*, 31 (*Teiōbu* 11); *KST*, 5: 172.

58. Kurahayashi, *Kyōen no kenkyū*, 434.

59. Yamaguchi Hiroshi, *Ōchō kadan no kenkyū: Kammu Ninmyō Kōkō-chō hen*, 325.

60. Usuda Jingorō, "Rokkasen jidai no bungei bunka," 107.

61. Kasuga features prominently throughout the Heian period as a symbolic center for the Fujiwara clan. Its location on the outskirts of Nara, situated in a liminal space between the city proper and the countryside, marked the Fujiwara clan's role as gatekeepers between the sovereign and his subjects. For more on its history, see Furuhashi Nobuyoshi, *Kodai toshi no bungei seikatsu*, 190–200.

62. There are scattered precedents for this equivalence. The literary Chinese preface to *Man'yōshū* poem 17: 3967, for example, uses the phrase *yamato shi* (倭詩) to describe native poetry (*SNKBZ*, 9: 180). Despite these earlier suggestions of a similarity between *shi* and *uta* as written forms of poetry, however, it would only be from the mid ninth century that *yamato uta* attained the same place in rituals of inscription that *shi* had long occupied.

63. The poem consists of 211 lines, making it significantly larger than the 149 lines that constitute the longest *chōka* in the *Man'yōshū*.

64. *Shoku nihon kōki*, Kajō 2/3/26; *KST*, 3: 2: 223. For a complete translation of this *chōka*, see Appendix D.

65. Konishi Jin'ichi, *The Early Middle Ages*, 2: 112–114.

66. Abe, *The Weaving of Mantra*, 368–390.

67. *Shoku nihon kōki*, Kajō 2/3/26; *KST*, 3: 2: 224.

68. Ibid., 225. Here and elsewhere in the six histories I have rendered the character compound 倭歌 as *yamato uta* rather than *waka* with the assumption that it is possible for these characters to be glossed in this manner, and that a semantic distinction obtained between the graphs 倭 as a mythically founded polity and 和 as a form of poetic practice.

69. *Kokinshū*, poem 52; *SNKBZ*, 11: 48.

70. As Helen McCullough notes in her exhaustive study of the *Kokinshū*, there are forty-one poems in the Spring section describing cherry blossoms, as opposed to only twenty-three on plum blossoms (*Brocade by Night*, 353–354). She further notes that the motif of cherry blossoms was relatively rare in early poetry matches, something that in itself indirectly attests to their strong association with the Fujiwara clan by virtue of the fact that such matches were chiefly sponsored by members of the royal family, as argued in Chapter 2.

71. Imai, *Kokin-fū no kigen to honshitsu*, 211.

72. *Montoku jitsuroku*, Ninju 1/3/10; *KST*, 3: 3: 27.

73. Mezaki, *Kizoku shakai to koten bunka*, 23–40.

74. Seiwa's ties to his grandfather's mansion were close throughout his life, and he appears to have resided there with his mother after his abdication, suggesting that he was dependent on his maternal relatives for material support during that period.

75. *Montoku jitsuroku*, Ninju 3/2/30; *KST*, 3: 3: 49.

76. For the passages in question, see *Sandai jitsuroku*, Jōgan 6/3/21 (*KST*, 4: 132) and Jōgan 8/3*/1 (*KST*, 4: 179–180).

77. For an account of these conventions in Chinese court banquet poetry, see Stephen Owen, *The Poetry of the Early Tang*, 264–266.

78. *Gosen wakashū*, poem 56; *SNKBT*, 6: 20.

79. Ōzuka Hideko, "Saga Tennō to 'hana no en no sechi,'" 29–32.

80. *Kokinshū*, poem 8; *SNKBZ*, 11: 33.

81. See Abe, ed., *Kodai kanshoku jiten*, 83–84.

82. *Kokinshū*, poem 53; *SNKBZ*, 11: 48.

83. *Ise monogatari*, episode 82; *SNKBZ*, 12: 183–186.

84. Robert Borgen, *Sugawara no Michizane and the Early Heian Court*, 154.

85. *Sandai jitsuroku*, Gangyō 6/8/29; *KST*, 4: 525.

86. *Shaku nihongi*; *KST*, 8: 2: 4.

87. Text as cited in Yamaguchi, *Ōchō kadan no kenkyū: Kammu Ninmyō Kōkō-chō hen*, 621. In keeping with Yamaguchi's citation, I have rendered the phonetic glosses for the Chinese characters in *katakana*.

88. Tokumori Makoto, "'Nihongi kyōen waka' ni okeru Nigihayai," 24–25.

89. One noteworthy exception is Hashimoto Fumio, who mentions this phenomenon in *Ōchō wakashi no kenkyū*, 14–25.

Chapter Two / Household Harmony in Uda's Poetry Matches

1. According to Hagitani Boku, the acknowledged authority on early Heian poetry matches, the earliest such collection, known as the Jūkan-bon ("Ten-Scroll Text"), was compiled after 1058. See *Nihon koten bungaku daijiten* 1: 283.

2. Ueno, *Goshūishū zengo*, 7.

3. LaMarre, *Uncovering Heian Japan*, 155–160.

4. For a detailed account of the history and significance of the terms *hare* and *ke*, see Kudō Shigenori, "*Gosen wakashū*," 266–275.

5. *Mumyōshō*; *NKBT*, 65: 44.

6. Sivin, "State, Cosmos, and Body in the Last Three Centuries B.C.," 7.

7. For an account of the cosmological and architectural dimensions of the emperor's person, see Zito, *Of Body & Brush*, 133–142.

8. Takinami, *Heian kento*, 67–68.

9. Katō Tomoyasu, "Chōgi no kōzō to sono tokushitsu," 153. On the connections between social identity and physical placement in court ritual, see also Igami Wataru, "Chakuza, chakujin ni tsuite," 29–30.

10. Fukui Toshihiko, "Heianchō ni okeru kanshoku ikai," 23.

11. For the full version, see Hagitani Boku, ed., *Heianchō uta-awase taisei*, 1: 541. This text can also be found under the title *Sanjō Sadaijin den senzai no uta-awase* in *KT*, 5: 1: 60.

12. We know from other sources that Tsurayuki was already writing poems for both teams in his earliest known match, the Kanpyō Empress's Palace Poetry Match (*Kanpyō no ōntoki kisai no miya no uta-awase*, ca. 893).

13. Borgen, *Sugawara no Michizane and the Early Heian Court*, 156.

14. *Sandai jitsuroku*, Gangyō 8/2/28; *KST*, 4: 552.

15. Text as cited in Yamaguchi, *Ōchō kadan no kenkyū: Uda, Daigo, Suzaku-chō hen*, 30.

16. In this regard, it is significant that the *Yijing* text to which Uda appended his commentary was a locus classicus for continental theories of the cosmological origins of writing. See Mark Edward Lewis, *Writing and Authority in Early China*, 241–286.

17. One instance of Uda's continued involvement in such rites after his abdication can be found in *Nihon kiryaku, Uda Tennō*; *KST*, 11: 4.

18. For an outline of the Seiryōden's architectural features and placement vis-à-vis other buildings in the Inner Palace, see Itō Hiroshi, "Dairi," 78–80. For a detailed account of Uda's alterations to the palace, see Tsunoda Bun'ei, *Nihon no kōkyū*, 92–93.

19. Yamanaka Yutaka, "Heianchō ni okeru nenjū gyōji," 55–56.

20. *Uda tennō shinki*, Ninna 4/10/19; *ST*, 1: 7.

21. Okada Shōji, *Heian jidai no kokka to saishi*, 248. The term *tenjōbito* first appears in Uda's diary under the entry for Kanpyō 1/4/24 (*ST*, 1: 10). Interestingly, this reference is in the context of a song and dance performance.

22. Fukui Toshihiko, "Heianchō ni okeru jige," 45.

23. *Makura no sōshi*, section 84; *SNKBZ*, 18: 166–167.

24. Takinami, *Heian kento*, 200–202.

25. For more on the changing status of women officials at the Heian court, see Yoshikawa Shinji, "Ritsuryō kokka to jokan," 118–120.

26. Hashimoto Yoshinori, "Kōkyū no seiritsu," 97.

27. The tendency to refer to women by the title of their father can be seen as part of a growing propensity to view rank and post as masculine markers at the Heian court.

28. *Daigo tennō gyoki*, Engi 5/1/1; *ST*, 1: 33.

29. *Teishin kōki*, Engi 19/1/1; *DNK*, 8: 60.

30. Nishimura Satomi, "Heian jidai no kizoku to mono-awase," 2–7.

31. These poetry matches are hereafter referred to as the Teiji Villa Match and the Kyōgoku Consort Match respectively.

32. Fujiwara no Atsuko's name is also often rendered as Onshi. I have chosen the

former pronunciation here in order to avoid confusion with her younger sister Yasuko, whose name is also pronounced "Onshi" (albeit with different characters).

33. Yamaguchi, *Ōchō kadan no kenkyū: Uda, Daigo, Suzaku-chō hen*, 65.

34. Despite the tantalizing suggestion of a distinction here between *omoi* and *koi* as two different forms of desire, their respective significances remain unclear.

35. One scholar has gone so far as to suggest that its chief aim was to integrate its poems in a single organized body, rather than represent competition between isolated pairs. See Tokuhara Shigemi, "Uta-awase no seiritsu to tenkai," 160.

36. Izumi Kazuko, "*Kokin wakashū* to *Shinsen man'yōshū*," *IKKW*, 543.

37. Yamaguchi, *Ōchō kadan no kenkyū: Uda, Daigo, Suzaku-chō hen*, 65–75.

38. For a concise account of the sorts of accretion that the text underwent, see Kyūsojin Hitaku, "*Shinsen man'yōshū* to *Kanpyō no ontoki kisai no miya no uta-awase*," 41.

39. Murase Toshio, *Kokinshū no kiban to sono shūhen*, 46.

40. For more on Hanshi's political influence at court see Fukutō Sanae and Takeshi Watanabe, "From Female Sovereign to Mother of the Nation," 26–27.

41. Borgen, *Sugawara no Michizane and the Early Heian Court*, 271.

42. Mezaki, *Kizoku shakai to koten bunka*, 74–83.

43. This tendency to link poems into sequences can be seen in the first extant poetry match. See Toku'ue Toshiyuki, "Zai minbukyō ke uta-awase ni tsuite," 29.

44. Yamazaki Kenji, "*Shinsen man'yōshū* ominaeshi no bu no keisei," 15.

45. Edward Kamens, "Dragon-Girl, Maiden-flower, Buddha," 419–420.

46. See Ōno Yukiko, "Heianchō waka ni okeru ominaeshi," 26.

47. *Kokinshū*, poem 439; *SNKBZ*, 11: 186. My use of bold font to highlight the acrostic effects of this verse, along with a translation that attempts to preserve them in English, is inspired by Thomas LaMarre's experiments in this area.

48. Mezaki, *Kizoku shakai to koten bunka*, 54–88. Mezaki describes Uda's political career in full both before and after the enthronement of his son, providing a detailed historical context for the period in which the *Kokinshū* was being compiled.

49. Tanaka Shin'ichi, *Heianchō bungaku ni miru nigenteki shikikan*, 126–145.

50. Obinata, *Kodai kokka to nenjū gyōji*, 235–248. The creation of such homogenous temporal settings in which events unfold and are shared in time across geographically disparate regions is arguably similar in effect, if not in scope or technical means, to the "imagined communities" that have been identified in the creation of modern nationalisms with the advent of the print capitalism and mass media in nineteenth-century Europe. See Benedict Anderson, *Imagined Communities*, 22–36.

51. Furuhashi Nobuyoshi, "*Man'yōshū* kara *Kokin wakashū* e," 27.

52. One characteristic of Heian verse is its dramatic expansion of this poetic topography related to the exurban periphery. The word "mountain retreat" (*yamazato*), for example, first appears in *Kokinshū* poetry, where it is used to denote the dwellings of capital residents situated on the edges of urban space. See Imanishi Yūichirō, "Yamazato," 114–115.

53. Go Tetsuo, "Sono no keifu," 67.

54. See Thomas Keirstead, "Gardens and Estates," 297.

55. Takei Jirō and Marc P. Keane, *Sakuteiki*, 17.

56. Mori Asao, "*Kokinshū* shiki uta no ichi," 1–3.

57. Imai, *Kokin-fū no kigen to honshitsu*, 303–346.

58. Yamagishi Tokuhei, *Waka bungaku kenkyū*, 91–95.

59. In addition to names such as Asuka, Yodo, and Minase, many rivers that appear in anonymous *Kokinshū* love poems bear suggestive designations such as Natori (Gossip), Otowa (Wings of Sound), and Mitarashi (Ritual Rinsing).

60. *Shoku nihongi*, Keiun 3/3/14; *SNKBT*, 12: 102–103.

61. Mori Asao, *Kodai waka to shukusai*, 48–58.

62. The list of things that could be compared in *mono-awase* was extensive, including maiden-flowers, sweet-flag roots, garden plants, plum blossoms, autumn leaves, insects, fireflies, small birds, incense, baskets, fans, and paper.

63. For a similar observation, see also Hashimoto Masayo, "'Fuyu' no tokushoku to kōzō," *IKKW*, 97–104.

64. Yoshikawa Eiji, "*Kokin wakashū* to *Kudai waka*," *IKKW*, 558.

65. Shinozaki Yukie, "Dai'ei," *IKKW*, 661.

66. *Kyōgoku no miyasundokoro uta-awase*, *NKBT*, 74: 70.

67. Yamada Kenzō, "Nara Heian jidai no jisho," 72.

68. LaMarre, *Uncovering Heian Japan*, 71–73.

69. Izumi Kazuko, "Uta-awase no seiritsushi," 138–149.

70. For the full text of this *kana* record, see Hagitani Boku, ed., *Heianchō uta-awase taisei zōho shintei*, 1: 15–16.

71. For an account of the ritual dimensions of *suhama* and their connections with earlier practices, see Motoi Jun, "*Kokinshū* zōka jō no umibe no kagun kō," 17–20.

72. For more on the rhetorical conventions used in shrine songs, see Komaki Satoshi, "Gengo no jusei to yōshiki," 57–63.

73. *Kagura uta* 6; *SNKBZ*, 42: 31.

74. It is only from the twelfth century in texts such as the *Fukurozōshi* that the procedures involved in poetry matches begin to be outlined in a programmatic form. See Hagitani Boku, "Kaisetsu," 13–19.

75. For more on the genres of record keeping in circulation at the Heian court, see my article, "Writing Like a Man," 12–16.

76. Hagitani, "Kaisetsu," 8–18.

77. For an account of the historical and ritual dimensions of *sumō* wrestling at the Heian court, see Obinata, *Kodai kokka to nenjū gyōji*, 91–131.

78. The *Dairi shiki* ritual formulary compiled at Saga's court specifies that team members known as "wrestling officials" (*sumai no tsukasa*) include courtiers of the Third, Fourth, and Fifth Ranks.

79. Kōda Kazuhiko, "Teiji-in uta-awase no katōdo ni tsuite," 35–37.

80. *Teiji-in uta-awase*; *SNKBZ*, 11: 495.

81. Ihara Akira, "Uta-awase ni okeru ichi seikaku," 39.

82. Such associations between colors and court ranks were often made in Heian poems. See, for example, poem 1123 in the *Gosen wakashū* (*SNKBT*, 6: 335).

83. Uda's new title of "tonsured sovereign" might have enabled such an unprecedented claim to parity with a reigning sovereign. Certainly, it suggested an entirely new relation to the latter that was distinct from that of a retired sovereign (*in*).

84. Tokuhara Shigemi, "Uda, Daigo-chō no utameshi o megutte," 25.

85. Tsuchihashi Yutaka, *Kodai kayō to girei no kenkyū*, 356.

86. Fujii, *Monogatari bungaku seiritsushi*, 516–519. For more on the corporeality of *utau*, see Furuhashi Nobuyoshi, "Waka no kōshōsei to kisaisei," 77–80.

87. Kamitani, *Kana bungaku no bunshōshiteki kenkyū*, 23.

88. For a concise summary of scholarly debates over the meaning of *utau* in the Nara period, see Yoshida Shūsaku, *Kotoba no jusei to seisei*, 114–115. Yoshida himself argues that the character 誦 denoted a style of singing which accompanied zither music and could be associated with either *uta* or *shi*.

89. Examples of these uses of the word *yomu* include *Man'yōshū* poems 17: 3982 (*SNKBZ*, 9: 195), and 18: 4101 (*SNKBZ*, 9: 262).

90. Shin'ya Tomiichi, "*Kinkafu* 'yomi uta' kō," 9.

91. Matsu'ura Tomohisa, "Shikei to shite no 'waka,'" 140–145. For a detailed and informative overview of approaches to metrics in Japanese verse, see Kawamoto Kōji, *The Poetics of Japanese Verse*, 173–297.

92. Hyōdō Hiromi, *Ōken to monogatari*, 183.

93. Kondō Nobuyoshi, "Makurakotoba, jokotoba, utamakura," 161.

94. Shin'ya Tomiichi, "'Uta o yomu' koto," 13.

95. As Walter Ong notes, the acts of writing and reading were invested with a residual orality in most manuscript cultures: any text worth reading was read aloud, and the act of writing was as much a dictation to oneself as a silent act of inscription (*Orality & Literacy*, 119).

96. Hyōdō, *Ōken to monogatari*, 175.

97. David Bialock, "Voice, Text, and the Question of Poetic Borrowing in Late Classical Japanese Poetry," 189. With regard to this link between poetry and "pattern" (*aya*), we should keep in mind here that *yomu* itself had strong ties to the recitation of canonical texts.

98. *Fusō ryakki*; *KST*, 12: 1: 168.

99. *Fukurozōshi*; *SNKBT*, 29: 18.

100. One example of a proxy composition being used in such a setting is poem 177 in the *Kokinshū*, which was originally composed by Ki no Tomonori for the use of one of Uda's hall courtiers at a Double Seventh banquet (*SNKBZ*, 11: 91–92).

101. Writing was described with only two terms in the Heian period, neither of which was reducible to the modern concept. *Kaku* could refer to painting, and *shirusu* was used also to indicate the marking of events by month or day. See Kamitani, *Kana bungaku no bunshōshiteki kenkyū*, 98.

102. Ibid., 10.

103. *Yomu* is first used for imperial poems in early Heian *monogatari* such as the *Tales of Yamato* (*Yamato monogatari*), where it is contrasted to the more prosaic *iu*. Given the association between such tales and the rise of the Fujiwara regency, it is interesting to speculate that this might have reflected a desire to "humanize" the emperor, placing him within the circuit of social relations that *uta* enabled, rather than making him the audience to which all poems were directed.

Chapter Three / Compiling Community in the *Kokinshū*

1. Masuda Shigeo, "Chokusenshū to wa nani ka," 41. See also *Fukurozōshi*; *SNKBT*, 29: 34.

2. For a concise account of textual variants, as well as text-critical approaches to them, see Katagiri, "*Kokin wakashū* no honbun," *IKKW*, 7–16.

3. In addition to complete manuscripts of the *Kokinshū*, there are more than three hundred fragmentary versions in the form of sections of old calligraphy (*kohitsu-gire*) and partial texts (*reihon*). Such fragments are often all that remain from the extensive body of manuscripts lost to fire or other causes.

4. For the full text of this account, see *Fukurozōshi*; *SNKBT*, 29: 56.

5. Nishishita Kyōichi, *Kokinshū no denpon no kenkyū*, 17–25.

6. Kyūsojin Hitaku, *Kokin wakashū seiritsu ron*, 2–15. While few scholars today follow Kyūsojin in seeing different texts as different stages in the compilation process, his study continues to be valuable insofar as it categorizes differences not only in the wording of individual poems, but also in the names of the topical categories used, styles for writing prose prefaces, and the manner in which authors' names are recorded.

7. Since then the major supplement has been provided by Nishishita Kyōichi and Takizawa Sadao who bring sixty-nine textual versions together along with old commentaries in *Kokinshū kōhon*. Recent scholarship has tended to emphasize the role played by later copyists in the evolution of textual variants, rather than following Kyūsojin's lead.

8. See for example, Tanaka Kimiharu, "Ausaka no tamuke uta," 55–56.

9. For a detailed overview of scholarly debates concerning the dating of the *Kokinshū*, see Yamaguchi, *Ōchō kadan no kenkyū: Uda, Daigo, Suzaku-chō hen*, 282–344. A more concise and recent summary can be found in Murase Toshio, "*Kokinshū* no seiritsu," 42–46.

10. Scholars who have focused on poetry circles (*kadan*) tend to share this view. See, for example, Okumura Tsuneya, "*Kokinshū* no seiritsu," 272–273.

11. Murase Toshio makes the argument about Tokihira's initial role in his book *Kokinshū no kiban to sono shūhen*, 129–134. For his account of Uda's subsequent role in the anthologizing process, see *Ki no Tsurayuki den kenkyū*, 139–145.

12. Tanaka Kimiharu, "Daigo tennō no *Kokinshū* kaishū," 45–46.

13. Mezaki, *Ki no Tsurayuki*, 21–22. For an account of the ways in which the anthology also hints at the links between the Ki clan and Heizei, see Hasegawa Masaharu, "*Kokinshū* no seiritsu to sono haikei," 45–47.

14. *Honchō monzui*, 8: 201; *SNKBT*, 27: 255.

15. Takigawa Kōji, "Uda, Daigo-chō no kadan to waka no dōkō," 233.

16. For more on the political situation during the first years of Tokihira's ascendancy, see Kumagai Naoharu, *Heianchō zenki bungakushi no kenkyū*, 243–253.

17. *Daigo tennō gyoki*, Engi 2/3/20; *ST* 1: 26.

18. For an overview of the practice of *hōken* in the early Heian period, see Mezaki, *Heian bunka shiron*, 75–136.

19. Although it was held in her quarters, there is no mention of Yasuko or any other woman participating in the wisteria blossom banquet.

20. *Kokinshū*, Mana Preface; *SNKBZ*, 11: 428–429. For my complete translation of the Mana Preface, see Appendix H.

21. The aim of reasserting harmony in the aftermath of political upheaval at court would also make the *Kokinshū* similar to Saga's anthologies, which, as I argued in Chapter 1, were produced under similar circumstances.

22. Yamaguchi, *Ōchō kadan no kenkyū: Uda, Daigo, Suzaku chō-hen*, 109–113.

23. *Kokinshū*, poem 1002; *SNKBZ*, 11: 381–382.

24. Kawaji Osamu, "*Kokin wakashū* ron," 34–35. The anthology's inclusion of poems from Uda's household poetry matches can be seen as an extension of this appropriative strategy.

25. In distinction from other scribal offices in the palace which were charged with copying out court documents for general use, the Uchi no Gosho-dokoro compiled and edited texts exclusively for the emperor's personal library. See Nagata Kazuya, "Gosho-dokoro to Uchi no Gosho-dokoro," 366.

26. Mezaki, *Ki no Tsurayuki*, 18–22. See also Murase Toshio, *Kyūtei kajin Ki no Tsurayuki*, 23. The prose preface to poem 456 in the *Shūi wakashū* (*SNKBT*, 7: 129) portrays Tsurayuki performing a ritual dance at the Sumiyoshi shrine, suggesting again that he may have received training in the Naikyōbō.

27. For example, one paired *kagura* chorus has been detected in poems 1076 and 1077 (*SNKBZ*, 11: 409). See Furuhashi Nobuyoshi, "*Kokin wakashū* to denshō kayō," 278–280.

28. The connections between these anonymous songs and similar ones in the *Man'yōshū* (particularly in Scrolls 7, 10, and 11) has been long recognized by scholars, perhaps most extensively and influentially by Yasuda Kiyomon in his *Kokinshū jidai no kenkyū*.

29. Yoshikawa Eiji, "*Kokinshū* senjutsu shiron," 21.

30. Sada Kimiko, "'Zō' no tokushoku to kōzō," *IKKW*, 156.

31. Akiyama Ken, "Nihon bungakushi ni okeru waka," 16.

32. *Daigo tennō gyoki*, Engi 6/1/9; *ST*, 1: 36.

33. For the full text, see *TSZ*, 576–577.

34. Itō Hiroshi, "Kōkyū," 85.

35. Arai Eizō, "Ōchō kannin Ki no Tsurayuki no shokumu," 143–144.

36. Mitani Kuniaki, "Chi = kankaku to tennōsei," 38.

37. Robert Ellwood, *The Feast of Kingship*, 143–148. For a discussion of the place of song in enthronement ceremonies, see Kurahayashi, "'Kami asobi no uta' no tokushoku to kōzō," *IKKW*, 178.

38. The connection between poems and food is also suggested by the word *utage* used to refer to court banquets in the six official dynastic histories. This term can be glossed as a compound formed from the words *uta* (verse) and *ke* (food / to eat). See Mezaki, "Nihon bunkashi ni okeru waka," 39.

39. *Chōya gunsai*; *KST*, 29: 1: 475.

40. *Makura no sōshi*, section 21; *SNKBZ*, 18: 54.

41. It is important to keep in mind that not all anonymous verses in the anthology are transcriptions of songs. For more on this issue, see Ueno, "Yomibito shirazu," 215–216.

42. Pauline Yu, "Poems in Their Place," 170.

43. One example of the way in which social status was more important than gender in determining nomenclature is the Assistant Imperial Handmaid Fujiwara no Yoruka, who is granted the title of "lord" (*ason*) in the anthology because she possessed Junior Fourth Rank. See *Kokinshū*, poem 80; *SNKBZ*, 11: 58.

44. Okumura, *Kokinshū no kenkyū*, 134–157.

45. *Ryō no gige*, 7; *KST*, 22: 244–245.

46. Kudō Shigenori, *Heianchō ritsuryō shakai no bungaku*, 8–10.

47. Although there appears to be no precedent for the ways in which the *Kokinshū* represents its poets, the practice of organizing imperial anthologies around the rubric of particular ritual contexts might have one precedent in the *Bunka shūreishū* which, as Wiebke Denecke notes, seems to preserve a vague narrative order replicating the practices of imperial outings and banquets ("Chinese Antiquity and Court Spectacle in Early *Kanshi*," 108).

48. This convention for limiting honorifics to the immediate line of succession was also observed in the next seven imperial anthologies. See Tamagami Takuya, "Keigo to mibun," *Genji monogatari kenkyū*, 26–41.

49. The earliest known instance of the word *kotobagaki* comes in section 138 of the fourteenth-century miscellany *Tsurezuregusa* (*SNKBT*, 44: 193).

50. The *Man'yōshū*, for example, uses *dai* in this broad sense to refer to the act of writing down a poem. For a detailed account of the history of the term, see Yoshikawa Eiji, "'Dai shirazu' to iu go ni tsuite," 178–189.

51. Ozawa, *Kokinshū no sekai*, 219–246.

52. Uchida, "*Kokinshū*," 41–42.

53. Katagiri, *Kokin wakashū no kenkyū*, 195. See also his essay "Dai'ei, sono keisei to ba."

54. For an overview of the use of the term *ba* in modern scholarship, see Kikuchi Yasuhiko, "*Kokinshū* no ba to sono hōhō," 89–91.

55. Takizawa Sadao, "Chokusen wakashū no kotobagaki ni tsuite," 12.

56. Okumura, *Kokinshū Gosenshū no shomondai*, 167–187.

57. We should also keep in mind that the roles of editor and reciter were usually distinguished in the court banquets on which the *Kokinshū* was modeled.

58. Kawamura Teruo, "Kotobagaki no imi suru mono," 37–38.

59. One precedent for this historical form of criticism can be found in the *Kakyō hyōshiki*, where *kokoro* is used in the sense of the author's original intentions. See Inomata Tokiwa, " 'Uta no 'kokoro' to 'mushin shochaku-ka,' " 199.

60. Some of these "after comments" appear to have been written as early as Daigo's reign; an example is the one that follows poem 1086 (*SNKBZ*, 11: 412), which refers to him as the current monarch. See Tanaka Kimiharu, "Uta no hairetsu," 46. For an account of the way anonymous poems in the *Kokinshū* are treated as song traditions with alternate wording, see Yoshiumi Naoto, "*Kokin wakashū* to denshō bungaku," *IKKW*, 270–276.

61. Takizawa Sadao, " 'Haru' no tokushoku to kōzō," *IKKW*, 71–72.

62. Matsuda Takeo, *Kokinshū no kōzō ni kansuru kenkyū*, 136–150.

63. Konishi Jin'ichi, "Association and Progression," 126–127.

64. For paradigmatic examples of this approach, see Arai, "*Kokin wakashū* shiki no bu no kōzō ni tsuite no ichi kōsatsu"; and "*Kokinshū* no kōzō," 55–57.

65. For an overview of structural approaches to this scroll, see Kuboki Hisako, "'Aishō' no tokushoku to kōzō," *IKKW*, 148–152.

66. Misaki Hayashi, " 'Ribetsu' no tokushoku to kōzō," *IKKW*, 114–115.

67. Some scholars have noted that there is a general distinction in the *Kokinshū* between the word *miyako*, which appears in poems as a way of denoting a nostalgic perspective on life within Heiankyō from a location outside it, and the word *kyō*, which appears in the prose prefaces to poems and emphasizes the capital's geographic location. See Takada Hirohiko "Kyō no bungaku *Kokinshū*," 183.

68. Kikuchi Yasuhiko, " 'Mono no na' " no tokushoku to kōzō, *IKKW*, 135.

69. Soda, "*Kokin wakashū* 'mono no na' kō," 41.

70. Because these three poems are personal messages to the emperor, the word *tanka* here could be the authors' expression of humility toward their personal poems rather than a reference to the 31-syllables metrical form (as would be the case in later times). See Tokuhara Shigemi, "*Kokinshū* zattei 'tanka' kō," 27.

71. Kubukihara Rei, " 'Zattei' no tokushoku to kōzō," *IKKW*, 165–171. For a more detailed treatment of these poems see also her essay "Haikai uta."

72. Okumura, "*Kokinshū* no zōtōteki hairetsu to chūshaku," 44.

73. Katagiri's thesis is outlined in a series of three articles: "*Kokinshū* ni okeru waka no kyōju"; and the two-part "*Kokin wakashū* no ba."

74. By contrast, poems 869 and 870 in the Miscellaneous Verse section of the *Kokinshū* (*SNKBZ*, 11: 330–331) are examples of congratulory verses marking the promotions of male officials.

75. Tanaka Kimiharu, "*Kokinshū* ga no uta ron," 8.

76. Murakami Miki, "Heian jidai no sanga," 45.

77. Matsuda, *Kokinshū no kōzō ni kansuru kenkyū*, 335–354.

78. Arai, "*Kokin wakashū* budate kō," 1018.

79. *Kokinshū*, Kana Preface; *SNKBZ*, 11: 29.

80. Due to the large number of poems from Blessings mentioned in this section, I will only provide page numbers for the edition I have used in those cases where poems are cited in full. The reader is referred to *SNKBZ*, 11: 148-156, for the relevant section of the *Kokinshū*. The central role played by women in defining the sort of kinship ties that birthday celebrations formally acknowledged at the Heian court is indirectly attested to by the fact that the only retainers who received the high honor of having an emperor or retired emperor host their birthday celebrations were maternal relatives, with many being Fujiwara regents (Murakami, "Heian jidai no sanga," 45).

81. The presence of a group of anonymous verses preceding ones by named authors in Blessings is characteristic of many other categories, such as Longing. See Yoshikawa Eiji, "*Kokinshū* senjutsu shiron," 32–33.

82. Igawa Kenji, "'Ga' no tokushoku to kōzō," *IKKW*, 109.

83. *Sandai jitsuroku*, Jōgan 17/5/19; *KST*, 4: 362.

84. The Yoshimine family was descended from a son of Emperor Kammu, making its members distant relations of the imperial house.

85. Igawa, "'Ga' no tokushoku to kōzō," 111–112.

86. *Kokinshū*, poem 364; *SNKBZ*, 11: 156.

87. Ibid., poem 343; *SNKBZ*, 11: 148.

88. Kyūsojin Hitaku, *Kokin wakashū seiritsu ron*, 249. In my subsequent discussion of Travel, I have observed the same policy for citing poems that was used in my earlier account of Blessings (see note 80). The reader is referred to *SNKBZ*, 11: 172–180 for the relevant section of the *Kokinshū*.

89. Matsuda, *Kokinshū no kōzō ni kansuru kenkyū*, 376–391.

90. See Arai, "*Kokin wakashū* kenkyū kiryobu no kōzō shōkō."

91. Mori Asao, "'Kiryo' no tokushoku to kōzō," *IKKW*, 122–124.

92. Shuen-fu Lin, "The Nature of the Quatrain from the Late Han to the High T'ang," 304.

93. *Kokinshū*, poem 343; *SNKBZ*, 11: 148.

94. Nakanishi Susumu, "*Kokin wakashū* kiryo kaken no seiritsu," 162.

95. Ebersole, *Ritual Poetry and the Politics of Death*, 45–50.

96. The choice of cuckoos and snow for describing Summer and Winter reflect the predominance of these words in the poems of these two small sections of the anthology. See Hirasawa Ryūsuke, "'Natsu' no tokoshoku to kōzō," and Hashimoto Masayo, "'Fuyu' no tokushoku to kōzō," in *IKKW*, 80–87 and 97–103, respectively.

97. Zito, *Of Body & Brush*, 147.

98. Takizawa Sadao, "'Haru' no tokushoku to kōzō," *IKKW*, 74. See also the entry for *uguisu* in Yamamoto Kenkichi et al., eds., *Nihon daisaijiki*, 296.

99. *Kokinshū*, poem 1; *SNKBZ*, 11: 31.

100. Ibid., poem 2; *SNKBZ*, 11: 31.

101. Suzuki Hideo, *Kodai waka shiron*, 435–458.

102. Takada Hirohiko, "*Kokin wakashū* no yu," *IKKW*, 458.

103. In a similar vein, one scholar has argued that *Kokinshū* poetry, and the anthology's Kana Preface in particular, are primarily concerned with the ways in which the subject creates relations between separate external objects, thereby investing those objects with the poet's subjectivity. See Kajimoto Kazuyoshi, "*Kokin*-ka no kōzō to sono isō," 15–17.

104. Imai, *Kokin-fū no kigen to honshitsu*, 180–184.

105. Many of the songs sung at such performances appear in Scroll 20, thus beginning and ending the two halves of the *Kokinshū* with the New Year's Day rituals. See Tanaka Shin'ichi, "*Kokin wakashū* to nenjū gyōji," *IKKW*, 285–286. The first verse in Scroll 20 (poem 1069; *SNKBZ*, 11: 407) itself is probably a *kagura uta* sung as part of the New Year's Day festivities. See Hirota Osamu, "'Ōuta-dokoro no on'uta' no tokushoku to kōzō," *IKKW*, 173.

106. *Kokinshū*, poem 3; *SNKBZ*, 11: 32.

107. Ibid., poems 4 and 5; *SNKBZ*, 11: 32.

108. For a version of this song that preserves its *hayashi kotoba*, see *Saibara* 28; *SNKBZ*, 42: 138.

109. *Kokinshū*, poem 8; *SNKBZ*, 11: 33.

110. The only other annual observance to receive any attention in the *Kokinshū*, the Tanabata festival of the Double Seventh, was not even mentioned in the taxonomy of major court rituals included in the *Engi shiki*. See Arai, "'*Kokin wakashū*' to nenjū gyōji," 103. Both Takaiko and her son were still alive in the early 900s.

111. Richard H. Okada, *Figures of Resistance*, 105-108. Although I agree with Okada's emphasis on the indeterminate nature of time and meaning presented in the opening section of Spring, the argument for a sustained calendrical reading of this sequence cannot be entirely dispensed with when specific ritual practices (rather than incantatory rhetoric) is stressed.

112. Tanaka Shin'ichi, *Heianchō bungaku ni miru nigenteki shikikan*, 65–146.

113. By contrast, Summer and Winter begin with monthly designations in the Fourth and Tenth Months respectively. The opening poems of Spring and Autumn can also be contrasted on the basis of their relative emphases on abstract reckoning and sensation respectively. Autumn in particular is pronouncedly more aural than Spring. See Taiyō Kazutoshi, "'Aki' no tokushoku to kōzō," *IKKW*, 89.

114. Tanaka Kimiharu, "Chūkō waka no genri," 24–27. On the links between poetry and textiles, as well as the overall cultural significance of the latter, see Carole Cavanaugh, "Text and Textile," 613–617.

115. Akimoto Morihide, "Mitate no kazai to hyōgen ruikei," 637. For a comparison of *miyu*'s use in *Man'yōshū* and Heian poetry, see Takahashi Bunji, *Fūkei to kyōkankaku*, 246–268.

116. *Kokinshū*, poem 469; *SNKBZ*, 11: 196.

117. By contrast, poems from the editors' period diversify the human element and conventionalize landscape depictions, a phenomenon that I discuss in Chapter 4.

118. Arai, "Wago to kango," 400.

119. For an informative overview of structural approaches to Longing, see Satō Kazuyoshi, " 'Koi' no tokushoku to kōzō," *IKKW*, 139–141.

120. See for example, McCullough, *Brocade by Night*, 453–456; and Gotō Yoshiko, "Joryū ni yoru danka," 305–306.

121. Suzuki Hideo, *Kodai waka shiron*, 547–551.

122. *Kokinshū*, poem 387; *SNKBZ*, 11: 165.

123. For one account of these earlier female entertainers, see Fukutō Sanae, "Ukareme kara asobi e," *Nihon josei seikatsushi* 1, 217–246. For a detailed study of Heian women performers, see Janet Goodwin, *Selling Songs and Smiles*, 11–40. The designation "Shirome" appears to have been used by more than one *asobi*.

124. Nakakōji Kimie, "Heianchō waka ni okeru 'hito' to 'kimi' no hyōgen," 3.

125. *Kokinshū*, poem 736; *SNKBZ*, 11: 282.

126. This indeterminacy is generally true of premodern Japanese. As the scholar Noguchi Takehiko has noted, grammatical person was not a recognized linguistic category prior to modern times (*Sanninshō no hakken made*, 7).

127. For an account of linguistic deixis in Japanese, see Patricia Wetzel, "A Movable Self," 73–79.

128. Paul Rouzer, *Articulated Ladies*, 117-156. For a detailed and thought-provoking account of the history of this trope in Chinese poetry, see Maija Bell Samei, *Gendered Persona and Poetic Voice*, 43–90.

129. Gotō, "Joryū ni yoru danka," 307.

130. Katagiri, "Kanshi no sekai, waka no sekai," 184–186.

131. *Kokinshū*, poem 656; *SNKBZ*, 11: 256.

132. Ibid., poem 559; *SNKBZ*, 11: 223.

133. Terry Kawashima, *Writing Margins*, 123–126.

134. Mezaki, *Ariwara no Narihira, Ono no Komachi*, 176.

135. *Kokinshū*, poem 797; *SNKBZ*, 11: 303.

136. Ibid., poems 552-554; *SNKBZ*, 11: 221-222.

137. Kojima Naoko, "Renka to jendaa," 59.

138. *Kokinshū*, poems 656-658; *SNKBZ*, 11: 256–257.

139. Gotō Yoshiko, "Ono no Komachi shiron," 24–25.

140. Komachi's manipulation of this trope is especially significant given the strong connections between subjectivity and sight that typify *uta* in her period. Unlike their poetic predecessors in the *Man'yōshū*, Heian modes of seeing often foregrounded the psychological dimension to this act by stressing the gap between its subject and object. See Hirasawa Ryūsuke, "*Man'yō* kara *Kokin* e," 48–49.

Chapter Four / Writing Yamato Verse in the Kana Preface

1. Kumagai Naoharu, "*Kokinshū* no seiritsu nendai ni tsuite," 10.
2. Yamaguchi, *Ōchō kadan no kenkyū: Uda, Daigo, Suzaku-chō hen*, 309.
3. For a discussion of these conventions, see Ozawa Masao, *Kodai kagaku no keisei*,

21–33. Ozawa's study of the Kana Preface is among the most thorough in its comparisons of this text with classical continental poetics and other early Japanese treatises such as the *Kakyō hyōshiki*, *Kisen shiki*, and *Shinsen zuinō waka*.

4. See *SNKBT*, 29: 53–54, for the full text in the *Fukurozōshi*.

5. Katagiri, "*Kokinshū* kanajo no bunshō," 225.

6. Murase, *Kokinshū no kiban to sono shūhen*, 91–92. As I mentioned in Chapter 3, the *Fukurozōshi* notes that two of the three versions in Tsurayuki's hand had *kana* prefaces. The one exception is the text initially presented to Daigo..

7. E. B. Ceadel, "The Ōi River Poems and Preface," 69–71. Ceadel's study and translation remains the most exhaustive and informative treatment of this text. My own translation of the preface is provided in Appendix G.

8. Owen, *The Poetry of the Early Tang*, 274–280.

9. For Tsurayuki's list of poems presented to Daigo, see *Kokinshū*, poem 1002; *SNKBZ*, 11: 381–382.

10. Yamaguchi, *Ōchō kadan no kenkyū: Uda, Daigo, Suzaku-chō hen*, 486.

11. Yamamoto Toshitatsu, "Tsurayuki no jo," 40–47.

12. Noda Hiroko, *Man'yōshū no jokei to shizen*, 9–16.

13. Satō Kazuyoshi, *Heian waka bungaku hyōgen ron*, 64.

14. The text cited here is from Owen, *Readings in Chinese Literary Thought*, 40–45. The translation is my own.

15. *Liji*, Book 19; *SKT*, 28: 556.

16. *Kokinshū*, Mana Preface; *SNKBZ*, 11: 422–423. A translation of the complete Mana Preface is provided in Appendix H.

17. Kenneth DeWoskin, "Early Chinese Music and the Origins of Aesthetic Terminology," 187–188.

18. For more on the emphasis placed on the musical qualities of poetry in both the Great Preface and authoritative early Tang commentaries to that text, see Steven Van Zoeren, *Poetry and Personality*, 108–111 and 139–145.

19. Kawada Yutaka, "Shirabe," 37.

20. See Kawahira Hitoshi, "Kokoro to kotoba," *IKKW*, 647–651. In the *Kokinshū*, the phrase "leaves of words" (*koto no ha*) appears in reference to epistles (poems 736 and 737 and 854), and to a *chōka* that acts as a prefatory table of contents for a collection of poems which Tsurayuki offers up to Daigo (poem 1002). The textual connotations of this word could also explain why leaves feature so prominently in the titles of anthologies such as the *Man'yōshū* and in such Six Dynasties works as the *Wenfu* (*The Poetic Exposition on Literature*, ca. 300) by Lu Ji (261–303). For an account of the way leaves are used in the latter text, see Owen, *Readings in Chinese Literary Thought*, 113.

21. *Hakushi monjū*, 22, "Letter to Yuan Zhen"; *SKT*, 101: 307.

22. *Kokinshū*, Kana Preface; *SNKBZ*, 11: 17.

23. For a convincing example of this counter argument, see Imazeki Toshiko, "'Izure ka uta o yomazarikeru' kō," 44–48. For an overview of scholarly debates about this passage, see Fujii, "Kanajo," *IKKW*, 55–63.

24. *Kokinshū*, Mana Preface, *SNKBZ*, 11: 422–423.

25. Ibid., Kana Preface; *SNKBZ*, 11: 17.

26. Hirasawa Ryūsuke, "*Kokinshū* no gengo ishiki," 9.

27. Owen, *Readings in Chinese Literary Thought*, 39–45.

28. Okumura, *Kokinshū no kenkyū*, 21–46.

29. The cosmological origins of Yamato verse are also suggested by the opening passage of the Kana Preface, in which its ability to exert influence is described as "effortless" (*chikara o irezu shite*), making it a spontaneous, self-generating force. The fact that this phrase is an addition to the otherwise similar account in the Mana Preface suggests Tsurayuki's specific concern with marking *yamato uta* as something extrahuman.

30. Connery, *The Empire of the Text*, 34–35.

31. James Hightower, "The *Wen Hsüan* and Genre Theory," 518.

32. Ozawa, *Kodai kagaku no keisei*, 95.

33. Mori Masamori, "*Kokinshū* no ji-amari," 1–2.

34. *Kokinshū*, Kana Preface; *SNKBZ*, 11: 18.

35. Ibid. (interpolated commentary); *SNKBZ*, 11: 18.

36. For more on the polyvocal nature of early poetry and its transformation into a more human-centered narrative form of voice in Heian times, see Satō Kazuyoshi, "Tasei no katai kara tansei no katai e," 164–165.

37. Nintoku's name literally denotes "benevolent virtue," making this association between Confucian kingship and poetic power even more overt.

38. For a comprehensive overview of these debates about the identity of the first poem, see Takeoka Masao, *Kokin wakashū zenhyōshaku*, 1: 74–76.

39. *Nihon shoki*; *SNKBZ*, 2: 126–127.

40. One version of the Naniwazu poem was scrawled on the roof of a five-storied pagoda at the temple of Daigo-ji when it was being repaired in the mid tenth century, suggesting that this poem was familiar to many different social classes. See Komatsu Shigemi, *Kana*, 106–107.

41. Arai, "'Jishin' kō," 15–25.

42. Takahashi Kazuo, "Gyōji to waka," 19–21.

43. Imai, *Kokin-fū no kigen to honshitsu*, 146.

44. Okumura, *Kokinshū no kenkyū*, 47–62. One example of such incantatory verse can be found in the *Man'yōshū*, poems 16: 3885 and 3886; *SNKBZ*, 9: 138–141.

45. By way of example, Imai cites one official edict from Jōgan 8/1/23 (866) which describes beggar-monks as willful fellows who barge into households and demand food in payment for not uttering curses (*Kokin-fū no kigen to honshitsu*, 327).

46. Fujii, "*Kokinshū* no kokoro to kotoba," 38–40.

47. *Kokinshū*, Kana Preface; *SNKBZ*, 11: 24.

48. Oda Shōkichi, *Kokin wakashū no nazo o toku*, 66–78.

49. An anonymous verse likening the Tatsuta River to brocade is attributed to this Nara sovereign in the commentary following it (*Kokinshū*, poem 283; *SNKBZ*, 11: 128), and subsequently in episode 151 in *Tales of Yamato* (*SNKBZ* 12: 385).

50. Imai, *Kokin-fū no kigen to honshitsu*, 14–16.

51. Kurahayashi, *Kyōen no kenkyū*, 692–695.

52. Satō, *Heian waka bungaku hyōgen ron*, 66–67.

53. Arai, "Kanajo manajo dokuyō no koto," 28–29.

54. *Ryō ni gige*; *KST*, 22: 30.

55. I do not mean to imply by this that the *Kokinshū* itself was intended for an exclusively male audience. As I have stressed at the beginning of this chapter, the Kana Preface is best seen a text that was separable from the anthology and intended for a particular readership known to Tsurayuki.

56. Tanaka Yutaka, "Kafū yōshiki ron," 273.

57. Owen, *Readings in Chinese Literary Thought*, 59–62. See also John Timothy Wixted, "The Nature of Evaluation in the *Shih-p'in*," 225 and 232–233.

58. Owen, *Readings in Chinese Literary Thought*, 210.

59. Sivin, "State, Cosmos, and Body in the Last Three Centuries B.C.," 14.

60. John Hay, "The Human Body as a Microcosmic Source of Macrocosmic Values in Calligraphy," 88.

61. Kōzen Hiroshi, "*Kokinshū* manajo oboegaki," 178–181. Subsequent citations from the *Gujin shuping* are drawn from pages 180–181 in this article.

62. *Nihon shoki*, Ingyō Tennō 7/12; *SNKBZ*, 3: 114–115.

63. Fujii, "Sotōrihime no nagare," 94–95.

64. *Kakyō hyōshiki*, *NKT*, 1:16. This mention of Sōtorihime occurs only in the *shōhon* [excerpted version] of the text, and is usually associated with the preface to the mid-Heian treatise *Hikohime shiki* ("Princess Hiko Formulary").

65. One scholar has recently suggested that the gendering of Komachi's style in the Kana Preface was perhaps intended to provide a prescriptive model for women poets at court. See Edith Sarra, *Fictions of Femininity*, 13–18.

66. Origuchi Shinobu, "Nyonin tanka josetsu," 448.

67. *Mumyōzōshi*; *SNKBZ*, 40: 263.

68. Ōno Susumu, Satake Akihiro, and Maeda Kingorō, eds., *Iwanami kogo jiten*, 587.

69. Yoshikawa Eiji, "*Kokinshū* jo no karon," 78.

70. *Kokinshū*, Kana Preface; *SNKBZ*, 11: 19.

71. Tsunoda Hiroko, "*Kokinshū* jobun ni okeru 'sama' no kōsatsu," 28.

72. Pauline Yu, *The Reading of Imagery in the Chinese Poetic Tradition*, 44–83.

73. Ozawa, *Kodai kagaku no keisei*, 184.

74. Takeoka, *Kokin wakashū zenhyōshaku* 1, 91–105.

75. Suzuki Hideo, *Kodai waka shiron*, 380–394.

76. McCullough, *Brocade by Night*, 364.

77. In my translations I use a bold font to represent *mono* and italics to represent *kokoro*. Both fonts are used together to represent points at which these elements overlap.

78. *Kokinshū*, Kana Preface; *SNKBZ*, 11: 20.

79. *Nihon shoki*, Jimmu Tennō 1/1/1; *SNKBZ*, 2: 232.

80. *Kokinshū*, Kana Preface; *SNKBZ*, 11: 20.

81. Matsumoto Hiroshi, "On'inshi kara mita mono no na uta," 19.

82. Dore Levy, "Constructing Sequences," 475. Another definition of *fu* describes it as a style of plain narration devoid of figuration. See David Knechtges, trans., *Wenxuan or Selections of Refined Literature*, 1: 20. As we shall see, however, this type of verse corresponds more closely to the category of "plain verse" in the Kana Preface than to "enumerative verse."

83. Soda Fumio, "*Kokin wakashū* 'mono no na' kō," 35.

84. *Maoshi zhengyi*; *Shisan jing zhushu*, 271.

85. For an extended discussion of the difference between allegorical and analogical ways of reading, see Yu, *The Reading of Imagery in the Chinese Poetic Tradition*, Chapter 1.

86. *Kokinshū*, Kana Preface; *SNKBZ*, 11: 20.

87. Fujii, "Kanajo," *IKKW*, 59.

88. *Iwanami kogo jiten*, 980.

89. *Kokinshū*, Kana Preface; *SNKBZ*, 11: 21.

90. Ibid.; *SNKBZ*, 11: 21.

91. A precursor to this use of the term *tada uta* appears in the *Kakyō hyōshiki* where it is written 直語 (*NKT*, 1: 5), and similar forms of plain narration can be found in Scrolls 11 and 12 of the *Man'yōshū* where they are categorized as a "forthright relation of the heart's feelings" (*shōjutsu shinsho*). In his *Tosa Diary*, Tsurayuki uses the related term *tadagoto* to criticize a poem for its prosaic quality (entry for 2/1; *SNKBZ*, 13: 43).

92. *Kokinshū*, Kana Preface; *SNKBZ*, 11: 22.

93. Yoshida, *Kotoba no jusei to seisei*, 184–193.

94. *Saibara* 44; *SNKBZ*, 42: 151. Italic font in the translation is used to indicate *hayashi kotoba* refrains.

95. I differ here from John Timothy Wixted's opinion that there is no new critical theory in the prefaces ("The *Kokinshū* Prefaces," 38). Wixted's painstaking analysis of the two prefaces is, however, enormously helpful in locating continental precedents for their language and structure.

96. Thomas LaMarre, following the work of Amagasaki Akira and Yoshino Tatsunori, provides one exception to this tendency (*Uncovering Heian Japan*, 63–64). My aim here is to expand on the history of such visual forms of rhetoric that he outlines by positing an initial shift toward sound in the medieval period, rather than under the aegis of modern nationalism.

97. For an account of these orthographic conventions and their potential for multiple interpretations of a poem, see Joshua S. Mostow, *Pictures of the Heart*, 45.

98. Akinaga Kazue, "*Kokin wakashū* no hyōki," *IKKW*, 296–297. Akinaga provides a singularly extensive analysis of these texts in his four-volume study *Kokin wakashū shōtenbon no kenkyū*.

99. Yanagawa Kiyoshi, "*Kokinshū* ni mirareru kakekotoba no akusento," 17. The fact

that Yanagawa's groundbreaking observations have largely been ignored in mainstream scholarship attests to the strength of the modern tendency to see pivot-words as puns.

100. Akahane Shuku, "Kakekotoba," *IKKW*, 633. For a detailed account of various definitions of *kakekotoba*, see Jon LaCure, *Rhetorical Devices of the Kokinshū*, 61–87. LaCure describes *kakekotoba* as a combination of human and natural elements. He also notes the problematic nature of identifying them in many cases due to the variety of definitions provided.

101. For an overview of *mitate* and the ways this rhetorical form impacted *Kokinshū* poetry, see Igawa Hiroko, "Mitate," *IKKW*, 678–682.

102. The expansion of pivot-words is commonly associated with the *rokkasen*-period poets who were active in the mid ninth century. See Hirano Yukiko, "Ninmyō-chō no wafū bunka to rokkasen," 226–227.

103. As LaMarre notes, there is a political dimension to this historical emphasis on visual doubles, which asserted similarities between different entities in a multipolar court where sovereigns were interchangeable with their retired fathers and maternal uncles (*Uncovering Heian Japan*, 73–74).

104. Sugitani Jurō, "*Kokin wakashū* to uta-awase," *IKKW*, 509–522.

105. Although most *Man'yōshū* pivot-words are syntactically related to the poem's sentence structure, a few "*Kokinshū*-style" ones in which this is not the case appear and are enabled by the strategic choice of a particular Chinese character to write the word. (See Ide Itaru, "Kakekotoba no genryū," 428). This suggests once again the strong links between pivot-words and writing.

106. Suzuki Hiroko, *Kokin wakashū hyōgen ron*, 4–5. This could be one reason why pivot-words transform only a small number of proper nouns. Most *furugoto* phrases might have been deeply tied to a particular sacral or mythical location, as opposed to the more generic categories of human emotions and natural settings.

107. One scholar has argued that *kakekotoba* were derived from the tonal and rhetorical concerns of *shi* poetics, which included 29 categories of parallelism in Kūkai's *Bunkyō hifuron* (*Secret Treasure-house of the Mirrors of Poetry*, ca. 809–820). See Watanabe Hideo, "Ōchō waka to kanshibun," 122–125.

108. Yanagawa, "*Kokinshū* ni okeru kakekotoba no akusento," 21.

109. Music first begins to figure prominently in poetics with Fujiwara no Shunzei's *Korai fūteishō* (*Poetic Styles from the Past*, 1197), a treatise that borrowed such musicological terminology as "clean sounding" (*kiyoge*) to develop a critical vocabulary for evaluating *uta*, and which placed emphasis on the aesthetic effects poems have when recited (*SNKBZ*, 87: 251–252).

110. Akahane Shuku, "Waka no inritsu," 140–143.

111. Hijikata Yōichi, "Waka hyōgenshi ni okeru 'yu' no isō,'" 27–28.

Chapter Five / Screen Poetry and Reflections of Power

1. Nothing is known for certain about the history of the *Tsurayuki-shū*. Two broad textual lineages exist today, one arranged by topic and the other with no apparent or-

ganizational scheme. The *TSZ* edition used here belongs to the former category. The earliest mention of Tsurayuki's poetry collection appears in the preface to poem 158 in the *Egyō hōshi shū* ("Reverend Egyō's Collection"), which mentions this contemporary of Tsurayuki borrowing a scroll from his household collection (*KT*, 3: 1: 183).

2. Fujioka Tadaharu, *Heian wakashi ron*, 16.

3. Shimada Ryōji, "*Kokinshū* no renka ni okeru hiyuteki hyōgen ni tsuite," 32.

4. Shimada, "*Kokinshū* no kōteki seikaku ni tsuite," 3.

5. For this use of the term *yamato-e*, see *Gonki*, Chōho 1/10/20; *ST*, 4: 83.

6. Minamoto Toyomune, *Yamato-e no kenkyū*, 14. Minamoto's account treats *yamato-e* as essentially interchangeable with *onna-e*, although the latter term, which first appears in the *Kagerō nikki* and *Makura no sōshi*, could refer simply to pictures produced by women rather than a particular style of painting.

7. One recent example of this tendency to associate the Yamato style with feminine qualities can be seen in an influential article by the art historian Chino Kaori, who characterizes the former as small, delicate, and gentle ("Gender and Japanese Art," 27).

8. *Kokinshū*, poem 930; *SNKBZ*, 11: 352.

9. Akiyama Terukazu, *Heian jidai sezokuga no kenkyū*, 6.

10. Watanabe Hideo, "Ki no Tsurayuki no isō," 29–30.

11. *Okikaze-shū*, poem 14 (*KT*, 3: 1: 28); *Yorimoto-shū*, poems 4–7 (*KT*, 3: 1: 77); *Tadamine-shū* poems 173 and 151 (*KT*, 3: 1: 41).

12. Richard Bowring, "The *Ise monogatari*: A Short Cultural History," 413–414.

13. This important collection, as Richard Okada has noted, can be seen as an early form of fictional romance (*Figures of Resistance*, 112–130). More recently, Joshua Mostow has argued that such narratives were produced under the aegis of the Northern House (*At the House of Gathered Leaves*, 35–38), a thesis that would accord well with Atsuko's position at court as a representative of her brother Tokihira's interests.

14. Tajima Satoko, "*Kokinshū* jidai no byōbu uta no eihō," 19–21.

15. *Tsurayuki-shū*, poems 417–446; *TSZ*, 328–344. For an analysis of this sequence that emphasizes its narrative qualities, see Suzuki Michiko, "Byōbu uta kajin to shite no Tsurayuki," 31–36.

16. Watada Yasuyo, "Tsurayuki ni okeru byōbu uta hyōgen no ichi tokushitsu," 85. Another scholar has suggested that Tsurayuki's narrative sequences of screen poems from this same period could also have inspired the relationship between male author and female narrator in his *Tosa Diary*, a relationship that could be likened to one between the screen poet and a fictional figure within the painted screen. See Horikawa Noboru, "*Tosa nikki* no hōhō keisei shiron," 76–77.

17. Inventories at temples such as Tōdai-ji are a major source of our knowledge concerning early Japanese painting. See Ienaga Saburō, *Jōdai yamato-e zenshi*, 72–75. For a detailed chronology of early Japanese paintings see also his *Jōdai yamato-e nenpyō*.

18. *Man'yōshū*, poem 9: 1682; *SNKBZ*, 7: 395.

19. Andō Tarō, *Heian jidai shikashū kajin no kenkyū*, 248–250.

20. Kierstead, "Gardens and Estates," 306–309.

21. Katagiri, *Kokin wakashū no kenkyū*, 50–71.

22. For a discussion of similar links among poetic descriptions of landscapes, gardens, and maps in China, see Xiaoshan Yang, *Metamorphosis of the Private Sphere*, 32–33.

23. For a detailed account of these early Japanese maps, see Ienaga, *Jodai yamato-e zenshi*, 437–438.

24. Ibid., 245.

25. *Wenxuan*, *Xijing fu*; *SKT*, 79: 82–133.

26. No doubt part of the rationale behind asserting such equivalences between Heiankyō and Luoyang was to fortify Saga's claim to maintaining the former as his capital in the face of potential challenges by Heizei's supporters.

27. *Keikokushū*, poem 827; *GR*, 8: 533. For a translation into English, see Joshua S. Mostow, "*E no Gotoshi*," 38.

28. Yamanaka Yutaka, *Heian jidai no kokiroku to kizoku bunka*, 289. Neither the format and nature of this text—known as the *Nenjū gyōji goshōji no fumi* ("Text for His Majesty's Screen of Annual Observances")—nor the way it might have related to painted depictions of annual observances at the palace are known.

29. *Shūi wakashū*, poem 1091; *SNKBT* 7: 313.

30. Takano Yasuhiro, "Ninna gobyōbu saikō," 1–9.

31. *Kokinshū*, poem 352; *SNKBZ*, 11: 151.

32. Yoshikawa, "*Kokinshū* izen no byōbu uta," 66.

33. For the respective versions of this verse, see *Kokinshū*, poem 214 (*SNKBZ*, 11: 103) and *Tadamine-shū*, poem 31 (*KT*, 3: 1: 38). Whereas the *Shinpen kokka taikan* version of this poem associates it with the Koresada poetry match, the same poem in the *Shikashū taisei* (no. 19) is associated with a screen painting belonging to an imperial consort. See Wakashi kenkyūkai, ed. *Shikashū taisei*, 1: 173.

34. Yamanaka Yutaka, "Heianchō ni okeru tsūka girei," 67.

35. Tokuhara Shigemi, "Byōbu uta no gūtaisō," 28–30.

36. Ozawa, *Kodai kagaku no keisei*, 256–257.

37. It is also possible that these screens were inspired by the series depicting annual rituals that had been commissioned by Kōkō. Regardless, this form of pictorial and poetic display can also be seen as a ritual assertion of Yasuko's authority on a par with that of the reigning sovereign.

38. *Mitsune-shū*, poems 156–166; *KT*, 3: 1: 33.

39. *Gosen wakashū*, poem 1105; *SNKBT*, 6: 328.

40. Fujita Isson, "Heianchō byōbu uta no shiteki kōsatsu," 24.

41. For a detailed history of the screen poetry used in Heian enthronement rites, see Fujita Yuriko, "Daijōe byōbu uta no seikaku o megutte," 47–60.

42. Yagi Ichio, *Daijōe waka no sekai*, 26–35 and 94–148.

43. Tokuhara Shigemi, "Ga no byōbu to byōbu uta," 25–26.

44. Fujita Isson, "Byōbu e to byōbu uta no sōkansei o megutte," 75.

45. *Tsurayuki-shū*, poems 3–22; *TSZ*, 74–87.

46. Tokuhara, "Byōbu uta no gūtaisō," 35.

47. The significance of these decades is derived from a passage in *Analects* 2: 4 in which Confucius describes his personal development at each stage (*SKT*, 1: 40).

48. *Kanke bunsō*, poems 174–178; *NKBT*, 72: 240–243. One scholar has noted that the scale of the quasi-urban scenes described in these poems is far more circumscribed than those in *shi* written for Saga's landscape mural, in keeping with the overall tendency to focus on more constricted spatial representations of natural settings as the Heian period progressed. See Kawaguchi Hisao, "Waga kuni ni okeru daiga bungaku no tenkai," 193.

49. *Sandai jitsuroku*, Ninna 1/12/18; *KST*, 4: 600.

50. As mentioned previously, the earliest poem in the *Kokinshū* clearly written for inclusion on a screen is from the first year of Daigo's reign (poem 352; *SNKBZ*, 11: 151–152). This dating suggesting that the techniques for composing screen poetry developed by Atsuko's salon spread quickly among her kin in the Northern House.

51. Tanaka Kimiharu and Kyōko, "Kaisetsu," *TSZ*, 31–35.

52. *Tsurayuki-shū*, poem 1; *TSZ*, 73.

53. Tajima Satoko, "Byōbu uta kajin to shite no Tsurayuki," 3.

54. *Tsurayuki-shū*, poem 91; *TSZ*, 127.

55. Ibid., poem 5; *TSZ*, 76.

56. The same style of calligraphy could be literally inscribed in a garden as well, suggesting once again their similarity with screens in creating an ordered regime through the combination of written signs and landscape depictions. The mid-Heian gardening treatise *Sakuteiki* mentions an "*ashide* style" of landscape which used the imagery of hills and fauna depicted in poems written in this style. Other garden features such as ponds could be designed to mimic specific *kana* letters (Takei and Keane, *Sakuteiki*, 30).

57. Motoi Jun, "Ki no Tsurayuki no byōbu uta hyōgen," 73.

58. Two such *kazashi* can be seen in the Kamakura-period *Nenjū gyōji emaki* ("Picture Scroll of Annual Court Rites"). See Komatsu Shigemi, *Nenjū gyōji emaki*, 23.

59. Fujioka Tadaharu, "Byōbu uta no honshitsu," 44.

60. *Midō kanpakki*, Chōhō 1/10/21 and 1/10/27; *DNK*, 1: 1: 35 and 36.

61. *Shōyūki*, Chōhō 1/10/23; *DNK*, 10: 2: 66.

62. Ibid., Chōhō 1/10/28; *DNK*, 10: 2: 67.

63. Ibid., Chōhō 1/10/30; *DNK*, 10: 2: 67–68.

64. Shimizu Yoshiko, *Genji monogatari no buntai to hōhō*, 239–254.

65. *Kagerō nikki*; *SNKBZ*, 13: 184.

66. Fujita Isson, "Byōbu uta no seisaku hō bekken," 11–17.

67. *Konjaku monogatari-shū*, story 24: 31; *SNKBZ*, 37: 321–327.

68. Tamagami Takuya, "Byōbu e to uta to monogatari to," 9.

69. *Shūishō chū*; *GR*, 16: 235.

70. Katano Tatsurō, *Nihon bungei to kaiga no sōkansei no kenkyū*, 181–182.

71. Kawamura Hiroko, "Byōbu uta ni tsuite," 36.

72. Tokuhara Shigemi, "*Tsurayuki-shū* byōbu uta no eihō," 4. Although we typically refer to the persona articulated in a poem as its "speaker," the word "onlooker" might be a more appropriate term for the visual subjectivity produced through a screen poem's perspective. Consequently, I will be using this term whenever applicable in the following discussion.

73. *Tsurayuki-shū*, poem 10; *TSZ*, 79.

74. Ibid., poem 51; *TSZ*, 104.

75. Motoi Jun, "Ki no Tsurayuki no byōbu uta hyōgen," 84–92.

76. *Tsurayuki-shū*, poem 14; *TSZ*, 82.

77. Kamishino Shōji, "Tsurayuki 'Mochizuki no koma' ei kō," 47–49.

78. Nakajima Terumasa, "Ki no Tsurayuki no mitate hyōgen," 48.

79. *Man'yōshū*, poem 8: 1435; *SNKBZ*, 7: 298–299. The *yamabuki* is a species of yellow flowering shrub often referred to as the kerria rose in English translation. I have used a more literal rendering of its name ("mountain-breeze") to emphasize the way that the word potentially adds further details to the poem's setting.

80. Mizutani Takashi, "Ki no Tsurayuki ni mirareru *Man'yō* uta no riyō ni tsuite," 15.

81. Tsurayuki is believed to have been Palace Librarian (*Gosho-dokoro no azukari*) while also occupying his post in the palace kitchen. For a concise chronology of his career during this period, see Hagitani Boku, *Tosa nikki zenchūshaku*, 465.

82. Nakano Masako, "Ki no Tsurayuki no uta to kanshibun," 20.

83. Tsurayuki's familiarity with *shi* poetry is suggested in part by his tendency to use parallelisms or contrastive balances in his own verses. See Watanabe Hideo, "Ki no Tsurayuki," 270.

84. Nakano Masako, "*Kokinshū* ni okeru 'beranari,'" 33. In the case of screen poetry, the textually based mode of inference marked by *beranari* might also refer to the written topics through which the poet would be informed about the painted scene.

85. Inukai Kimiyuki, *Kage no kodai*, 3.

86. Ōoka Makoto, *Ki no Tsurayuki*, 45. For a detailed analysis of Tsurayuki's screen poems with reflections, see Tajima Satoko, "*Kokinshū* izen no byōbu uta."

87. Komachiya Teruhiko, *Kokin wakashū to uta kotoba hyōgen*, 228. The earliest text identifying *mitate* as a distinct form of rhetoric is Fujiwara no Kiyosuke's *Waka shogaku shō* ("A *Waka* Primer," 1169), which refers to such forms of visual likeness as "resemblances between things" (*niru mono*). See *NKT*, 2: 199–201.

88. Tsurayuki's interest in pitting fictive alternatives against actual situations in screen poems can also be seen in his frequent use of the contra-factual verbal auxiliary *mashi* (it would be so), which ends many of these verses (Hasegawa Masaharu, *Ki no Tsurayuki ron*, 149).

89. Konishi, "The Genesis of the *Kokinshū* Style," 152.

90. Nakajima, "Ki no Tsurayuki no mitate hyōgen," 45–49.

91. *Kokinshū*, poem 89; *SNKBZ*, 11: 61.

92. Watanabe Hideo, *Heianchō bungaku to kanbun sekai*, 147–152.

93. *Tsurayuki-shū*, poems 890–891; *TSZ*, 644–645.
94. Katō Kōichi, "Tsurayuki no hyōgen," 14–15.
95. *Tsurayuki-shū*, poem 804; *TSZ*, 575.
96. Gotō Yoshiko, "Tsurayuki uta no haramu mono," 64.

Epilogue / Yamato Verse and Yamato Japan

1. Kamiya Masaaki, "Heian jidai no sesshō to gishiki," 132.
2. Murai Yasuhiko, "Heian kizoku to wa," 14.
3. Komachiya Teruhiko, *Genji monogatari no uta kotoba hyōgen*, 7.
4. Susan B. Klein, *Allegories of Desire*, 43–47.
5. The other two instances in which the word *yamato uta* appears in *kana* are in the entry for 12/26 in the *Tosa Diary* (*SNKBZ*, 13:16) and episode 82 in *Tales of Ise* (*SNKBZ*, 12: 184). Tsurayuki, of course, wrote the first of these two texts and in this particular instance appears to use the term in deliberate contrast to *kara uta* (Tang verse). There has been frequent speculation that he also had some relation to the *Tales of Ise*, although the occurence of *yamato uta* in episode 82 is harder to explain.
6. LaMarre, *Uncovering Heian Japan*, 1–4. Chino Kaori's essay "Gender and Japanese Art" provides another example of the ways in which a *kara/yamato* binary system has been seen as endemic to the structures of cultural expression and self-imagination in Heian Japan.
7. For the earliest instances of this binary representation of authority, see Joan Piggott, "Chieftain Pairs and Co-rulers," 40–42. In a similar vein, Peter Nickerson has argued that such binaries were intrinsic to Heian notions of power; see "The Meaning of Matrilocality," 466.
8. I use the term "zones" here to refer to a porous liminal space between polities, as opposed to a precise linear boundary that clearly demarcates these entities. See Bruce Batten, *To the Ends of Japan*, 24.
9. Mimi Hall Yiengpruksawan, *Hiraizumi*, 10.
10. *Shaku nihongi*; *KST*, 8: 2: 6.
11. Amino Yoshiko, *'Nihon' to wa nani ka*, 221.
12. Donald H. Shively and William McCullough, eds., *The Cambridge History of Japan*, 2: 89–94.
13. *Kokinshū*, poem 1100; *SNKBZ*, 11: 416.
14. Tsuchihashi Yutaka and Konishi Jin'ichi, eds., *Kodai kayō shū*, *NKBT*, 3: 424.
15. Mizushima Yoshiharu, "'Azuma uta' no tokushoku to kōzō," *IKKW*, 184.
16. Inukai Kimiyuki, "Kayō to Ōuta-dokoro," 347–352.
17. Mimi Hall Yiengpruksawan, "What's in a Name?" 424.
18. Thomas Kierstead, "The Gendering and Regendering of Medieval Japan," 78.
19. Yoda, *Gender and National Literature*, 25–40. See also Peter Nosco, *Remembering Paradise*, 148–149.
20. Nakanishi Susumu, "Onna kara onna e: kodai wakashi no sobyō," 77–87.

21. *Honchō monzui*, 1: 15; *SNKBT*, 27:130.

22. Donald H. Shively and William H. McCullough, eds., *Cambridge History of Japan*, 2: 134.

23. Sugiyama Hideaki, "Heian kizoku no densha to chōdo," 105.

24. Takinami, *Heian kento*, 318. Would-be clients (often known literally as "housemen" or *kenin*) would call on a patron's mansion to request an audience, after which they would present their name placard. For a brief description of this procedure; see Karl Friday, *Hired Swords*, 78.

25. Watanabe Hideo, "*Kokinshū* jo no bungakushi," 130–136.

Appendix A / Preface to the *Ryōunshū*

1. Otherwise known as Cao Pi, the citation is from the opening passage of his *Discourse on Literature*.

2. In chapter 20 of *Laozi*, one of the joys of life is described as ascending a high pavilion in spring to clear one's spirits (*SKT*, 7: 43).

3. A phrase from *Laozi*, 74; *SKT*, 7: 121. Its use here appears to be a disclaimer with respect to any expertise on the part of Minemori and his fellow editors.

4. The proverbially limited perspective of a frog in the well is taken from the "Autumn Floods" chapter of *Zhuangzi*, as is the image of the Yellow River god praising the ocean's lord for its vastness (*SKT*, 8: 461).

5. The trope likening virtue's suasive powers to wind bending the grass is taken from *Analects* 12: 19; *SKT*, 1: 274.

6. The phrase "broadening oneself through culture" (*wen*) is derived from *Analects* 9: 11; *SKT*, 1: 203.

7. The imagery here appears to be derived from the *Wenfu*, where the overall effect on a text of beautiful phrasing in one particular passage is likened to pearls that impart richness to their surrounding waters (Owen, *Readings in Chinese Literary Thought*, 152–153).

Appendix B / Preface to the *Bunka shureishū*

1. There is a lacuna after this sentence, the fragments of which suggest a rhetorical question of some sort.

2. The author of the preface is here dividing contemporary poetry into two schools according to critical commonplaces employed in continental criticism. The first of these schools is said to aspire to the edifying values of classical poetry embodied in the *Guofeng* ("The Airs of the States") in the *Classic of Poetry* and the *Lisao* ("Encountering Sorrow") in the *Chuci*. The other school is said to aim for the beauty and ornamentation found in so-called "palace poems" of the Six Dynasties, which were often characterized by Confucian critics as superficial and lascivious. Similar distinctions between

serious and frivolous forms of verse can also be seen at work in the prefaces to the *Kokinshū*.

3. The description of plain carts being transformed into grand carriages and water into ice is taken from the preface to the *Wenxuan*, where both images are used to refer to the historical evolution of poetry from simpler forms into more elaborate ones (Knechtges, *Wenxuan or Selections of Refined Literature*, 73–75). The implication here could be that the *Bunka shūreishū* is an improvement on the *Ryōunshū*. The corresponding passage in the *Wenxuan* preface, however, also suggests that both the simplicity of antiquity and complexity of more recent times each have their own virtues. The denial of distinctions that is asserted in the passage following this one in the preface to the *Bunka shūreishū* would accord with this latter reading.

Appendix C / Preface to the *Keikokushū*

1. This is probably a reference to the tradition that officials of the ancient Zhou dynasty selected popular songs in order to gauge the feelings of the common people, a practice that was said to have led to the compiling of the *Classic of Poetry*.

2. This emphasis on the balance between form and content is adapted from a famous passage in *Analects* 6: 18 where the ideal gentleman is described as combining the qualities of inner feeling and external etiquette (*SKT*, 1: 139).

3. Chu and Han are likely references to the earliest poetry anthologies, the *Chuci* and *Classic of Poetry*. The Luo River runs by Luoyang, the capital of the Han dynasty. The following phrase refers to the region around Yangzhou. Note the additional meaning of "current" as "literary movement."

4. *Model Sayings* (*Fayan*) is a treatise by the Confucian scholar Yang Xiong (53 B.C.E.–18 C.E.) dealing with various topics in philosophy, governance, and literature. The *Keikokushū* preface is perhaps rejecting his criticism of the *fu* poetic genre for its overly seductive and ornate rhetoric.

5. This is a reference to Cao Pi and his *Discourse on Literature*.

6. There is no known source for the remarkably detailed literary history of the Six Dynasties presented in the *Keikokushū*, although its critical stance toward preceding dynasties would suggest the source was Tang-period.

7. This is probably a reference to Prince Xiao Tang (501–531). A son of Emperor Wu, he was a major patron of poetry at the Liang court and the editor of the *Wenxuan*.

8. According to Confucian tradition, the sage king Yao voluntarily abdicated in favor of Shun on account of the latter's moral worthiness. The analogy here seems to be with Saga and Junna respectively. The succeeding sentence appears to be referring to Heizei when it describes a departed sovereign.

9. Master He is said to have suffered the loss of his limbs when a stone he presenteds to several rulers was not recognized as precious jade. The preface appears to be saying that both exalted and common poems have been included in the anthology, and

that the imperial reader (the anthologizer hopes) will be able to recognize the relative merits of each one.

10. This is the same Isayama no Fumitsugu who was mentioned in the preface to the *Bunka shūreishū* as one of its editors. He received the surname Yasuno at the end of the Kōnin era.

Appendix D / *Chōka* for Ninmyō's Fortieth Birthday Celebration

1. *Kongō jumyō darani-kyō*. This text was originally a Sanskrit scripture translated into Chinese by Amoghavajra (705–774). As its title suggests, it consisted of incantatory phrases whose recitation was designed to ensure long life.

2. These two images allude to popular analogies for the enormous amount of time encompassed by a Buddhist eon. The *kalpa* is said to be a greater span of time than it would take for a walled enclosure forty miles high and wide to be emptied of mustard seeds if only one was taken every hundred years or, alternately, the time it would take for a mountain forty *li* high to be worn down if the robe of a heavenly being brushed against it only once in a hundred years. In each case the number forty is used to reflect Montoku's age. The static nature of these depictions refers to the images that have been crafted, while also perhaps implying that time has stopped still during the ceremony.

3. The ensuing poem seems to mention the dioramas that were presented to Ninmyō repeatedly. Since the *chōka* claims that both "seeing and hearing" the tales it relates confers immortality, both the narration and the image that accompanied it appear to have been integral elements in this rite.

4. In the version of Urashimako's tale told in *Man'yōshū* poem 9: 1740 (*SNKBZ*, 7: 414–416) he marries the daughter of the sea god in the mythical land of Tokoyo and gains immortality until he opens a casket she has given him, whereupon the many years he has spent in the sea god's magical realm catch up with him and he dies of old age. Here, as in the *chōka*'s ensuing account of the Yoshino legend, the protagonist appears to fly away at some point. Overall, the account of Urashimako provided here is strikingly different from the *Man'yōshū* version, which makes no overt mention of Urashimako traveling up to the Milky Way.

5. This legend has not survived, although passing mention of it is made in a note appended to *Man'yōshū* poem 3: 385 (*SNKBZ*, 6: 223). According to this note, a man named Umashine built a fishing weir in the Yoshino River, where he caught a branch of mountain mulberry. When he brought it home, the branch became a beautiful maiden whom he then married. Judging from the reference here and in the ensuing poem, she left her mortal husband in the same manner as the celestial maiden immortalized in the Hagoromo legend.

6. A "long poem" (*chōka*) is defined as a poem with alternating lines of 5 and 7 syllables, ending with a final three lines in a 5-7-7 syllable pattern. The 211 lines of this *chōka* make it far longer than any of its predecessors.

7. Sukanabikona no Kami is a deity who is said to have had a small frame but a strong constitution. He was often associated with medicine and charms to preserve health.

8. A reference to Ninigi no Mikoto, the grandson of Amaterasu and the first mortal ruler.

9. The teachings expounded by the historical Buddha. They are specifically associated in the following passage with the regulations for monastic conduct that the sovereign is charged with enforcing.

10. There is no other mention made of this person in the histories. Judging from his clan name, he was probably a relative of Empress Kachiko, who was a political ally of Yoshifusa.

Appendix E / *Kana* Record of the Teiji Villa Poetry Match

1. Otherwise known as Princess Kaishi (d. 952), her maternal grandfather Fujiwara no Arizane also appears on her team. Her brothers mentioned in the following sentence are Princes Atsuyoshi (887–930) and Atsukata (d. 926) respectively. All three were children of Uda.

2. The poets in fact usually contributed poems to both sides at a match and were not themselves present. It is somewhat unusual that the record here affiliates them with particular teams.

3. Nothing about these two men is known except that they also contributed poems to two other poetry matches. Muneyuki is identified elsewhere as a member of the Minamoto clan (not to be confused with the more famous Minamoto no Muneyuki, who was one of Uda's half brothers). Yoshikaze is either Fujiwara no Yoshikaze or Taira no Yoshikaze, the latter being a close follower of Uda after he took the tonsure.

4. Princess Yoriko (895–936) was a daughter of Uda. As with the Left, the captain's maternal grandfather Minamoto no Noboru is also a member of her team. The princes for the Right have been identified as Uda's son Prince Atsumi (893–967) and Prince Sadakazu (875–916), a son of Seiwa. The latter's mother was a daughter of Ariwara no Yukihira.

5. "Ise Sea" (*Ise no umi*): "On Ise Sea's, sparkling shoreline, between the tides, let's harvest name-me seaweed! Let's gather shells! Let's gather shining pebbles!" (*Ise no umi no / kiyoki nagisa ni / shiogai ni / nanoriso ya tsumamu / kai ya hirowamu ya / tama ya hirowamu ya*). For the original text, see *Saibara* 10; *SNKBZ*, 42: 126. Perhaps the *suhama* accompanying this song represented just such a seaside landscape.

6. "Bamboo River" (*Takekawa*): "At Bamboo River, by the base of the bridge, by the base of the bridge, lies a flower-filled garden, *hare*! In that flower-filled garden, set me free! Oh set me free! Together with my girl." (*Takekawa no / hashi no tsume naru ya / hashi no tsume naru ya / hanazono ni / hare / hanazono ni / ware oba hanate ya / ware oba hanate ya / mezashi taguete*). For the original text, see *Saibara* 33; *SNKBZ*, 42: 143. This river is also located in Ise. Perhaps the Right's *suhama* was intended to represent

a complementary landscape to the one presented by the Left, matching one body of water (the ocean) with another (a river). "Bamboo River" was often sung at the beginning of court banquets.

7. Prince Atsumi was governor of the province of Kōzuke at the time.

8. *Nyokurōdo* (lady chamberlains) were low-ranking women officials responsible for various menial tasks connected with the palace's day-to-day operations and official events. Most were recruited from the daughters of retainers to the nobility and families associated with major shrines.

9. Judging from the emphasis given here, it appears to have been somewhat unusual at the time for women to recite the poems presented to the emperor on formal occasions.

Appendix F / *Kana* Record of Kyōgoku Consort Poetry Match

1. Unlike the previous record, this one appears to observe the conventions used in official court records more closely by beginning with the precise date of the event. The Kyōgoku Consort mentioned here was Fujiwara no Hōshi. Also known as Rokujō no Miyasundokoro, she was the eldest daughter of Tokihira and one of Uda's more important consorts, eventually holding the position of *naishi no kami* and Junior Second Rank. Prince Masaakira (920–929) was her first son.

2. Fujiwara no Tadafusa was one of Uda's chief allies at court and appears to have been closely involved with its cultural activities. In addition to his role in this and the previous poetry match, he was also famed for his skill at playing the flute, and is credited with composing the *gagaku* piece *Kochōraku*. He was appointed governor of Yamashiro province in Engi 20 (920).

3. One variant of this text specifies that the match was held at Hōshi's mansion on the Sixth Avenue.

4. The identity of this woman is not known for certain, but possibly she was Minamoto no Junshi, wife of Fujiwara no Tadahira and mother of the future regent Saneyori (900–970).

5. Fujiwara no Korehira (876–938), the third son of the poet Fujiwara no Toshiyuki, would have been forty-six at the time. Ki no Yoshimitsu was the third son of the famed scholar Ki no Haseo.

Appendix G / Preface to Poems for the Royal Procession to the Ōi River

1. The briefer *mana* preface to the *Ōigawa gyōkō waka* which precedes the *kana* preface is separated by a space from the latter in my translation. The Ōi River runs due west of the capital in the vicinity of Mount Ogura. Tonase is a waterfall descending into the western bank of the river from the foot of Mount Arashi (Storm Mountain).

2. The Double Ninth (*chōyō*) observance that took place on the ninth day of the Ninth Month was intended to renew energy and vitality. Chrysanthemum blossoms were viewed at a palace banquet as part of the ritual. The phrase "revive" (*okoshimi-*

tamawan) here portrays Uda's ritual actions as ones that invigorates the natural world as well as the celebrants.

3. Every place mentioned in this and the preceding sentence is accompanied by a poetic epithet that plays off the literal meaning of that place's name. A *katsura* (cassia) was believed to grow on the moon, hence the epithet used here to describe the Katsura River, which forms the southern extension of the Ōi River. The Ōi River itself, whose name means "Greatwell," is prefaced here by the expression *yuku mizu* (onrushing waters). "Plum Ford" (Umezu), which is preceded by the phrase "springtime" (*haru no*), was located just north of Katsura. Mount Ogura, whose name can also be taken to mean "slight darkness," is prefaced by the epithet *yūzukuyo* (twilight moon). It lies on the eastern side of the Ōi River.

4. The first eight topics mentioned here are arranged in complementary pairs of natural phenomena: the first referring to the landscape (in the form of mountains and rivers); the second to plants (leaves and blossoms), the third to animals (cranes and monkeys), and the fourth to birds in flight (geese and gulls). The final image of a long-lived pine tree probably alludes to poems praying for the emperor's long life, or possibly Tsurayuki himself.

Appendix H / Mana Preface to the *Kokinshū*

1. This is the only time that the word for "heart" appears in the entire Mana Preface. The description of poetry's genesis is taken from a letter by Bo Juyi (*Hakushi monjū*, 28; *SKT*, 101: 347).

2. These two functions of poetry are taken from the *Maoshi zhengyi* commentary to the Great Preface (*Shisan jing zhushu*, 270).

3. The terms used here for the six principles of *feng*, *fu*, *bi*, *xing*, *fu*, *ya*, and *song* departs somewhat from Leonard Grzanka's translation in Laurel Rodd and Mary Henkenius, *Kokinshū*, 379. Grzanka renders the six principles as "Suasive," "Narration," "Analogy," "Evocative Imagery," "Elegantia," and "Eulogies," respectively. In his translation of the Great Preface, Stephen Owen renders them as "Airs," "exposition," "comparison," "affective image," "Odes," and "Hymns" (*Readings in Chinese Literary Thought*, 45), with the capitalized terms referring to genres as opposed to rhetorical modes. David Knechtges's translation of the six principles as they appear in the preface to the *Wenxuan*, uses Latinate terms and treats them as rhetorical methods for conveying moral and political messages (*Wenxuan or Selections of Refined Literature*, 74). My translation seeks to suggest social contexts and purposes for the first, fifth, and sixth principles in particular.

4. This description of song as a natural phenomenon is possibly derived from a passage in the *Maoshi zhengyi* where birds are said to dance and sing in the same manner as people (*Shisan jing zhushu*, 270).

5. This historical account of poetry appears to be derived from the preface to the *Wenxuan*, where a pristine state of simplicity is said to have preceded the development of writing and literature (Knechtges, *Wenxuan or Selections of Refined Literature*, 73).

6. 31-syllable envoy verses (*hanka*) were attached to the end of longer *chōka* poems. This is not the case with Susanoo's poem, however. Insofar as it tends to repeat the words of its longer predecessor, however, *hanka* poems can be considered "responses" to the former in the manner of harmonizing verse, which is perhaps why the term is used here to refer to the first 31-syllable *waka*.

7. This is a reference to the deities Hikohohodemi no Mikoto and Toyotama Hime who exchange poems in the *Nihon shoki* affirming their regard for one another after they have parted ways, giving them the name *age uta* (praise songs). For the passage in question, see *SNKBZ*, 2: 178-181. This is the first pair of songs in the *Nihon shoki* in which the second verse is a response to the first.

8. At the time, the "age of mortals" was seen as beginning either with Amaterasu or Emperor Jimmu, depending on the way the *Nihon shoki* was interpreted. The latter is probably more likely, given that current versions of the history end the age of the gods with the story of Hikohohodemi no Mikoto and Toyotama Hime, whose grandchild becomes the first human ruler.

9. The first three metrical forms of poetry can be found in both the *Man'yōshū* and *Kokinshū*. The final verse form *konponka* does not appear anywhere else. It is assumed to be shorter than the other forms, possibly consisting of three lines in the manner of a *kata uta* (half song). Another possibility is that it corresponds to the form of poetry known as *hitamoto* in the *Kakyō hyōshiki*.

10. For a discussion of the Naniwazu poem, see note 5 in my translation of the Kana Preface. The story connected with the second poem can be found in the *Nihon shoki*, the *Nihon ryōiki* (*Record of Miraculous Events in Japan*, ca. 822), and in the *Shūi wakashū* anthology. According to these sources, it was composed by a beggar and addressed to Shōtoku Taishi out of gratitude for having received a robe from the prince regent. The verse appears as poem 1351 in the *Shūi wakashū*: "Only when the Tomi stream / in Ikaruga / ceases to flow / will my lord's name / ever be forgotten." (*Ikaruga ya / Tomi no ogawa no / taeba koso / waga ōkimi no / mina o wasureme*). Note that this poem is a response to a previous one by Shōtoku Taishi. For the full text of both poems, see *SNKBT*, 7: 397.

11. Prince Ōtsu (663–686) was the third son of Emperor Temmu. Although his *shi* poems are among the earliest written in Japan, there are others by earlier figures in the first anthology the *Kaifūsō*. In claiming he began the custom of composing poetry in literary Chinese, the Mana Preface is drawing on the brief biography provided for him in the *Nihon shoki* (Shuchō 1/10/3; *SNKBZ*, 4: 477). As a result of these claims, the preface to the *Kaifūsō* is often ascribed to him.

12. The number given here is usually rendered as "two or three," but it can also be "six," a reading that lends more specificity to the significance of the six poets who are mentioned in the following section.

13. Henjō here is named after the Kazan region where the temple with which he was affiliated was located.

14. Fun'ya no Yasuhide's name has been altered here to conform to literary Chinese

conventions, possibly as a way of marking his status as a literati and a scholar affiliated with the university. The description of a merchant wearing colorful robes (as opposed to the yellow or dark grey colors reserved for commoners) implies an infringement on social distinctions.

15. Sōtori Hime was a consort of the legendary fifth-century emperor Ingyō. For a discussion of her significance here, see Chapter 4.

16. Sarumaru is a legendary figure whose historical circumstances remain unknown.

17. The phrase "ten reigns and a hundred years" is adopted from the *Wenxuan* and not to be taken literally. The ascription of the *Man'yōshū* to Heizei was often made in the Heian period.

18. The author here is possibly referring to the reputations of these two men presented in the official historical chronicles. The obituary for Ono no Takamura (802–852) in the *Montoku jitsuroku* praises him for his skill at writing in literary Chinese (Ninju 2/12/22; *KST*, 3: 3: 43), while the *Sandai jitsuroku* singles out Ariwara no Yukihira for his moral rectitude (Ninna 2/5/12; *KST*, 4: 609–610). Neither history makes any mention of *waka* in relation to the two.

19. This phrase observes the conventions for praising emperors used in the official histories.

20. A similar phrase appears in the Kana Preface. In both cases, it echoes a famous sentence in *Analects* 9: 5 (*SKT*, 1: 198–199) in which Confucius lauds the cultural legacy (*wen*) of King Wen (1099–1050 B.C.E.), the legendary founder of the Zhou dynasty, for continuing after his death.

21. The fact that Tsurayuki's name heads the final sentence suggests that the first senior editor Ki no Tomonori had already passed away at the time the Mana Preface was presented. The actual writer of the preface would not necessarily have been the person who formally addresses the emperor in it.

Appendix I / Kana Preface to the *Kokinshū*

1. My translation omits the later interpolated commentary included in most modern versions. In my rendering of the opening line, I have sought to suggest the alternate reading of *hito no kokoro* (people's hearts) as *hitotsu kokoro* (the loyal subject's devoted heart).

2. According to the *Nihon shoki*, Shitateru Hime was the daughter of a local deity who married Amewaka no Miko when the latter descended from Heaven to subdue the Earth. After Prince Amewaka was executed for failing to return to Heaven, Shitateru Hime composed a song praising the beauty of her elder brother Ajisukitakahikone no Kami at the funeral of her husband (*SNKBZ*, 2: 126–127).

3. The association between Susanoo no Mikoto and the age of mortals here differs somewhat from the chronology presented in the *Nihon shoki* and the Mana Preface. In some cases, however, the "age of the gods" was associated with the first seven generations of deities prior to Amaterasu no Ōmikami and her brother.

4. This sentence alludes to two lines from a poem by Bo Juyi in *Hakushi monjū*, Book 22; *SKT*, 101: 3.

5. Although it is nowhere specified in the Kana Preface, most scholars have followed the interpolated commentary and taken this as a reference to the reign of Nintoku, whose palace was situated at Naniwazu in present-day Ōsaka. The Naniwazu poem, which is provided later as an example of *soe uta* (the first of the six *sama*) does not appear in any other extant source. According to the interpolated commentary, the Paekche scholar Wani composed this poem to urge Nintoku to ascend the throne. The *Nihon shoki* relates that he and his younger brother deferred the throne to one another for three years until the latter's death.

6. This verse has been identified as *Man'yōshū* poem 16: 3807 (*SNKBZ*, 9: 102–103): "I do not think it to be / a heart as shallow / as the mountain well / whose reflection reveals / Mount Asaka." (*Asaka yama / kage sae miyuru / yama no i no / asaki kokoro o / waga omowanaku ni*). According to tradition, the woman composed this poem in order to mollify a royal prince who she was serving at a banquet held in his honor by the governor of Michinoku.

7. For an explanation of my use of different fonts in translating these poems, see Chapter 4.

8. This is the only one of the example poems to appear in another extant text, in this case as the anonymous poem 712 in the Longing section of the *Kokinshū* (*SNKBZ*, 11: 274).

9. This example poem is an adaptation of a *saibara* sung by guests at a banquet in praise of their host (*SNKBZ*, 42: 151). Some commentators take the phrase *mitsuba yotsuba ni* to refer to the hall's ridgepoles.

10. The verb used here to describe the allegorical symbolism of blossom imagery (*sou*) is related to the term *soe uta* used to describe the first of the six *sama*.

11. The following paragraph concerns social occasions on which poems are addressed to people in situations other than annual court banquets. Because each example phrase refers to a poem or poems that appear in the *Kokinshū*, I have sought to specify the social context implied by the source poem(s) in my translation. In each case, the phrases appear to form complementary pairings.

12. These two example phrases are of tropes used to praise a member of the royal family. The first phrase refers to poem 343 (*SNKBZ*, 11: 148), which opens the Blessings section of the anthology. The second phrase alludes to poem 966 (*SNKBZ*, 11: 365), in the Miscellaneous Verse section, which was composed as an entreaty to Crown Prince Yasuakira, and to poem 1095 (*SNKBZ*, 11: 415), which is an *azuma uta* from Hitachi that was probably sung as part of a court ritual, perhaps at an enthronement rite.

13. These phrases again form a pair. The first refers to poem 865 (*SNKBZ*, 11: 329), an anonymous song from the first scroll of Miscellaneous Verse. The third poem in this scroll, it occupies a portion of the anthology which chiefly concerns expressions of thanks for favors received from a superior. The second phrase refers to poem 1069 (*SNKBZ*, 11: 407), the first of the ritual songs in Scroll 20. It is identified there as a

ōnaobi no uta, which traditionally inaugurated the banquet following a rite worshiping some divinity.

14. These phrases form a pair referring to unrequited longing for lovers and missing distant friends respectively. The first phrase can be found in poem 534 (*SNKBZ*, 11:215), which is an anonymous song in Longing, and the second in 1028 (*SNKBZ*, 11: 393) which is a *haikai* verse by Ki no Menoto. The image of a pine cricket can be found in a series of four anonymous Autumn verses (poems 200–203; *SNKBZ*, 11: 99–100).

15. This pairing suggests a long-lived couple, with the Suminoe pine (referred to as *hime matsu* or "princess pine") constituting the female partner. The pines of Takasago and Suminoe are mentioned in two separate pairs of poems adjacent to one another in the first scroll of Miscellaneous Verse: poems 908–909 (*SNKBZ*, 11: 343–344) and 905–906 (*SNKBZ*, 11: 343) respectively. This placement possibly explains the Kana Preface's description of them as "twined together" (*aioi*). Poem 909 by Fujiwara no Okikaze is the only one in this group which is not anonymous. All four poems emphasize the distance between the long-lived pines and the mortals who address them.

16. In contrast to the long-lived marriage suggested in the preceding passage, the two phrases here point to men and women who find it increasingly difficult to attract a partner as their physical charms decline with age. The first phrase references poem 889 (*SNKBZ*, 11: 338), an anonymous composition in the first scroll of Miscellaneous Verse that bemoans the loss of male virility. The second phrase is usually seen as referencing poem 1016 (*SNKBZ*, 11: 390), a *haikai* verse in the Miscellaneous Forms scroll by the priest Henjō.

17. The first phrase alludes to a series of Spring verses beginning with poem 104 (*SNKBZ*, 11: 66) which describe scattering blossoms. The second phrase references a series of Autumn verses beginning with poem 281 (*SNKBZ*, 11: 127) describing scattering autumn foliage.

18. In contrast to the brevity of seasonal phenomena in the previous pairing, this one expresses the brevity of human life. Taken together, they progress from old age to death. The first phrase references poem 460 (*SNKBZ*, 11: 193), a *mono no na* by Tsurayuki. The images of dew and foam in the second phrase refer respectively to poems 860 (*SNKBZ*, 11: 326) in Lamentations by Fujiwara no Koremoto and 827 (*SNKBZ*, 11: 312) by Tomonori near the end of Longing.

19. This first part of this phrase references poem 888 (*SNKBZ*, 11: 337), an anonymous verse from the first scroll of Miscellaneous Verse. The second part of this passage corresponds to a sequence of verses in the second scroll of the same section, beginning with anonymous poem 981 (*SNKBZ*, 11: 371), that describe people who have left capital society.

20. In this pair, fidelity is contrasted to the fickleness of the preceding section. The first phrase references an *azuma uta* from Scroll 20 (poem 1093; *SNKBZ*, 11: 414). The second phrase echoes an anonymous verse from the first scroll of Miscellaneous Verse (poem 887; *SNKBZ*, 11: 337). This second example is perhaps related to the "old song" Kammu cites in his exchange with Myōshin (see Chapter 1).

21. In this pair, a neglected lover is contrasted with the declarations of fidelity made in the preceding pair of poems. The first phrase appears in an anonymous verse from Autumn (poem 220; *SNKBZ*, 11: 105). The second phrase alludes to an anonymous verse from the final scroll of the Longing section (poem 761; *SNKBZ*, 11: 292).

22. The first phrase echoes poem 958 in the second scroll of Miscellaneous Verse (*SNKBZ*, 11: 362). The second one refers to the very last poem in Longing (poem 828; *SNKBZ*, 11: 312).

23. Both of these phrases contrast present times with the situation expressed in earlier poems. The first phrase refers to poems 534 (*SNKBZ*, 11: 215) and 1028 (*SNKBZ*, 11: 393). The trope of the dilapidated Nagara Bridge is used to bewail the speaker's age in an anonymous song found in the first scroll of Miscellaneous Verse and in a *haikai* verse by Lady Ise (poem 1051; *SNKBZ*, 11:400).

Glossary

Abe no Nakamaro	阿部仲麻呂	Atsumi	敦実
Abe no Yoshihito	阿部吉人	Atsuyoshi	敦慶
agaseko	吾背子	Ausaka	逢坂
age uta	挙歌	*Awazu kuni no Ōzu shozu*	阿波国大豆処図
aishō no uta	哀傷歌		
Ajisukitakahikone no Kami	味耜高彦根神	*aya*	文
		ayame	文目
Akashi	明石	*ayamegusa*	菖蒲草
Akitsushima	秋津洲	*azana*	字
akō	阿衡	Azuma	東
Amaterasu no Ōmikami	天照大御神	*azuma asobi no uta*	東遊歌
Amewaka Miko	天稚御子	*Azuma kudari*	東下り
aouma no sechie	白馬節会	*azuma kuni no uta*	東国歌
Arashiyama	嵐山	*azuma uta*	東歌
aratama	荒魂		
Ariwara no Motokata	在原元方	*ba*	場
Ariwara no Narihira	在原業平	Ban	班
Ariwara no Tomoyuki	在原友于	*banzai*	万歳
Ariwara no Yukihira	在原行平	*benji*	本紀
ashide	葦手	*bixing*	比興
Asakayama	安積山	Bizen	備前
asobi	遊	*Bo Juyi*	白居易
ason	朝臣	*budate*	部立
Asuka	飛鳥	*Bunka shūreishū*	文華秀麗集
Atsuhito	敦仁	*Bunkyō hifuron*	文鏡秘府論
Atsukata	敦固	Bunrin	文琳

buntai	文体	*ei*	詠
byōbu e uta	屏風絵歌	Emishi	蝦夷
byōbu uta	屏風歌	*en*	艶
		Enchō	延長
Cao Pi	曹丕	En'en	延円
Chang'an	長安	Engi	延喜
chiyo	千代	Engi gyohon	延喜御本
chō	帖	*Engi igo shi jo*	延喜以後 詩序
chōga	朝賀	*Engi kyaku*	延喜格
Chōhō	長保	*Engi shiki*	延喜式
chōka	長歌	Enryaku	延暦
chōkin no miyuki	朝覲行幸		
chokusenshū	勅撰集	*Fayan*	法言
Chōya gunzai	朝野群載	*feng*	風
chōyō	重陽	*fu*	賦
Chuci	楚辞	*fudoki*	風土記
		Fuji	富士
dai	題	*fujibakama*	藤袴
Daidō	大同	Fujiwara	藤原
Daigaku	大学	Fujiwara no Akirakeiko	藤原明子
Daigo	醍醐	Fujiwara no Arizane	藤原有実
Daigo tennō gyoki	醍醐天皇御記	Fujiwara no Atsuko	藤原温子
Daigokuden	大極殿	Fujiwara no Fuyutsugu	藤原冬嗣
daikyaku	題脚	Fujiwara no Hōshi	藤原褒子
daimoku	題目	Fujiwara no Inshi	藤原胤子
dainagon	大納言	Fujiwara no Kaneie	藤原兼家
Dairi shiki	内裏式	Fujiwara no Kanesuke	藤原兼輔
Dajōkan	太政官	Fujiwara no Kanshi	藤原歓子
dakuten	濁点	Fujiwara no Kenshō	藤原顕昭
Danjo kon'in fu	男女婚姻賦	Fujiwara no Kintō	藤原公任
Daxu	大序	Fujiwara no Kiyosuke	藤原清輔
Dezongdi	徳宗帝	Fujiwara no Korehira	藤原伊衡
darani	陀羅尼	Fujiwara no Koremoto	藤原惟幹
dōji igi	同字異義	Fujiwara no Kunitsune	藤原国経
dōon igi	同音異義	Fujiwara no Kusuko	藤原薬子
		Fujiwara no Michinaga	藤原道長
ebisu uta	夷歌	Fujiwara no Miyoshi	藤原三善
Egyō hōshi shū	恵慶法師集	Fujiwara no Moromasa	藤原師伊

Fujiwara no Mototsune 藤原基経
Fujiwara no Nakahira 藤原仲平
Fujiwara no Okikaze 藤原興風
Fujiwara no Sadakata 藤原定方
Fujiwara no Sadakuni 藤原定国
Fujiwara no Sanesuke 藤原実資
Fujiwara no Saneyori 藤原実頼
Fujiwara no Shunzei 藤原俊成
Fujiwara no Sonondo 藤原園人
Fujiwara no Sugane 藤原菅根
Fujiwara no Sumitomo 藤原純友
Fujiwara no Tadafusa 藤原忠房
Fujiwara no Tadahira 藤原忠平
Fujiwara no Takafuji 藤原高藤
Fujiwara no Takaiko 藤原高子
Fujiwara no Teika 藤原定家
Fujiwara no Tokihira 藤原時平
Fujiwara no Toshiyuki 藤原敏行
Fujiwara no Tsugutada 藤原継縄
Fujiwara no Yasuko 藤原穏子
Fujiwara no Yoritada 藤原頼忠
Fujiwara no Yoruka 藤原因香
Fujiwara no Yoshifusa 藤原良房
Fujiwara no Yukinari 藤原行成
Fukurozōshi 袋草子
fuku-shudai 副主題
Fun'ya no Yasuhide 文屋康秀
furugoto 古言 or 古事
furumichi 古道
Fusō ryakki 扶桑略記

ga 賀
ga no uta 賀歌
gagaku 雅楽
Gangyō 元慶
ganying 感応
Geibun ruijū 芸文類聚
Genji monogatari 源氏物語
Gen'ei-bon 元永本
gishōka 戯笑歌
Gonki 権記
Go-Reizei 後冷泉
goryaku no sō 御暦の奏
Gosen wakashū 後撰和歌集
Gosho-dokoro no azukari 御書所預
Guanshan yue 関山月
Gujin shuping 古今書評
Guofeng 国風

hadai 破題
Hagoromo 羽衣
haikai 誹諧
Hakushi monjū 白氏文集
Han 漢
Han Feizi 韓非子
hana no en 花宴
hana no en no sechi 花宴節
Hanazono no safu gyohon 花園左府御本
handen 班田
hanka 反歌
Hanshi 斑子
hare 晴れ
Harima 播磨
Hayabusawake 隼総別
hayashi kotoba 囃子詞
Hayato 隼人
hayato-shi no kami 隼人司正
he 和
Heguri no Kazemaro 平群賀是麻呂
Heian chūki 平安中期
Heian kōki 平安後期
Heian shoki 平安初期
Heiankyō 平安京
Heizei 平城
Henjō 遍昭
Higyōsha 飛香舎

Hikohime shiki	孫姫式
Hikohohodemi no Mikoto	彦火火出見尊
hinaburi	夷曲
hinami no niezukai	日次贄使
hi no tameshi	氷の様
Hitachi	常陸
Hitachi fudoki	常陸風土記
hitamoto	双本
hito	人
hito no kokoro	人の心
hito no yo	人代
hitotsu kokoro	一つ心
hiyu	譬喩
Hōjōki	方丈記
hōken	奉献
hōkō	法皇
Hokuzanshō	北山抄
Honchō monzui	本朝文粋
hōwa	奉和
hote	最手
Huang	黄
Hyōe	兵衛
hyōgen	表現
ie	家
Ikaruga	斑鳩
imina	諱
in	院
Inaba	因幡
Inari	稲荷
Ingyō	允恭
Isayama no Fumitsugu	勇山文継
Ise monogatari	伊勢物語
Ise no umi	伊勢海
Ise-shū	伊勢集
Iyo	伊予
Izanagi	伊邪那岐

Izanami	伊邪那美
Izumi	和泉
Izumo	出雲
Jiang	江
Jijūden	仁寿殿
Jikiro	直廬
Jimmu	神武
Jingikan	神祇官
jintaku no sai	人宅祭
jogaku	女楽
Jōgan	貞観
Jōgan shiki	貞観式
jokan	女官
jokotoba	序詞
jōshi	上巳
Jōwa	承和
jueju	絶句
Jūkan-bon	十巻本
jukkai	述懐
Junna	淳和
kabane	姓
kachō no tsukai	花鳥之使
kadan	歌壇
kado	門
Kagenori	景式
Kagerō nikki	蜻蛉日記
kagura uta	神楽歌
Kai	甲斐
Kaifūsō	懐風藻
Kaishi	誨子
Kajō	嘉祥
kakekotoba	掛詞
Kakinomoto no Hitomaro	柿本人麻呂
Kakyō hyōshiki	歌経標式
kami	神

kami no ku	上句	*kibutsu chinshi*	寄物陳思
kami no yo	神世	*kiden*	紀伝
Kammu	桓武	*kimi*	君
Kamo	賀茂	Kinai	畿内
Kamo no Chōmei	鴨長明	*Kindai shūka*	近代秀歌
Kamo no Mabuchi	賀茂真淵	*kinka*	琴歌
kana	仮名	*Kinkafu*	琴歌譜
kanajo	仮名序	Ki no Haseo	紀長谷雄
kanden	官田	Ki no Menoto	紀乳母
Kanemi	兼覧	Ki no Natora	紀名虎
Kannon	観音	Ki no Shizuko	紀静子
kanpaku	関白	Ki no Tomonori	紀友則
Kanpyō	寛平	Ki no Tsurayuki	紀貫之
Kanpyō no ōntoki kisai no miya no uta-awase	寛平御時后宮歌合	Ki no Yoshimitsu	紀淑光
		kiryo no uta	羇旅歌
Kara	唐	Kisen	喜撰
kara zu	唐図	Kitano	北野
kashū	家集	*kiyoge*	清げ
Kasuga	春日	Kiyomichi	きよみち
kata uta	片歌	Kiyosuke-bon	清輔本
katami	形見	Kiyotsura	清貫
Katano	交野	*kochōhai*	小朝拝
kataribe	語部	*Kochōraku*	胡蝶楽
kataudo	方人	*kodai*	古代
katsura	桂	Kōen	皇円
Kaya no Toyotoshi	賀陽豊年	Kōfuku-ji	興福寺
kayō	歌謡	*Kogo shūi*	古語拾遺
Kazan	華山	*kohitsu-gire*	古筆切れ
Kazan'in	花山院	*koi*	恋
kazashi	指頭	*kōi*	更衣
ke	褻	*koi no uta*	恋歌
kei	経	*Kokin wakashū*	古今和歌集
Keichū	契沖	*Kokin wakashū mokuroku*	古今和歌集目録
Keikokushū	経国集	*Kokin wakashū uchigiki*	古今和歌集打聞
Keiun	慶雲	*Kokin yozaishō*	古今余材抄
Kenpō jūshichi jō	憲法十七条	*Kokinshū*	古今集
Khitan	契丹	*Kokinshū jo chū*	古今集序注

Kōkō	光孝
kokoro	心
Kōkyū	後宮
koma-mukae	駒迎え
Kongō jumyō darani-kyō	金剛寿命陀羅尼経
Kong Yingda	孔穎達
Kōnin	弘仁
Konjaku monogatari-shū	今昔物語集
Konmei-chi no shōji	昆明池障子
Konoefu	近衛府
konpon	混本
Korai fūteishō	古来風躰抄
Korenori	是則
Koresada	是貞
Koretada	是忠
Koretaka	惟喬
Koryo	駒麗
Kose no Hirotaka	巨勢広貴
Kose no Kanaoka	巨勢金岡
kōshi	講師
Koshi no kuni	越国
koto no ha	言の葉
kotobagaki	詞書
kotodama	言霊
kotogaki	事書
koyomi	暦
Kōzuke	上野
ku	句
Kudai waka	句題和歌
Kudara no Kawanari	百済川成
Kudara no Kokishi Myōshin	百済王明信
Kujō	九条
Kūkai	空海
Kume uta	久米歌
kunimi	国見
Kurōdo-dokoro	蔵人所
kurōdo no tō	蔵人頭
Kurōdo shiki	蔵人式
Kuwahara no Haraaka	桑原腹赤
kyō	京
kyōdōtai	共同体
Kyōgoku no miyasundokoro Hōshi no uta-awase	京極御息所褒子歌合
kyokuen	曲宴
kyokusui no en	曲水宴
Kyūshū	九州
Laozi	老子
lei	類
leishu	類書
li	礼
Li Sao	離騒
Liang	梁
Liang Wudi	梁武帝
liezhuan	列伝
Liji	礼記
liuhe	六合
Lu Ji	陸機
Lunwen	論文
Lunyu	論語
Luo	洛
Luoyang	洛陽
Maboroshi	幻
machi	町
Makura no sōshi	枕草子
mana	真名
manajo	真名序
Man'yō daishōki	万葉代匠記
Man'yōshū	万葉集
Maoshi zhengyi	毛詩正義

Masaakira 雅明
Masaoka Shiki 正岡子規
Masatsune-bon 雅経本
masurao-buri 益荒男振り
matsurigoto no itoma 政の暇
Mibu no Tadamine 壬生忠岑
Michitsuna no haha 道綱の母
Midō kanpakki 御堂関白記
Mikawa 三河
mikotomochi 命持 / 宰 / 司
Minabuchi no Hirosada 淵弘貞
Minamoto no Junshi 源順子
Minamoto no Noboru 源昇
Minamoto no Sane 源実
Minamoto no Shitagō 源順
Minamoto no Tōru 源融
Minamoto no Toshikata 源俊賢
Minamoto noYoshiari 源能有
Minatsuki no tsugomori 水無月の晦
misogi 禊
Mitarashi 御手洗
mitate 見立て
Mitsune-shū 躬恒集
miyako 都
miyasundokoro 御息所
Mizushi-dokoro 御厨子所
Mochizuki 望月
moji 文字
monjō 文章
monjō keikoku 文章経国
monnin 文人
mono 物
mono no na 物名
Montoku 文徳
Montoku jitsuroku 文徳実録
moto no ku 本句
motomego uta 求子歌
Motoori Norinaga 本居宣長
Motoyasu 本康
Mumyōshō 無名抄
Mumyōzōshi 無名草子
Muneyuki 致行
Murakami 村上
Musashino 武蔵野
myōbu 名簿

Nagara 長柄
Nagatsuki no tsugomori no hi 長月の晦の日
Nagisa 渚
naien 内宴
Naiki-dokoro 内記所
Naikyōbō 内教房
Naikyōbō no Machi 内教房町
nairan 内覧
naishi no kami 尚侍
naishi no suke 典侍
naizen no tenzen 内膳典膳
Nakao 仲雄
Nakatomi 中臣
Naniwazu 難波津
Nara 奈良
natori 名取り
natsu no sōmon 夏相聞
Nenjū gyōji goshōji no fumi 年中行事御障子文
ne no hi 子の日
Nihon 日本
Nihon kiryaku 日本紀略
Nihon kōki 日本後紀
Nihon ryōiki 日本霊異記
Nihon shoki 日本書紀
Nihongi kyōen waka 日本紀竟宴和歌
nikitama 和魂

Ninigi no Mikoto	邇邇芸命
Ninjū	仁寿
Ninmyō	仁明
Ninna	仁和
Ninna-ji	仁和寺
Nintoku	仁徳
niru mono	似物
Nōin	能因
Nonaka	野中
norito	祝詞
nuidono no suke	縫殿助
nyokurōdo	女蔵人
Ōe no Asatsuna	大江朝綱
Ōe no Chisato	大江千里
Ōe no Masahira	大江匡衡
Ogura	小倉
Ōharano	大原野
Ōigawa gyōkō waka no jo	大井川行幸和歌序
Okikaze-shū	興風集
Ōmi	近江
ominaeshi	女郎花
omoi	思
ōmu uta	御歌
Ō no Yasumaro	多安
ōnaobi no uta	大直毘歌
onna-e	女絵
onna no uta	女の歌
Ono no Komachi	小野小町
Ono no kōtaigōgū no gyohon	小野皇太后宮御本
Ono no Minemori	小野岑守
Ono no Takamura	小野篁
Ononomiya	小野宮
onritsu	音律
Osakabe	忍壁
ōsei	応制
Ōshikōchi no Mitsune	凡河内躬恒
ōshō	応詔
osu kuni	食す国
Ōtenmon	大天門
otoko no uta	男の歌
Ōtomo no Kuronushi	大友黒主
Otowa	音羽
Ōtsu	大津
ōuta	大歌
Ōuta-dokoro	大歌所
Paekche	百済
Parhae	渤海
qi	気
Qi	斉
Rakuyō	洛陽
reihon	零本
reki hakase	暦博士
rekishi monogatari	歴史物語
renga	連歌
rentaikei	連体形
ribetsu no uta	離別歌
ritsu	律
ritsuryō	律令
rokkasen jidai	六歌仙時代
Rokujō no Miyasundokoro	六条御息所
Ruijū kokushi	類聚国史
Ryō no gige	令義解
Ryōunshū	凌雲集
sachū	左註
Sadakazu	貞数
Saga	嵯峨
saibara	催馬楽
Saijibu	歳時部
Saikyūki	西宮記

sakaki 榊
sakashima-goto 倒語
Sakuteiki 作庭記
Sandai jitsuroku 三代実録
Sanjō Sadaijin den senzai no uta-awase 三条左大臣殿前栽歌合
Sanjō no Machi 三条町
Sanuki 讃岐
Sarumaru 猿丸
sechien 節宴
sechiroku 節禄
sedōka 旋頭歌
sei 声
Sei Shōnagon 清少納言
seigi 晴儀
Seiryōden 清涼殿
Seiwa 清和
sekiten 釈奠
sen 扇
senmyō 宣命
senmyōgaki 宣命書
senshū 撰集
senzai awase 前栽合
Senzai wakashū 千載和歌集
sesshō 摂政
Settsu 摂津
shansui 山水
shi 詩
Shigeno no Sadanushi 滋野貞主
shihōhai 四方拝
Shiji 史記
Shijing 詩経
shiki 私記
shiki 式
shiki no uta 四季歌
shikishi 色紙
Shimada no Yoshiomi 嶋田良臣
shimeno 標野
shimo no ku 下句
Shimotsufusa 下総
Shin kokin wakashū 新古今和歌集
Shingon 真言
shinkō 新皇
Shinsen-en 神泉苑
Shinsen jikyō 新撰字鏡
Shinsen man'yōshū 新撰万葉集
Shinshoku kokin wakashū 新続古今和歌集
Shipin 詩品
Shirome 白女
Shishinden 紫宸殿
Shitateru Hime 下照姫
Shoekishō 周易抄
shōen 荘園
shōhon 抄本
shōjutsu shinsho 正述心緒
Shoku kokin wakashū 続古今和歌集
Shoku man'yōshū 続万葉集
Shoku nihongi 続日本紀
Shoku nihon kōki 続日本後記
Shōkyōden 承香殿
Shōmu 聖武
Shōshi 彰子
Shōtai 昌泰
shōten 声点
shōtenbon 声点本
Shōtoku Taishi 聖徳太子
Shōyūki 小右記
shudai 主題
Shūi wakashū 拾遺和歌集
Shūishō chū 拾遺抄註
Shun 舜
Shungen 春源
Shun'ōten 春鶯囀
Shunrai zuinō 俊頼随脳
Shunzei-bon 俊成本

shūshikei	終止形	Tang	唐
shushō	首唱	*tanka*	短歌
Silla	新羅	*tansaku*	短冊
soe uta	諷歌	*tatsu*	裁つ
Sōgi	宗祇	Tatsuta	竜田
sokutai	束帯	*taoyame-buri*	手弱女振り
Somedono	染殿	Teiji-in	亭子院
song	頌	*Teiji-in no uta-awase*	亭子院歌合
sōranbon	奏覧本	Teika-bon	定家本
Sosei	素性	*Teiōbu*	帝王部
Sotōri Hime	衣通姫	Teishi	禎子
sue no ku	末句	*Teishin kōki*	貞信公記
Sugawara no Kiyoyoshi	菅原清公	Temmu	天武
Sugawara no Michizane	菅原道真	Tenchi	天智
suhama	州浜	Tenchō	天長
Sui	隋	Tenjō no Ma	殿上間
Sukanabikona no kami	少彦名神	*tenjō no warawa*	殿上童
Sukemichi	如道	*tenjōbito*	殿上人
suki	主基	Tenpyō hōji	天平宝字
Suma	須磨	*Tentoku dairi uta-awase*	天徳内裏歌合
sumai no tsukasa	相撲司	*ti*	躰
Sumida	隅田	*tō*	頭
Suminoe	住江	Tōdai-ji	東大寺
sumō	相撲	Tōji	東寺
Susanoo no Mikoto	素盞烏尊	*tōka*	踏歌
Suzaku-in	朱雀院	*tokoro*	所
		Tokoyo	常世
Tachibana no Kachiko	橘嘉智子	*toku*	徳
Tadamine-shū	忠岑集	Tomi-no-ogawa	富緒河
Taira no Masakado	平将門	Tonase	戸無瀬
Taira no Tadanori	平忠度	*tono*	殿
Tajima	但馬	*torimono*	取物
Takasago	高砂	*Tosa nikki*	土佐日記
Takekawa	竹河	*toshi no hate*	年のはて
Tamuke	手向け	Toyo-oka Hime	豊岡姫
Tanabata	七夕	Toyotama Hime	豊玉姫
tandai	探題	*tsugomori*	晦

Tsukuba	筑波	*Wenxuan*	文選
tsukurimono	作り物	*wu*	誤
Tsurayuki-shū	貫之集		
Tsurezuregusa	徒然草	*xangbiaowen*	上表文
		Xiao Tong	蕭統
Uchi no Gosho-dokoro	内御書所	*Xijing fu*	西京賦
uchi no gosho-dokoro no azukari	内御書所預	*xing*	興
Uda	宇多	*ya*	雅
Uda tennō shinki	宇多天皇宸記	Yamabe no Akahito	山部赤人
Uda-in	宇多院	*yamagata*	山形
ugi	雨儀	Yamashiro	山城
uguisu	鶯	Yamato	大和 or 倭
Uji	宇治	*yamato no shi*	倭詩
Umashine	味稲	*yamato uta*	倭歌
Umezu	梅津	*yamato-e*	大和絵
uneme	釆女	Yamazaki	山崎
unohana	卯の花	*yamazato*	山里
Urashimako	浦島子	Yang Xiong	楊雄
urate	占手	Yangzhou	楊州
uta	歌	Yao	堯
uta nushi	歌主	Yasuakira	保明
uta-awase	歌合	Yasuno no Fumitsugu	安野文継
utagaki	歌垣	*Yayoi no tsugomori*	弥生の晦
utage	宴	*yi*	疑
utayomi	歌よみ	*Yijing*	易経
		ying	応
wa	和	*yin-yang*	陰陽
wagimoko	我妹子	Yodo	淀
waka	和歌	Yōmeimon'in-bon	陽明門院本
waka no meishi	和歌名士	*yomibito*	読人
Waka shogaku shō	和歌初学抄	*yomikudashi*	読み下し
Wani	王仁	*yomi-uta*	余美歌
waza kurabe	技競	*yo no naka*	世の中
Wei Wendi	魏文帝	Yoriko	依子
wen	文	*Yorimoto-shū*	頼基集
Wenfu	文賦	Yoshibuchi no Aisei	善淵愛成

Yoshida Kenkō 吉田兼好
Yoshikaze 好風
Yoshimine no Tsunenari 良岑経也
Yoshimine no Yasuyo 良岑安世
Yoshino 吉野
Yoshino no Kuzu 吉野国巣
Yōzei 陽成
Yuefu 楽府
yuefu 楽府
Yueji 楽記
yuki 悠紀
yūsoku kojitsu 有職故実

zattei no uta 雑躰歌
zhengming 正名
Zhou 周
Zhuangzi 荘子
zō no uta 雑歌
zōgaku 雑楽

Works Cited

Primary Sources

Bunka shūreishū. In Kojima Noriyuki, ed., *NKBT*, vol. 69 (1964).
Chōya gunsai. *KST*, vol. 29, pt. 1 (1938).
Daigo tennō gyoki. In *ST*, vol. 1 (1965).
Daxu. In Stephen Owen, *Readings in Chinese Literary Thought*. Cambridge, MA: Harvard Council on East Asian Studies, 1992.
Egyō hōshi shū. In *KT*, vol. 3, pt. 1 (1985).
Engi shiki. *KST*, vol. 26 (1965).
Fukurozōshi. Fujioka Tadaharu, ed., *SNKBT*, vol. 29 (1995).
Fusō ryakki. *KST*, vol. 12, pt. 1 (1932).
Gonki. *ST*, vols. 4–5 (1965).
Gosen wakashū. Katagiri Yōichi, ed., *SNKBT*, vol. 6 (1990).
Hakushi monjū. Okamura Shigeru, ed., *SKT*, vols. 97–102 (1988–1993).
Hikohime shiki. In Sasaki Nobutsuna, ed., *NKT*, vol. 1 (1957).
Hōjōki. In Kanda Hideo, Nagazumi Yasuaki, and Yasuraoka Kōsaku, eds., *SNBKZ* , vol. 44 (1995).
Honchō monzui. In Ōsone Shōsuke, Kinpara Tadashi, and Gotō Akio, eds., *SNKBT*, vol. 27 (1992).
Ise monogatari. In Katagiri Yōichi, et al., eds., *SNKBZ*, vol. 12 (1994).
Kagerō nikki. In Kikuchi Yasuhiko, Kimura Masanori, and Imuta Tsunehisa, eds., *SNKBZ*, vol. 13 (1995).
Kagura uta. In Usuda Jingorō, Shinma Shin'ichi, Tonomura Natsuko, and Tokue Gensei, eds., *SNKBZ*, vol. 42 (1994).
Kakyō hyōshiki. In Sasaki Nobutsuna, ed., *NKT*, vol. 1 (1957).
Kanke bunsō. In Kawaguchi Hisao, ed., *NKBT*, vol. 72 (1966).
Keikokushū. In *GR*, vol. 8 (1983).
Kenpō jūshichi jō. In Ienaga Saburō et al., eds., *Shōtoku Taishi shū*, *Nihon shisō taikei*, vol. 2. Tokyo: Iwanami shoten, 1975.
Kokin wakashū. Ozawa Masao and Matsuda Shigeo, eds., *SNKBZ*, vol. 11 (1994).

Konjaku monogatari-shū. Mabuchi Kazuo, Kunisaki Fumimaro, and Inagaki Taiichi, eds., *SNKBZ*, vols. 35–38 (1999–2002).
Korai fūteishō. In Hashimoto Fumio, Ariyoshi Tamotsu, and Fujihira Haruo, eds., *SNKBZ*, vol. 87 (2002).
Kyōgoku no miyasundokoro Hōshi no uta-awase. In Hagitani Boku and Taniyama Shigeru, eds., *NKBT*, vol. 74 (1965).
Laozi (*Rōshi*). Abe Yoshio and Yamamoto Toshio, eds., *SKT*, vol. 7 (1966).
Liji (*Raiki*). Takeuchi Teruo, ed., *SKT*, vols. 27–29 (1971–1979).
Lunwen. In Stephen Owen, *Readings in Chinese Literary Thought*. Cambridge, MA: Harvard Council on East Asian Studies, 1992.
Lunyu (*Rongo*). Yoshida Kenkō, ed., *SKT*, vol. 1 (1961).
Makura no sōshi. Matsuo Satoshi and Nagai Kazuko, eds., *SNKBZ*, vol. 18 (1997).
Man'yōshū. Kojima Noriyuki, Kinoshita Masatoshi, and Tōno Haruyuki, eds., *SNKBZ*, vols. 6–9 (1994).
Maoshi zhengyi. Zhonghua shuju bianjibu, ed., *Shisan jing zhushu: Fujiao kanji shangce*. Beijing: Zhonghua shuju, 1979.
Midō kanpakki. *DNK*, vol. 1, pts. 1–3 (1952–1954).
Mitsune-shū. In *KT*, vol. 3, pt. 1 (1983).
Montoku jitsuroku. *KST*, vol. 3, pt. 3 (1934).
Mumyōshō. In Hisamatsu Sen'ichi and Nishio Minoru, eds., *NKBT*, vol. 65 (1961).
Mumyōzōshi. In Higuchi Yoshimaro and Kuboki Tetsuo, eds., *SNKBZ*, vol. 40 (1999).
Nihon kiryaku. *KST*, vols. 10–11 (1929).
Nihon shoki. Kojima Noriyuki et al., eds., *SNKBZ*, vols. 2–4 (1994).
Ōigawa gyōkō waka no jo. E. B. Ceadel, *Asia Major*, n.s. 3: 1 (1953).
Okikaze-shū, in *KT*, vol. 3, pt. 1 (1983).
Ruijū kokushi. *KST*, vols. 5–6 (1933–1934).
Ryō no gige. *KST*, vol. 22 (1939).
Ryōunshū. In *GR*, vol. 8 (1983).
Saibara. In Usuda Jingorō, Shinma Shin'ichi, Tonomura Natsuko, and Tokue Gensei, eds., *SNKBZ*, vol. 42 (1994).
Sandai jitsuroku. *KST*, vol. 4 (1934).
Sanjō Sadaijin den senzai no uta-awase. In *KT*, vol. 5, pt. 1.
Senzai wakashū. Katano Tatsurō and Matsuno Yōichi, eds., *SNKBT*, vol. 10 (1993).
Shaku nihongi. *KST*, vol. 8, pt. 2 (1932).
Shoku nihongi. Aoki Kazuo et al., eds., *SNKBT*, vols. 12–16 (1989–1998).
Shoku nihon kōki. *KST*, vol. 3, pt. 2 (1934).
Shōyūki. *DNK*, vol. 10, pts. 1–11 (1959–1986).
Shūishō chū. In *GR*, vol. 16.
Shūi wakashū. Komachiya Teruhiko, ed., *SNKBT*, vol. 7 (1990).
Tadamine-shū. In *KT*, vol. 3, pt. 1 (1983).
Teiji-in no uta-awase. In Ozawa Masao and Matsuda Shigeo, eds., *SNKBZ*, vol. 11 (1994).

Teishin kōki. *DNK*, vol. 8 (1956).
Tosa nikki. In Kikuchi Yasuhiko, Kimura Masanori, and Imuta Tsunehisa, eds., *SNKBZ*, vol. 13 (1995).
Tsurayuki-shū. Tanaka Kimiharu and Tanaka Kyōko, eds., *Tsurayuki-shū zenshaku*. Tokyo: Kazama shobō, 1996.
Tsurezuregusa. In Kanda Hideo, Nagazumi Yasuaki, and Yasuraoka Kōsaku, eds., *SNBKZ*, vol. 44 (1995).
Uda tennō shinki. In *ST*, vol. 1 (1965).
Waka shogaku shō. In Sasaki Nobutsuna, ed., *NKT*, vol. 2 (1956).
Wenfu. In Stephen Owen, *Readings in Chinese Literary Thought*. Cambridge, MA: Harvard Council on East Asian Studies, 1992.
Wenxuan (*Monzen*). Uchida Sennosuke, ed., *SKT*, vols. 14–15 (1963–1964). Preface cited from David R. Knechtges, trans., *Wenxuan or Selections of Refined Literature*, vol. 1, *Rhapsodies on Metropolises and Capitals*. Princeton, NJ: Princeton, 1985.
Yamato monogatari. In Katagiri Yōichi, et al., eds., *SNKBZ*, vol. 12 (1994).
Yorimoto-shū. In *KT*, vol. 3, pt. 1 (1983).
Zhuangzi (*Sōshi*). Endō Tetsuo and Ichikawa Yasuji, eds., *SKT*, vols. 7–8 (1966–1967).

Secondary Works

Abe, Ryūichi. *The Weaving of Mantra: Kūkai and the Construction of Esoteric Buddhist Discourse*. New York: Columbia University Press, 1999.
Abe Takeshi, ed. *Nihon kodai kanshoku jiten*. Tokyo: Takashina shoten, 1995.
Akahane Shuku. "Kakekotoba." *IKKW*, 632–634.
_____. "Waka no inritsu." In Fujihira Haruo, ed., *Waka no honshitsu to hyōgen*, *Waka bungaku kōza*, vol. 1. Tokyo: Benseisha, 1993. 131–146.
Akimoto Morihide. "Mitate no kazai to hyōgen ruikei: 'miru,' 'miyu' o chūshin to shite." *Ryūgoku daigaku ronshū*, 433–434 (November 1989): 635–650.
Akinaga Kazue. "*Kokin wakashū* no hyōki." *IKKW*, 291–297.
_____. *Kokin wakashū shōtenbon no kenkyū*, 4 vols. Tokyo: Azekura shobō, 1972–1991.
Akiyama Ken. "Nihon bungakushi ni okeru waka." In Fujihira Haruo, ed., *Waka no honshitsu to hyōgen*, *Waka bungaku kōza*, vol. 1. Tokyo: Benseisha, 1993. 7–24.
_____. "Rokkasen jidai to wa nani ka." *Kokubungaku kaishaku to kyōzai no kenkyū*, 28: 9 (July 1983): 23–31.
Akiyama Terukazu. *Heian jidai sezokuga no kenkyū*. Tokyo: Yoshikawa kōbunkan, 1964.
Amagasaki Akira. "Waka no retorikku." In Fujihira Haruo, ed., *Waka no honshitsu to hyōgen*, *Waka bungaku kōza*, vol. 1. Tokyo: Benseisha, 1993. 147–162.
Amino Yoshihiko. *"Nihon" to wa nani ka*. Tokyo: Kōdansha, 2000.
Anderson, Benedict. *Imagined Communities: Reflections on the Origin and Spread of Nationalism*. London: Verso, 1991.

Andō Tarō. *Heian jidai shikashū kajin no kenkyū*. Tokyo: Ōfūsha, 1982.

Arai Eizō. "'Jishin' kō: *Kokin wakashū* kajin no kanshoku to ritsuryō." In Wakan hikaku bungakkai, ed., *Chūko bungaku to kanbungaku*, vol. 1, 3–26. Tokyo: Kyūko shoin, 1986.

_____. "Kanajo manajo dokuyō no koto: *Kokin wakashū* kō." *Kokugo to kokubungaku*, 57: 11 (November 1980): 24–35.

_____. "*Kokin wakashū* budate kō: maki nana gabu ni tsuite." *Bungaku*, 43: 8 (August 1975): 1000–1018.

_____. "*Kokin wakashū* kenkyū kiryobu no kōzō shōkō." *Kokugo kokubun*, 42: 2 and 42: 5 (February and August 1973): 13–31 and 17–31.

_____. "*Kokin wakashū* renbu no budate shōkō." *Kokugo kokubun*, 43: 6 (June 1974): 40–58.

_____. "*Kokin wakashū* shiki no bu no kōzō ni tsuite no ichi kōsatsu: tairitsuteki kikō ron no tachiba kara." *Kokugo kokubun*, 41: 8 (August 1962): 1–30.

_____. "'*Kokin wakashū*' to nenjū gyōji: shōgatsu mikka to shichigatsu nanoka to o megutte." In Hamada Keisuke, ed., *Ronshū nihon bungaku nihongo*, vol. 2. Tokyo: Kadokawa shoten, 1977. 95–105.

_____. "*Kokinshū* no kōzō." In Ueno Osamu, ed., *Kokinshū*, *Waka bungaku kōza*, vol. 4. Tokyo: Benseisha, 1993. 51–68.

_____. "Ochō kannin Ki no Tsurayuki no shokumu." *Bungaku*, 54: 2 (February 1986): 141–150.

_____. "Wago to kango: *Kokinshū* renbu kantōka shiken." *Kokugo kokubun*, 46: 5 (May 1977): 393–401.

Austin, John L. *How to Do Things with Words*. Cambridge, MA: Harvard University Press, 1962.

Barlow, Tani E. "Theorizing Woman: *Funu*, *Guojia*, and *Jiating* (Chinese Women, Chinese State, Chinese Family)." In Angela Zito and Tani Barlow, eds., *Body, Subject & Power in China*, 253–289. Chicago: University of Chicago Press, 1994.

Batten, Bruce. *To the Ends of Japan: Premodern Frontiers, Boundaries, and Interactions*. Honolulu: University of Hawai'i Press, 2003.

Bell, Catherine. *Ritual Theory, Ritual Practice*. New York: Oxford University Press, 1992.

Bialock, David T., "Voice, Text, and the Question of Poetic Borrowing in Late Classical Japanese Poetry." *HJAS*, 54: 1 (June 1994): 181–231.

Bloch, Maurice. *Ritual, History and Power: Selected Papers in Anthropology*. London: Athlone Press, 1989.

Borgen, Robert. *Sugawara no Michizane and the Early Heian Court*. Cambridge, MA: Harvard Council on East Asian Studies, 1986.

Bourdieu, Pierre. *The Field of Cultural Production*. New York: Columbia University Press, 1993.

Bowring, Richard. "The *Ise monogatari*: A Short Cultural History." *HJAS*, 52: 2 (December 1992): 401–480.

Cavanaugh, Carole. "Text and Textile: Unweaving the Female Subject in Heian Writing." *positions*, 4: 3 (Winter 1996): 593–636.

Ceadel, E. B. "The Ōi River Poems and Preface." *Asia Major*, n.s. 3: 1 (1953): 65–106.

Chartier, Roger. *The Order of Books: Readers, Authors, and Libraries in Europe Between the Fourteenth and Eighteenth Centuries*. Lydia G. Cochrane, trans. Stanford, CA: Stanford University Press, 1994.

Cheng, François. "Some Reflections on Chinese Poetic Language and Its Relation to Chinese Cosmology." Stephen Owen, trans. In Shuen-fu Lin and Stephen Owen, eds., *The Vitality of the Lyric Voice: Shih Poetry from the Late Han to the T'ang*. Princeton, NJ: Princeton University Press, 1986. 32–48.

Chino Kaori. "Gender in Japanese Art." In Norman Bryson, Joshua S. Mostow, and Maribeth Graybill, eds., *Gender and Power in the Japanese Visual Field*. Honolulu: University of Hawai'i Press, 2003. 17–34.

Connery, Christopher Leigh. *The Empire of the Text: Writing and Authority in Early Imperial China*. Lanham, MD: Rowman and Littlefield, 1998.

Denecke, Wiebke. "Chinese Antiquity and Court Spectacle in Early *Kanshi*." *Journal of Japanese Studies*, 30:1 (Winter 2004): 97–122.

Derrida, Jacques. *Limited Inc*. Evanston, IL: Northwestern University Press, 1988.

DeWoskin, Kenneth. "Early Chinese Music and the Origins of Aesthetic Terminology." In Susan Bush and Christian Murck, eds., *Theories of the Arts in China*. Princeton, NJ: Princeton University Press, 1983. 187–214.

Ebersole, Gary. *Ritual Poetry and the Politics of Death in Early Japan*. Princeton, NJ: Princeton University Press, 1989.

Ellwood, Robert S. *The Feast of Kingship: Accession Ceremonies in Ancient Japan*. Tokyo: Sophia University Press, 1973.

Enokimura Hiroyuki. "No no miyuki no seiritsu: kodai no ōken girei to shite no shuryō to henshitsu." *Hisutoria*, 141 (January 1993): 114–133.

Foucault, Michel. "What Is an Author?" In Josue V. Harari, ed., *Textual Strategies: Perspectives in Post-Structuralist Criticism*. Ithaca, NY: Cornell University Press, 1979. 141–160.

Friday, Karl F. *Hired Swords: The Rise of Private Warrior Power in Early Japan*. Stanford, CA: Stanford University Press, 1992.

Fujihira Haruo. "Dai'ei seiritsu zenshi." In Ozawa Masao, ed., *Sandaishū no kenkyū*. Tokyo: Meiji shoin, 1981. 57–70.

Fujii Sadakazu. "Kanajo." *IKKW*, 55–63.

_____. "*Kokinshū* no kokoro to kotoba: 'irogonomi no ie,' 'kisshoku no kaku.'" In Masuda Shigeo et al., eds., *Kokin wakashū no seisei to honshitsu, Kokin wakashū kenkyū shūsei*, vol. 1. Tokyo: Kazama shobō, 2004. 25–54.

_____. "Kōzō, yu, kokoro to kotoba: *Kakyō hyōshiki* kara *Kokin wakashū* e." *Bungaku*, 54: 2 (February 1986): 47–57.

_____. *Monogatari bungaku seiritsushi: furukoto, katari, monogatari*. Tokyo: Tokyo daigaku shuppankai, 1987.

_____. "Sotōrihime no nagare: Komachi o sakanoboru." *Kokubungaku kaishaku to kyōzai no kenkyū*, 28: 9 (July 1983): 90–95.

Fujioka Tadaharu. "Byōbu uta no honshitsu." In Waka bungaku ronshū henshū iinkai, ed., *Byōbu uta to uta-awase*. Tokyo: Kazama shobō, 1995. 29–50.

_____. *Heian waka shiron: Sandaishū jidai no kichō*. Tokyo: Ōfūsha, 1966.

Fujita Isson. "Byōbu e to byōbu uta to no sōkansei o megutte." *Nihon bungaku kenkyū*, 30 (January 1991): 61–78.

_____. "Byōbu uta no seisakuhō bekken." *Nihon bungaku ronshū*, 13 (March 1989): 5–23.

_____. "Heianchō byōbu uta no shiteki kōsatsu: jūseiki kōhan no dōkō to tokuchō." *Daitō bunka daigaku nihon bungaku kenkyū*, 32 (February 1993): 22–36.

Fujita Yuriko. "Daijōe byōbu uta no seikaku o megutte." *Kokugo to kokubungaku*, 55: 4 (April 1978): 47–60.

Fukui Toshihiko. "Heianchō ni okeru jige." In Yūseidō henshūbu, ed., *Heian kizoku no seikatsu*. Tokyo: Yūseidō, 1985. 41–47.

_____. "Heianchō ni okeru kanshoku ikai." In Yūseidō henshūbu, ed., *Heian kizoku no seikatsu*. Tokyo: Yūseidō, 1985. 18–24.

Fukutō Sanae. "Ukareme kara asobi e." In Joseishi sōgō kenkyūkai, ed., *Nihon josei seikatsushi*, vol. 1. Tokyo: Tokyo daigaku shuppankai, 1990. 217–246.

Fukutō Sanae and Takeshi Watanabe. "From Female Sovereign to Mother of the Nation." In Mikael Adolphson and Edward Kamens, eds., *Heian Japan, Centers and Peripheries*. Honolulu: University of Hawai'i Press, 2007. 15–34.

Furuhashi Nobuyoshi. *Kodai toshi no bungei seikatsu*. Tokyo: Taishūkan shoten, 1994.

_____. *Kodai waka no hassei: uta no jusei to yōshiki*. Tokyo: Tokyo daigaku shuppankai, 1988.

_____. "*Kokin wakashū* to denshō kayō." *IKKW*, 277–283.

_____. "*Man'yōshū* kara *Kokin wakashū* e." *Kokubungaku kaishaku to kyōzai no kenkyū*, 40: 10 (August 1995): 26–32.

_____. "Waka no kōshōsei to kisaisei." In Fujihira Haruo, ed., *Waka no honshitsu to hyōgen, Waka bungaku kōza*, vol. 1. Tokyo: Benseisha, 1993. 77–92.

Furuse Natsuko. "Kyakushiki, gishiki no hensan." In Iwanami kōza nihon tsūshi henshū iinkai, ed., *Iwanami kōza nihon tsūshi*, 347–366. Tokyo: Iwanami shoten, 1994.

Go Tetsuo. "Sono no keifu: *Kokinshū* to gaibu." *Bungaku*, 54: 2 (February 1986): 58–69.

Goodwin, Janet. *Selling Songs and Smiles: The Sex Trade in Heian and Kamakura Japan*. Honolulu: University of Hawai'i Press, 2007.

Gotō Akio. "Montoku-chō izen to igo." *Bungaku*, 53: 12 (December 1985): 53–66.

Gotō Yoshiko. "Joryū ni yoru danka: Shikishi Naishinnō uta e no ichi shiten." In Kubukihara Rei, ed., *Waka to wa nani ka, Nihon bungaku o yomikaeru*, vol. 3. Tokyo: Benseisha, 1993. 302–323.

_____. "Ono no Komachi shiron." *Nihon joshi daigaku kiyō (bungaku-bu)*, 27 (1977): 17–28.

_____. "Tsurayuki uta no haramu mono." *Kokubungaku kaishaku to kanshō*, 44: 2 (February 1979): 57–64.

Haga Tsunao. "*Man'yōshū* ni okeru 'hō' to 'wa' no mondai: shidai shokan to no kanren o megutte." In Yoshii Iwao sensei koki kinen ronshū kankōkai, ed., *Nihon koten no chōbō*, 17–55. Tokyo: Ōfūsha, 1991.

Hagitani Boku, ed., *Heianchō uta-awase taisei* (*zōho shintei*, vol. 1). Kyoto: Dōhōsha, 1995.

_____. "Kaisetsu." In Hagitani Boku and Taniyama Shigeru, eds., *Uta-awase shū*, *NKBT*, vol. 74. Tokyo: Iwanami shoten, 1965. 7–74.

_____. *Tosa nikki zenchūshaku*. Tokyo: Kadokawa shoten, 1967.

Hasegawa Masaharu. *Ki no Tsurayuki ron*. Tokyo: Yūseidō, 1984.

_____. "*Kokinshū* no seiritsu to sono haikei: kōtōfu to Kishi to Ōmi to." In Nihon bungaku kenkyū shiryō kankōkai, ed., *Kokin wakashū*. Tokyo: Yūseidō, 1976. 45–54.

_____. Hashimoto Fumio. *Ōchō wakashi no kenkyū*. Tokyo: Kasama shoin, 1972.

Hashimoto Masayo. "'Fuyu' no tokushoku to kōzō." *IKKW*, 97–104.

Hashimoto Yoshinori. "'Kōkyū' no seiritsu: kōgō no henbō to kōkyū no saien." In Murai Yasuhiko, ed., *Kuge to buke: sono hikaku bunmeishiteki kōsatsu*. Kyoto: Shibunkaku, 1995. 81–122

Hatooka Akira. *Jōdai kanshibun to chūgoku bungaku*. Tokyo: Kasama shoin, 1989.

Hay, John. "The Human Body as a Microcosmic Source of Macrocosmic Values in Calligraphy." In Susan Bush and Christian Murck, eds., *Theories of the Arts in China*. Princeton, NJ: Princeton University Press, 1983. 74–103.

Heldt, Gustav. "Writing Like a Man: Poetic Literacy, Textual Property, and Gender in the *Tosa Diary*." *Journal of Asian Studies*, 64: 1 (February 2005): 7–34.

Hightower, James R. "The *Wen Hsüan* and Genre Theory." *HJAS*, 20 (1957): 512–533.

Hijikata Yōichi. "Waka hyōgenshi ni okeru 'yu' no isō: uta to 'kaku koto.'" *Nihon bungaku*, 31: 5 (May 1982): 23–33.

Hirano Yukiko. "Ninmyō-chō no wafū bunka to rokkasen: kakekotoba, mono no na, *Taketori monogatari*." In Masuda Shigeo et al., eds. *Kokin wakashū no seisei to honshitsu, Kokin wakashū kenkyū shūsei*, vol. 1. Tokyo: Kazama shobō, 2004. 201–230.

Hirasawa Ryūsuke. "*Kokinshū* no gengo ishiki." *Mozu joshi daigaku kenkyū kiyō*, 24 (1988): 1–26.

_____. "*Man'yō* kara *Kokin* e: shikaku hyōgen o tōshite." *Shirayuri joshi daigaku kenkyū kiyō*, 27 (December 1991): 25–76.

_____. "'Natsu' no tokushoku to kōzō." *IKKW*, 80–87.

Hirota Osamu. "'Ōutadokoro no on'uta' no tokushoku to kōzō." *IKKW*, 171–176.

Holcombe, Charles. "*Ritsuryō* Confucianism." *HJAS*, 57: 2 (December 1997): 543–573.

Horikawa Noboru. "*Tosa nikki* no hōhō keisei shiron: byōbu uta no hyōgen kōzō to no kanren o chūshin ni shite." *Gengo to bungei*, 79 (November 1974): 61–80.

Hyōdō Hiromi. *Ōken to monogatari*. Tokyo: Seikyūsha, 1989.

Ide Itaru. "Kakekotoba no genryū." *Jinbun kenkyū*, 21: 6 (1970): 420–440.

Ienaga Saburō. *Jōdai yamato-e nenpyō*. Tokyo: Meicho kankōkai, 1988.

_____. *Jōdai yamato-e zenshi*. Tokyo: Bokusui shobō, 1966.

Igami Wataru. "Chakuza, chakujin ni tsuite: kodai kizoku no 'ba' no shinsei." *Kodai bunka*, 47: 7 (July 1995): 23–30.

Igawa Hiroko. "Mitate." *IKKW*, 678–682.

Igawa Kenji. "'Ga' no tokushoku to kōzō." *IKKW*, 104–113.

Ihara Akira. "Uta-awase ni okeru ichi seikaku: akairo to aoiro to." *Wayō kokubun kenkyū*, 9 (September 1972): 34–43.

Imai Yutaka. *Kokin-fū no kigen to honshitsu*. Tokyo: Izumi shoin, 1986.

Imanishi Yūichirō. "Yamazato." *Kokubungaku kaishaku to kyōzai no kenkyū*, 28: 16 (December 1983): 114–117.

Imazeki Toshiko. "'Izure ka uta o yomazarikeru' kō: kanajo sakusha no gengo ishiki." *Nihon bungaku*, 41: 2 (February 1992): 43–55.

Inomata Tokiwa. "Jusei: kotoba no kodai." *Kodai bungaku*, 28 (1989): 39–47.

_____. "Uta no 'kokoro' to 'mushin shochaku-ka.'" In Kubukihara Rei, ed. *Waka to wa nani ka, Nihon bungaku o yomikaeru*, vol. 3. Tokyo: Yūseidō, 1996. 180–199.

Inukai Kimiyuki. *Kage no kodai*. Tokyo: Ōfūsha, 1991.

_____. "Kayō to Ōuta-dokoro." In Masuda Shigeo et al., eds. *Kokin wakashū no seisei to honshitsu, Kokin wakashū kenkyū shūsei*, vol. 1. Tokyo: Kazama shobō, 2004. 323–353.

Ishimoda Shō. *Kodai makki seijishi josetsu*. Tokyo: Miraisha, 1956.

Itō Hiroshi. "Dairi." In Yūseidō henshūbu, ed. *Heian kizoku no seikatsu*. Tokyo: Yūseidō, 1985. 73–82.

_____. "Kōkyū." In Yūseidō henshūbu, ed. *Heian kizoku no seikatsu*. Tokyo: Yūseidō, 1985. 83–88.

Izumi Kazuko. "*Kokin wakashū* to *Shinsen man'yōshū*." *IKKW*, 543–554.

_____. "Uta-awase no seiritsu." In Waka bungaku ronshū henshū iinkai, ed., *Byōbu uta to uta-awase*. Tokyo: Kazama shobō, 1995. 135–162.

Kajimoto Kazuyoshi. "*Kokin*-ka no kōzō to sono isō." *Nihon bungaku*, 26: 5 (May 1977): 13–24.

Kamens, Edward. "Dragon-Girl, Maiden-flower, Buddha: The Transformation of a *Waka* Topos, 'The Five Obstructions.'" *HJAS*, 53: 2 (December 1993): 389–442.

Kamishino Shōji. "Tsurayuki 'Mochizuki no koma' ei kō." *Bungaku* 39: 10 (October 1971): 47–65.

Kamitani Kaoru. *Kana bungaku no bunshōshiteki kenkyū*. Osaka: Izumi shoin, 1993.

Kamiya Masaaki. "Heian jidai no sesshō to gishiki." In Hayashi Rokurō and Suzuki Haruuji, eds., *Nihon kodai no kokka to saigi*, 118–139. Tokyo: Yūzankaku, 1996.

Katagiri Yōichi. "Dai'ei, sono keisei to ba: sandaishū no jidai." In Waka bungakukai, ed., *Ronshū 'dai' no waka kūkan*. Tokyo: Kasama shoin, 1992. 39–57.

_____. "Kanshi no sekai, waka no sekai: chokusen sanshū to *Kokinshū* o megutte no danshō." *Bungaku*, 53: 12 (December 1985): 183–196.

_____. "*Kokin wakashū* no ba." *Bungaku*, 47: 7 and 8 (July and August 1979): 38–48 and 86–95.

_____. "*Kokin wakashū* no honbun." *IKKW*, 7–16.

_____. *Kokin wakashū no kenkyū*. Tokyo: Meiji shoin, 1991.

_____. "*Kokinshū* kanajo no bunshō: sono seikaku to seiritsu." In Tsuruhisa kyōju taikan kinen kokugogaku ronshū kankōkai, ed., *Tsuruhisa kyōju taikan kinen kokugogaku ronshū*. Tokyo: Ōfūsha, 1993. 210–229.

_____. "*Kokinshū* ni okeru waka no kyōju." *Bungaku*, 43: 8 (August 1975): 924–935.

_____. "Utamakura no seiritsu: *Kokinshū* hyōgen kenkyū no ichibu to shite." *Kokugo to kokubungaku*, 47: 4 (April 1970): 22–33.

Katano Tatsurō. *Nihon bungei to kaiga no sōkansei no kenkyū*. Tokyo: Kasama shoin, 1975.

Katō Kōichi. "Tsurayuki no hyōgen: *Tsurayuki-shū* shoshū mondōka niso o megutte." *Chūko bungaku*, 41 (1988): 10–18.

Katō Tomoyasu. "Chōgi no kōzō to sono tokushitsu: Heianki o chūshin to shite." In Nagahara Keiji, ed., *Sekaishi no naka no tennō*. Tokyo: Aoki shoten, 1995. 149–190.

Kawada Yutaka. "Shirabe: Heianchō karon o chūshin to shite." *Oto*, 3: 5 (May 1984): 34–37.

Kawaguchi Hisao. "Waga kuni ni okeru daiga bungaku no tenkai." In Yamagishi Tokuhei, ed., *Nihon bungakushi ronkō*. Tokyo: Iwanami shoten, 1974. 188–214.

Kawahira Hitoshi. "Kokoro to kotoba." *IKKW*, 647–653.

Kawaji Osamu. "*Kokin wakashū* ron: 'Tennō no kashū' moshiku wa 'kashū' no kaitai." *Tōyō*, 12 (December 1994): 26–37.

Kawamoto Kōji. Stephen Collington, Kevin Collins, and Gustav Heldt, trans. *The Poetics of Japanese Verse: Imagery, Structure, Meter*. Tokyo: University of Tokyo Press, 2000.

Kawamura Hiroko. "Byōbu uta ni tsuite." *Rikkyō daigaku nihon bungaku*, 41 (January 1979): 35–44.

Kawamura Teruo. "Kotobagaki no imi suru mono." *Kokubungaku kaishaku to kyōzai no kenkyū*, 40: 10 (August 1995): 33–39.

Kawashima, Terry. *Writing Margins: The Textual Construction of Gender in Heian and Kamakura Japan*. Cambridge, MA: Harvard University Asia Center, 2001.

Kierstead, Thomas. "Gardens and Estates: Medievality and Space." *positions*, 1: 1 (Fall 1993): 289–320.

_____. "The Gendering and Regendering of Medieval Japan." *U.S.-Japan Women's Journal*, 9 (1995): 77–92.

Kikuchi Yasuhiko. "*Kokinshū* no ba to hōhō." In Ueno Osamu, ed., *Kokinshū*, *Waka bungaku kōza*, vol. 4. Tokyo: Benseisha, 1993. 89–108.

_____. "'Mono no na' no tokushoku to kōzō." *IKKW*, 130–137.

Klein, Susan Blakeley. *Allegories of Desire: Esoteric Literary Commentaries of Medieval Japan*. Cambridge, MA: Harvard University Asia Center, 2002.

Kōda Kazuhiko. "Teiji-in uta-awase no katōdo ni tsuite." *Kokugakuin zasshi*, 90: 7 (July 1989): 30–43.

Kojima Naoko. "Renka to jendaa: Narihira, Komachi, Henjō," *Kokubungaku kaishaku to kyōzai no kenkyū*, 41: 12 (October 1996): 56–62.

Kojima Noriyuki. *Kokinshū izen: shi to uta no kōryū*. Tokyo: Hanawa shobō, 1976.

_____. *Kokufū ankoku jidai no bungaku*, vol. 2, no. 3. Tokyo: Hanawa shobō, 1973.

Komachiya Teruhiko. *Genji monogatari no uta kotoba hyōgen*. Tokyo: Tokyo daigaku shuppankai, 1984.

_____. *Kokin wakashū to uta kotoba hyōgen*. Tokyo: Iwanami shoten, 1994.

Komaki Satoshi. "Gengo no jusei to yōshiki: mondō kayō no jirei ni soku shite." In Tsuchihashi Yutaka, ed., *Kodai bungaku no yōshiki to kinō*. Tokyo: Ōfūsha, 1988. 52–69.

Komatsu Shigemi. *Kana: sono seiritsu to hensen*. Tokyo: Iwanami shoten, 1986.

_____. *Nenjū gyōji e-maki, Nihon emaki taisei,* vol. 8. Tokyo: Chūō kōronsha, 1977.

Kondō Miyuki. "*Kokinshū* no 'kotoba' no kata: gengo hyōshō to jendaa." In Kokubungaku kenkyū shiryōkan, ed., *Jendaa no seisei: Kokinshū kara Kyoka made.* Kyoto, Rinsen shoten, 2002. 2–61.

Kondō Nobuyoshi. "Makurakotoba, jokotoba, utamakura." In Furuhashi Nobuyoshi, Miura Sukeyuki, and Mori Asao, eds., *Kotoba no shinwagaku, Kodai bungaku kōza*, vol. 7. Tokyo: Benseisha, 1996. 156–169.

_____. "*Shoku nihongi* ikō no kayō: inishie no nonaka furu michi." In Furuhashi Nobuyoshi, Miura Sukeyuki, and Mori Asao, eds., *Kayō, Kodai bungaku kōza*, vol. 9. Tokyo: Benseisha, 1996. 34–49.

Konishi Jin'ichi. *The Early Middle Ages, A History of Japanese Literature*, vol. 2. Aileen Gatten, trans. Princeton, NJ: Princeton University Press, 1986.

_____. "Association and Progression: Principles of Integration in Anthologies and Sequences of Japanese Court Poetry, A.D. 900–1350." Robert H. Brower and Earl Miner, trans. *HJAS*, 21 (1958): 67–127.

_____. "The Genesis of the *Kokinshū* Style." Helen McCullough, trans. *HJAS*, 38: 1 (June 1978): 61–170.

Kōzen Hiroshi. "*Kokinshū* manajo oboegaki." *Bungaku*, 53: 12 (December 1985): 169–182.

Kubota Utsubo. *Kokin wakashū hyōshaku*. Tokyo: Tōkyōdō, 1937.

Kuboki Hisako. "'Aishō' no tokushoku to kōzō." *IKKW*, 148–155.

Kubukihara Rei. "Haikai uta: wakashi no kōsō josetsu." In Kubukihara Rei, ed., *Waka to wa nani ka, Nihon bungaku o yomikaeru,* vol. 3. Tokyo: Yūseidō, 1996. 99–125

_____. "'Zattei' no tokushoku to kōzō." *IKKW*, 165–171.

Kudō Shigenori. "*Gosen wakashū*: waka ni okeru ke, hare to wa nani ka." In Waka bungaku ronshū henshū iinkai, ed., *Kokinshū to sono zengo.* Tokyo: Kazama shobō, 1994. 257–286.

_____. *Heianchō ritsuryō shakai no bungaku*. Tokyo: Perikansha, 1993.

Kumagai Naoharu. *Heianchō zenki bungakushi no kenkyū*. Tokyo: Ōfūsha, 1992.

_____. "*Kokinshū* no seiritsu nendai ni tsuite." *Kokubungaku kenkyū*, 42 (June 1970): 1–12.

Kurahayashi Shōji. "'Kami asobi no uta' no tokushoku to kōzō." *IKKW*, 177–183.

_____. *Kyōen no kenkyū* (*bungaku hen*). Tokyo: Ōfūsha, 1969.

Kyūsojin Hitaku. *Kokin wakashū seiritsu ron*. Tokyo: Kazama shobō, 1961.

_____. "*Shinsen man'yōshū* to *Kanpyō no ontoki kisai no miya no uta-awase*." *Bungaku*, 54: 2 (February 1986): 34–46.

LaCure, Jon. *Rhetorical Devices of the Kokinshū: A Structural Analysis of Japanese Waka Poetry*. Lewiston, NY: Edwin Mellen Press, 1997.

LaMarre, Thomas. *Uncovering Heian Japan: An Archeology of Sensation and Inscription*. Durham, NC: Duke University Press, 2000.

Lewis, Mark Edward. *Writing and Authority in Early China*. Albany: SUNY Press, 1999.

Levy, Dore J. "Constructing Sequences: Another Look at the Principle of Fu Enumeration." *HJAS*, 46: 2 (December 1986): 471–493.

Lin, Shuen-fu. "The Nature of the Quatrain from the Late Han to the High T'ang." In Shuen-fu Lin and Stephen Owen, eds., *The Vitality of the Lyric Voice: Shih Poetry from the Late Han to the T'ang*. Princeton, NJ: Princeton University Press, 1986. 296–331.

Major, John S. *Heaven and Earth in Early Han Thought: Chapters Three, Four, and Five of the Huainanzi*. Albany: SUNY Press, 1993.

Marra, Michele. *The Aesthetics of Discontent: Politics and Reclusion in Medieval Japanese Literature*. Honolulu: University of Hawai'i Press, 1991.

Masuda Shigeo. "Chokusenshū to wa nani ka." In Waka bungaku ronshū henshū iinkai, ed., *Kokinshū to sono zengo*. Tokyo: Kazama shobō, 1994. 41–67.

_____. "*Kokinshū* no chokusensei: waka to seiji, shakai, rinri." In Nihon bungaku kenkyū shiryō kankōkai, ed., *Kokin wakashū, Nihon bungaku kenkyū shiryō sōsho*, vol. 15. Tokyo: Yūseidō, 1976. 31–44.

_____. "*Kokinshū* no hyōgen." *Kokugo to kokubungaku*, 52: 9 (September 1975): 13–26.

_____. "*Kokinshū* to kizoku bunka." In Masuda Shigeo et al., eds. *Kokin wakashū no seisei to honshitsu, Kokin wakashū kenkyū shūsei*, vol. 1. Tokyo: Kazama shobō, 2004. 1–24.

Matsuda Takeo. *Kokinshū no kōzō ni kansuru kenkyū*. Tokyo: Kazama shobō, 1965.

Matsumoto Hiroshi. "On'inshi kara mita mono no na uta." *Miyagi kyōiku daigaku kokugo kokubun*, 13–14 (August 1984): 18–25.

Matsu'ura Tomohisa. "Shikei to shite no 'waka': chūgoku kotenshi no hikaku ni oite." *Bungaku*, 53: 12 (December 1985): 140–154.

McCullough, Helen Craig. *Brocade by Night: 'Kokin Wakashū' and the Court Style in Japanese Classical Poetry*. Stanford, CA: Stanford University Press, 1985.

_____. *Kokin Wakashū: The First Imperial Anthology of Japanese Poetry*. Stanford, CA: Stanford University Press, 1985.

McCullough, William H., and Helen Craig, trans. *A Tale of Flowering Fortunes: Annals of Japanese Aristocratic Life in the Heian Period*. 2 vols. Stanford, CA: Stanford University Press, 1980.

Mezaki Tokue. *Ariwara no Narihira, Ono no Komachi*. Tokyo: Chikuma shobō, 1970.

_____. *Heian bunka shiron*. Tokyo: Ōfūsha, 1968.

_____. *Ki no Tsurayuki*. Tokyo: Yoshikawa kōbunkan, 1985.

_____. *Kizoku shakai to koten bunka*. Tokyo: Yoshikawa kōbunkan, 1995.

_____. "Nihon bunkashi ni okeru waka." In Fujihira Haruo, ed., *Waka no honshitsu to hyōgen, Waka bungaku kōza*, vol. 1. Tokyo: Benseisha, 1993. 25–40.

Miao, Ronald. "Literary Criticism at the End of the Eastern Han." *Literature East and West*, 16: 3 (September 1972): 1013–1034.

Minamoto Toyomune. *Yamato-e no kenkyū*. Tokyo: Kadokawa shoten, 1976.

Mine Yōko. "Kodai nihon ni okeru tōka no igi to sono tenkai." *Kodai nihonshi no kenkyū*, 10 (June 1995): 13–29.

Miner, Earl. "*Waka*: Features of Its Constitution and Development." *HJAS*, 50: 2 (December 1990): 669–706.

Misaki Hisashi. "'Ribetsu' no tokushoku to kōzō." *IKKW*, 114–121.

Mitani Kuniaki. "Chi = kankaku to tennōsei: kodai ōken to 'shoyū' arui wa daijōsai no ronri." In Saitō Hideki, ed., *Nihon shinwa: sono kōzō to seisei*. Tokyo: Yūseidō, 1995. 36–52.

Mizushima Yoshiharu. "'Azuma uta' no tokushoku to kōzō." *IKKW*, 183–189.

Mizutani Takashi. "Ki no Tsurayuki ni mirareru *Man'yō* uta no riyō ni tsuite." *Waka bungaku kenkyū*, 56 (June 1988): 10–20.

Mori Asao. "'Kiryo' no tokushoku to kōzō." *IKKW*, 122–129.

_____. *Kodai waka to shukusai*. Tokyo: Yūseidō, 1988.

_____. "*Kokinshū* shiki uta no ichi: yu no kanten kara." *Kokugo to kokubungaku*, 72: 5 (May 1996): 1–10.

Mori Masamori. "*Kokinshū* no ji-amari." *Shinwa kokubun*, 15 (December 1980): 1–13.

Morris, Mark. "*Waka* and Form, *Waka* and History." *HJAS*, 46: 2 (December 1986): 551–610.

Mostow, Joshua S. "*E no Gotoshi*: The Picture Simile and the Feminine Re-Guard in Japanese Illustrated Romances." *Word & Image*, 11: 1 (January–March 1995): 37–40.

_____. *At the House of Gathered Leaves: Shorter Biographical and Autobiographical Narratives from Japanese Court Literature*. Honolulu: University of Hawai'i Press, 2004.

_____. *Pictures of the Heart: The Hyakunin Isshu in Word and Image*. Honolulu: University of Hawai'i Press, 1996.

Motoi Jun. "Ki no Tsurayuki no byōbu uta hyōgen: eisha no shisen o megutte." *Kokugakuin daigaku daigakuin kiyō (bungaku kenkyūkai)*, 26 (1994): 71–95.

_____. "*Kokinshū* zōka jō no umibe no kagun kō: enka to shite no shiza kara." *Nihon bungaku ronkyū*, 53 (March 1994): 13–23.

Murai Yasuhiko. "Heian kizoku to wa." In Yūseidō henshūbu, ed., *Heian kizoku no seikatsu*. Tokyo: Yūseidō, 1985. 7–17.

Murakami Miki. "Heian jidai no sanga." *Nara shien*, 40 (February 1995): 38–52.

Murase Toshio. *Ki no Tsurayuki den kenkyū*. Tokyo: Ōfūsha, 1981.

_____. *Kokinshū no kiban to sono shūhen*. Tokyo: Ōfūsha, 1971.

_____. "*Kokinshū* no seiritsu." In Ueno Osamu, ed., *Kokinshū*, *Waka bungaku kōza*, vol. 4. Tokyo: Benseisha, 1993. 31–50.

_____. *Kyūtei kajin Ki no Tsurayuki*. Tokyo: Shintensha, 1987.

Nagata Kazuya. "Gosho-dokoro to Uchi no Gosho-dokoro." *Kokugakuin daigakuin bungakubu kiyō*, 20 (1989): 354–379.

Nakajima Terumasa. "Ki no Tsurayuki no 'mitate' hyōgen: 'jitsuzō' to 'kyozō' no nijū eizō." *Kodai kenkyū*, 28 (January 1995): 43–52.

Nakakōji Kimie. "Heianchō waka ni okeru 'hito' to 'kimi' no hyōgen." *Shigadai kokubun*, 23 (June 1985): 1–7.

Nakanishi Susumu. "*Kokin wakashū* kiryo kaken no seiritsu: kentōshi to Ki-shi." *Bungaku*, 54: 2 (February 1986): 152–166.

_____. "Onna kara onna e: kodai wakashi no sobyō." *Kokugo to kokubungaku*, 43: 4 (April 1966): 77–87.

Nakano Masako. "Ki no Tsurayuki no uta to kanshibun: keionshi no eikyō." *Waka bungaku kenkyū*, 71 (November 1995): 12–23.

_____. "*Kokinshū* ni okeru 'beranari': yu ni shōsetsu suru jodōshi." *Ochanomizu joshi daigaku kokubun*, 86 (January 1997): 20–33.

Nickerson, Peter. "The Meaning of Matrilocality: Kinship, Property, and Politics in Mid-Heian," *MN*, 48: 4 (Winter 1994): 429–467.

Nihon koten bungaku daijiten iinkai, ed. *Nihon koten bungaku daijiten*. 6 vols. Tokyo: Iwanami shoten, 1983–1985.

Nishimura Satomi. "Heian jidai no kizoku to mono awase." *Nara shien*, 34 (February 1989): 1–23.

Nishishita Kyōichi. *Kokinshū no denpon no kenkyū*. Tokyo: Meiji shoin, 1954.

Nishishita Kyōichi and Takizawa Sadao, eds. *Kokinshū kōhon*. Tokyo: Kasama shoin, 1977.

Noda Hiroko. *Man'yōshū no jokei to shizen*. Tokyo: Shintensha, 1995.

Noguchi Takehiko. *Sanninshō no hakken made*. Tokyo: Chikuma shobō, 1994.

Nomura Seiichi. "*Kokinshū* uta no shisō." In Nihon bungaku kenkyū shiryō kankōkai, ed., *Kokin wakashū*, *Nihon bungaku kenkyū shiryō sōsho*, vol. 15. Tokyo: Yūseidō, 1976. 55–64.

Nosco, Peter. *Remembering Paradise: Nativism and Nostalgia in Eighteenth-Century Japan*. Cambridge, MA: Harvard Council on East Asian Studies, 1990.

Obinata Katsumi. *Kodai kokka to nenjū gyōji*. Tokyo: Yoshikawa kōbunkan, 1993.

Oda Shōkichi. *Kokin wakashū no nazo o toku*. Tokyo: Kōdansha, 2000.

Okada, Richard H. *Figures of Resistance: Language, Poetry, and Narrating in* The Tale of Genji *and Other Mid-Heian Texts*. Durham, NC: Duke University Press, 1992.

Okada Shōji. *Heian jidai no kokka to saishi*. Tokyo: Zoku gunsho ruijū kanseikai, 1994.

Okumura Tsuneya. *Kokinshū Gosenshū no shomondai*. Tokyo: Kazama shobō, 1971.

_____. *Kokinshū no kenkyū*. Kyoto: Rinsen shoten, 1980.

_____. "*Kokinshū* no seiritsu: Kanpyō to Engi." *Kokugo kokubun*, 23: 5 (May 1954): 272–283.

_____. "*Kokinshū* no zōtōteki hairetsu to chūshaku." *Kokugo kokubun*, 46: 1 (January 1977): 38–44.

Ōmuro Mikio. *Gekijō toshi: kodai chūgoku no sekaizō*. Tokyo: Chikuma shōbō, 1994.

Ong, Walter J. *Orality & Literacy: The Technologizing of the Word*. London: Routledge, 1982.

Ōno Susumu, Satake Akihiro, and Maeda Kingorō, eds. *Iwanami kogo jiten*. Tokyo: Iwanami shoten, 1990.

Ono Yasuo. "Heianchō no kōenshi ni okeru jukkai ni tsuite." *Kokugo to kokubungaku*, 74: 9 (September 1997): 11–24.

Ōno Yukiko. "Heianchō waka ni okeru ominaeshi: *Kokinshū*-teki hyōgen no ikkan to shite." *Ochanomizu joshi daigaku kokubun*, 81 (July 1994): 22–30.

Ōoka Makoto. *Ki no Tsurayuki*. Tokyo: Chikuma shobō, 1971.

Origuchi Shinobu. "Nyonin tanka josetsu." In Origuchi hakase kinen kodai kenkyūjo, ed., *Origuchi Shinobu zenshū*, vol 47. Tokyo: Chūō kōronsha, 1976. 447–465.

Owen, Stephen. "The Formation of the Tang Estate Poem." *HJAS*, 55: 1 (August 1995): 39–59.

_____. *The Making of Early Chinese Classical Poetry*. Cambridge, MA: Harvard University Asia Center, 2006.

_____. *The Poetry of the Early Tang*. New Haven: Yale University Press, 1977.

_____. *Readings in Chinese Literary Thought*. Cambridge, MA: Harvard Council on East Asian Studies, 1992.

_____. *Traditional Chinese Poetry and Poetics: Omen of the World*. Madison: University of Wisconsin Press, 1985.

Ozawa Masao. *Kodai kagaku no keisei*. Tokyo: Hanawa shobō, 1963.

_____. *Kokinshū no sekai*. Tokyo: Hanawa shobō, 1961.

Ōzuka Hideko. "Saga Tennō to 'hana no en no sechi.'" *Kodai bunkashi ronkō*, 6 (1986): 21–44.

Pekarik, Andrew Joseph. "Poetics and the Place of Japanese Poetry in Court Society through the Early Heian Period." Ph.D. dissertation, Columbia University, 1983.

Piggott, Joan R. "Chieftain Pairs and Co-rulers: Female Sovereignty in Early Japan." In Hitomi Tonomura, et al., eds. *Women and Class in Japanese History*. Ann Arbor: University of Michigan Center for Japanese Studies, 1999. 17–52.

_____. *The Emergence of Japanese Kingship*. Stanford, CA: Stanford University Press, 1997.

Rodd, Laurel Rasplica, and Mary Catherine Henkenius, trans. *Kokinshū: A Collection of Poems Ancient and Modern*. Princeton, NJ: Princeton University Press, 1984.

Rouzer, Paul. *Articulated Ladies: Gender and the Male Community in Early Chinese Texts*. Cambridge, MA: Harvard University Asia Center, 1999.

Sada Kimiko. "'Zō' no tokushoku to kōzō." *IKKW*, 156–164.

Samei, Maija Bell. *Gendered Persona and Poetic Voice: The Abandoned Woman in Early Chinese Song Lyrics*. Lanham, MD: Lexington Books, 2004.

Sarra, Edith. *Fictions of Femininity: Literary Inventions of Gender in Japanese Court Women's Memoirs*. Stanford, CA: Stanford University Press, 1999.

Sato, Hiroaki. "Lineation of Tanka in English Translation." *MN*, 42: 3 (Autumn 1987): 347–356.

Satō Kazuyoshi. *Heian waka bungaku hyōgen ron*. Tokyo: Yūseidō, 1993.

_____. "'Koi' no tokushoku to kōzō." *IKKW*, 138–147.

_____. "Tasei no katai kara tansei no katai e: uta monogatari no seisei." In Kubukihara Rei, ed., *Waka to wa nani ka, Nihon bungaku o yomikaeru*, vol. 3. Tokyo: Yūseidō, 1996. 163–178.

Satō Shin'ichi. "*Keikokushū* no hyōgen ni tsuite." *Shirayuri joshi daigaku kenkyū kiyō*, 28 (December 1992): 43–56.

Shimada Ryōji. "*Kokinshū* no kōteki seikaku ni tsuite." *Kokugo to kokubungaku*, 54: 11 (November 1977): 1–13.

_____. "*Kokinshū* no renka ni okeru hiyuteki hyōgen ni tsuite." *Kokugo to kokubungaku*, 47: 9 (September 1970): 27–41.

_____. *Kokinshū to sono shūhen*. Tokyo: Kasama shoin, 1987.

Shimizu Yoshiko. *Genji monogatari no buntai to hōhō*. Tokyo: Tokyo daigaku shuppankai, 1980.

Shinozaki Yukie. "Dai'ei." *IKKW*, 661–663.

Shin'ya Tomiichi. "*Kinkafu* 'yomi uta' kō." *Kokugo kokubun*, 66: 9 (September 1997): 1–23.

_____. "'Uta o yomu' koto." *Kokugo kokubun*, 48: 3 (March 1979): 1–17.

Shively, Donald H., and William H. McCullough, eds., *Heian Japan, The Cambridge History of Japan*, vol. 2. Cambridge: University of Cambridge Press, 1999.

Sivin, Nathan. "State, Cosmos, and Body in the Last Three Centuries B.C." *HJAS*, 55: 1 (June 1995): 5–37.

Soda Fumio. "*Kokin wakashū* 'mono no na' kō." *Tōdai kokubun*, 1 (August 1942): 34–41.

Sugitani Jurō. "*Kokin wakashū* to uta-awase." *IKKW*, 509–522.

Sugiyama Hideaki. "Heian kizoku no densha to chōdo." In Yūseidō henshūbu, ed., *Heian kizoku no seikatsu*. Tokyo: Yūseidō, 1985. 102–115.

Suzuki Hideo. "Kodai waka ni okeru shinbutsu taiō kōzō." *Kokugo to kokubungaku*, 47: 4 (April 1970): 1–21.

_____. *Kodai waka shiron*. Tokyo: Tokyo daigaku shuppankai, 1990.

Suzuki Hiroko. *Kokin wakashū hyōgen ron*. Tokyo: Kasama shoin, 2000.

Suzuki Michiko. "Byōbu uta kajin to shite no Tsurayuki." *Nihon bungaku nōto*, 31 (January 1996): 26–37.

Taiyō Kazutoshi. "'Aki' no tokushoku to kōzō." *IKKW*, 88–97.

Tajima Satoko. "Byōbu uta kajin to shite no Tsurayuki: 'sōmoku' o megutte." *Shirin*, 9 (April 1991): 1–9.

_____. "*Kokinshū* izen no byōbu uta." In Waka bungaku ronshū henshū iinkai, ed., *Byōbu uta to uta-awase*. Tokyo: Kazama shobō, 1995. 51–80.

_____. "*Kokinshū* jidai no byōbu uta no eihō: takagari o chūshin to shite." *Kokugo kokubun*, 61: 4 (April 1992): 13–28.

_____. "Tsurayuki byōbu uta no seikaku to hyōgen: mizu ni utsutta kage no uta o megutte." *Machikaneyama ronsō (bungaku hen)*, 23 (December 1989): 1–12.

Takada Hirohiko. "*Kokin wakashū* no yu." *IKKW*, 453–462.

_____. "Kyō no bungaku *Kokinshū*." In Masuda Shigeo et al., eds., *Kokin wakashū no seisei to honshitsu, Kokin wakashū kenkyū shūsei*, vol. 1. Tokyo: Kazama shobō, 2004. 173–199.

Takahashi Bunji. *Fūkei to kyōkankaku: ōchō bungaku shiron*. Tokyo: Shunjūsha, 1985.

Takahashi Kazuo. "Gyōji to waka." In Waka bungaku ronshū henshū iinkai, ed., *Byōbu uta to uta-awase*. Tokyo: Kazama shobō, 1995. 1–28.

Takano Yasushiro. "Ninna gobyōbu saikō." *Waka bungaku kenkyū*, 63 (November 1991): 1–9.

Takei Jirō, and Marc P. Keane. *Sakuteiki: Visions of the Japanese Garden*. Rutland, VT: Tuttle Publishing, 2001.

Takeoka Masao. *Kokin wakashū zenhyōshaku*. 2 vols. Tokyo: Yūbun shoin, 1976.

Takeuchi Michiko. *Heian jidai wabun no kenkyū*. Tokyo: Meiji shoin, 1986.

Takigawa Kōji. "Uda, Daigo-chō no kadan to waka no dōkō." In Masuda Shigeo, et al., eds., *Kokin wakashū no seisei to honshitsu, Kokin wakashū kenkyū shūsei* vol. 1. Tokyo: Kazama shobō, 2004. 231–268.

Takinami Sadako. *Heian kento, Nihon no rekishi*, vol. 5. Tokyo: Shūeisha, 1991.

Takizawa Sadao. "Chokusen wakashū no kotobagaki ni tsuite: *Kokin wakashū* no baai." *Waka bungaku kenkyū*, 52 (April 1986): 1–12.

_____. "'Haru' no tokushoku to kōzō." *IKKW*, 71–80.

Tamagami Takuya. "Byōbu e to uta to monogatari to." *Kokugo kokubun*, 22: 1 (January 1953): 1–20.

_____. *Genji monogatari kenkyū*. Tokyo: Kadokawa shoten, 1966.

Tanaka Kazuo. "*Kokin wakashū* to chūgoku bungaku." *IKKW*, 482–492.

Tanaka Kimiharu. "Ausaka no tamuke uta." *Sanukidai kokugo kokubungaku*, 15 (March 1982): 49–56.

_____. "Chūkō waka no genri." *Kokugo to kokubungaku*, 69: 12 (December 1992): 13–32.

_____. "Daigo tennō no *Kokinshū* kaishū." *Kokugo to kokubungaku*, 58: 4 (April 1981): 28–46.

_____. "*Kokinshū* ga no uta ron." *Waka bungaku kenkyū*, 44 (August 1981): 1–10.

_____. "Uta no hairetsu." *Kokubungaku kaishaku to kyōzai no kenkyū*, 40: 10 (August 1995): 40–47.

Tanaka Kimiharu and Kyōko, eds. *Tsurayuki-shū zenshaku*. Tokyo: Kazama shobō, 1997.

Tanaka Shin'ichi. *Heianchō bungaku ni miru nigenteki shikikan*. Tokyo: Kasama shoin, 1990.

_____. "*Kokin wakashū* to nenjū gyōji." *IKKW*, 284–290.

Tanaka Yutaka. "Kafū yōshiki ron: *Kokinshū* kanajo to *Wakatei jisshu* ni tsuite." In Fujihira Haruo, ed., *Waka no honshitsu to hyōgen, Waka bungaku kōza*, vol. 1. Tokyo: Benseisha, 1993. 265–282.

Toby, Ronald. "Why Leave Nara? Kammu and the Transfer of the Capital." *MN*, 40: 3 (Autumn 1985): 331–347.

Tokieda Motoki. *Kokugogaku genron*. Tokyo: Iwanami shoten, 1941.

Tokuhara Shigemi. "Byōbu uta no gutaisō." *Kokugo to kokubungaku*, 55: 6 (June 1978): 24–36.

_____. "Ga no byōbu to byōbu uta." *Heian bungaku kenkyū*, 64 (December 1980): 19–26.

_____. "*Kokinshū* zattei 'tanka' kō," *Heian bungaku kenkyū*, 66 (November 1981): 20–27.

_____. "*Tsurayuki-shū* byōbu uta no eihō." *Kokubungaku kenkyū nōto*, 7 (October 1976): 1–9.

_____. "Uda, Daigo-chō no utameshi o megutte." *Chūko bungaku*, 26 (October 1980): 25–32.

_____. "Uta-awase no seiritsu to tenkai." In Ueno Osamu, ed., *Ōchō no waka*. Tokyo: Benseisha, 1993. 145–164.

Tokumori Makoto. "'*Nihongi kyōen waka*' ni okeru Nigihayai: Heianki no *Nihongi* gensetsu." *Kokugo to kokubungaku*, 72: 10 (October 1995): 14–26.

Toku'ue Toshiyuki. "Zai minbukyō ke uta-awase ni tsuite." *Heian bungaku kenkyū*, 77 (May 1987): 20–37.

Tsuchihashi Yutaka. *Kodai kayō to girei no kenkyū*. Tokyo: Iwanami shoten, 1965.

Tsuchihashi Yutaka and Konishi Jin'ichi, eds. *Kodai kayō shū*, *NKBT*, vol. 3. Tokyo: Iwanami shoten, 1957.

Tsuda Hiroyuki. "Ōken no kotoba." In Akasaka Norio, ed., *Ōken no kisō e*. Tokyo: Shin'yōsha, 1992. 68–116.

Tsunoda Bun'ei. *Nihon no kōkyū*. Tokyo: Gakutōsha, 1973.

Tsunoda Hiroko. "*Kokinshū* jobun ni okeru 'sama' no kōsatsu: rokkasen hyō o chūshin ni." *Nihon bungei kenkyū*, 48: 1 (June 1996): 21–40.

Uchida Yoshiko. "*Kokinshū*: chokusen to iu koto." *Kokugo kokubun*, 58: 8 (August 1989): 38–54.

Ueno Osamu. *Goshūishū zengo*. Tokyo: Kasama shoin, 1976.

_____. "Heianchō wakashi ni okeru ke to hare." *Bungaku*, 34: 1 (December 1965): 77–88.

_____. "Yomibito shirazu." In Ueno Osamu, ed., *Kokinshū*, *Waka bungaku kōza*, vol. 4. Tokyo: Benseisha, 1993. 201–220.

Usuda Jingorō. "Rokkasen jidai no bungei bunka: Ninmyō-chō ni sotte." *Bungaku*, 54: 2 (February 1986): 103–113.

Van Zoeren, Steven. *Poetry and Personality: Reading, Exegesis, and Hermeneutics in Traditional China*. Stanford, CA: Stanford University Press, 1991.

Wakashi kenkyūkai, ed. *Shikashū taisei*, vol. 1. Tokyo: Meiji shoin, 1973.

Watada Yasuyo. "Tsurayuki ni okeru byōbu uta hyōgen no ichi tokushitsu: Atsutada-ke byōbu uta o megutte." *Heian bungaku kenkyū*, 55 (June 1976): 77–85.

Watanabe Hideo. *Heianchō bungaku to kanbun sekai*. Tokyo: Benseisha, 1991.

_____. "Ki no Tsurayuki no isō." *Kokubungaku kenkyū*, 54 (October 1974): 19–30.

_____. "Ki no Tsurayuki: utakotoba no sōzō." In Ueno Osamu, ed., *Kokinshū*, *Waka bungaku kōza*, vol. 4. Tokyo: Benseisha, 1993. 256–274.

_____. "*Kokinshū* jo no bungakushi." In Masuda Shigeo et al., eds. *Kokin wakashū no seisei to honshitsu*, *Kokin wakashū kenkyū shūsei*, vol. 1. Tokyo: Kazama shobō, 2004. 109–142.

_____. "Ōchō waka to kanshibun: *Kokinshū* o chūshin ni." In Wakan hikaku bungakkai, ed., *Wakan hikaku bungaku kenkyū no kōsō*, vol. 1. Tokyo: Kyūko shoin, 1986. 111–127.

Watanabe Mio. "Saga Tennō kōki-den (jō): *Man'yō* kara *Kokin* e." *Komazawa kokubun*, 18 (March 1981): 15–24.

Wetzel, Patricia J. "A Movable Self: The Linguistic Indexing of *Uchi* and *Soto*." In Jane M. Bachnik and Charles J. Quinn, Jr., eds., *Situated Meaning: Inside and Outside Japanese Self, Society, and Language*. Princeton, NJ: Princeton University Press, 1994. 73–88.

Wixted, John Timothy. "The *Kokinshū* Prefaces: Another Perspective." *HJAS*, 43: 1 (June 1983): 215–238.

_____. "The Nature of Evaluation in the *Shih-p'in* ('Grading of Poets') by Chung Hung (A.D. 469–518)." In Susan Bush and Christian Murck, eds., *Theories of the Arts in China*. Princeton, NJ: Princeton University Press, 1983. 225–264.

Yagi Ichio. *Daijōe waka no sekai*. Tokyo: Kōgakukan daigaku shuppanbu, 1986.

Yamada Kenzō. "Nara Heian jidai no jisho." In Nishizaki Tōru, ed., *Nihon kojisho o manabu hito no tame ni*. Tokyo: Sekai shisōsha, 1995. 68–118.

Yamagishi Tokuhei. *Waka bungaku kenkyū*. Tokyo: Yūseidō, 1941.

Yamaguchi Hiroshi. *Ōchō kadan no kenkyū: Kammu Ninmyō Kōkō-chō hen*. Tokyo: Ōfūsha, 1982.

_____. *Ōchō kadan no kenkyū: Uda Daigo Suzaku-chō hen*. Tokyo: Ōfūsha, 1967.

Yamamoto Kenkichi, et al., eds. *Nihon daisaijiki*. Tokyo: Kōdansha, 1982.

Yamamoto Toshitatsu. "Tsurayuki no jo: *Ōigawa gyokō waka* no jo o megutte." *Kokugo kokubun*, 39: 4 (April 1970): 44–52.

Yamanaka Yutaka. *Heian jidai no kokiroku to kizoku bunka*. Kyoto: Shibunkaku, 1988.

_____. "Heianchō ni okeru nenjū gyōji." In Yūseidō henshūbu, ed., *Heian kizoku no seikatsu*. Tokyo: Yūseidō, 1985. 48–64.

_____. "Heianchō ni okeru tsūka girei." In Yūseidō henshūbu, ed., *Heian kizoku no seikatsu*. Tokyo: Yūseidō, 1985. 65–72.

_____. *Heianchō no nenjū gyōji*. Tokyo: Hanawa shobō, 1972.

Yamazaki Kenji. "*Shinsen man'yōshū* ominaeshi no bu no keisei: Uda jōkō shūhen ni okeru waka no kyōju." *Kokugo kokubun*, 59: 3 (March 1990): 1–16.

Yanagawa Kiyoshi. "*Kokinshū* uta ni mirareru kakekotoba no akusento." *San'yō joshi tanki daigaku kenkyū kiyō*, 12 (March 1986): 13–21.

Yang, Xiaoshan. *Metamorphosis of the Private Sphere: Gardens and Objects in Tang-Song Poetry*. Cambridge, MA: Harvard University Asia Center, 2003.

Yasuda Kiyomon. *Kokinshū jidai no kenkyū*. Tokyo: Rokubunkan, 1932.

Yiengpruksawan, Mimi Hall. *Hiraizumi: Buddhist Art and Regional Politics in Twelfth-Century Japan*. Cambridge, MA: Harvard University Asia Center, 1998.

_____. "What's in a Name? Fujiwara Fixation in Japanese Cultural History." *MN*, 49: 4 (Winter 1993): 423–453.

Yoda, Tomiko. *Gender and National Literature: Heian Texts in the Constructions of Japanese Modernity*. Durham, NC: Duke University Press, 2004.

Yoshida Shūsaku. *Kotoba no jusei to seisei: konton kara no koe*. Tokyo: Ōfūsha, 1996.

Yoshikawa Eiji. "'Dai shirazu' to iu go ni tsuite." In Heian bungaku ronkyūkai, ed., *Kōza Heian bungaku ronkyū*, vol. 2. Tokyo: Kazama shobō, 1985. 175–211.

_____. "*Kokin wakashū* to *Kudai waka*." *IKKW*, 555–560.

_____. "*Kokinshū* izen no byōbu uta." In Waka bungaku ronshū henshū iinkai, ed., *Byōbu uta to uta-awase*. Tokyo: Kazama shobō, 1995. 51–80.

_____. "*Kokinshū* jo no karon." In Ueno Osamu, ed., *Kokinshū*, *Waka bungaku kōza*, vol. 4. Tokyo: Benseisha, 1993. 69–88.

_____. "*Kokinshū* senjutsu shiron: yomibito shirazu uta no hairetsu o megutte." *Waseda daigaku kokubungaku kenkyū*, 82 (March 1984): 21–33.

Yoshikawa Shinji. "Ritsuryō kokka to jokan." In Joseishi sōgō kenkyūkai, ed., *Nihon josei seikatsushi*, vol. 1. Tokyo: Tōkyō daigaku shuppankai, 1990. 105–142.

Yoshiumi Naoto. "*Kokin wakashū* to denshō bungaku." *IKKW*, 270–276.

Yu, Pauline. "Poems in Their Place: Collections and Canons in Early Chinese Literature." *HJAS*, 50: 1 (June 1990): 163–196.

_____. *The Reading of Imagery in the Chinese Poetic Tradition*. Princeton, NJ: Princeton University Press, 1987.

Zito, Angela. *Of Body & Brush: Grand Sacrifice as Text/Performance in Eighteenth-Century China*. Chicago: University of Chicago Press, 1997.

Index

CORNELL EAST ASIA SERIES

4 Fredrick Teiwes, *Provincial Leadership in China: The Cultural Revolution and Its Aftermath*

8 Cornelius C. Kubler, *Vocabulary and Notes to Ba Jin's Jia: An Aid for Reading the Novel*

16 Monica Bethe & Karen Brazell, *Nō as Performance: An Analysis of the Kuse Scene of Yamamba*

18 Royall Tyler, tr., *Granny Mountains: A Second Cycle of Nō Plays*

23 Knight Biggerstaff, *Nanking Letters, 1949*

28 Diane E. Perushek, ed., *The Griffis Collection of Japanese Books: An Annotated Bibliography*

37 J. Victor Koschmann, Ōiwa Keibō & Yamashita Shinji, eds., *International Perspectives on Yanagita Kunio and Japanese Folklore Studies*

38 James O'Brien, tr., *Murō Saisei: Three Works*

40 Kubo Sakae, *Land of Volcanic Ash: A Play in Two Parts,* revised edition, tr. David G. Goodman

44 Susan Orpett Long, *Family Change and the Life Course in Japan*

48 Helen Craig McCullough, *Bungo Manual: Selected Reference Materials for Students of Classical Japanese*

49 Susan Blakeley Klein, *Ankoku Butō: The Premodern and Postmodern Influences on the Dance of Utter Darkness*

50 Karen Brazell, ed., *Twelve Plays of the Noh and Kyōgen Theaters*

51 David G. Goodman, ed., *Five Plays by Kishida Kunio*

52 Shirō Hara, *Ode to Stone,* tr. James Morita

53 Peter J. Katzenstein & Yutaka Tsujinaka, *Defending the Japanese State: Structures, Norms and the Political Responses to Terrorism and Violent Social Protest in the 1970s and 1980s*

54 Su Xiaokang & Wang Luxiang, *Deathsong of the River: A Reader's Guide to the Chinese TV Series* Heshang, trs. Richard Bodman & Pin P. Wan

55 Jingyuan Zhang, *Psychoanalysis in China: Literary Transformations, 1919–1949*

56 Jane Kate Leonard & John R. Watt, eds., *To Achieve Security and Wealth: The Qing Imperial State and the Economy, 1644–1911*

57 Andrew F. Jones, *Like a Knife: Ideology and Genre in Contemporary Chinese Popular Music*

58 Peter J. Katzenstein & Nobuo Okawara, *Japan's National Security: Structures, Norms and Policy Responses in a Changing World*

59 Carsten Holz, *The Role of Central Banking in China's Economic Reforms*

60 Chifumi Shimazaki, *Warrior Ghost Plays from the Japanese Noh Theater: Parallel Translations with Running Commentary*

61 Emily Groszos Ooms, *Women and Millenarian Protest in Meiji Japan: Deguchi Nao and Ōmotokyō*

62 Carolyn Anne Morley, *Transformation, Miracles, and Mischief: The Mountain Priest Plays of Kōygen*

63 David R. McCann & Hyunjae Yee Sallee, tr., *Selected Poems of Kim Namjo,* afterword by Kim Yunsik

64 Hua Qingzhao, *From Yalta to Panmunjom: Truman's Diplomacy and the Four Powers, 1945–1953*

65 Margaret Benton Fukasawa, *Kitahara Hakushū: His Life and Poetry*

66 Kam Louie, ed., *Strange Tales from Strange Lands: Stories by Zheng Wanlong,* with introduction

67 Wang Wen-hsing, *Backed Against the Sea,* tr. Edward Gunn

69 Brian Myers, *Han Sōrya and North Korean Literature: The Failure of Socialist Realism in the DPRK*

70 Thomas P. Lyons & Victor Nee, eds., *The Economic Transformation of South China: Reform and Development in the Post-Mao Era*

71 David G. Goodman, tr., *After Apocalypse: Four Japanese Plays of Hiroshima and Nagasaki,* with introduction

72 Thomas Lyons, *Poverty and Growth in a South China County: Anxi, Fujian, 1949–1992*

74 Martyn Atkins, *Informal Empire in Crisis: British Diplomacy and the Chinese Customs Succession, 1927–1929*

76 Chifumi Shimazaki, *Restless Spirits from Japanese Noh Plays of the Fourth Group: Parallel Translations with Running Commentary*

77 Brother Anthony of Taizé & Young-Moo Kim, trs., *Back to Heaven: Selected Poems of Ch'ŏn Sang Pyŏng*

78 Kevin O'Rourke, tr., *Singing Like a Cricket, Hooting Like an Owl: Selected Poems by Yi Kyu-bo*

79 Irit Averbuch, *The Gods Come Dancing: A Study of the Japanese Ritual Dance of Yamabushi Kagura*

80 Mark Peterson, *Korean Adoption and Inheritance: Case Studies in the Creation of a Classic Confucian Society*

81 Yenna Wu, tr., *The Lioness Roars: Shrew Stories from Late Imperial China*

82 Thomas Lyons, *The Economic Geography of Fujian: A Sourcebook,* Vol. 1

83 Pak Wan-so, *The Naked Tree,* tr. Yu Young-nan

84 C.T. Hsia, *The Classic Chinese Novel: A Critical Introduction*

85 Cho Chong-Rae, *Playing With Fire,* tr. Chun Kyung-Ja

86 Hayashi Fumiko, *I Saw a Pale Horse and Selections from Diary of a Vagabond,* tr. Janice Brown

87 Motoori Norinaga, *Kojiki-den, Book 1*, tr. Ann Wehmeyer

88 Chang Soo Ko, tr., *Sending the Ship Out to the Stars: Poems of Park Je-chun*

89 Thomas Lyons, *The Economic Geography of Fujian: A Sourcebook*, Vol. 2

90 Brother Anthony of Taizé, tr., Midang: *Early Lyrics of So Chong-Ju*

92 Janice Matsumura, *More Than a Momentary Nightmare: The Yokohama Incident and Wartime Japan*

93 Kim Jong-Gil tr., *The Snow Falling on Chagall's Village: Selected Poems of Kim Ch'un-Su*

94 Wolhee Choe & Peter Fusco, trs., *Day-Shine: Poetry by Hyon-jong Chong*

95 Chifumi Shimazaki, *Troubled Souls from Japanese Noh Plays of the Fourth Group*

96 Hagiwara Sakutarō, *Principles of Poetry (Shi no Genri)*, tr. Chester Wang

97 Mae J. Smethurst, *Dramatic Representations of Filial Piety: Five Noh in Translation*

98 Ross King, ed., *Description and Explanation in Korean Linguistics*

99 William Wilson, *Hōgen Monogatari: Tale of the Disorder in Hōgen*

100 Yasushi Yamanouchi, J. Victor Koschmann and Ryūichi Narita, eds., *Total War and 'Modernization'*

101 Yi Ch'ŏng-jun, *The Prophet and Other Stories*, tr. Julie Pickering

102 S.A. Thornton, *Charisma and Community Formation in Medieval Japan: The Case of the Yugyō-ha (1300–1700)*

103 Sherman Cochran, ed., *Inventing Nanjing Road: Commercial Culture in Shanghai, 1900–1945*

104 Harold M. Tanner, *Strike Hard! Anti-Crime Campaigns and Chinese Criminal Justice, 1979–1985*

105 Brother Anthony of Taizé & Young-Moo Kim, trs., *Farmers' Dance: Poems by Shin Kyŏng-nim*

106 Susan Orpett Long, ed., *Lives in Motion: Composing Circles of Self and Community in Japan*

107 Peter J. Katzenstein, Natasha Hamilton-Hart, Kozo Kato, & Ming Yue, *Asian Regionalism*

108 Kenneth Alan Grossberg, *Japan's Renaissance: The Politics of the Muromachi Bakufu*

109 John W. Hall & Toyoda Takeshi, eds., *Japan in the Muromachi Age*

110 Kim Su-Young, Shin Kyong-Nim, Lee Si-Young; *Variations: Three Korean Poets;* trs. Brother Anthony of Taizé & Young-Moo Kim

111 Samuel Leiter, *Frozen Moments: Writings on* Kabuki, *1966–2001*

112 Pilwun Shih Wang & Sarah Wang, *Early One Spring: A Learning Guide to Accompany the Film Video* February

113 Thomas Conlan, *In Little Need of Divine Intervention: Scrolls of the Mongol Invasions of Japan*

114 Jane Kate Leonard & Robert Antony, eds., *Dragons, Tigers, and Dogs: Qing Crisis Management and the Boundaries of State Power in Late Imperial China*

115 Shu-ning Sciban & Fred Edwards, eds., *Dragonflies: Fiction by Chinese Women in the Twentieth Century*

116 David G. Goodman, ed., *The Return of the Gods: Japanese Drama and Culture in the 1960s*

117 Yang Hi Choe-Wall, *Vision of a Phoenix: The Poems of Hŏ Nansŏrhŏn*

118 Mae J. Smethurst and Christina Laffin, eds., *The Noh* Ominameshi*: A Flower Viewed from Many Directions*

119 Joseph A. Murphy, *Metaphorical Circuit: Negotiations Between Literature and Science in Twentieth-Century Japan*

120 Richard F. Calichman, *Takeuchi Yoshimi: Displacing the West*

121 Fan Pen Li Chen, *Visions for the Masses: Chinese Shadow Plays from Shaanxi and Shanxi*

122 S. Yumiko Hulvey, *Sacred Rites in Moonlight: Ben no Naishi Nikki*

123 Tetsuo Najita and J. Victor Koschmann, *Conflict in Modern Japanese History: The Neglected Tradition*

124 Naoki Sakai, Brett de Bary, & Iyotani Toshio, eds., *Deconstructing Nationality*

125 Judith N. Rabinovitch and Timothy R. Bradstock, *Dance of the Butterflies: Chinese Poetry from the Japanese Court Tradition*

126 Yang Gui-ja, *Contradictions*, trs. Stephen Epstein and Kim Mi-Young

127 Ann Sung-hi Lee, *Yi Kwang-su and Modern Korean Literature:* Mujŏng

128 Pang Kie-chung & Michael D. Shin, eds., *Landlords, Peasants, & Intellectuals in Modern Korea*

129 Joan R. Piggott, ed., *Capital and Countryside in Japan, 300–1180: Japanese Historians Interpreted in English*

130 Kyoko Selden and Jolisa Gracewood, eds., *Annotated Japanese Literary Gems: Stories by Tawada Yōko, Nakagami Kenji, and Hayashi Kyōko* (Vol. 1)

131 Michael G. Murdock, *Disarming the Allies of Imperialism: The State, Agitation, and Manipulation during China's Nationalist Revolution, 1922–1929*

132 Noel J. Pinnington, *Traces in the Way: Michi and the Writings of Komparu Zenchiku*

133 Charlotte von Verschuer, *Across the Perilous Sea: Japanese Trade with China and Korea from the Seventh to the Sixteenth Centuries*, Kristen Lee Hunter, tr.

134 John Timothy Wixted, *A Handbook to Classical Japanese*

135 Kyoko Selden and Jolisa Gracewoord, with Lili Selden, eds., *Annotated Japanese Literary Gems: Stories by Natsume Sōseki, Tomioka Taeko, and Inoue Yasushi* (Vol. 2)

136 Yi Tae-Jin, *The Dynamics of Confucianism and Modernization in Korean History*

137 Jennifer Rudolph, *Negotiated Power in Late Imperial China: The Zongli Yamen and the Politics of Reform*

138 Thomas D. Loooser, *Visioning Eternity: Aesthetics, Politics, and History in the Early Modern Noh Theater*

139 Gustav Heldt, *The Pursuit of Harmony: Poetry and Power in Late Heian Japan*

140 Joan R. Piggott and Yoshida Sanae, *Teishinkōki: The Year 939 in the Journal of Regent Fujiwara no Tadahira*

141 Robert Bagley, *Max Loehr and the Study of Chinese Bronzes: Style and Classification in the History of Art*

142 Edwin A. Cranston, *The Secret Island and the Enticing Flame: Worlds of Memory, Discovery, and Loss in Japanese Poetry*

143 Sung-Il Lee, *Blue Stallion: Poems of Yu Chi-Whan*

DVD Monica Bethe and Karen Brazell: "Yamanba: The Old Woman of the Mountains" to accompany CEAS Volume 16 *Noh As Performance*

Order online at www.einaudi.cornell.edu/eastasia/publications or contact
Cornell University Press Services, P. O. Box 6525, 750 Cascadilla Street,
Ithaca, NY 14851, USA.
Tel: 1-800-666-2211 (USA or Canada), 1-607-277-2211 (International);
Fax: 1-800-688-2877 (USA or Canada), 1-607-277-6292 (International);
E-mail orders: orderbook@cupserv.org

CPSIA information can be obtained
at www.ICGtesting.com
Printed in the USA
LVHW091940301019
635851LV00010B/51/P